OXFORD THEOLOGY AN

OXFORD THEOLOGY AND RELIGION MONOGRAPHS

Qur'an of the Oppressed

*Liberation Theology and Gender
Justice in Islam*

SHADAAB RAHEMTULLA

Great Clarendon Street, Oxford, OX2 6DP,
United Kingdom

Oxford University Press is a department of the University of Oxford.
It furthers the University's objective of excellence in research, scholarship,
and education by publishing worldwide. Oxford is a registered trade mark of
Oxford University Press in the UK and in certain other countries

First published 2017
First published in paperback 2018

Published in the United States of America by Oxford University Press
198 Madison Avenue, New York, NY 10016, United States of America

British Library Cataloguing in Publication Data
Data available

Library of Congress Cataloging in Publication Data
Data available

ISBN 978-0-19-879648-0 (Hbk.)
ISBN 978-0-19-882009-3 (Pbk.)

In loving memory of Malcolm X
(1925–65)

Acknowledgements

This book would not have been possible without the loving support of my family. Throughout my education, my parents—Mehfuza and Haiderali Rahemtulla—have been my rock, an unwavering source of comfort and encouragement. It is because of them that I was able to enter graduate school, let alone complete it. I cannot separate this book, which is based on my doctoral dissertation, from the beautiful and radiant face of Sara Ababneh, my life partner and comrade in struggle. This is not only because, throughout the research and writing, I was in a perpetual conversation with her about my work, but also because we met during my very first week in Oxford as a graduate student. Her presence, insight, and love therefore are an integral aspect of my learning. I would also like to express my deepest gratitude to Sara's family—Mahmoud, Dorothee, Nora, and Hanna—for their friendship and hospitality in Jordan. From the moment I arrived in Amman, they made me feel like a part of their family. Our children Leila and Ali arrived shortly after we moved to Jordan. I cannot express in words the joy that they bring to my life, and I pray that they will grow up to become conscientious human beings committed to the values that lie at the core of this book, namely: justice, compassion, and solidarity.

I am truly blessed to have had wonderful teachers. I wish to express my gratitude to Derryl MacLean, Paul Sedra, Thomas Kuehn, and the late William Cleveland, all at Simon Fraser University, and James Piscatori, now at the University of Durham, for their teaching, support, and unceasing encouragement. I am forever indebted to Christopher Rowland and James McDougall, both at the University of Oxford. I could not have asked for more engaging and selfless supervisors. James pushed me in my writing to be as detailed, as exhaustive, as rigorous as possible. If this book is meticulous, it is because of him. Chris was not only an outstanding teacher and mentor, but he is the scholar—indeed, he is the human being—that I want to be. Without words and through his actions alone, Chris taught me what a genuine commitment to liberation means, and that is translating one's social and political ideals into one's personal life.

The revisions for this book were completed while teaching at the University of Jordan's School of International Studies in Amman, and I would like to thank all the faculty and administrative staff for their warm collegiality and friendship, especially university president Azmi Mahafzah and deans Abdullah Nagrash, Faisal Al-Rfouh, and Zaid Eyadat. A special shout out goes to my brilliant and inspiring students, including (but certainly not limited to) Ayesha al-Omary, Wesam Wekhyan, Rita Adel, and Laila Meloelain.

Having now written a monograph, I have come to appreciate the truly exacting work that goes into the production process. I want to express my gratitude to everyone at Oxford University Press and beyond: Tom Perridge, Karen Raith, Kavya Ramu, Francesca White, Joy Mellor, Martin Noble, Hannah Chippendale, and Diarmaid MacCulloch, the chair of the Oxford Theology and Religion Monographs Committee. I am grateful to Diarmaid for inviting me to be a part of the series. I am indebted to the anonymous external reviewer at OUP, whose perceptive and deeply learned comments significantly improved the manuscript. This book would not have been possible without the funding that I received for my doctorate. I thank the Social Sciences and Humanities Research Council of Canada and the Clarendon Fund at the University of Oxford for their scholarship support.

Finally, I would like to thank the intellectuals studied in this book—Farid Esack, the late Asghar Ali Engineer (may he rest in peace), Amina Wadud, and Asma Barlas—for doing what they do, for being who they are. While I have striven to be critical of their work, I have learned immensely from their insights. They have opened up new horizons for me, giving me a language, a vocabulary, a space with which to bring together the two callings that lie closest to my soul: faith and social justice. For this, I thank them from the bottom of my heart.

Table of Contents

1

Introduction

Over the past two centuries the slogan 'reform and renewal' (*islah wa tajdid*) has swept through Islamic intellectual circles, as Muslims have sought to reinterpret their faith afresh in light of modernity. Insofar as Islamic texts are concerned, the majority of literature on contemporary Islamic reform has focussed on the *shari'a* (the inherited legal tradition).[1] Indeed, the law has dominated discussions of Islam in general. Less attention has been given to reformism based on the Qur'an,[2] despite the significance of this scripture both in terms of Muslim theology, in which it is understood as being the Word of God (*kalam Allah*), and of the current state of Islamic thought. Far from being a marginal text, the Qur'an has emerged as a rich resource for theological reflection and sociopolitical action. Specifically, it has become a source of empowerment, speaking to structures of oppression. This book offers a comprehensive survey and analysis of the commentaries of four Muslim intellectuals who have turned to scripture as a liberating text to confront an array of problems, from

---

[1] See, among others: Abbas Amanat and Frank Griffel eds., *Shari'a: Islamic Law in the Contemporary Context* (Stanford: Stanford University Press, 2009); Abdullahi an-Na'im, *Islam and the Secular State: Negotiating the Future of the Shari'a* (Cambridge, MA: Harvard University Press, 2010); Khaled Abou El Fadl, *Speaking in God's Name: Islamic Law, Authority and Women* (Oxford: Oneworld, 2001); Tariq Ramadan, *To Be a European Muslim: A Study of Islamic Sources in the European Context* (Markfield, Leicestershire: The Islamic Foundation, 1999); and Ziba Mir-Hosseini, *Islam and Gender: The Religious Debate in Contemporary Iran* (London: I.B. Tauris, 2000).

[2] For surveys of contemporary Muslim engagement with the Qur'an, see: Part Three—'Contemporary Readings'—in Jane D. McAuliffe ed., *The Cambridge Companion to the Quran* (Cambridge: Cambridge University Press, 2006); Rotraud Wielandt, 'Exegesis of the Qur'an: Early Modern and Contemporary', in *Encyclopaedia of the Qur'an*, ed. Jane D. McAuliffe (Georgetown University, Washington, DC), consulted online on 8 May 2012; and Suha Taji-Farouki ed., *Modern Muslim Intellectuals and the Qur'an* (Oxford: Oxford University Press, 2004).

patriarchy, racism and empire to poverty and interreligious communal violence.[3] In particular, I explore the exegeses of the South African
Farid Esack (b. 1956), the Indian Asghar Ali Engineer (1939–2013),
the African American Amina Wadud (b. 1952) and the Pakistani
American Asma Barlas (b. 1950),[4] supplemented by in-depth interviews with each of them.

The following question frames the study: How have these exegetes
been able to expound this seventh-century Arabian text in a socially
liberating way, addressing their own realities of oppression and thus
contexts (as diverse as twentieth-century and twenty-first-century
South Africa, India and America) that are worlds removed from that
of the text's immediate audience? For a believing Muslim, the divinity
of the Qur'an as the Word of God may well suffice as an answer, for the
Word is meant for all times and places. The following passage, depicting an exchange between a knowledge seeker and a major Islamic
scholar in the eighth century, captures this deep-seated conviction:

> A man asked Imam Ja'far al-Sadiq, 'Why does the Qur'an, despite the
> coming of new and passing of old generations, only increase in its

[3] For existing studies on liberationist and women's gender egalitarian Qur'anic
exegesis—the vast majority of attention focussing on the latter—see, among others:
Asma Barlas, 'Amina Wadud's Hermeneutics of the Qur'an: Women Rereading
Sacred Texts', in *Modern Muslim Intellectuals and the Qur'an*, ed. Suha Taji-Farouki
(Oxford: Oxford University Press, 2004); Aysha A. Hidayatullah, *Feminist Edges of the
Qur'an* (Oxford: Oxford University Press, 2014); Juliane Hammer, 'Identity, Author-
ity, and Activism: American Muslim Women Approach the Qur'an', *The Muslim
World* 98 (2008): 443–64; Nimat Hafez Barazangi, *Women's Identity and the Qur'an:
A New Reading* (Gainesville: University Press of Florida, 2004); Chapter Seven—' "If
you have touched women": Female Bodies and Male Agency in the Qur'an'—in
Kecia Ali, *Sexual Ethics and Islam: Feminist Reflections on Qur'an, Hadith, and
Jurisprudence* (Oxford: Oneworld, 2006); and Chapter Four—'The Qur'an and the
Hermeneutics of Liberation'—which examines Esack's and Wadud's readings, in
Massimo Campanini, *The Qur'an: Modern Muslim Interpretations* (London: Routle-
dge, 2011).
[4] While, strictly speaking, this book focuses on Qur'anic commentary, as opposed
to a study of scripture itself, over the course of my research I have had to refer to the
Qur'an as much as to the writings of these exegetes. As no single translation can
definitively represent the original text, in this study I have drawn on three English
translations, supplemented by my own knowledge of Arabic, to arrive at, at least what
I believe to be, the most accurate and faithful rendering of the text. Specifically, I have
consulted the works of the Sunni scholar Ahmed Ali, *Al-Qur'an: A Contemporary
Translation* (Princeton: Princeton University Press, 1993); the Shi'a scholar Ali Quli
Qara'i, *The Qur'an, with a Phrase-by-Phrase Translation* (London: Islamic College for
Advanced Studies, 2004); and the Sunni scholar Muhammad Asad, *The Message of the
Qur'an* (Bristol: The Book Foundation, 2003).

freshness?' The Imam replied, 'Because God did not make it for one specific time or people, so it is new in every age, fresh for every people, until the Day of Judgement.'[5]

Hence the ability, the power of the Word to speak to the pressing problems of the present, however disparate that present may be, however differently societal relations may be understood and practiced politically, economically, sexually and ethnically, is taken as a given, intuitive. To be sure, my grievance with this answer—that the Qur'an is meant for all times and places—is not its faith-based epistemology. I myself am a believing Muslim and also approach the Qur'an as the Word of God, a concept that will be unpacked shortly. Rather, my grievance with this answer is that it lacks an analytical dimension, and I do not view faith and critical reflection as mutually exclusive categories.

Through my analysis of the works of Esack, Engineer, Wadud and Barlas, I argue that their interpretations of the Qur'an are able to confront oppression in the present time due to three principal reasons. Firstly, the substantive content of the text itself, that is, its accent on social justice and descriptions of God as a compassionate and just deity. Secondly, their critique of existing reading practices, which (according to them) pose obstacles in arriving at an egalitarian and inclusive understanding of the text. Thirdly, their adoption of new reading practices that enable them to arrive at precisely such an understanding, thereby making the text directly relevant to their own contexts of oppression. These reading practices include:

- *Praxis*-based reflection, entailing a dialectic between, on the one hand, the lived experience of marginalization and the ensuing struggle against it and, on the other hand, scriptural exegesis.

- Historical criticism, unearthing not only the specific circumstances but also the broader social, cultural, gendered, political and economic milieu in which the text was revealed.

- This is textual holism, treating the Qur'an as a unified, indivisible whole and thus understanding a given verse or passage through the prism of the rest of the text, such as in terms of its underlying themes and principles.

---

[5] Al-Khatib al-Baghdadi, *Tarikh Baghdad* [A History of Baghdad] (Beirut: Dar al-Kutub al-'Ilmiyya, n.d.), 6:115.

- Careful literary analysis, discerning what exactly the text itself
  states and, just as importantly, what it does not: its silences.

In sum, I argue that the methods with which the Qur'anic text is
approached, conceptualized and expounded are as consequential as
its substantive letter.

In addition to their manifest social relevance, the readings of these
exegetes are significant, as I discuss in the concluding chapter. They
shed critical insight into the character of 'thematic exegesis' (*tafsir
mawdu'i*) of the Qur'an, which was (and continues to be) largely
interpreted through a sequential, verse-by-verse format (*tafsir musalsal*),
beginning from the first verse of the opening chapter and proceeding,
in a linear manner, to the last verse of the closing chapter. Specifically,
I argue that their interpretations offer three insights into thematic exegesis of the Qur'an. Firstly, the desire to partake in a direct engagement
with scripture and, therefore, one that is unmediated by the inherited
exegetical tradition. Secondly, the foregrounding of the reader's subject
position in the thematic interpretive process, which suggests a hermeneutical linkage between thematic reflection and 'contextual theology'
(a discipline that consciously uses one's context as the point of departure
for theological reflection). Thirdly, the seminal role that modern print
culture has played in shaping the formats of Qur'anic commentary,
massifying both the producers and consumers of religious knowledge.[6]

ONTOLOGY AS METHODOLOGY

While the ensuing chapters will provide in-depth discussions of these
exegetes' methodological approaches, it is necessary to say a few words,
right from the outset, about what exactly these exegetes mean when
they state, often emphatically, that the Qur'an is the Word of God.
The conception of the Qur'an as the Word, after all, does not reflect
even a remote departure from historic Muslim understandings of
the text. Indeed, all Muslims, irrespective of ideological or sectarian
persuasion, believe in the divine ontology of the Qur'an: that the

---

[6] In this book, I will use the term hermeneutics in two distinct senses: the first as
the *way* in which a text is interpreted and the second as the *study* of the strategies and
problems of interpretation.

revelations that the Prophet received between *c.* 610 and 632, through the mediation of the archangel Gabriel, are the very words of the one God.[7] What does represent a departure in these exegetes' understanding of the term (at least in my reading of their works) is that the Qur'an's ontological status has inescapable implications in regard to methodology, in terms of how authoritative Islamic normative thinking is, or rather ought to be, produced. Specifically, the unique nature of the Qur'an as the Word necessitates the hermeneutical *elevation* of that text over all other Islamic texts and traditions, which are created by fallible human beings and thus lie within a wholly different, and significantly less authoritative, ontological category. I write elevation because these exegetes, as will be demonstrated at various points in this book, do not sweepingly reject the inherited intellectual tradition but rather directly engage the Qur'an and privilege it over other Islamic texts. Invoking the Qur'an's hallowed status as the Word, they use it as the framework, the criterion with which to engage other Islamic texts, often (though not always) critically. It is crucial to appreciate that this connection—linking ontological status with methodological approach—was not considered, by any means, intuitive in classical Islamic thought. For classical scholars, the *sunna* (literally precedent, referring to the custom of Prophet Muhammad) was on a par with the Qur'an in terms of authority.[8] In fact, they even considered the *sunna* to be a form of revelation (*wahy*), while at the same time acknowledging that the *sunna* did not reflect the words of God.[9] My point here is that while classical scholars may not have translated the Qur'an's ontological status into method, while they may not have prioritized the text's substantive content over that of other Islamic texts, they certainly did not consider the Qur'an as being anything *less* than the Word of God.

These exegetes' particular understanding of the Qur'an as the Word poses, of course, a direct challenge to established religious hierarchy, especially the authority of the historic interpreters of the

---

[7] It is worthwhile noting that these exegetes also adhere to the wider Muslim consensus that the Qur'anic codex (*mushaf*) that we have today replicates, verbatim, the revelations that the Prophet received, notwithstanding a different ordering of the chapters. This codex emerged during the caliphal reign of 'Uthman b. 'Affan (r. 644–656) and thus roughly a quarter century after the Prophet's death.

[8] Daniel Brown, *Rethinking Tradition in Modern Islamic Thought* (Cambridge: Cambridge University Press, 1996), 15–16.

[9] Ibid, 7.

faith: the *'ulama*. The Qur'anic scholar Walid Saleh has described the genre of Qur'anic commentary (*tafsir*) as a 'genealogical tradition'.[10] That is, a commentator did not simply expound the Qur'an itself, but did so through the prism of the commentorial tradition, either reproducing existing exegetical insights or adding new insights to that pool,[11] the former being more common than the latter. And it is through these accumulated layers of exegesis, spread over a millennia of scriptural reflection, that the religious authority of the *'ulama*—in this specific case, those specialized in the art of exegesis (*mufassirun*)—was sustained, consolidated. In linking the Qur'an's ontological status with method and, by extension, seeking a direct audience, an unmediated encounter, with the text, these exegetes bypass the commentorial tradition and the broader Islamic intellectual heritage.[12] In so doing, they undercut the *'ulama's* authority as an interpretive class. Unsurprisingly, as a result of their Islamic writings, coupled with their justice-based activism, these exegetes have been controversial within Muslim circles, eliciting suspicion and distrust. Though they have attained modest followings among progressively minded Muslims, they are generally not accepted by the authorities

---

[10] Walid A. Saleh, *The Formation of the Classical Tafsir Tradition: The Qur'an Commentary of al-Tha'labi (d. 427/1035)* (Leiden: Brill, 2004), 14.

[11] Ibid.

[12] To be sure, circumventing the inherited intellectual tradition is a major theme in contemporary Islamic thought and thus is hardly confined to these exegetes' writings. Beginning in the eighteenth century, Muslim reformists emphasized the necessity of engaging the Qur'an and the *hadith*—the reported sayings and actions of the Prophet—directly, seeking to emulate the actions of the first generation of Muslims (*al-salaf al-salih*, literally, the righteous predecessors). What sets the exegetes of this study apart is that they focus on the Qur'an in particular, discerning a critical distinction in the authority of the Qur'an and other Islamic texts, such as the *hadith*. That being said, these exegetes also differ from the Qur'an-only movement, which grew out of the *Ahl-i Qur'an* (People of the Qur'an) school in early twentieth-century India. Making a similar connection between ontology and method, the Qur'an-only movement calls for a 'return' to the Qur'an and the Qur'an alone, categorically rejecting other Islamic texts and especially the *hadith*. As discussed earlier, the exegetes of this study do not categorically reject other Islamic texts. Instead, they call for a hermeneutical privileging of the Qur'an as the Word of God, assessing other human-made textual sources through a Qur'anic framework. For examples of Qur'an-only literature, see: Abdur Rab, *Exploring Islam in a New Light: An Understanding from the Qur'anic Perspective* (New York: iUniverse, 2008); Edip Yuksel, *Manifesto for Islamic Reform* (Breinigsville, PA: Brainbow Press, 2009); Khalid Sayyed, *The Qur'an's Challenge to Islam: The Clash Between the Muslim Holy Scripture and Islamic Literature* (Dooagh, Ireland: Checkpoint Press, 2009); and The Monotheist Group, *The Natural Republic: Reclaiming Islam from Within* (Breinigsville, PA: Brainbow Press, 2009).

in any Islamic school of law or established institution within centres of Islamic learning. In contrast, they have had a largely positive reception among non-Muslim Western audiences, particularly within the academy. This is partially due to their educational backgrounds, having been schooled in so-called secular universities (as we will see shortly, Esack is the only exegete who attended an Islamic seminary). My interest in this book, however, is not to evaluate their Islamic orthodoxy or to document how they have been received by varying readerships.[13] My focus lies in expounding and assessing their ideas, and it is to the structure of this exposition and assessment that we turn to in the following section.

THE STUDY

Comparative textual analysis is my prime methodology. The writings of Esack, Engineer, Wadud, and Barlas are readily accessible, appearing as book-length monographs, as individual chapters in edited volumes and as articles in both academic and non-academic journals. As such, when I refer to a respective intellectual's 'commentary,' a term that I use interchangeably with 'exegesis' and 'interpretation', I am referring not to a physical book but to her/his Qur'anic *discourse*, which encompasses all of these media. However, at various points in this book, particularly in the concluding chapter, I will refer to their principal monographs on the Qur'an: namely, Esack's *Qur'an, Liberation and Pluralism: An Islamic Perspective of Interreligious Solidarity Against Oppression* (1997); Wadud's *Qur'an and Woman: Rereading the Sacred Text from a Woman's Perspective* (1999); and Barlas' *'Believing Women' in Islam: Unreading Patriarchal Interpretations of the Qur'an* (2002).[14] Engineer is the only exegete who has not produced a single-volume text devoted solely to his Qur'anic commentary. Rather, his hermeneutic is spread throughout a number of books and articles. Therefore, while I will use 'commentary' to denote their Qur'anic

[13] For a concise but insightful analysis of how modern Muslim intellectuals have been received in Muslim and non-Muslim contexts, see Taji-Farouki, 5–8.
[14] Farid Esack, *Qur'an, Liberation, and Pluralism: An Islamic Perspective of Interreligious Solidarity Against Oppression* (Oxford: Oneworld, 1997); Amina Wadud, *Qur'an and Woman: Rereading the Sacred Text from a Woman's Perspective* (Oxford: Oxford University Press, 1999); Asma Barlas, *'Believing Women' in Islam: Unreading Patriarchal Interpretations of the Qur'an* (Austin: University of Texas Press, 2002).

discourses, I will use 'Commentary'—that is, with an upper-case 'C'—
to refer to their main exegetical monographs. In addition to engaging
in a close reading of their publications, I have undertaken in-depth
interviews with these exegetes. I organized these semi-structured interviews into three sections—biography, interpretive methodology, and
discourses on justice—in order to mirror the layout of the chapters,
which will be discussed shortly. To clarify, I have privileged these
intellectuals' publications. The intended function of the interviews was
to play a supplementary role to their written works, such as elucidating
and fleshing out vague aspects of their arguments and filling in gaps,
particularly in terms of biographical and historical context.

Why have I picked these exegetes in particular? There were two
fundamental criteria for the selection of the cases: firstly, that the
intellectual's principal interests are social justice and liberation, as
opposed to Islamic reform in general, and, secondly, that s/he focuses
on expounding the Qur'an, as opposed to other Islamic texts and
traditions. Since my aim is not to write a panoramic account of all
Muslim intellectuals who could be examined within this dual frame,
I have focussed on the best-known intellectuals: namely, the two
leading Qur'anic liberation theologians (Esack and Engineer) and the
two leading gender-egalitarian interpreters of the Qur'an (Wadud and
Barlas). Collectively, their scholarship provides ample material to
address my research question and evidence my argument. That being
said, a few words are in order as to why the British-Pakistani intellectual Shabbir Akhtar (b. 1960) is not included in this comparison. While
he has written on both liberation theology and the Qur'an, I am not
convinced that he fits well into this comparative study because his
acutely philosophical writings (drawing on his disciplinary background
in the philosophy of religion) are less grounded than the aforemen-
tioned exegetes', all of whom focus and reflect on concrete categories,
on lived realities of marginalization, such as sexism, poverty and
racism. In contrast, Akhtar's main interests lie in broader and much
more abstract debates about secular humanism, Western modernity
and the relationship between Islam and politics.[15]

---

[15] See: Shabbir Akhtar, *A Faith for All Seasons* (Chicago: Ivan R. Dee, 1990); *Islam
as Political Religion: The Future of an Imperial Faith* (Abingdon, UK: Routledge,
2011); *The Final Imperative: An Islamic Theology of Liberation* (London: Bellew,
1991); and *The Qur'an and the Secular Mind: A Philosophy of Islam* (Abingdon,
UK: Routledge, 2007).

The book is comprised of four core chapters, each devoted to a specific exegete. Chapter 2 will focus on Esack; Chapter 3 on Engineer; Chapter 4 on Wadud; and Chapter 5 on Barlas. The first part of each chapter will provide some contextual background on the exegete in question, such as key biographical information and a brief historical survey of the country from which s/he hails. The second part of each chapter will address issues of interpretive method: How exactly ought the Qur'an to be read? Who has the authority to expound the text? What are the problems with existing modes of interpretation? Why precisely does scripture, as opposed to other Islamic texts, assume a central place in her/his Islamic discourse? In turn, what role do extra-Qur'anic sources like the *hadith* and the *shari'a* play in the exegetical enterprise? What are the principal hermeneutical strategies for the reinterpretation of the text? In the third section of each chapter, I will explore how the interpreter approaches liberation and its relationship to Islam: What does the Qur'an have to say about socioeconomic justice, gender equity and/or religious pluralism? How does one stand against oppression? That is, what modes of resistance are sanctioned by the text? What is the scope of the exegete's discourse on liberation? Does it extend to other struggles and, if so, how are the linkages made?

These questions, which will function more as general guidelines than steadfast rules, have been conceptualized broadly to allow for the specificities of the intellectuals' societal contexts to come through. Because of their different subject positions, these exegetes emphasize certain struggles over others. As women, Wadud and Barlas foreground the struggle for gender equality. Meanwhile, questions of religious pluralism play a more central role in Esack's hermeneutic, as he resisted alongside non-Muslim activists in the anti-apartheid struggle. This is not to suggest that gender justice is not an important part of Esack's thinking—it certainly is—but rather that one's priorities are determined by context. Throughout the book, I will think comparatively, contrasting and drawing connections between these thinkers. The Conclusion, as discussed earlier, will reflect on the significance of their works in terms of the thematic exegesis of the Qur'an. Finally, for the convenience of the reader I have provided a select glossary of terms, located at the end of the book.

2

Theology of the Margins

The Reading of Farid Esack

INTRODUCTION

This chapter is devoted to the Qur'anic exegesis of the South African theologian Farid Esack. The first part of the chapter will focus on hermeneutical method: how does Esack read the text and how is his reading a departure from other interpretive methods? Here, I will demonstrate that, although the Qur'anic text certainly plays a prime role in Esack's commentary, the experiences of the marginalized coupled with struggle against oppression constitute as important a text that is to be read alongside scripture. This will then lead into a discussion of how Esack interprets justice in the text. According to Esack, the God of the Qur'an is not only a just deity, but is in solidarity with the marginalized—a preferential option that is embodied in the Exodus. In this section, I critique Esack's usage of the Exodus as the key paradigm in his liberationist exegesis, pointing to its centrality in Christian liberation theology and, in its stead, proposing a more organic paradigm, one that can underline the distinctiveness of Muslim theology and experience. This chapter will then explore the scope of Esack's discourse on justice. I will argue that while the genesis of his radical theology lies in the South African struggle against apartheid, it cannot be reduced to this struggle. Indeed, to do so would undermine his very conception of justice. Esack's articulation of liberation is a fully comprehensive one and cannot be confined to a specific struggle. 'Prophetic'—or a principled—solidarity, therefore, is a fundamental component of liberation and lies at the heart of a meaningful commitment to social justice. The final section of this chapter will deal with the wider significance of Esack's hermeneutic, which, I argue, is twofold. Firstly, his pluralistic reading of the Qur'an speaks to the potential of liberation theology, as an approach that is not only critical of power relations but built on the struggle against oppression, to act as an effective, interfaith alternative to the problematic and simplistic language of religious dialogue. Secondly, Esack's hermeneutic undermines any objective, disembodied claim to 'Islam'. In so doing, he forces Muslims to raise larger questions of whose Islam is being articulated in a given context and whose interests are being served by this particular understanding. This chapter will first set the stage for discussion by providing a short history of South Africa and some biographical background on Esack.

Historical Context

Over the course of its modern history South Africa became an increasingly racist state, as a White minority came to dominate an indigenous Black majority, leading to an anti-apartheid movement that toppled the regime in 1994. The Dutch first arrived in South Africa as part of a shipping cartel in the late seventeenth century, followed by the first wave of the British in the late eighteenth century.[1] The burgeoning White settler community confiscated land from the indigenous people and created a racially stratified society. Separation—or apartheid, as it later came to be termed—between Coloureds and Whites became an integral part of the social order and was institutionalized in law.[2] The Urban Areas Act of 1923, for example, made it illegal for Blacks to live in the cities.[3] Three hundred years of White supremacy came to a head in 1948 with the electoral victory of the National Party, which sought to institutionalize racial hierarchy in every aspect of South African life.[4] Though a mass

---

[1] Esack, *Qur'an, Liberation, and Pluralism*, 19.

[2] For useful surveys of South Africa and its history of apartheid, see Leonard Thompson, *A History of South Africa* (New Haven: Yale University Press, 2000) and William Beinart, *Twentieth-Century South Africa* (Oxford: Oxford University Press, 2001).

[3] Bernard Magubane, 'Introduction: The Political Context', in *The Road to Democracy in South Africa, Vol. 1*, ed. South African Democracy Education Trust (Cape Town: Zebra Press, 2004), 8.

[4] Esack, *Qur'an, Liberation, and Pluralism*, 24.

resistance movement had existed since the early 1930s,[5] it took on a more radicalized and militant colouring with the rise of the National Party.[6] The anti-apartheid struggle gained great momentum over the second half of the twentieth century, despite the ruthless manner in which the state clamped down on activists, ranging from imprisonment to torture to outright murder. The internal liberation struggle was also strengthened by a formidable international solidarity movement, arguably the largest in world history,[7] successfully calling for a global boycott of the South African state. In 1994, the regime fell and democratic elections were held, ushering in Nelson Mandela—the leader of the main resistance organization, the African National Congress—as president.

Trained in Qur'anic studies and active as a religious scholar, Esack played a leading role in the anti-apartheid struggle. He was born in 1956 in the Cape Town suburb of Wynberg,[8] and experienced the racism of apartheid at a very early age. As a result of the Group Areas Act of 1961, Esack, his mother, and five siblings—his father had abandoned his mother when Esack was only three weeks old—were forced to move from their home, which was now rendered 'White', to the ghettos of the Cape Flats.[9] It was here, in the Coloured township of Bonteheuwel, that Esack was raised. He recounts vividly his experience of growing up in poverty: 'Long periods passed during which we had no shoes and I recall running across frost-covered fields to school so that the frost could not really bite into my feet.'[10] These formative experiences led Esack to join the anti-apartheid struggle while still a child. Indeed, he was first detained by the South African Security Police at the age of nine. Esack was awarded a scholarship when he was seventeen to undertake Islamic studies in a *madrasa* in Karachi, Pakistan. Eight years later he completed his studies, specializing in *'ulum al-Qur'an* (the Sciences of the Qur'an). After his return to South Africa, he and several friends formed the Islamic anti-apartheid group 'The Call of Islam' in 1984. The Call worked closely with the United Democratic Front (est. 1983), a mass-based coalition

---

[5] Magubane, 31.   [6] Ibid, 29.

[7] Esack, *Qur'an, Liberation, and Pluralism*, 240.

[8] Esack (in discussion with the author) preferred that his full date of birth not be disclosed.

[9] Farid Esack, *On Being a Muslim: Finding a Religious Path in the World Today* (Oxford: Oneworld, 1999), 95.

[10] Esack, *Qur'an, Liberation, and Pluralism*, 2.

of organizations that emerged in response to the National Party's proposed Tricameral Parliament giving Coloureds and Indians limited political representation while continuing to exclude the Black majority.[11] After the fall of apartheid, Esack travelled to Germany to study biblical hermeneutics and then to the UK, where he earned a Ph.D. in Qur'anic hermeneutics at the University of Birmingham. Having studied in the *madrasa* and the so-called secular university, Esack is reflective of a growing class of Muslim scholars schooled in both systems of knowledge.[12] He has taught at numerous seminaries and universities around the world, such as Union Theological Seminary in New York City and Harvard University. Esack returned to South Africa in 2009 and is, at the time of writing, Professor in the Study of Islam at the University of Johannesburg.

INTERPRETIVE METHOD

The Order of the Texts

Insofar as the textual sources of Islam are concerned, the Qur'an lies at the core of Esack's Islamic discourse. He focuses on the Qur'an because, as the Word of God, it is the only source of Islam that is deemed by all Muslims, irrespective of sectarian allegiance, to be completely authentic. To be sure, for Esack the Qur'an being the Word of God is not synonymous with the Qur'an being a closed corpus—a concept that will be explored later in this chapter. Conversely, the *hadith* do not have a prominent place in his Islamic discourse because they are highly contested amongst Muslims.[13] He also finds the *hadith* difficult to negotiate due to the sheer number of prophetic reports—there are six canonical collections for Sunni Muslims and three separate collections for Shi'a Muslims—as well as the fact that the content of some of the reports are acutely misogynistic.[14] This is not to imply, however, that Esack rejects *hadith* altogether, but rather that he privileges the Qur'an as the supreme

[11] Jill E. Kelly, '"It is because of our Islam that we are there": The Call of Islam in the United Democratic Front Era', *African Historical Review* 41:1 (2009): 121.

[12] Taji-Farouki, 5.

[13] Esack, *Qur'an, Liberation, and Pluralism*, 15.

[14] Esack Interview, 2009.

textual source of religious enquiry. As we shall see in subsequent
chapters, the prioritization of the Qur'an—as opposed to the exclusive use of the Qur'an—is a common thematic thread running
through the exegetes studied in this book. In fact, Esack makes use
of prophetic reports in his work. In an article calling for compassion
and solidarity with victims of AIDS, for example, he draws upon the
following *hadith*, in which God, on the Day of Judgement, will
address the believer who neglects the sick:

> 'O child of humankind, I was sick and you did not visit me!' I will say:
> 'My Lord! How could I visit You when You are the Sustainer of the
> Universe?' And God will reply: 'Did you not know that my servant so-
> and-so was sick and you did not bother to visit him? Did you not realize
> that if you had visited him, you would have found me with him?'
> (*Tirmidhi*, 2:438)[15]

It is telling that Esack's book *On Being a Muslim: Finding a Religious
Path in the World Today*—a deeply personal collection of writings—is
prefaced not with a Qur'anic verse but a *hadith*, related to him by a
dying friend afflicted with cancer, Shamima Shaikh. It reads, 'If the Last
Hour strikes and finds you carrying a sapling to the grove for planting,
go ahead and plant it.'[16] Every *hadith* is comprised of a chain of
narration (*sanad*), which traces itself back to Prophet Muhammad,
and the substantive content of the report (*matn*)—the former historically receiving far more attention in Islamic scholarship than the latter—
and it is interesting to note that the chains of narration are almost always
absent in the *hadiths* that Esack cites. This is not because who narrated
what, and thus the question of authenticity, is irrelevant to Esack, but
rather because what the text actually says is the most important issue.
Indeed, when I asked him if the *hadith* literature would figure more
prominently in his work if there were to be a systematic rethinking of the
hadith sciences—a scholarly shift from focussing on the chain of narration to the actual content of the *hadith* and how congruent this content
is with the Qur'an—he promptly agreed.[17]

Just as Esack prioritizes the Qur'an over the *hadith* so, too, does he
privilege the Qur'an over the historic intellectual tradition. Esack is at

[15] Farid Esack, 'Care in a Season of AIDS: An Islamic Perspective', in *Restoring
Hope: Decent Care in the Midst of HIV/AIDS*, eds. Ted Karpf, Jeffrey V. Lazarus, and
Todd Ferguson (New York: Palgrave Macmillan, 2008), 66.
[16] Esack, *On Being a Muslim*, xi.   [17] Esack Interview, 2009.

home with this immense corpus of knowledge, particularly the field of classical commentary, which is a direct result of his own traditional training.[18] In his textbook on the Qur'an, for instance, he cites such celebrated scholars as Abu Ja'far al-Tabari (d. 923), Abu al-Qasim al-Zamakhshari (d. 1144), Fakhr al-Din al-Razi (d. 1210), Ibn Qayyim al-Jawziyyah (d. 1350) and Jalal al-Din al-Suyuti (d. 1505), as well as modern commentators like Rashid Rida (d. 1935) and Abu al-Qasim al-Khoei (d. 1992). Indeed, Esack's hermeneutical theory of 'progressive revelation'—which will be discussed shortly—builds upon the exegetical writings of the eighteenth-century Indian scholar Shah Wali Allah Dehlawi (d. 1762).[19] Esack engages the tradition in a highly critical manner, however. The Qur'an reigns supreme in his thinking and where there is any conflict between the two, the Qur'an squarely takes precedence. As he succinctly sums it up, 'You trump all other arguments with the Qur'an.'[20]

Contests over Contexts: From Scholarly Project to Liberating Exegesis

The question of context has become an increasingly salient feature of Qur'anic exegesis. This is quite a recent hermeneutical development, as classical commentators concentrated on the linguistic study of the text, such as its philology and grammar.[21] The Pakistani Islamic scholar Fazlur Rahman (d. 1988) played a pioneering role in raising the question of historical context in commentary, engineering an entirely new method in approaching scripture: namely, the 'double movement theory'. It was historical criticism par excellence. The first 'movement', Rahman proposed, was an exhaustive examination of the immediate setting of revelation—that is, seventh-century Arabia—and thus a comprehensive study of the societal, cultural, political and economic milieu of Meccan life.[22] Broader socio-moral

---

[18] Jane D. McAuliffe, 'Reading the Qur'an with Fidelity and Freedom', *Journal of the American Academy of Religion* 73 (2005): 629.

[19] Esack, *Qur'an, Liberation, and Pluralism*, 55.

[20] Esack Interview, 2009.

[21] Abdullah Saeed, *Interpreting the Qur'an: Towards a Contemporary Approach* (London: Routledge, 2006), 117.

[22] Fazlur Rahman, *Islam and Modernity: The Transformation of an Intellectual Tradition* (Chicago: University of Chicago Press, 1982), 6.

objectives would be extracted from this classical context and then, in the second movement, these general Islamic principles would be applied to the specificities of the present.[23] An interesting aspect of this interpretive strategy is that the *'ulama* (the traditionally trained and historic interpreters of the faith) and lay experts in fields of knowledge outside Islam like sociology, law, history and philosophy would have to work together in order to see both movements through.[24] This was a shared scholarly project, therefore, between lay and learned. Islamic scholars have built on this notion of a shared *ijtihad*, or critical intellectual enquiry. The Muslim reformist Tariq Ramadan, for example, has classified scholars into two groups: *'ulama al-nusus* ('text scholars'), denoting specialists in Islam, and *'ulama al-waqi'* ('context scholars'), or those who are experts in other fields of learning.[25] And it is through the collaboration of both, Ramadan argues, that an Islam that speaks to the challenges of modernity can be articulated.

Esack's principal interest is not the classical context, however, but the immediate present. The historical criticism of Rahman denotes a certain distance, a rift between the average, contemporary reader and the Qur'anic text. The underlying assumption of his scholarly project is that the Qur'an, as a historical document, had a primary audience and that this was the Prophet's community in seventh-century Arabia. With the passing of generations, then, distance is inevitably created between the initial act of revelation and the present. The following description of the text by the Islamic scholar Bruce Lawrence, clearly conditioned by the logic of historical criticism, encapsulates this assumption:

> The Qur'an as *written* in Arabic is less than the revelation given to Muhammad; it is a second-order revelation. The Qur'an written, then *translated* from Arabic into English, becomes a third-order revelation. Distance from the source handicaps us, yet we can still learn about Islam by engaging with the Qur'an, even as a written text, translated from Arabic into English.[26] (My italics)

[23] Ibid, 7.
[24] Abdullah Saeed, 'Fazlur Rahman: A Framework for Interpreting the Ethico-Legal Content of the Qur'an', in *Modern Muslim Intellectuals and the Qur'an*, ed. Suha Taji-Farouki (Oxford: Oxford University Press, 2004), 58.
[25] Tariq Ramadan, *Radical Reform: Islamic Ethics and Liberation* (Oxford: Oxford University Press, 2009), 121.
[26] Bruce Lawrence, *The Qur'an: A Biography* (London: Atlantic Books, 2006), 8.

The subtext here is that the most authentic encounter with the text is as an essentially oral, Arabic discourse. There exists an enduring and inherent hermeneutical gap, rooted in time, which cannot be bridged. But where a connection can be made, however limited it may be, is through the mediation of the immediate audience of the text: the very first generation of Muslims to whom God revealed the Word. And it is precisely because the Qur'an, Esack interjects, is not speaking primarily to the community of Muhammad in seventh-century Arabia but to all of humanity,[27] that his key interest is the contemporary context of the reader. This is not to say that Esack ignores the conditions of seventh-century Arabian life. In fact, he devotes the second chapter of his textbook on the Qur'an, entitled *The Word Enters the World*, to this topic, examining the prior circumstances and immediate social context of revelation.[28] Furthermore, because the Qur'an and its interpretation cannot be stripped of time and locale, and because the Qur'an was undoubtedly revealed in a particular historical moment, that historical moment must always, to some degree, be engaged.[29] Rather, my point is that the chief, the overarching framework of Esack's hermeneutic is the here and now—not late antiquity—and that he consciously privileges the former over the latter.

It is worthwhile noting that Esack's emphasis on the present bears a striking resemblance to Islamist readings. Leading Islamist thinkers, such as the Egyptian Sayyid Qutb (d. 1966) and the Pakistani Abu'l-A'la Mawdudi (d. 1979), urged ordinary Muslims to read the Qur'an themselves—and, therefore, to bypass the accumulated scholarly commentary on the text—arguing that the Qur'an spoke directly to the believers, addressing their immediate circumstances and struggles.[30] The following is an excerpt from a set of guidelines on how to read the Qur'an by Khurram Murad, a member of the Jama'at-i Islami—the most influential Islamist movement in South Asia—and a student of Mawdudi:

> Be aware that you are always in Allah's presence.
> Feel, as though you hear the Qur'an from Allah.

[27] Farid Esack, 'Islam and Gender Justice: Beyond Simplistic Apologia,' in *What Men Owe Women: Men's Voices from World Religions*, eds. John C. Raines and Daniel C. Maguire (Albany, NY: State University of New York Press, 2001), 195.
[28] Farid Esack, *The Qur'an: A User's Guide* (Oxford: Oneworld, 2005), 56.
[29] Farid Esack, 'Qur'anic Hermeneutics: Problems and Prospects', *The Muslim World* 83:2 (1993): 119.
[30] McAuliffe, 'Reading the Qur'an with Fidelity and Freedom', 623.

> Feel, as though the Qur'an addresses you directly...
> Consider each *aya* [verse] as relevant today, not as a thing
>   of the past...
> Reflect deeply upon what you read...
> Take each passage of the revelation as addressed to you.[31]

In other words, scripture does not speak through the mediation of a
primary audience (classical Arabia) to a secondary audience (the
present). Rather, a direct hermeneutical link is forged between God
and the faithful, transcending time and space. Another common
characteristic between Esack's readings and those of Islamists, then,
is their markedly lay character. South African Muslims engaged in the
anti-apartheid struggle routinely came together in religious circles
(*halaqat*) to reflect collectively on a translation of the Qur'an, asking
one another what they felt the various verses meant and how these verses
spoke to their experiences.[32] Such communitarian exegesis and direct
access to the Qur'anic text—a hallmark of Islamist interpretation—
stands in stark contrast to the elite manner in which sacred authority
operated historically in Muslim societies, wherein the *'ulama* functioned
as the main arbiters of Islam.[33] Unsurprisingly, these reading practices
have been met with much antagonism by the *'ulama*, who have been
quick to dismiss such readings as skewed, as lacking requisite exegetical
skills. According to the *'ulama*, without the guidance of a scholar well
versed in the Qur'an and its interpretation, a lay reader will go astray.[34]
And it is this scholarly claim to *own* the Qur'an that violates, for Esack,
the profoundly universal spirit of the text. In our interview, he described

---

[31] Khurram Murad, as quoted in Ahmad von Denffer, *'Ulum al-Qur'an: An
Introduction to the Sciences of the Qur'an* (Leicestershire: The Islamic Foundation,
2007), 179.
[32] Esack Interview, 2009. The founders of the Call of Islam (Esack included) were
former, disillusioned members of the Islamist-inspired Muslim Youth Movement
(MYM), breaking away from the latter due to a number of ideological reasons. See
Kelly, 128. The parallels that exist between Esack's and Islamist hermeneutics, therefore, are not a coincidence. For a historical analysis of how Islamism (and humanism)
influenced South African Muslim discourse, see Matthew Palombo, 'The Emergence
of Islamic Liberation Theology in South Africa', *Journal of Religion in Africa* 44
(2014): 28–61.
[33] Taji-Farouki, 12.
[34] Farid Esack, 'Contemporary Religious Thought in South Africa and the Emergence of Qur'anic Hermeneutical Notions', *Islam and Christian-Muslim Relations* 2:2
(1991): 210–11.

the *'ulama's* deep-seated reservations about direct access to the Qur'an as follows:

> I think it has something to do with control. You have all of these barricades, all these walls, and they are not just walls. All these walls, all of these barricades have gatekeepers. And the gatekeepers derive their own meaning from their role as controllers or managers of the sacred. So once you say that, look, I want to parachute into the centre and seek an audience with the centre, all these people who have made their livings and have derived meanings from being interlocutors with the centre, you are threatening them. So they have sacralised all these borders, all these boundaries and so on, but it is also really about their authority. They will say we want to protect the centre.[35]

This points to another problem in Rahman's approach: that it is an essentially elitist enterprise. For if the classical context is to be hermeneutically positioned between the Creator and the contemporary reader then so, too, must religious authority be delegated to those very few people, traditionally trained or otherwise, who can partake in this scholarly project.

In Esack's reading of the Qur'an through the lens of the present, he consciously privileges the perspective of the poor and the oppressed. The following guideline from Murad's essay on how to approach the text betrays a key difference between the readings of Esack and contemporary Islamists: 'Read the Qur'an with a mind free from bias and preconceived ideas, as otherwise you will read your own notions into the book.'[36] There is no acknowledgement, therefore, that the reader brings a *pretext*, conditioned by class, religion, ethnicity, gender, time, and place, among other factors, to the text and that this contextual baggage constitutes an inescapable reality of reading. This is not to imply, however, that classical Islamic scholars acknowledged their own biases when approaching scripture. Within traditional exegesis—a dense body of knowledge built on the continuous accumulation of commentary over the generations—interpretations that lay outside the fold of orthodoxy were hastily consigned to the categorical dustbin of *tafsir bi'l-ra'y*, or 'commentary by opinion'.[37] In contrast to this lack of reflexivity, Esack is keenly aware that he

---

[35] Esack Interview, 2009.
[36] Murad, as quoted in von Denffer, *'Ulum al-Qur'an: An Introduction to the Sciences of the Qur'an*, 180.
[37] Esack, *Qur'an, Liberation, and Pluralism*, 75.

cannot approach the Qur'an as a disembodied figure, appreciating that he brings to the text limited horizons rooted in his own reality.[38] And it is through this acknowledgement that all readings are contextual that he chooses to favour a specific context: that of the oppressed. The principal subjects of Esack's interpretation are not the powerful and the affluent, but the marginalized (*al-aradhil*) and the downtrodden (*al-mustad'afun*).[39] It is important to clarify here that he is not interested in merely including the perspective of the marginalized into a growing pool of existing accounts. Esack's hermeneutic is not one in which the discourses of the powerful and the powerless weigh in side-by-side. Instead, he privileges the vantage point, the experiences of the oppressed.[40]

But Esack does not read from the perspective of the oppressed as a neutral and disinterested observer. Rather, he approaches the text as an ally actively engaged in struggle with the oppressed against their oppressor. Esack's understanding of Islam is one that emerges in the heat of resistance, for 'understanding is viewed as the product of engagement for justice combined with reflection'.[41] *Praxis*—the idea that the struggle against oppression ought to form the framework through which theology emerges[42]—is a cornerstone of his exegesis. And it is precisely this overtly political aspect of Esack's reading that makes his hermeneutic a hermeneutic of liberation. The pioneering Christian liberation theologian, Gustavo Gutiérrez, sums up the difference between liberating and conventional exegesis:

> the theology of liberation offers us not so much a new theme for reflection as a new *way* to do theology. Theology as critical reflection on historical praxis is a liberating theology.[43] (My italics)

Theology and struggle, therefore, are inextricably interwoven into a dialectical paradigm of action, religious reflection, and renewed action—a mode of reading sanctioned, Esack argues, by the very

---

[38] Esack, *The Qur'an: A User's Guide*, 192.

[39] Farid Esack, 'In Search of Progressive Islam Beyond 9/11', in *Progressive Muslims: On Justice, Gender, and Pluralism*, ed. Omid Safi (Oxford: Oneworld, 2003), 81.

[40] Esack Interview, 2009.

[41] Esack, 'In Search of Progressive Islam Beyond 9/11', 80.

[42] Christopher Rowland ed., *The Cambridge Companion to Liberation Theology* (Cambridge: Cambridge University Press, 2007), xix.

[43] Gustavo Gutiérrez, *A Theology of Liberation: History, Politics, and Salvation* (Maryknoll, New York: Orbis Books, 1973), 15.

nature of the Qur'an's revelation. For the text never presented itself as a coherent and closed scripture, but as 'a revealed discourse unfolding in response to the requirements of a society over a period of twenty-three years (Q. 17:82; 17:106)'.[44] God was thoroughly immersed in the struggles of the early Muslim community, manifesting the divine presence, through the act of revelation, in response to various situations as they emerged. In other words, the seemingly insulated categories of text and context were collapsed into a hermeneutical circle of liberation: struggle, followed by revelation and introspection, followed by further struggle.[45] Hence, the Qur'an's revelation reflects a deity who engages history and whose discourse is shaped by that history, intervening in and conversing with the affairs of humankind. Esack calls this Qur'anic commitment to *praxis* 'progressive revelation'—a form of scriptural engagement that characterized the lives of the first Muslims. And it is because the text speaks to all times and places that the principle of progressive revelation, too, is universal. To be sure, Esack clarifies that the process of *revelation* was completed with Muhammad as the Final Messenger and Seal of the Prophets—a key Muslim belief—and so when Esack refers to interacting with the Qur'an today through *praxis* he is referring to the process of *understanding*.[46] Through this commitment to *praxis*, the Qur'an becomes alive and speaks in a liberating way to every generation of Muslims, who draw their own distinctive meanings and inspiration from the text.[47]

It is misleading and simplistic to dismiss interpretations rooted in *praxis* as being politicized or contextual, for all readings are inescapably shaped by context and reflect vested political interests. Many contemporary Islamic scholars, traditional or otherwise, have hastily dismissed what they have deemed as politicized readings of Islam. Rahman is a compelling case in point. Operating on the assumption

---

[44] Esack, *Qur'an, Liberation, and Pluralism*, 53.

[45] Esack, *On Being a Muslim*, 3.

[46] Esack, 'Contemporary Religious Thought in South Africa and the Emergence of Qur'anic Hermeneutical Notions', 222. While Esack focuses on the progressive nature of the Qur'an's revelation in seventh-century Arabia when arguing for a *praxis*-based hermeneutical precedent in Islam, he also points to Q. 29:69, which reads: 'To those who strive for Us, We will surely guide them to our ways, and indeed God is with the doers of good.' To quote Esack's reflection on Q. 29:69: 'This verse implies a dialectical process whereby struggle informs guidance as much as guidance informs struggle.' See ibid, 221.

[47] Esack, 'Islam and Gender Justice', 206.

that there exists a pristine, apolitical state of being, Rahman criticized the mixing of religion and politics which, he argued, had led to disastrous consequences for Islamic thought.[48] What is even more problematic in Rahman's discourse is that while he was reluctant to partake in political activity, justice remained a core component of his exegesis, reiterating time and again that a key objective of scripture was the attainment of a socially just order.[49] This incongruence between Rahman's emphasis on Qur'anic justice on the one hand and his criticism of the mixing of religion and politics on the other— or, to put it another way, speaking of justice in purely abstract terms and thus divorced from specificity, from concrete contexts of oppression—raises larger ethical questions about those who preach justice but who are not, at the same time, engaged in struggle. The refusal to locate oneself within a decidedly political context is not restricted to Rahman, however. During the anti-apartheid movement the *'ulama*, many of whom chose to remain silent and complicit in the face of oppression, kept an arm's length from Muslim youth in confrontation with the state, dismissing them as having radicalized and politicized Islam.[50] Not only are detachment and neutrality hermeneutical impossibilities, but, within a context of manifest injustice, the claim to be apolitical, and thus to allow one's passivity to justify the existing status quo, constitutes the very foil of liberation: a theology of accommodation.[51]

Indeed, within the expressly politicized discourse of liberation theology, *praxis* is a central text that is to be read alongside the Qur'anic text. Most Islamic reformists who have sought to reread scripture in light of contemporary circumstances have, in spite of their differing methods, searched for the right way to expound the text. Rahman, for instance, was pre-occupied with finding the 'correct method' of interpreting the Qur'an, and this objective lay at the heart of his pioneering scholarship.[52] His interest in unearthing the proper methodology of Qur'anic exegesis, culminating in the double

---

[48] Dale F. Eickelman and James Piscatori, *Muslim Politics* (Princeton: Princeton University Press, 1996), 53.

[49] Fazlur Rahman, *Major Themes of the Qur'an* (Minneapolis, US: Bibliotheca Islamica, 1994), 37.

[50] Farid Esack, 'Three Islamic Strands in the South African Struggle for Justice', *Third World Quarterly* 10 (1988): 478.

[51] Esack, *Qur'an, Liberation, and Pluralism*, 7.

[52] Rahman, *Islam and Modernity*, 1.

movement theory, was premised on the deep-seated conviction that there exist concrete and unchanging principles within the text. The trick was simply to discern the universals from the particulars. And it is here that a fundamental divergence emerges between Rahman and Esack, for *whose* understanding of the universal gets universalized? As Esack exclaims: 'It's not just: Oh, the Qur'an must be studied in its context. Whose context?'[53] The context and vantage point of the slave is radically different from that of the slave-master—a lived experience that will inevitably shape the type of exegesis that emerges. Thus, within a theology of liberation, lived realities of inequality and oppression constitute the interpretive point of departure, reflecting an embodied text ('life') that is as significant as the written text ('scripture').[54] Because context is never universal or stable, and because context is hermeneutically on a par with scripture, truth— what Rahman calls *the* underlying principles of the Qur'an—can never be singular and absolute, timeless and disembodied. Rather, through the process of *praxis* truth manifests itself, in complex and manifold ways, as an ever-unfolding discourse to those immersed in struggle.[55]

ISLAM AND THE TASK OF LIBERATION

On Divine Justice

Justice is a crucial part of the Qur'anic message. In fact, it constitutes such an important component of the Qur'anic worldview that, Esack reminds us, justice is one of the reasons as to why God created the universe (Q. 45:22):[56] so that every human being, via the Day of Reckoning, will receive exactly what s/he sows and thus no soul shall be oppressed. Justice, therefore, is a distinctly divine quality. God can never act unjustly. This is the natural state of the universe and humankind is obligated to act in a fair, equitable manner with others and to avoid partaking in oppression, as this would run

---

[53] Esack Interview, 2009.   [54] Rowland, 7–8.

[55] Esack, *Qur'an, Liberation, and Pluralism*, 111.

[56] Farid Esack, *But Musa Went to Fir-aun! A Compilation of Questions and Answers about the Role of Muslims in the South African Struggle for Liberation* (Maitland, South Africa: Call of Islam, 1989), 77.

contrary to the nature of God.[57] Moreover, humankind is commanded to establish an enduring, ethically based order on Earth,[58] thereby mirroring the divine justice of the Heavens. Action is thus located at the very heart of Islamic theology, for true faith is belief wedded to action. The Arabic word for faith in the Qur'an—*iman*—entails not only believing in God, but also observing righteous conduct, such as treating others in a just manner, giving charity and performing prayers.[59] The overwhelming emphasis on action in Esack's Islamic discourse—as we have just seen with regard to *praxis*—bears remarkable resemblance, yet again, to Islamist approaches to the text, in which Qur'anic reading is not an abstract, intellectual exercise but a solemn act of submission, of translating the Qur'an's teachings into one's daily life. Indeed, it is only through action, through putting the divine word into practice, that the text's meaning is unlocked to the reader. As Murad, the Islamist writer whom we met earlier, cautions: 'Do not forget that the real key to understanding the Qur'an is the practical application of its meaning.'[60]

The Qur'an does not only mandate the believers to act justly, argues Esack, but expresses a preferential option for the oppressed and explicitly sides with them. Just as justice is a core theme, so is its antithesis: oppression (*zulm*), a ubiquitous term in the Qur'an. In fact, the linguistic root of *zulm* appears in various forms on almost every page of the text.[61] Upon making a clear distinction between the opposing states of justice and oppression, Esack writes, the Qur'an takes an unqualified stance with those who are being wronged—the downtrodden (*al-mustad'afun*)—over those responsible for such oppression (*al-mustakbirun*) and who have therefore transgressed the bounds of just conduct (Q. 7:136–137; 28:5).[62] It is important to note here that within a theology of liberation, God does not side with those who are oppressed but who, nonetheless, have faith and do righteous works. Rather, divine solidarity with the oppressed is unconditional, unqualified: God stands with the downtrodden

---

[57] Toshihiko Izutsu, *Ethico-Religious Concepts in the Qur'an* (Montreal: McGill-Queen's University Press, 2002), 18.

[58] Rahman, *Major Themes of the Qur'an*, 37.

[59] Michael Sells, *Approaching the Qur'an: The Early Revelations* (Ashland, Oregon: White Cloud Press, 1999), 37.

[60] Murad, as quoted in von Denffer, 180.   [61] Izutsu, 164.

[62] Esack, *Qur'an, Liberation, and Pluralism*, 98.

precisely because they have been wronged and exploited.[63] The question of their belief or righteousness is irrelevant. This notion of God as exerting a preferential option for the oppressed became common currency amongst South African Muslims during the anti-apartheid struggle. Specifically, verses five and six of *Surat al-Qasas* (The Chapter of the Story; Chapter 28) became the most significant Qur'anic passages quoted time and again by activist Muslims of all ideological strands.[64] Referring to the ancient Israelites suffering under the yoke of Pharaoh's oppression, the verses read:

> It is Our Will to bestow Our grace upon the downtrodden of the Earth, and to make them the leaders and to make them the inheritors of the Earth. And to establish them securely on the Earth, and to let Pharaoh and Haman and their hosts experience through them (the Children of Israel) the very thing against which they sought to protect themselves.

The commitment of God to the oppressed, then, is sacralised in a solemn covenant: that injustice, soon, will be dismantled through a radical reconfiguration of the existing status quo, wherein those who were at the very bottom of society will inherit the Earth.[65]

Esack and the Exodus: A Critique and a Proposal

Indeed, the Exodus is the central paradigm in Esack's liberation theology—an aspect of his Qur'anic hermeneutic that bears a striking similarity to Christian liberation theology. The Exodus is an exemplary model of interfaith solidarity with the oppressed, Esack argues, for it not only reflects a deity who sided with the enslaved Israelites against Pharaoh, but did so in spite of the Israelites' constant displays of disbelief (Q. 2:51; 2:55; 26:67), refusing to leave their side until they had reached the Promised Land.[66] God stood with the faithless

---

[63] Leonardo Boff and Clodovis Boff, *Introducing Liberation Theology* (Maryknoll, New York: Orbis Books, 1999), 48.

[64] Esack, *Qur'an, Liberation, and Pluralism*, 101. Q. 2:193 and 4:75—both calling on believers to struggle against oppression—also became popular Qur'anic passages in South African anti-apartheid Muslim circles. See Palombo, 44.

[65] Esack is not the only Muslim, of course, to have been inspired by the story of Moses and the Israelites. For an analysis of how Sayyid Qutb interprets this story, see Anthony H. Johns, 'Let my people go! Sayyid Qutb and the Vocation of Moses', *Islam and Christian-Muslim Relations* 1:2 (1990): 143–70.

[66] Esack, *Qur'an, Liberation, and Pluralism*, 195–6.

Israelites, then, because they were being oppressed.[67] Yet as compelling as the Exodus is as a pluralistic model of liberation, it is important to note that Christian liberation theology, too, builds heavily on the Exodus experience. In addition to drawing great inspiration from the example of Jesus Christ as the struggle for justice personified,[68] Gutiérrez—a founding figure of Latin American liberation theology whom we mentioned earlier—drew extensively upon the Exodus when putting to paper his pioneering tract on liberation theology in the 1960s. In fact, according to Gutiérrez, the Exodus represented a 'paradigmatic' event in biblical history, constituting a liberating hermeneutical lens with which to reinterpret the Old and New Testaments.[69] In other words, when reading Esack in light of Christian liberation theology, one wonders how organic an Islamic theology of liberation built upon the Exodus experience truly is? This is not to imply that the Exodus is an exclusively biblical event and, as such, Islamically inauthentic. On the contrary, the Qur'an lays a powerful claim over all the Abrahamic prophets, embracing them as part and parcel of the monotheistic call.[70] In fact, Moses is the most mentioned prophet in the text, his name surfacing approximately 140 times.[71]

Rather, my argument is that because of the power differential that exists between Christianity and Islam, it is necessary to foreground the specificity of Islam in order to counter a universalizing Christian framework. As a result of over 200 years of world dominance through colonialism and imperialism, Europe and North America have come to occupy very different positions within the global power structure than the rest of the world. This disparity, in turn, has had tremendous consequences in terms of modern knowledge production. As the South Asian historian, Dipesh Chakrabarty, sums it up:

---

[67] The faithlessness of the Israelites is further evidenced, as Esack points out, by Q. 10:83, which states that only a small group of them (*dhurriyyatun*) believed in the God of Moses. See ibid. In a separate study, it is worth noting, Esack has explored the complex manner in which Jews are represented in the Qur'an, underlining a plurality of Qur'anic narratives and thereby challenging mainstream Muslim assumptions that the Jews have incurred divine wrath. See Farid Esack, "The Portrayal of Jews and the Possibilities for Their Salvation in the Qur'an," in *Between Heaven and Hell: Islam, Salvation, and the Fate of Others*, ed. Mohammad Hassan Khalil (Oxford: Oxford University Press, 2013).

[68] Gutiérrez, 35.   [69] Ibid, 158–9.

[70] Omid Safi, *Memories of Muhammad: Why the Prophet Matters* (New York: HarperOne, 2009), 196.

[71] Esack, *The Qur'an: A User's Guide*, 154.

insofar as the academic discourse of history—that is, 'history' as a
discourse produced at the institutional site of the university—is concerned, 'Europe' remains the sovereign, theoretical subject of all histories, including the ones we call 'Indian,' 'Chinese,' 'Kenyan,' and so on.
There is a peculiar way in which all these other histories tend to become
variations on a master narrative that would be called 'the history of
Europe.'[72]

In other words, Europe has become universalized as an intellectual
frame of reference. Or, to put it another way, non-European histories
have been stripped of their specificities, becoming homogenized in
their incorporation as backward into a grand narrative defined by (an
idealized reading of) European historical experience. There is, therefore, an intellectual culture of inequality. Asian and African historians
are often expected, for example, to refer to the histories of Europe and
North America while European and North American historians sel-
dom feel the need to cite the histories of Asia and Africa.[73] And
because Christianity in general, and the figures, stories, and imageries
of the Bible in particular, were—and to varying degrees remain—a
major source of European culture,[74] the language and experience of
(Western) Christianity, too, has become universalized.[75] This phenomenon is particularly acute in the modern academic discipline of
Religion, also known as Theology, which originated in Catholic and
Protestant circles.[76] Within the field of Religion, students of Islam are
expected to be familiar with Christianity, Christian debates, and the
Bible in a way that is rarely reciprocated by their Christian counterparts. Indeed, the very terms of discourse reflect a history rooted in a
distinctly Christian past. For instance, the idea of religious tolerance,
which is routinely used nowadays to refer to mutual understanding

[72] Dipesh Chakrabarty, *Provincializing Europe: Postcolonial Thought and Historical Difference* (Princeton: Princeton University Press, 2000), 27.
[73] Talal Asad, *Genealogies of Religion: Discipline and Reasons of Power in Christianity and Islam* (Baltimore: Johns Hopkins University Press, 1993), 1.
[74] John Riches, *The Bible: A Very Short Introduction* (Oxford: Oxford University
Press, 2000), 100.
[75] To be sure, the power differential between Islam and Christianity is not necessarily material, but rather epistemic. This is particularly true in the context of
liberation theology, since Latin America has been the continental wellspring of
Christian liberation theology. Radical exegesis of the Bible, then, has emerged from
a region of the world that has been as economically exploited as Africa and Asia.
[76] Carl W. Ernst, *Following Muhammad: Rethinking Islam in the Contemporary
World* (Chapel Hill: University of North Carolina Press, 2003), 47.

between different faith traditions, emerged in the aftermath of Europe's wars of religion, seeking to underline the plurality of paths *within* Christianity.[77] In other words, just as non-European historians need to struggle against the grain of the European experience as an underlying, universalizing tendency in the discipline of History, so must non-Christian theologians struggle against the epistemic might of the Christian experience as a homogenizing force in Religion. And it is in this pursuit to craft an Islamic theology of liberation that becomes more than simply a variation on a master narrative called Christianity, I argue, that historical and theological difference—that is, the specificity of Islam and Muslim experiences—ought to be foregrounded.[78]

An alternative point of departure that may be more promising in conceptualizing an Islamic liberation theology that explicitly embraces this question of difference is that of *tawhid*—or the Divine Unity (the absolute Oneness) of God—and the ensuing social, economic, and political implications of this central Islamic belief. This liberating idea that the Oneness of a just God must be paralleled by the Oneness of a single humanity, and thus that anything that divides the creation into hierarchies violates the divine unity of the Creator, was first articulated amongst Islamic radicals during the Iranian Revolution of 1978–9, in particular the Mujahidin-i Khalq.[79] Combining Islamic and Marxist teachings, the Mujahidin-i Khalq was a resistance group committed to armed struggle against the Shah's regime.[80] Ali Shari'ati (d. 1977)—a leading revolutionary figure and intellectual in Iran—became a chief exponent of the sociopolitical implications of *tawhid*. As a divine concept built on the intrinsic unity of all beings, argued Shari'ati, *tawhid* cannot accept any

---

[77] Ibid, 39–43.

[78] For a more extensive exposition of this critique, see Shadaab Rahemtulla, 'Im Schatten des Christentums? Die Herausforderung islamischer Befreiungstheologie' [In the Shadow of Christianity? The Challenge of an Islamic Liberation Theology], in *Gott und Befreiung. Befreiungstheologische Konzepte in Islam und Christentum* [God and Liberation: Concepts of Liberation Theology in Islam and Christianity], eds. Klaus von Stosch and Muna Tatari (Paderborn, Germany: Schöningh, 2012).

[79] Esack, *Qur'an, Liberation, and Pluralism*, 83.

[80] The Mujahidin emerged in the 1960s as an outgrowth of the religious faction of the wider national struggle. Its members were initially part of the Freedom Movement of Iran, which underscored the compatibility between Shi'a Islam and modernity, and was thus largely liberal in scope. However, state suppression, especially in 1963, radicalized segments of the Freedom Movement and the origins of the Mujahidin are to be found in this transformation. See Nikki R. Keddie, *Modern Iran: Roots and Results of Revolution* (New Haven: Yale University Press, 2003), 220–2.

'contradictions', such as those of economic, social, legal, geographical or racial hierarchy.[81] Whereas Shari'ati and the Mujahidin-i Khalq approached *tawhid* primarily from the perspective of class, two decades later gender activists would draw on *tawhid* extensively when critiquing patriarchy and male privilege. As we shall see in the following chapters on Wadud and Barlas, Islamic monotheism is a core paradigm in women's gender egalitarian readings of the Qur'an. This doctrine, therefore, has been invoked increasingly as a guiding hermeneutical principle in liberationist expositions of Islam.

Two points of clarification are in order here. Firstly, I do not wish to imply that *tawhid* is entirely absent from Esack's hermeneutic. In weaving together an Islamic theology of liberation, he redefines, in light of his own experience and struggles against apartheid, a number of Qur'anic concepts, such as *al-mustad'afun fi al-ard* ('the oppressed on the Earth'), *jihad* ('struggle and praxis'), *al-nas* ('the people', that is, in the popular sense of the word), *taqwa* ('integrity and awareness in relation to the presence of God'), and *tawhid* ('divine unity').[82] And in his reading of *tawhid*, Esack echoes the earlier arguments of Shari'ati by unpacking the sociopolitical implications of this key tenet. But Esack consigns *tawhid* to the back of his theology and devotes far more attention to the Exodus, despite the fact that the language of *tawhid* became widely circulated amongst South African Muslims during the anti-apartheid struggle. As he himself notes, Islamic activists used terms like 'tawhidi society' and 'the sociological implications of tawhid' in their demands for a qualitatively different order, condemning apartheid as a form of *shirk*—the cardinal sin of associating partners with God and, thus, the theological foil of *tawhid*—since apartheid undermined the unity of God by dividing humanity into unequal racial camps.[83]

Secondly, I do not mean to suggest that contemporary Muslim thinkers have drawn upon *tawhid* in solely progressive terms. Consider the Wahhabi movement or, as they refer to themselves, the *muwahhidun* (literally, the monotheists). *Tawhid* was a central aspect of the revivalist discourse of the Najd-based scholar Muhammad ibn 'Abd al-Wahhab (d. 1792). Calling for a return to the Qur'an and

---

[81] Ali Shari'ati, 'On the Sociology of Islam: The World-View of Tawhid', in *Introduction to Islam: A Reader*, ed. Amina Wadud (Dubuque, Iowa: Kendall/Hunt Publishing, 2007), 3.

[82] Esack, *Qur'an, Liberation, and Pluralism*, 83.   [83] Ibid, 91–2.

sunna, he and his followers maintained that Islam needed to be cleansed from so-called deviant beliefs and practices—especially Sufi Islam and its emphasis on saintly veneration, as well as heterodox sects like Shi'a Islam—which, they claimed, were guilty of *shirk*.[84] Wahhabism thus reflects a sharply puritan, literalist approach to Islam, fixated on dogma and ritual practice and with little interest in questions of social justice. The political thought of Mawdudi is another example of a non-progressive exegesis of *tawhid*. Islamic monotheism was central for Mawdudi, and his reflections would have a lasting impact on Qutb. For Mawdudi, to accept *tawhid* is to acknowledge the 'sovereignty of God' with all its political and legal consequences, namely, that 'God alone is the source of the law, all people must submit to this law, and the sole mandate of the Islamic state is to implement this law.'[85] *Tawhid*, then, has become an increasingly prominent theme in contemporary Islamic thought, and progressives like Shari'ati, Wadud, and Barlas are a part of this broader trend while, at the same time, departing from it by reinterpreting monotheism in significant and unique ways.[86]

What makes *tawhid* so provocative as a point of departure for a liberating Islamic theology is that it not only weds the struggle for justice to the single most important tenet in Islam, but also foregrounds the specificity of Muslim theology. Christ stands at the centre of Christianity in general,[87] and of Christian liberation theology in particular,[88] and the nature of the biblical text mirrors the distinctiveness of this theology. Indeed, in traditional Christianity it is not the Bible that is considered to be the Word of God but Christ himself.[89]

---

[84] There is a dearth of serious scholarship (as opposed to sensationalist writings) on the history and politics of Wahhabism. For two refreshingly sober and nuanced accounts, see David D. Commins, *The Wahhabi Mission and Saudi Arabia* (London: I.B. Tauris, 2009) and Natana J. DeLong-Bas, *Wahhabi Islam: From Revival to Reform to Global Jihad* (Oxford: Oxford University Press, 2004).

[85] Roxanne L. Euben and Muhammad Q. Zaman eds., *Princeton Readings in Islamist Thought: Texts and Contexts from al-Banna to Bin Laden* (Princeton: Princeton University Press, 2009), 81. To clarify, here I am quoting Euben and Zaman.

[86] I am grateful to James McDougall for this insight.

[87] Christopher Rowland and Jonathan Roberts, *The Bible for Sinners: Interpretation in the Present Time* (London: Society for Promoting Christian Knowledge, 2008), 21.

[88] Boff and Boff, 4.

[89] This is not the case, of course, for many conservative Protestant Christians, who view the Bible as God's Word, as 'God-breathed', and hence holding a similar ontological status as the Qur'an for Muslims.

The Bible represents a collection of texts, produced by individuals and communities, which reflect upon the example of Jesus and, as a sustained reflection, can never fully capture him, since the Son of God cannot be confined to a text. The roles of Prophet Muhammad and the Qur'anic text within the Islamic worldview, on the other hand, are markedly different. The Prophet of Islam holds no comparable position to the Christ of Christianity for, according to Muslims, Muhammad was a mortal man whose vocation was to deliver a divine message. The closest Islamic equivalent to the Christian Jesus is the Qur'an,[90] which is understood as the actual Speech of God. And it is precisely because Muslims perceive the Qur'an as being the Word that it is God, alone, who stands at the heart of the Islamic faith. The intrinsic value of *tawhid* as the conceptual framework for radical thought and action, then, is that it acknowledges the theological distinctiveness of Islam as a vigorously monotheistic religion. As Esack himself affirms, it is God and the belief in this single deity that comprises the crux of the Qur'anic call, receiving far more attention than any other topic in the text.[91]

Towards a Comprehensive Justice: Prophetic Solidarity

A crucial aspect of Esack's understanding of justice is its comprehensive character. Esack is usually associated with the anti-apartheid struggle in South Africa. As important as this struggle was for Esack, however, his Islamic liberation theology cannot be reduced to it because, as a Coloured South African, he had vested interests in seeing the struggle through. As integral as the commitment to the liberation of one's own oppressed social, religious or racial group is, warns Esack, a genuine commitment to morality lies in being moved not by one's own suffering but by the suffering of others.[92] This is the litmus test of the ethical, empathetic human being. Justice must be comprehensive—encompassing racial, class, and gender equality—and is the right of all of humanity, not a specific subsection of it. Esack's sense of liberation, then, is utterly universal. The South African struggle acted as a critical point of departure for this

---

[90] Esack, *The Qur'an: A User's Guide*, 16.   [91] Ibid, 147.
[92] Farid Esack, 'Open Letter', *Jewish Peace News* (2009), available at: http://jewishpeacenews.blogspot.co.uk/2009/04/farid-esacks-open-letter-is-inscribed.html accessed 3 September 2012.

understanding. His experience of growing up under apartheid not only allowed him, when travelling to Pakistan for Islamic training, to make connections with the discrimination of women in Muslim-majority societies,[93] but also the second-class status of Pakistani Christians.[94] It is due to the complexity, the multilayered basis of oppression that Esack's definition of liberation is equally complex and layered, entailing 'the freedom of all people from all those laws, social norms and economic practices that militate against them developing their potential to be fully human.'[95]

Because Esack's understanding of justice is universal, solidarity—what he calls 'prophetic Islam'—features prominently in his liberationist discourse. Simply translated, prophetic Islam is a *principled* practice of solidarity, whereby a Muslim stands with the oppressed while at the same time acknowledging that this analytical category—'the oppressed'—is not fixed or timeless but conditioned, and repeatedly reconditioned, by an ever-changing context, denoting different communities and individuals in different times and places.[96] Esack foregrounds this contextually contingent practice of solidarity since he has witnessed, at first hand, how an oppressed group can, with the passage of time, actually become the oppressing party: namely, the Afrikaners of South Africa. Initially the victims of the British, who placed them in concentration camps and destroyed almost a sixth of their population, the Afrikaners went on to consolidate their colonization of indigenous Black land, erecting a deeply authoritarian and White-supremacist state.[97] The case of European Jewry is another compelling example: the very people who experienced the horrors of the Nazi holocaust became staunch supporters of Israel—a settler-colonial state built on the ethnic cleansing of Palestine and that

[93] Farid Esack, 'Religio-Cultural Diversity: For What and With Whom? Muslim Reflections from a Post-Apartheid South Africa in the Throes of Globalization', in *Cultural Diversity in Islam*, eds. Abdul Aziz Said and Meena Sharify-Funk (Lanham, Maryland: University Press of America, 2003), 167.

[94] Michael Wolfe ed., *Taking Back Islam: American Muslims Reclaim their Faith* (Emmaus, Pennsylvania: Rodale Press, 2004), 15.

[95] Esack, *Qur'an, Liberation, and Pluralism*, xi.

[96] Farid Esack, 'The Contemporary Democracy and the Human Rights Project for Muslim Societies: Challenges for the Progressive Muslim Intellectual', in *Contemporary Islam: Dynamic, not Static*, eds. Abdul Aziz Said, Mohammad Abu-Nimr, and Meena Sharify-Funk (London: Routledge, 2006), 125.

[97] Esack, 'Open Letter'.

continues to occupy Palestinian land illegally.[98] A prophetic solidarity, therefore, is about being vigilant of the inherently fluid and dynamic nature of injustice. As Esack puts it:

> While I can, for example, be in solidarity with a male black worker in respect of the exploitation that he experiences at work, I ought to be in solidarity with his abused wife in the home context. While I can be in solidarity with the Muslim male who is being racially profiled at airports, I can be in solidarity with the marginalized Christian who lives in the same Muslim country that the Muslim male comes from.[99]

In other words, by avoiding sweeping affiliation with abstract, disembodied communities—Muslims or Blacks or workers—and instead constantly defining and redefining the categories of oppressor and oppressed within a complex, ever-changing web of power relations, the progressive Muslim intellectual is able to pre-empt the reproduction of the very inequality that s/he seeks to critique. Prophetic Islam and the type of principled solidarity that it espouses, then, is built on a keen sense of *vision*: that whatever struggle one may be engaged in at the moment, the ultimate objective is the establishment of a genuinely inclusive social order wherein all people are equal.[100]

Fitra, or human nature, is an interesting aspect of Esack's discourse on solidarity with the oppressed. Muslims often describe Islam as *din al-fitra*. Departing from mainstream Muslim understandings of *din al-fitra*, which views Islam as the natural religion of humankind, thereby treating other religions as abberations,[101] Esack understands Islam's description as *din al-fitra* as being a religion based on the natural state of humankind,[102] that is, on one's humanity. The Islamic scholars Kecia Ali and Oliver Leaman have a similar rendering of *fitra*, which they describe as the innate inclination of every human

---

[98] The underlying purpose behind Esack's reflection on the Afrikaner experience and their transition from oppressed to oppressor is to make a wider analogy between apartheid South Africa and the state of Israel, as this reflection commences an open letter that Esack wrote to the Palestinians in solidarity with their national struggle (see ibid). The letter will be discussed shortly.

[99] Esack, 'The Contemporary Democracy and the Human Rights Project for Muslim Societies', 125.

[100] Esack Interview, 2009.

[101] Farid Esack, 'Muslims Engaging the Other and the Humanum', in *Proselytization and Communal Self-Determination in Africa*, ed. Abdullahi A. An-Na'im (Eugene, OR: Wipf and Stock, 2009), 52.

[102] Esack, 'Islam and Gender Justice', 189.

being, from the beginning of time when God fashioned Adam, to yearn for goodness.[103] For Esack, the presence and persistence of injustice constitute a threat to this natural state of being and thus one's humanity is fundamentally compromised if one does not act.[104] Esack, therefore, has an acutely communitarian sense of selfhood, for his *fitra* is wedded to the well-being of those around him and by standing for others he is, in fact, standing for himself. The idea that the liberation of the Self is intrinsically tied to the liberation of the Other—that *I* am lacking because *you* are suffering—has deep roots in Islam. The *zaka*, or annual almsgiving, is one of the five pillars of the faith. Yet the actual definition of *zaka* is neither almsgiving nor charity. Literally, *zaka* means 'purification', referring to the idea that when a Muslim gives a portion of her/his accrued wealth to the needy, the remaining amount is purified in the eyes of God.[105] The concept of *fitra* is especially salient to solidarity and activism because it provides an alternative, theoretical framework to the patronizing discourse of benevolence and charity. Standing in solidarity with others, through the framework of *fitra*, is not about doing a favour to the less fortunate, for the favour, by affirming one's own humanity through the act of standing, is done to oneself. As Esack describes it within the context of gender justice:

> This is not a favour that I am doing for women. I have often used the analogy that if I am holding someone down, I am not free to be myself. I can't grow, I can't enjoy the sun, I just can't *be*.[106]

It is important to appreciate the significance of this point, as it raises crucial questions concerning the complex power dynamics at play in solidarity work. Is a White American activist's humanity fully intact if s/he, whilst standing in solidarity with Black Americans, reproduces racial inequality by speaking over the voices of the very people that s/he is standing with? Is a male feminist's humanity wholly intact if he, when articulating an anti-patriarchal platform, does so with a voice louder than the very women that he is in solidarity with? By acknowledging one's own complicity in complex systems of oppression, the concept of *fitra* forcefully shifts the battleground of liberation from

---

[103] Kecia Ali and Oliver Leaman, *Islam: The Key Concepts* (London: Routledge, 2008), 40.
[104] Esack, *On Being a Muslim*, 79.   [105] Ali and Leaman, 19.
[106] Esack Interview, 2009.

the Other to the Self. In so doing, it undercuts the consignment of the oppressed to the role of passive objects—that are to be pitied and patronized through benevolent acts of charity—encouraging, in its stead, reflexivity and humility on the part of those in solidarity with the oppressed.

Esack has been extensively involved in solidarity work, such as supporting the Palestinian cause and working with South African Muslims who have HIV/AIDS.[107] He has visited Palestine numerous times and has been a prominent participant in the international solidarity movement, regularly speaking at educational events like Israeli Apartheid Week.[108] In 2009, Esack wrote an open letter to the Palestinians, outlining the striking similarities between the Israeli occupation of Palestine and the oppression of Blacks under the apartheid regime in South Africa.[109] This letter was then spray-painted in large font on the so-called Security Fence in Palestine, the wording running for over two and a half kilometres. Drawing on his understanding of a prophetic Islam dedicated to the attainment of justice for all peoples, Esack describes his connection as a South African to Palestine as follows:

> Indeed, for those of us who lived under South African Apartheid and fought for liberation from it and everything that it represented, Palestine reflects in many ways the unfinished business of our own struggle.[110]

Here, again, liberation—although being waged in solidarity with the Other—is located within the Self. Esack's own humanity (*fitra*) is under siege so long as Israel continues to brutalize the Palestinians. He has also worked extensively with Muslims who are HIV-positive or have AIDS. Along with a number of colleagues, he established an

---

[107] While these are two prominent examples of his comprehensive approach to social justice, Esack has engaged numerous human rights issues. For instance, he has explored the rights of the child through an Islamic framework, focussing on the Qur'an's narratives on children and its discourse on parental obligations. See Farid Esack, "Islam, Children, and Modernity: A Qur'anic Perspective," in *Children, Adults, and Shared Responsibilities: Jewish, Christian, and Muslim Perspectives*, ed. Marcia J. Bunge (Cambridge: Cambridge University Press, 2014).

[108] Israeli Apartheid Week (IAW) is a weeklong series of lectures and activities held every spring that raise awareness about the Israeli occupation, promoting the global Boycott, Divestment, and Sanctions (BDS) campaign against the state of Israel. Initiated by Palestinian students at the University of Toronto in 2005, IAW has since spread to over fifty cities across the world and has aroused the ire of Zionist groups and conservative forces. See www.apartheidweek.org

[109] Esack, 'Open Letter'.   [110] Ibid.

organization in 2000 called Positive Muslims. In addition to creating a support network for victims, the group seeks to challenge dominant Muslim attitudes towards HIV/AIDS, exposing Muslim complicity in the stigmatization of those afflicted with the disease.[111] In his struggle to combat AIDS, Esack has repeatedly emphasized the socioeconomic roots of the pandemic. A meaningful struggle against AIDS, then, must include the critique of a cruel economic establishment that prioritizes profit over human welfare.[112] Capitalism, Esack laments, is a principal cause of global suffering, effectively cleaving the world into two unequal halves: the affluent North, comprising Western Europe and North America, which continues to become exponentially wealthier at the expense of the impoverished South—Africa, Asia, Latin America—leading to immense suffering for the vast majority of the Earth's inhabitants.[113]

It is the struggle for gender justice, however, that is most intimately tied to Esack's own liberation. Growing up in a single-parent family— recall that his father had abandoned his mother when Esack was only three weeks old, leaving her to raise six children on her own—Esack discerned the demons of patriarchy at a very young age. Furthermore, he experienced first-hand the close collusion of patriarchy, racism, and capitalism, as his mother laboured long hours every day as an underpaid factory worker, eventually succumbing to her crippling circumstances.[114] Indeed, the roots of Esack's liberationist discourse are to be found in this painful, formative period. Due to the efforts of South African Muslim feminists, including Esack, gender equality became an integral component of anti-apartheid discourse within the Muslim community. Wadud, whose hermeneutic we will explore in the fourth chapter, visited South Africa in 1994 and was struck by the centrality of gender justice amongst Muslims, who were even talking about the possibility of women leading ritual worship.[115] The following passage captures the critical linkages Esack draws between racism and patriarchy, underscoring their common denominator of inequality:

---

[111] Farid Esack, *HIV, AIDS and Islam: Reflections based on Compassion, Responsibility and Justice* (Cape Town: Positive Muslims, 2004), 5–6.

[112] Farid Esack and Sarah Chiddy eds. *Islam and AIDS: Between Scorn, Pity and Justice* (Oxford: Oneworld, 2009), 7.

[113] Esack, 'In Search of Progressive Islam Beyond 9/11', 91.

[114] Esack, *Qur'an, Liberation, and Pluralism*, 2.

[115] Amina Wadud, *Inside the Gender Jihad: Women's Reform in Islam* (Oxford: Oneworld, 2006), 166.

Every single argument, religious or cultural, that is employed to keep women in the kitchen or in the house has a parallel in racist discourse. 'Our traditional way of life,' 'Allah made them inferior,' 'No they are not inferior, merely different,' 'What would happen if women were to control the world?' . . . 'Of course women can govern, if they are capable.'[116]

In other words, to call for racial or economic justice without at the same time taking a firm stand against patriarchy (and vice versa) is hypocrisy. Inconsistency—the selective application of justice, restricting it to only certain struggles—is an act of *in*justice.

The realm of gender relations is illustrative of how, within Esack's hermeneutic, *praxis* constitutes as important a text that is to be read alongside the text of scripture. As central as the theme of justice is within the Qur'an, Esack is wary of idealizing the text. In particular, he notes that with regard to social and legal matters, the Qur'an presupposes male control over women, in that women are to be economically maintained and protected by men, scolded, and even beaten if they are disobedient.[117] The literal wording of the text, then, is essentially androcentric: a number of passages like Q. 4:34—the so-called Beating Verse, which we will engage in detail when examining women's gender egalitarian exegesis—clearly address men and speak of women in the third person, and therefore as objects to be acted upon by men.[118] Q. 4:34 reads:

Men are the guardians of women, because of the advantage God has granted some of them over others and by virtue of their spending out of their wealth. So righteous women are obedient, safeguarding what is unseen of what God has enjoined them to guard. As for those wives whose misconduct you fear, (first) advise them, and (if ineffective) keep away from them in the bed, and (as a last resort) beat them. Then if they obey you, do not seek any course (of action) against them. Indeed, God is all-Exalted, all-Great.

This critical take on the Qur'an stands in contrast, as we will see later in this book, to the exegeses of Engineer and Barlas, who insist that the text affirms the complete equality of women and men. It is necessary to clarify here that Esack does not view the Qur'an as an obstacle to gender justice. He writes that the text 'contains sufficient

[116] Esack, *On Being a Muslim*, 127–8.
[117] Esack, 'Islam and Gender Justice', 193.
[118] Ali, *Sexual Ethics and Islam*, 125–6.

seeds for those committed to human rights and gender justice to live in fidelity to its underlying ethos.'[119] But this does not entail partaking in, Esack stresses, simplistic apologia. He thus seeks to navigate a complex middle way between what he sees as two interpretive extremes: classical commentators who read far more patriarchy into the Qur'an than there actually was and, now, modern-day apologists—women and men alike—who are reading absolute gender justice into the Qur'an despite the fact that several verses presume male listeners and male control over women's bodies.[120] These are verses, argues Esack, which ought to be confronted, not ignored. And in this hermeneutical endeavour contemporary standards of justice, as defined through *praxis*, need to be taken as seriously as scripture itself. There are, then, two principal texts—the text of the Qur'an and the text of *praxis*—that must be reconciled through various reading strategies, one such strategy being an emphasis on the spirit over the letter: that whenever a seeming contradiction may emerge between scripture and *praxis*, the Qur'anic spirit, or what he refers to as 'its underlying ethos', is privileged over the Qur'anic letter. In so doing, Esack is able to acknowledge unapologetically the androcentrism of the text while, at the same time, using its gender egalitarian spirit to uphold contemporary understandings of justice.

In addition to the centrality of *praxis*, Esack's writings on gender are illustrative of his commitment to approaching social justice in a comprehensive fashion, namely, supporting queer Muslims through an anticolonial lens. Esack, and coauthor Nadeem Mahomed, a South African legal scholar, have argued that while Muslims need to be more tolerant of homosexuality, recent attempts at a 'homosexual friendly Islamic jurisprudence' ought to be critiqued.[121] Here, the authors refer to the work of the American Islamic scholar Scott Siraj al-Haqq Kugle, who has made a case for homosexuality through an Islamic framework, systematically expounding the Qur'an, *hadith*, and legal tradition.[122] Specifically, Esack and Mahomed contend that, in positing a sexually-sensitive reading of Islamic jurisprudence, Kugle plays into Western colonial notions of sexuality as a fixed, singular,

---

[119] Esack, 'Islam and Gender Justice', 203.

[120] Ali, *Sexual Ethics and Islam*, 126.

[121] Farid Esack and Nadeem Mahomed, 'Sexual Diversity, Islamic Jurisprudence and Sociality', *Journal of Gender and Religion in Africa* 17:2 (2011): 41.

[122] Scott Siraj Al-Haqq Kugle, *Homosexuality in Islam: Critical Reflection on Gay, Lesbian, and Transgender Muslims* (Oxford: Oneworld, 2010).

and stable category, thereby undermining sexuality's fluidity, complexity, and acutely unstable character, especially in non-Western societies.[123] In other words, while sexual justice is squarely a component of Esack's understanding of gender justice, he raises the following key question: sexuality on whose epistemological terms and based on whose lived experiences—that of the hegemonic West (read secular modernity) or the two-third world? In offering this postcolonial perspective the authors draw on, among others, the Palestinian intellectual Joseph Massad. Massad has argued that the 'Gay International', defined as the discourse of Western-based LGBTQ (lesbian, gay, bisexual, trans, and queer) organizations who claim to defend and speak on behalf of homosexuals worldwide,[124] effectively 'produces homosexuals, as well as gays and lesbians, where they do not exist, and represses same-sex desires and practices that refuse to be assimilated into its sexual epistemology.'[125] This discursive production is a result of treating sexual categories–gay, lesbian, homosexual–as universal, timeless, and stable, and by presuming that sexual practice is intrinsically linked to *identity*: that is, that someone who practices same-sex contact necessarily identifies as a homosexual subject.[126] For Massad, this linkage is not axiomatic but socially created, a product of Western historical experiences that were universalized, and that continue to be universalized, through empire. Esack and Mahomed, too, underline the connections between discourses of gay rights and empire (past and present), noting, for example, how Israel portrays itself as a homosexual safehaven in the Middle East while simultaneously brutalizing the Palestinians, straight and queer, through military occupation.[127] To be sure, Esack and Mahomed also challenge Massad on various levels, such as his lack "of any recognition whatsoever of the harsh negative effects of heteronormative societal structures on Muslim or Arab societies"[128] and his dismissive attitude towards queer identity

---

[123] Esack and Mahomed, "Sexual Diversity, Islamic Jurisprudence and Sociality," 49–50.
[124] Joseph Massad, 'Re-Orienting Desire: The Gay International and the Arab World', *Public Culture* 14:2 (2002): 361–2.
[125] Ibid, 363.   [126] Ibid, 362–3.
[127] Nadeem Mahomed and Farid Esack, "The Normal and Abnormal: On the Politics of Being Muslim and Relating to Same-Sex Sexuality," *Journal of the American Academy of Religion*, advance access published 24 July 2016, doi: 10.1093/jaarel/lfw057.
[128] Ibid.

politics. For this can serve to ignore the genuine grievances of (and, by extension, deny justice for) marginalized queer Muslims "struggling for acceptance and recognition, both spiritually and socially, as individuals, activists, and groups."[129]

INTERFAITH SOLIDARITY AND A COMMITMENT TO THE MARGINS

Beyond Dialogue

In this final section, I will reflect upon the significance of Esack's hermeneutic, beginning with its implications in terms of religious pluralism. The interfaith character of the anti-apartheid movement forced Esack to raise larger questions concerning the very nature of salvation. Solidarity amongst Muslims, Christians, and other religious groups became an integral component of the collective struggle, especially during the uprisings of the 1980s.[130] To be sure, not all South African Muslims resisted apartheid alongside the religious Other. The reluctance to partake in interfaith solidarity—particularly within the United Democratic Front—was actually a key reason why the founders of the Call of Islam (Esack included) broke away from the Muslim Youth Movement,[131] one of the most influential Islamic organizations in South Africa. Though the Dutch Reformed Church was complicit in providing scriptural support to the status quo, other Christian elements were actively engaged in the struggle against apartheid. The Kairos Document is a classic case in point. Published in 1985 by Christian clerics, it argued that the moment of truth (*kairos*) had arrived for the Church and that it was an ethical obligation for every Christian to partake in the struggle to create a just society, calling for civil disobedience to undermine the regime.[132] The deeply moving experience of standing with the religious Other, while a number of his own co-religionists chose silence in the face of oppression, compelled Esack to question the exclusivist notion that

---

[129] Ibid.
[130] Esack, *Qur'an, Liberation, and Pluralism*, 8.   [131] Kelly, 129–30.
[132] 'The Kairos Document,' as cited in Andrew Bradstock and Christopher Rowland eds., *Radical Christian Writings: A Reader* (Oxford: Blackwell Publishers, 2002), 303.

Muslims alone would achieve salvation. Indeed, being born into the fold of the faith is, for most Muslims, sufficient to be included amongst the ranks of the *mu'minun* (literally, those who believe).[133] It is important to note that the anti-apartheid movement was not the first time that Esack was touched by the humanity of non-Muslims. Growing up in Bonteheuwel, an impoverished, Coloured township in the Cape Flats, many a time it was Esack's Christian neighbours, themselves struggling to make ends meet, who helped out his family when there was no food on the table.[134] This heartfelt experience was reaffirmed in Esack's youth, when he became close friends with the marginalized Christian community in Pakistan.[135]

As a result of this deeply moving encounter with the religious Other, pluralism and universal salvation constitute an intrinsic part of Esack's Qur'anic hermeneutic of liberation. Islam is simply one way of responding to the divine call. Genuine pluralism, he observes, must entail not the mere toleration of other religious communities, but the humble acknowledgement that there exist multiple paths to salvation.[136] In fact, in the Qur'an the words *islam* and *muslim* (submission and submitter, respectively) are not used to refer solely to those who accept the Qur'an as the final revelation and Muhammad as the last prophet. Rather, they encompass all those who have submitted themselves to God via the earlier prophets, who preached the same monotheistic message.[137] This acknowledgement of the *iman* (faith) of those who received scripture before Prophet Muhammad speaks to the universality of the Qur'anic worldview. To restrict salvation to Muslims, Esack argues, is to reduce God from a universal, indeed unfathomable, entity to one confined to the contextually contingent imagination of a specific socio-religious community.[138] Just as faith is a highly fluid and dynamic term in the Qur'an, so too is its counterpart: *kufr*, frequently translated as disbelief. But the meaning of the term is multilayered, Esack points out, as the linguistic root of *kufr* (*k-f-r*) denotes not simply disbelief but the notion of rejecting a gift, of being ungrateful for God's blessings and, as a result,

---

[133] Esack, *Qur'an, Liberation, and Pluralism*, 124.
[134] Esack, *On Being a Muslim*, 150.
[135] Esack, *Qur'an, Liberation, and Pluralism*, 5. Specifically, he got involved with 'Breakthrough', a student Christian group that addressed their lived experiences of oppression through a Christian lens.
[136] Ibid, xii.   [137] Safi, *Memories of Muhammad*, 202–3.
[138] Esack, *Qur'an, Liberation, and Pluralism*, 125.

exhibiting arrogant behaviour.[139] By underscoring the fluidity of Qur'anic concepts like *islam*, *iman*, and *kufr*, and thereby creating a theological space for the religious Other, Esack is able to shift the key criterion of salvation from membership in the *right* religious community to righteous conduct. Faith in and of itself is insufficient, for faith must be wedded to *praxis*. It is precisely because of the Qur'anic emphasis on action as an integral component of faith that one scholar of the Qur'an, Michael Sells, has translated *iman* as 'keeping the faith', and thus as a verb instead of a noun.[140]

Religious dialogue, particularly between Muslims and Christians, has become increasingly popular in recent years. In addition to hundreds of academic conferences and thousands of smaller meetings held by faith groups, entire centres have been constructed to promote religious dialogue. The Centre for the Study of Islam and Christian–Muslim Relations at the University of Birmingham; the Prince Alwaleed bin Talal Center for Muslim-Christian Understanding at Georgetown University in Washington, DC; and the Duncan Black MacDonald Center for the Study of Islam and Christian–Muslim Relations at Hartford Seminary in Connecticut are a few cases in point.[141] Keen to emphasize the scriptural similarities between Christianity and Islam, scholars of both religious traditions argued that it was necessary to foreground this theological common ground to counter the state of 'crisis' that had beset the world.[142] Another important factor behind the rise of religious dialogue was the radically changing demographics of European and North American societies, which now witnessed sizable religious minorities in their midst.[143] Religious dialogue has not been spearheaded by state bodies and Christian communities alone, for Muslims too have been actively involved. 'A Common Word between Us and You' is an illustrative example. Issued in October 2007 to the Pope by over a hundred Muslim scholars across the world, Common Word was a statement

---

[139] Ibid, 137–8. Here, Esack draws upon the earlier work of the Japanese Qur'anic scholar Toshihiko Izutsu, who cites a number of verses wherein *kufr* is used in this particular sense, such as Q. 14:34 and 26:18–19. See Izutsu, 120–1.

[140] Sells, 37.

[141] Hugh Goddard, *A History of Christian-Muslim Relations* (Edinburgh: Edinburgh University Press, 2000), 185.

[142] Kenneth Cragg, *A Christian-Muslim Inter-Text Now: From Anathemata to Theme* (London: Melisende, 2008), v.

[143] Goddard, 182.

of unity, underscoring the shared heritage of the two monotheistic religions and claiming that Christian-Muslim harmony was paramount in order to avert global crisis and ensure world peace.[144]

As the above statement suggests, the discourse of dialogue emerged largely as a response to the idea that a clash of civilizations between Islam and Christianity was imminent. Although popularized in the immediate post-9/11 environment, the clash of civilizations was a theory put forward by American political scientist Samuel Huntington in the 1990s. It posited that non-Western civilizations were growing in strength and Islam in particular, which was 'exploding demographically', was on a collision course with Western civilization and its core values,[145] especially democracy. Huntington's thesis was not uncontested. Countless voices spoke out in protest to this simplistic paradigm, and the phenomenon of religious dialogue needs to be situated within this discursive context. John Esposito—a scholar of Islamic studies and director of the Prince Alwaleed Bin Talal Center for Muslim-Christian Understanding—is a representative example. He countered that the vast majority of Islamists worldwide worked through the democratic system, and thus that Islam and democracy were compatible categories.[146] Richard Bulliet, a historian of Islam at Columbia University in New York City, offered another noteworthy critique of the Clash of Civilizations thesis, proposing that the primarily Muslim societies of the Middle East and North Africa and the predominantly Christian societies of Europe and North America comprised a single historical complex— what he coined, 'Islamo-Christian civilization'—and, therefore, that an imminent clash between the two was actually a definitional impossibility.[147]

So rather than unearthing the essentialism underlying the term civilization or questioning the universalist assumption that Western democracy was *the* political model that the whole world had to follow,

---

[144] 'A Common Word between Us and You (Summary and Abridgement),' *Common Word*, available at: www.acommonword.com/index.php?lang=en&page=option1 accessed 3 September 2012.

[145] Samuel P. Huntington, *The Clash of Civilizations and the Remaking of the World Order* (London: Touchstone Books, 1998), 20.

[146] Zachary Lockman, *Contending Visions of the Middle East: The History and Politics of Orientalism* (Cambridge: Cambridge University Press, 2004), 221–2.

[147] Richard W. Bulliet, *The Case for Islamo-Christian Civilization* (New York: Columbia University Press, 2004), 11.

most mainstream critics called for religious dialogue and peaceful co-existence. Though most of these accounts usually cited American foreign policy in the Middle East as a key reason as to 'why they hate us', a larger critique of global power relations was strikingly absent in the dominant discourse: specifically, that of American imperialism. Indeed, the USA is not only deeply resented in the Middle East, but throughout the global South, like in Latin America,[148] where US foreign policy has a far worse track record. Thus, the clash of civilizations paradigm was not challenged by mainstream critics as an ideological tool for the advancement of empire, despite the well-known fact that Huntington had a long history in the American foreign policy establishment, such as when he argued in favour of 'free-fire zones' in Vietnam to justify the US military's carpet-bombing of the countryside.[149]

The significance of Esack's hermeneutic, then, is that it speaks to the potential of liberation theology, as a contextual approach rooted in the realities of oppression and inequality, to act as an alternative, interfaith model to the discourse of religious dialogue. Because of his experience as a South African living under apartheid, Esack is wary of sweeping statements of peace and co-existence that do not take into account questions of power. The apartheid regime, when it realized that the country was going up in arms, openly called for 'peaceful co-existence' in order to maintain the status quo and thus resistance fighters, like Esack, saw it as their duty to make the state as ungovernable as possible.[150] In other words, within contexts of manifest inequality a stabilizing language of peace becomes the favoured discourse of the oppressor and, conversely, a subversive language of militancy that of the oppressed. And it is this appreciation of the political nature of dialogue that is largely missing from mainstream interfaith discourse. Common Word is a classic case in point. Despite its ceaseless calls for global peace and Christian–Muslim unity, nowhere in the document is there to be found a critique of power relations, an effort to locate the root source of 'global crisis'.[151] In so doing, Common Word only reinforced the discursive strength of the status quo by toeing the simplistic logic that peace and order are good, militancy and violence bad. By using a framework of social liberation,

---

[148] Esack, as cited in Wolfe, 17.   [149] Lockman, 142.
[150] Esack, 'Religio-Cultural Diversity', 167.
[151] 'A Common Word between Us and You.'

however, Esack is able to shift the discourse effectively from religious dialogue to interfaith solidarity against oppression. As he puts it:

> A theoretically postulated, dislocated or decontextualized passion for diversity and pluralism often becomes an excuse for not taking sides. This is the perfect ideology for the modern bourgeois mind . . . Interfaith and cross-cultural dialogue is empty without a firm grounding in solidarity with the oppressed and dispossessed.[152]

To be sure, Islamic scholars and community activists involved in interfaith exchange have also called for collaborative action in social justice works and solidarity with the marginalized, as opposed to meeting solely in a seminar setting.[153] The crucial difference with Esack's approach, however, is his emphasis that religious pluralism must be built on a principled, prophetic solidarity with the oppressed. The collective struggle against the unjust status quo, then, becomes *the* point of departure for all interreligious interaction.

Islam as a Theology of the Margins

Esack's exegesis is also significant because he forces Muslims to reconsider the context in which they articulate understandings of Islam. Since the 1990s, the question of whether Islam and Islamism are synonymous with terrorism has taken centre-stage in public discourse in Europe and North America.[154] The 9/11 attacks of 2001 have entrenched this discourse further. Indeed, 9/11 has become the overwhelming backdrop in which contemporary Islamic thinking has taken shape, with Muslim spokespeople and intellectuals eager to prove the compatibility of a peaceful, tolerant Islam with Western values. To quote Esack's words:

> All of us are forced by the context of 9/11 to find a moderate Islam, a beautiful Islam, a gentle Islam. Why should the context of occupation not force us to find an angry Islam?[155]

Common Word needs to be located within this larger post-9/11 project of presenting a good Islam—one that does not challenge the

---

[152] Esack, 'Religio-Cultural Diversity', 184.
[153] Tariq Ramadan, *Western Muslims and the Future of Islam* (Oxford: Oxford University Press, 2004), 212.
[154] Lockman, 223.   [155] Esack Interview, 2009.

powers that be but simply affirms empty expressions of religious tolerance, world peace, greater understanding—in juxtaposition to a bad Islam, which is confrontational, anti-imperialist, militant. This is not to imply that deep-seated misconceptions about Islam do not abound. Islam is often portrayed by Islamophobes as a violent, authoritarian faith of fear, as opposed to Christianity, which is presented as a religion that promotes love and tolerance.[156] Rather, my point here is that, for Esack, the most important question is: in *whose* context do we approach Islam? In a global context of manifest injustice, a friendly, law-abiding Islam projected through the lens of the powerful will inevitably devolve into a theology of accommodation, toeing the simplistic lines of peace and dialogue, while an Islam channelled through the experiences of the oppressed will take on a fundamentally different character. In fact, Esack writes, if one's eyes are those of the world and not of the USA, then it is capitalism, not religious fundamentalism, which represents the most devastating form of terrorism.[157] The very fact that one country—the USA—consumes half of the world's natural resources speaks volumes about the glaring maldistribution of wealth.[158] It is this stark reality of economic deprivation, in which the affluent North rides with complete impunity on the broken back of the South, that forms the principal context through which Esack articulates his faith.

Questions of authenticity are central to theologies that seek to accommodate the unjust status quo. In their hermeneutical quest to present a peaceful, passive, and beautiful Islam, critiques Esack, liberal Muslims persistently claimed that their reading of Islam was the only authentic one, that they alone adhered to 'true Islam' while other Muslims, particularly Wahhabis and militant oppositional figures like Osama Bin Laden, were not really Muslim, did not really practice Islam.[159] This desire to claim authenticity, however, is not restricted to post-9/11 liberal Muslim discourse, but is a signature trademark of accommodationist theology, which posits its understanding and practice of religion as the *correct* one.[160] Conversely,

---

[156] Sells, 23.   [157] Esack, 'Religio-Cultural Diversity', 184.
[158] Esack, *On Being a Muslim*, 105.
[159] Esack, 'In Search of Progressive Islam Beyond 9/11', 83.
[160] I do not mean to suggest that rhetorical claims of authenticity are the preserve of accommodationist theology, as dissident figures and groups routinely present themselves as the most authentic and genuine spokespersons of the faith. I am grateful to James McDougall and Paul Joyce (in discussion with the author) for this insight.

radical interpretations rooted in protest and the struggle for liberation are Othered within theologies of accommodation as inauthentic. A recurring frustration for Barlas (whose work we will engage in Chapter 5) was that the language she used in her gender-sensitive rereading of scripture—terms like anti-patriarchal, sexual inequality, and liberation—was hastily dismissed by mainstream Muslims as Western concepts alien to Islam.[161] Interpretations in confrontation with capitalism, too, have been disregarded by most Muslims as being nothing more than socialist and Marxist ideologies cloaked in Islamic garb,[162] and thus lacking genuine authenticity. Yet the fact that these very Muslims, by being complicit in and even actively promoting free-market policies, are as ideological in their (neoliberal) economic thinking does not seem to problematize their own incessant claims to authenticity.

On the contrary, a radical commitment to justice and economic equality has deep roots in the history of Islam. Esack does not claim to be an innovator. Rather, he argues that progressive Islam—one dedicated to the task of liberation for all of humanity—has been present, albeit in the shadows, right from the very beginning of Islamic history,[163] tracing all the way back to the practice of Prophet Muhammad. Having little interest in securing an audience within the Meccan corridors of power, Esack writes, the Prophet condemned wealth accumulation and spent his life serving the neglected, praying to God 'to let him live, die and be raised on the Day of Judgement with the poor.'[164] Indeed, the emergence of Islam represented a formidable challenge to the socioeconomic practices of seventh-century Mecca,[165] which was a rigidly stratified society. Intrinsic to the Islamic call was a comprehensive reconfiguration of the existing order, and it was because of the profound socioeconomic implications

---

That being said, I would argue that such dissident actors make assertions of authenticity precisely in order to challenge the entrenched authenticity claims of the status quo, which exercises hegemony over what constitutes truth.

[161] Barlas, *'Believing Women' in Islam*, xii.

[162] Omid Safi ed., *Progressive Muslims: On Justice, Gender, and Pluralism* (Oxford: Oneworld, 2003), 7. To be sure, Muslim Marxists have not made serious attempts to interpret Islamic texts, such as the Qur'an, in light of their ideological commitments. As Safi—a progressive Islamic scholar—observes, their lack of engagement with religious texts and traditions is one of the reasons why they have failed to attract mainstream Muslim audiences.

[163] Esack, as cited in Wolfe, 15.   [164] Esack, *On Being a Muslim*, 105.

[165] Izutsu, 16.

of Muhammad's monotheism that the Meccan elite rejected his prophecy.[166] But a liberating practice, Esack continues, was not just characteristic of Prophet Muhammad, but of all the prophets of God. Like Muhammad, the prophets of the Qur'an were firmly committed to the oppressed and their own social origins were largely humble, coming from peasant or other lowly backgrounds.[167] In other words, a radical religiosity devoted to justice is, insofar as Qur'anic and prophetic precedence is concerned, more orthodox than the very orthodoxy that dismisses it.

The Qur'anic hermeneutic of Esack thus forces Muslims to ask *whose* interests—the powerful or the powerless—are being served by their articulation of Islam. The call for reform has become a pervasive discourse in contemporary Islam. But the most important question in any discussion of reform, interjects Esack, should be 'in response to whose demands do I re-think the meaning and implications of my faith?'[168] That is, reform to what ends? The question of subject is paramount here: are the subjects—the primary actors—of my religious discourse the elites or the people? Is my Islam a theology of the centre or a theology of the margins? These questions are rarely raised in contemporary Islamic discourse. Esack gives the example of fasting in Ramadan. The rationale that is usually given as to why Muslims are commanded to fast in the holy month is in order to empathize with the poor. Yet this explanation is problematic, as it is founded on the presumption that the average Muslim is wealthy or at least self-sufficient.[169] By taking the affluent members of the faith as a default frame of reference, as the subject of Islamic discourse, the poor are Othered—indeed, poverty is treated as an essentially non-Muslim issue—and consigned to the passive role of objects that are to be empathized with through pity and charity. Muslim discourse over the AIDS pandemic, which adversely affects the poor, is another case in point. Esack notes that mainstream Muslim responses to AIDS have, in classic conservative fashion, portrayed the crisis as a form of divine retribution against people who practice the sins of

---

[166] Esack, *Qur'an, Liberation, and Pluralism*, 138. [167] Ibid, 99.
[168] Esack, 'The Contemporary Democracy and the Human Rights Project for Muslim Societies', 125.
[169] Esack, *On Being a Muslim*, 34. Significantly, the Qur'an's own stated rationale for fasting is solely to achieve *taqwa* (God-consciousness): 'O you who believe! Fasting has been prescribed for you as it was prescribed for those before you, so that you may attain *taqwa*' (Q. 2:183).

sexual perversity.[170] So not only is there a striking lack of socio-economic analysis behind the spread of the virus, such as the fact that the market actually profits from holding back treatments to victims through patents or even the basic knowledge that the most common form of transmission is not sex but contaminated needles, but the AIDS crisis is treated, too, as a non-Muslim problem. This is a pandemic that apparently affects other people, not us. The very idea of a Muslim afflicted with HIV or AIDS becomes an oxymoron, despite the reality that countless Muslims continue to live and die with the disease. The critical intervention of Esack's hermeneutic, therefore, is that it shifts the locus of Islam from the dominant centre to the much maligned margins, to those people—Muslim or otherwise—for whom poverty and disease, patriarchy and dispossession are inescapable facts of life. Furthermore, this hermeneutical transition in subject, Esack argues, will transform the language of Islam, thereby allowing for a more liberating vocabulary to emerge. Consider the revamping of the term *jihad* (sensationally rendered as Holy War but literally meaning struggle) in the discourse of progressive Muslims involved in the anti-apartheid movement. For these Muslims the objective of *jihad* was neither the Islamist project of creating an Islamic state nor the liberal Muslim project of inner exertion, of attaining spiritual enlightenment from within, but rather—through solidarity and struggle with the oppressed—the establishment of a just social order.[171]

CONCLUSIONS

Although the substance of the Qur'anic text occupies a central position in Esack's hermeneutic, *praxis* is treated as an equally important text. Esack's emphasis on the Qur'an stems from the fact that it is universally accepted by all Muslims as the actual Word of God, as opposed to the *hadith* and the inherited intellectual tradition, both of

[170] Esack and Chiddy, 4.
[171] For the references to liberationist versus Islamist understandings of *jihad*, see Esack, *Qur'an, Liberation, and Pluralism*, 107 and Esack, *The Qur'an: A User's Guide*, 178. For the reference to liberal Muslim interpretations of *jihad*, see Esack, 'In Search of Progressive Islam Beyond 9/11,' 83.

which are human-made and thus fallible and disputed. Esack does
not write them off altogether, however. Instead, he draws selectively
from them, privileging the Qur'an wherever a contradiction may
emerge. Scripture thus reigns supreme, and extra-Qur'anic texts
need to be understood through the framework of scripture. Yet who
gets to decide what the Qur'anic message is? In whose context is the
text to be understood? It is here that a fundamental difference
emerges between Esack's hermeneutical method and those of other
scholars, most notably the doyen of modernist Islamic thought,
Rahman. For the latter, seventh-century Arabia was the first context
to be studied, and therefore historical criticism, in which a double
movement theory would allow for the principles of the pre-modern
text to be extracted and then applied to the modern context, constituted the 'correct' method of reading the Qur'an. For Esack, however,
the most important context is the contemporary one, for the Qur'an
was sent for all peoples, irrespective of time and place. But even
within the present the text speaks to a more specific context: that of
oppression and poverty. The Qur'an, then, is the living speech of a
just deity addressed first and foremost to the downtrodden. The text
is only truly liberating, moreover, when those who are oppressed
struggle against their oppressors, and it is within this framework of
praxis that the text ought to be engaged: through a hermeneutical
dialectic of struggle, reflection, and further struggle. The Qur'an, by
the very nature of its own 'progressive revelation', affirms this liberating reading strategy. Truth is never timeless and absolute, therefore,
but continuously revealed to those who partake in critical reflection
based on struggle. Indeed, within Esack's exegesis, *praxis* functions as
the motor of theological enquiry, a central source that is hermeneutically on a par with scripture.

While the seeds of his radical commentary are to be found in the
anti-apartheid movement in South Africa, the larger vision of Esack's
liberation struggle is a thoroughly comprehensive one, and thus an
abiding commitment to solidarity lies at the heart of his Islamic
praxis. Justice is a fundamental component of the Qur'anic call,
commanding humankind to strive towards creating a lasting, egalitarian social order. According to the Qur'an, faith is inextricably
linked with the performance of righteous works. In fact, the text
makes an explicit, preferential option for the oppressed—irrespective
of their belief—promising that they will inherit the Earth. This pledge
is sacralised, according to Esack, in the Exodus experience. This is a

problematic paradigmatic move, however, given the overwhelming emphasis that Christian liberation theology has also placed on this event. Because of the universalizing tendency of Christianity, particularly in the academic discipline of Religion, Islamic liberation theology will have to speak to the question of difference, to foreground the specificity of Muslim theology and experience. And in this vein, the concept of *tawhid*—the central tenet of Islam—holds great potential as an alternative, theological paradigm. It is precisely because a genuine commitment to morality is gauged by the ability to be moved by the suffering of others, and not just of one's own community, that the South African struggle, although playing a formative role in Esack's hermeneutic, cannot capture the universality of his liberationist project. Solidarity has been a hallmark of Esack's activism, especially with regard to the struggle for gender justice, combating the stigmatization of Muslims afflicted with HIV/AIDS and supporting the Palestinian cause. Because the categories of oppressor and oppressed are dynamic and conditioned by an ever-changing context, solidarity ought to be principled—what Esack terms, 'prophetic'—so that the progressive Muslim intellectual does not end up reproducing relationships of inequality in her/his struggle for justice. Moreover, the impulse to stand with the oppressed must not be guided by benevolence and charity, but rather by the pressing need to keep one's own humanity (*fitra*) intact, for within contexts of oppression one's *fitra* is compromised if one does not act. The liberation of the Self, therefore, is intimately tied to the liberation of the Other.

Esack's liberating exegesis is significant, I argue, for two reasons. Firstly, he shows the potential of liberation theology to function as a viable, alternative framework to the otherwise deeply problematic discourse of religious dialogue. Interreligious solidarity became a crucial part of the South African struggle against apartheid. Standing next to and being touched by the humanity of the non-Muslim Other compelled Esack to find a pluralistic hermeneutic of liberation, disclosing the dynamism and fluidity of such key Qur'anic concepts as *iman*, *islam*, and *kufr*. The core criterion of salvation in Muslim scripture, Esack argues, lies in one's commitment to justice and not one's membership in a chosen ethno-religious community. And it is this emphasis on interreligious solidarity against oppression that can provide an effective alternative to the discourse of dialogue. What has been strikingly absent in the language of religious dialogue, bent on countering an imminent civilization clash between Islam and the

West, is a critical awareness of global politics. For religious dialogue has failed to address the root cause of world suffering, which is not a result of a misunderstanding between different 'civilizations' but rather the exploits of American imperialism and the brutality of a free-market capitalism that has long ravaged the South. Esack's emphasis on solidarity, therefore, allows the critique of power to act as the point of departure for all interfaith collaboration.

Esack's liberation theology is also significant because it forcefully undermines any essentialist, disembodied claim to 'Islam' by raising the larger question of whose context religion is being articulated within. Challenging 9/11 as the framework, the underlying backdrop within which contemporary Islamic thought has taken shape, Esack insists that Islam needs to be expounded through the context of the two-thirds world. This shift in the subject of one's discourse from the powerful to the powerless, such as the millions of people who die every year because of AIDS will, in turn, raise entirely different questions and spawn a new theological language firmly rooted in justice. So instead of pontificating as to how authentic a particular interpretation of Islam is—a theological obsession of accommodationist Islamic discourse—the progressive Muslim intellectual would ask how such an understanding can speak to the problems plaguing the vast majority of humanity: poverty, hunger, unemployment, homelessness, disease, occupation, death. Although the issue of authenticity is clearly consigned to the edges of Esack's hermeneutic, a radical commitment to justice has deep roots in Islamic history and Esack himself takes great inspiration from the examples of Muhammad and the earlier prophets of the Qur'an. The centring of liberation is a seminal contribution that Esack makes to Islamic thought, for it forces Muslims to confront the elitism and complicity of mainstream Islamic discourse, like its patronizing attitude towards the poor as passive objects to be empathized with and dismissive treatment of the AIDS pandemic as divine punishment and a non-Muslim problem. In so doing, Esack compels Muslims to rethink their Islam as a theology of the margins, as a faith defined by its commitment to the oppressed.

3

From the Hereafter to the Here and Now

The Reading of Asghar Ali Engineer

INTRODUCTION

This chapter explores the Qur'anic hermeneutic of the Indian theologian Asghar Ali Engineer. The first section will examine the interpretive order of the Islamic texts in Engineer's discourse. Specifically, I will show that, in a similar fashion to Esack, the Qur'an is the primary textual source that Engineer draws upon. This is not to say that he categorically rejects the *hadith* and the inherited, intellectual tradition, but rather that scripture authoritatively trumps all other Islamic sources. This hermeneutical privileging of the Qur'anic text, I argue, is intrinsically linked to Engineer's critique of clerical authority. This chapter will then examine the centrality of justice in his exegesis, exploring the relationship between the sacred text and social liberation. Because of his sharp emphasis on action as a mode of Qur'anic reading, Engineer's hermeneutic is first and foremost a hermeneutic of the here and now, of this world and *then* the next. Like Esack, he exhibits an awareness of the complexity of oppression, calling for a (generally) comprehensive commitment to justice and bringing together questions of class, gender, and pluralism. But whereas Esack draws upon the Exodus as a paradigm of struggle, Engineer turns to the Battle of Karbala (680), reflecting his background as a Shi'a Muslim. While this chapter seeks to underscore the striking similarities of Esack's and Engineer's Islamic discourses in spite of their very different geographical locations, I will conclude by highlighting some key hermeneutical disparities between these two exegetes. In particular, I will problematize three recurring themes in

Engineer's writings, namely: secularism, modernism, and peace. This chapter will first set the stage for discussion by providing a brief history of India and a biographical sketch of Engineer.

Historical Context

Though India achieved independence from the British in 1947, the country has been plagued by communal riots, especially between Hindus and Muslims, the seeds of which were sown in the colonial era. India was a principal colony of the British Empire, which had consolidated its control from the second half of the eighteenth century onwards, first economically and then through direct, imperial rule. Initially comprised of bourgeois intellectuals loyal to the British, the Indian National Congress (est. 1885) was gradually transformed into a major vehicle of nationalist, anti-colonial resistance, developing a popular following under the leadership of Mahatma Gandhi (d. 1948).[1] It would be elitist, however, to reduce the complex history of the South Asian liberation struggle to the activities of the Indian National Congress. As the Bengali historian Ranajit Guha has argued, India never had a 'national liberation movement', since upper-class Indians were unable to exert control over mass uprisings that were erupting throughout the country—particularly amongst peasants, workers, and the urban petty bourgeoisie—and to generalize them into a unified, nationalist movement.[2] India's independence would lead to Partition (1947)—one of the most horrific events in South Asian history and in which almost a million people were killed as Muslims frantically moved to newly-created Pakistan, Hindus and Sikhs to independent India. It is important to note that the roots of such communal violence, professing solid, hermetically sealed boundaries between Hindus, Sikhs, and Muslims, are to be found in the colonial period. In 1909, for example, the British set up separate electorates based on communal lines,[3] thereby laying the groundwork

---

[1] Robert Young, *Postcolonialism: An Historical Introduction* (Oxford: Blackwell Publishing, 2001), 309.

[2] Ranajit Guha, 'On Some Aspects of the Historiography of Colonial India', in *Selected Subaltern Studies*, eds. Ranajit Guha and Gayatri Chakravorty Spivak (Oxford: Oxford University Press, 1988), 42–3.

[3] Asghar Ali Engineer ed., *The Gujarat Carnage* (New Delhi: Orient Longman, 2003), 5.

for religious affiliation as a marker of political identity. Such colonial policies were informed by strategies of divide and rule, seeking to pre-empt political alignments between Hindus and Muslims against the British, as well as by the deep-seated assumption that communalism was 'an essential and unchanging feature of Indian society.'[4] Communal violence in contemporary India, then, is a lasting legacy of empire. A series of riots rocked the country in the late 1960s and early 1970s, in particular in Ahmadabad, in which a thousand people were killed, and in Bhivandi, claiming four hundred lives.[5] Communal conflict reared its ugly face again in the 1980s, culminating in the Mumbai riots of 1992–3. Perhaps the most shocking episode of communal violence, however, was that of Gujarat in 2002, wherein roughly eight hundred Muslims and two hundred Hindus were brutally massacred. This resurgence of sectarian strife is in large part due to the rise of Hindu nationalism (*hindutva*) since the 1980s, which has 'sought to establish India as a primarily Hindu nation (*rashtra*), based on a notion of Hindu ethos, values and religion', and views Muslims as a threat to Hindus and the nation as a whole.[6]

Raised in a traditional Muslim household, Engineer was an influential, progressive voice in India, writing widely on Islam and communal violence.[7] He was born on 10 March 1939 in Salumbar—a town in the Udaipur district—and brought up as a Dawudi Bohra, a sub-sect of Shi'a Isma'ili Islam based primarily in India and with a membership of roughly a million followers.[8] Although he never

---

[4] Anuradha D. Needham and Rajeswari S. Rajan eds., *The Crisis of Secularism in India* (Durham, US: Duke University Press, 2007), 12. For a study of how imperial discourses produced and solidified communal identities, see Gyanendra Pandey, *The Construction of Communalism in Colonial North India* (Delhi: Oxford University Press, 1990).

[5] Asghar Ali Engineer, 'How Secular is India Today?' *Secular Perspective*, 16 October 2008, available at: http://www.csss-isla.com/wp-content/uploads/2015/06/October-16-31-08.pdf, accessed 12 August 2016.

[6] Ornit Shani, *Communalism, Caste and Hindu Nationalism: The Violence in Gujarat* (Cambridge: Cambridge University Press, 2007), 1.

[7] While Engineer uses the terms 'communalism' and 'communal violence' interchangeably, I prefer to use the latter in my own writing. I avoid the word communalism in describing the historic tensions between Sikhs, Muslims, and Hindus because, by definition, communalism refers to a very different concept: namely, a form of sociopolitical organization built on fellowship, egalitarianism, and the commonwealth.

[8] Asghar Ali Engineer, *On Developing Theology of Peace in Islam* (New Delhi: Sterling Publishers, 2005), 166.

attended a *madrasa*, Engineer was exposed to classical Islamic subjects, such as Qur'anic exegesis, jurisprudence, and Muslim history, at
an early age, as his father was a traditionally trained Islamic scholar.[9]
At the same time, however, Engineer took an avid interest in secular
topics like Western philosophy and science.[10] Upon completing his
secondary education, he went on to study civil engineering at Vikram
University in Indore and eventually settled in Mumbai. While working as an engineer, he continued his readings in religion, literature,
and philosophy, and wrote on these topics in Urdu magazines and in
English newspapers like *The Times of India*. With the rise of communal riots between Muslims and Hindus in the late 1960s, Engineer
began to write on communal violence and, in particular, how religion
could work towards fostering peaceful dialogue between the two
communities.[11] Concurrently, he became a prominent voice in the
Bohra reform movement,[12] rebelling against the conservative and
exploitative practices of the religious leadership. Taking an early
retirement in 1972, he decided to dedicate himself fully to the task
of writing, publishing numerous articles and books on contemporary
Islam, social justice, and communal violence. Engineer founded a
number of educational and outreach organizations, including the
Institute for Islamic Studies (est. 1980) and, in order to further
research on communal violence and interfaith harmony, the Center
for the Study of Society and Secularism (est. 1993). He passed away
on 14 May 2013 in Mumbai.

ISLAMIC TEXTS AND SACRED AUTHORITY

Qur'an First

Like Esack, the Qur'an is the primary text that Engineer draws upon
in his Islamic discourse. This is because, writes Engineer, as the literal
Word of God the Qur'an is considered to be completely authentic by
all Muslims, irrespective of sectarian affiliation.[13] His foregrounding
of the Qur'an is at odds with traditionalist approaches to textual

---

[9] Engineer Interview, 2010.   [10] Ibid.   [11] Ibid.
[12] The Bohras will be discussed later on in this chapter.
[13] Engineer, *On Developing Theology of Peace in Islam*, 144.

authority, in which the *sunna* is also considered to be a form of divine revelation and, therefore, hermeneutically on a par with the Qur'an. Indeed, the only difference that classical theologians drew between the Qur'an and the *sunna* was that the former is to be used in recitation (*tilawa*), such as in religious rites and rituals, while the latter is unrecited (*ghayr matlu*).[14] This is not to imply that classical scholars understood the *sunna* as being the literal Word of God. Rather, they argued that while the Qur'an was the speech of God *in word*, the *sunna* reflected this divine speech *in spirit*.[15] Yet how can the disputed word of the Prophet, asks Engineer, compete with the authentic Word of God? Drawing upon the writings of the Egyptian Qur'anic scholar Nasr Hamid Abu Zayd (d. 2010), specifically the distinction that he draws between revelation (*tanzil*) and interpretation (*ta'wil*), Engineer argues that while the Qur'anic text constitutes revelation, the Prophet's explanations of these verses reflect his own interpretations.[16] So while these explanations may be of immense value, they are not authoritative and cannot override the dictates of the Qur'an. To put it another way: if any *sunna* is to be followed, it is that of the Qur'an and not of the Prophet. This is a compelling point given the striking absence of the much celebrated term *sunnat an-nabi*—the precedent of Prophet Muhammad—in the Qur'an. As the Islamic scholar Daniel Brown has noted, the Arabic root of *sunna* (S-N-N) surfaces only sixteen times in the text, emerging in two general contexts, both of which refer to God's judgement: firstly, as the precedent of—that is, the fate that befell—earlier communities (*sunnat al-awwalin*, such as in Q. 8:38; 15:13; 18:55; 35:43); and, secondly, as the precedent of God, or *sunnat Allah* (Q. 33:62; 35:43; 40:85; 48:23).[17]

That being said, the *hadith* literature is not entirely absent in Engineer's writings. Indeed, there are various *hadith* reports interspersed throughout his work. For instance, at one point he relates the prophetic prayer—'O Lord, I seek refuge in Thee from unbelief (*kufr*) and poverty (*faqr*)'[18]—while at another he recalls the famous prophetic maxim: 'Wisdom is the lost property of the faithful; he should acquire it wherever he finds it.'[19] What Engineer seeks to underscore,

---

[14] Brown, *Rethinking Tradition in Modern Islamic Thought*, 7.
[15] Von Denffer, 93.   [16] Engineer Interview, 2010.
[17] Brown, *Rethinking Tradition in Modern Islamic Thought*, 143.
[18] Engineer, *Islam and Liberation Theology*, 79.   [19] Ibid, 87.

however, is that the *hadith* are not a binding source. These reports are useful because they provide a historical window into how the Qur'an was understood in the classical world.[20] That is, the *hadith* reflect a particular culture and experience—namely, that of the first Muslims—and while this experience certainly holds much value for contemporary believers, it should never eclipse our own lived realities. Engineer's critique of *hadith* moves beyond the universalization of classical experiences, extending, like Esack, to issues of authenticity. Because many of the *hadith* came into being in the centuries following the Qur'anic revelation, Engineer writes, the veracity of these traditions is deeply contested. As such, the *hadith* reports need to be approached with caution and Muslims ought to avoid making any authoritative, legal pronouncements from this disputed body of literature.[21] His core grievance with the *hadith*, then, is its hermeneutical elevation to that of the Qur'an or, even worse, when these prophetic reports outright trump the Word of God.

The Islamic punishments for apostasy and illicit sexual relations are illustrative examples. Engineer points out that capital punishment for apostasy (*irtidad*) derives from the *hadith* and has no scriptural basis,[22] just as the penalty of stoning to death for unlawful sexual relations (*zina*), too, is based on *hadith*, while the Qur'an prescribes a hundred lashes.[23] Although the Qur'anic prescription is, technically speaking, a step up from stoning—the express objective of stoning is to kill whereas that of flogging is not—it is difficult to believe that someone could survive a hundred lashes. In reality, the outcome of both punishments may well be the same: death.[24] Instead of merely juxtaposing the *hadith*-based penalty with the almost equally violent scriptural one, a more persuasive line of argument would have been to highlight the wider message of the Qur'an's discourse on *zina*. For a necessary condition of any accusation of *zina*, the text goes on to state, is the testimony of four witnesses who saw the sexual act taking place, prescribing a punishment of eighty lashes for those who accuse chaste women without substantiating their claim with these four

[20] Engineer Interview, 2010.
[21] Asghar Ali Engineer, *The Rights of Women in Islam* (New York: St. Martin's Press, 1992), 13.
[22] Asghar Ali Engineer, *Islam: Misgivings and History* (New Delhi: Vitasta Publishing, 2008), 140.
[23] Ibid, 166. The punishment of one hundred lashes can be found in Q. 24:2.
[24] I am grateful to Tim Gorringe (in discussion with the author) for this insight.

witnesses (Q. 24:4–5).[25] Since it is highly unlikely that four witnesses (in addition to the couple) would be present during the act of sex—making it next to impossible for the punishment of a hundred lashes to be meted out—the Qur'an's intent is clearly not to give free license to flog fornicators. Rather, it seeks to emphasize the grave sinfulness (a) of illicit sexual relations and (b) of slander, of falsely accusing others of sexual immorality, especially women.

Engineer also engages the inherited, intellectual tradition, albeit in a critical manner, always making sure to privilege Qur'anic teachings over the *shari'a* whenever any conflict between the two may arise. Discussions of Islamic jurisprudence resurface at numerous points in Engineer's writings. When showing how earlier Muslim jurists had taken into account questions of oppression and social justice, for instance, Engineer refers to the following proverb by the medieval Islamic scholar Ahmad b. Taymiyya (d. 1328): 'The affairs of men in this world can be kept in order with justice and a certain connivance in sin is better than pious tyranny.'[26] As was noted at the beginning of this chapter, Engineer received training from his father in the Islamic intellectual tradition and therefore, like Esack, Engineer is conversant with this corpus of accumulated knowledge. His main contention with the tradition, however, is that it has come to dominate Islamic thinking and practice. As he put it in our interview:

> Still, take any *madrasa*. I'm talking of higher Islamic learning in *madrasas*. It is 100% based on medieval texts. Not even a 1% attempt to understand the Qur'an in the modern context ... So that [medieval] text is at the centre of traditional Islam. And what is needed to understand the Qur'an in its real, revolutionary spirit is not this medieval text but reason and reflection in the light of our own experiences, our own problems, our own issues.[27]

There are thus two fundamental concerns at stake here. Firstly, that the *shari'a* does not cater to contemporary circumstances. A key critique that Engineer levels against traditional Islamic scholars, particularly in the Indian context, is that they hastily apply medieval rulings without studying the particularities of present situations and

---

[25] These rules differ when a man accuses his own wife. In this case, both spouses take oaths that they are telling the truth, at which point, significantly, the wife's word is privileged over the husband's (Q. 24:6–9).

[26] Ahmad b. Taymiyya, as cited in Engineer, *Islam and Liberation Theology*, 26.

[27] Engineer Interview, 2010.

without applying *ijtihad*, which he describes as being 'creative re-interpretation'.[28] Secondly, in traditional Islam the *shari'a* supersedes the Qur'an rather than the other way around. On the contrary, he argues, the *shari'a* should be approached as an 'instrument'—a means of transmitting, of putting into practice scriptural values—as it is the Qur'an that is central to Islamic teaching and, as such, should take precedence over *shari'a* rulings.[29]

Between Exegesis and Essentialism

Though Engineer's and Esack's hermeneutics are similar in terms of their ordering of the Islamic texts, there is a crucial difference, as the feminist legal scholar Kecia Ali has pointed out, in their Qur'anic commentaries. Focussing on gender relations, Ali argues that Engineer's interpretation is an apologetic one, selectively sifting through various Qur'anic texts and singling out passages that support gender justice while overlooking those that suggest otherwise.[30] Citing Q. 2:228, for example, Engineer concludes that the Qur'an upholds the full equality of women and men:

> The real intention of the Qur'an—that of sexual equality—comes through several verses. Those verses need to be reemphasized . . . The rights of the wives (with regard to their husbands) are equal to (husbands') rights with regard to them . . . [*sic*](2:228) is quite definitive in this respect. It hardly needs any comment.[31]

A far more complicated picture emerges, however, when one actually looks up this verse:

> The divorced women shall undergo, without remarrying, a waiting-period of three monthly courses: for it is not lawful for them to conceal what God may have created in their wombs, if they believe in God and the Last Day. And during this period their husbands are fully entitled to take them back, if they desire reconciliation. The wives have rights

---

[28] Asghar Ali Engineer, 'Women's Plight in Muslim Society', *Secular Perspective*, 1 November 2006, available at: http://www.csss-isla.com/wp-content/uploads/2015/06/November-1-15-06.pdf accessed 12 August 2016.

[29] Engineer, *Islam: Misgivings and History*, 100.

[30] Ali, *Sexual Ethics and Islam*, 123–4.

[31] Asghar Ali Engineer, 'Islam, Women, and Gender Justice', in *What Men Owe Women: Men's Voices from World Religions*, eds. John C. Raines and Daniel C. Maguire (Albany, New York: State University of New York Press, 2001), 124.

similar to the obligations upon them, in accordance with honorable norms, and men have a degree (*daraja*) over them. And God is All-Mighty, All-Wise.

Engineer's reference to Q. 2:228 thus really refers, as Ali shows, to (a skewed reading of) a particular passage *within* the passage, dealing with rights and responsibilities, while conveniently omitting the final and overtly problematic section stating men's 'degree' (*daraja*) over women.[32] This verse can, of course, be contextualized and women's gender egalitarian readings, as we shall see shortly, have argued that the 'degree' refers to men's advantage in divorce proceedings—the main subject of Q. 2:228—rather than making a broader, ontological claim about male superiority. Yet Engineer does not even attempt here to grapple with this part of the verse, ignoring it altogether.

Indeed, the underlying problem in Engineer's exegesis is that he presents the Qur'an as a human rights document espousing absolute gender parity. At one point he proclaims—'Muhammad announced through the Qur'an a charter of rights for women'[33]—while at another he insists that the 'Qur'an is the first revealed book that accords equal rights to women.'[34] As Chapter 2 has shown, Esack's hermeneutical treatment of gender justice is more nuanced. Though Esack, like Engineer, approaches the text as an engaged reader who is in solidarity with women and their struggles against patriarchy, Esack argues that regardless of how the text may be reinterpreted, the Qur'an in certain ways remains an androcentric document, or one that addresses male audiences, while women 'are essentially subjects being dealt with—however kindly—rather than being directly addressed.'[35] This is not to imply that the Qur'an is completely male-centred, for it explicitly affirms the individual accountability of all people irrespective of gender, promising salvation for both believing men and believing women (Q. 33:35; 49:13).[36] That being said, the text ascribes greater moral agency to men in the spheres of sex and marriage.[37] The difference between Esack's and Engineer's

[32] Ali, *Sexual Ethics and Islam*, 123–4.
[33] Engineer, *Islam and Liberation Theology*, 33.
[34] Engineer, *Islam: Misgivings and History*, 98.
[35] Esack, 'Islam and Gender Justice', 195.
[36] In the following chapters it will be seen that these verses play a key role in women's gender egalitarian readings.
[37] Ali, *Sexual Ethics and Islam*, 131.

readings, then, is that whereas the former is willing to acknowledge, to wrestle with problematic passages, the latter simply refuses to do so, either explaining away or wholly ignoring those passages that do not fit into a liberating discourse.

The apologetics of Engineer's gendered reading reflect a deeper tendency in his exegesis to essentialize the Qur'an and, by extension, Islam. Despite acknowledging the subjectivity of the reader and the hermeneutical impossibility of interpreting the text in a contextual vacuum, he persists in claiming that there are no Qur'anic passages that can be used to support the status quo.[38] There is only one way to read scripture, and that is a liberating reading. This essentializing of the Qur'an, in turn, leads Engineer to essentialize the Muslim faith as a whole. With regard to religious pluralism, for example, he maintains that Islam 'does not even indirectly hint at coercion, let alone violence, when it comes to any religious or spiritual matter.'[39] Islam can thus only be a progressive force for social justice, and interpretations that suggest otherwise are not *really* Islamic. His essentialism, moreover, comes packaged with crude triumphalism, proclaiming that Islam was 'the first systematic attempt to bring a just society into existence in the history of mankind.'[40] This tendency to essentialize Islam stands in marked contrast, again, to Esack's liberating exegesis. As discussed in the previous chapter, a key critique that Esack levelled against liberal Muslims in post-9/11 America was their claim over Islamic authenticity, declaring that Islam can *only* be peaceful and that militant interpretations of Islam, such as that of Osama Bin Laden, are outside the fold of the faith.[41]

On Authority

Engineer's prioritization of the Qur'an over other Islamic texts is intrinsically linked, I argue, to his critique of clerical hierarchy. As the Islamic scholar Carl Ernst has observed, the most contentious issue in Islam is the question of sacred authority: that is, who has the right to partake in religious interpretation and, in so doing, to define

[38] Engineer, *On Developing Theology of Peace in Islam*, v.   [39] Ibid, 95.
[40] Engineer, *Islam: Misgivings and History*, 39.
[41] Esack, 'In Search of Progressive Islam Beyond 9/11', 83.

the faith?[42] In our interview, Engineer summed up his stance on this heated question:

There is no concept of authority as far as the Qur'an is concerned. As far as the Qur'an is concerned, it is the individual. Responsibility is with the individual. The Qur'an nowhere says that the Prophet will be responsible for what Muslims are doing. The Qur'an nowhere says that any caliph will be responsible or any *'alim* [religious scholar] will be responsible. If I am accountable on the Day of Judgement to Allah, I must accept my own authority.[43]

Engineer draws a compelling connection here between authority and accountability: that because each and every person will ultimately stand before God for what s/he has done, it is the individual's authority that is binding and not those of Islamic scholars or mystical intermediaries. The Islamic intellectual tradition, as an elite body of scholarship requiring years of intensive study in order to master medieval texts, poses a fundamental problem for such an inclusive approach to authority. While arguably more accessible than the intellectual tradition, the *hadith*, too, comprises a dense corpus involving the study of thousands of prophetic reports, including the substantive portions of these reports as well as their complex, convoluted and often contradictory chains of narration. Indeed, it is important to point out that the *'ulama* are not only staunch supporters of the intellectual tradition but also of the *hadith*, reflecting their sustained efforts to maintain their own position as the authoritative interpreters of the prophetic legacy.[44] Compared to the *hadith* and the tradition, the Qur'an is a simple (not to be confused with *simplistic*) and straightforward text, comprising a single-volume canon. And it is precisely because of the accessibility of the Qur'an, in addition of course to its hallowed status as the Word of God, that it takes centre-stage in Engineer's Islamic discourse. To be sure, successive layers of exegesis have accumulated around the Qur'anic text, embodied most evidently in *'ulum al-Qur'an* (the Sciences of the Qur'an), which deal with the text's *proper* exposition. A recurring theme in this genre, as in much of mainstream Islamic thought, is delineating who exactly has the authority to interpret. According to Islamic scholars, the qualified Qur'anic exegete must display such

---

[42] Ernst, 31.   [43] Engineer Interview, 2010.
[44] Brown, *Rethinking Tradition in Modern Islamic Thought*, 133.

qualities as soundness in *'aqida*, or creed (effectively ruling out heterodox Muslim groups), a mastery of the Arabic language and knowledge of the classical commentarial tradition.[45] The exegete should also refrain from using personal opinion, refer to *hadith* to advance understanding and consult the views of respected Islamic scholars.[46] Countering such interpretive hierarchy, Engineer argues that every Muslim should be able to expound the Qur'an, to draw authoritative meaning from the text. Furthermore, even if a Muslim cannot read classical Arabic—let alone display mastery over the language—s/he has the solemn responsibility to study the text through translations, though knowledge of Arabic would be an obvious advantage.[47]

Engineer's suspicion of religious authority is, in large part, a result of his own upbringing, in which he was exposed to the exploitative nature of entrenched, clerical hierarchy. Manipulating his spiritual credentials, the head of the Dawudi Bohras imposed heavy taxes on his followers in order to consolidate control and secure his family's financial standing.[48] What allowed him to do so was his own privileged position as the authoritative representative of the hidden *imam*.[49] As Shi'a Muslims, the Bohras believe in the institution of imamate. Starting from Ali b. Abi Talib (d. 661), the cousin and son-in-law of Prophet Muhammad, the imamate is understood by Shi'a Muslims as a divinely sanctioned and hereditary spiritual office, safeguarding the message of the Prophet, and the authority of which is vested in the Prophet's immediate family. Different Shi'a schools of thought, therefore, follow various hereditary lines of *imams*. After the disappearance of their twenty-first *imam*, Tayyib Abi al-Qasim (b. *circa* 1130), who is believed to have gone into seclusion at a very young age, the Bohra community began to follow the authority of a hereditary line of *da'is*, or representatives of the hidden *imam*. Engineer grew up under the leadership of Tahir Seifuddin (d. 1965), who assumed office as the fifty-first *da'i*. In addition to exploiting the community financially, Seifuddin essentially established himself as an intermediary between God and the faithful, claiming that any marriage contracted without his permission was Islamically unlawful—and, thus, any children borne of such

---

[45] Von Denffer, 122–3.   [46] Ibid.   [47] Engineer Interview, 2010.
[48] Engineer, *On Developing Theology of Peace in Islam*, 171–2.
[49] Engineer Interview, 2010.

wedlock illegitimate—and that no Bohra could lead the congrega-
tional prayers without his express consent.[50] The *da'i's* authority,
moreover, spread to the secular realm. For instance, elections could
not be contested and organizations such as schools and charities
could not be established without his permission.[51] A traditional
scholar, Engineer's father was an *'amil*, or a lower official whose
task was to execute the wishes of the *da'i*. In our interview, Engineer
recounted how his father encouraged him to follow a more 'secular'
education and become an engineer precisely so that Engineer would
not have to enter the acutely hierarchical clerical establishment and
become a 'slave' to the *da'i* like his father.[52] When the Bohra community in the city of Udaipur was driven to such an extreme that they
openly rebelled against the *da'i* in the early 1960s, Engineer joined the
uprising and became a leading figure in the reformist movement.[53]
This formative experience of witnessing first-hand the oppressive
potential of religious hierarchy has, in turn, led Engineer to become
deeply suspicious of sacred authority as a whole. The critique of the
'ulama is a prominent theme in his writings, which portray these
traditional scholars and especially their claim that the *shari'a* is divine
and unalterable—thereby consolidating their own authority—as a
prime obstacle towards progressive change within Islam.[54]

Engineer's critique of the Bohra clerical establishment has come
with severe personal consequences. *Barat* was a key tool that the
establishment used, and continues to use, against internal dissent in
general and the reformist movement in particular.[55] *Barat* is basically
a social boycott, with no Bohra allowed to speak with the targeted
individual. It thus entails complete isolation from the community,
including the targeted individual's family,[56] and is especially dam-
aging given how closely-knit Bohras are as a community. As soon as
Engineer spoke out against the clerical establishment, *Barat* was
imposed on him. In his memoirs, he relives the deep alienation and
tribulations that he faced, with relatives urging him to apologize to
the *da'i* and, if he failed to do so, that they would never speak to

---

[50] Engineer, *On Developing Theology of Peace in Islam*, 173.
[51] Asghar Ali Engineer, *A Living Faith: My Quest for Peace, Harmony and Social
Change: An Autobiography of Asghar Ali Engineer* (New Delhi: Orient Blackswan,
2011), 42.
[52] Engineer Interview, 2010.   [53] Ibid.
[54] Engineer, 'Women's Plight in Muslim Society'.
[55] Engineer, *A Living Faith*, 43.   [56] Ibid.

Engineer again.[57] He refused and was consequently ostracized from his family. This time was particularly painful for his mother, who was ridiculed in community circles and whom he could only meet in secret.[58] In addition to being rendered an outcast, Engineer has been physically assaulted by supporters of the Bohra clerical establishment, including in Hyderabad in 1977 and 1981; in Mumbai in 2001; and even in Cairo in 1983. The Bohras have a natural connection to Egypt, with its Isma'ili Fatimid legacy (909–1171). In 1983, the *da'i* decided to hold the Muharram lectures, which commemorate the death of the third *imam* Husayn b. Ali, in Cairo and thus a large number of Bohras assembled in the Egyptian capital. Engineer happened to be in Cairo at the same time for a conference. When he visited one of the Fatimid mosques—Jami' al-Hakim—he inadvertently ran into a group of Bohras, who recognized him and beat him unconscious.[59]

A REVOLUTIONARY FAITH

Islam and Liberation Theology

Indeed, this formative experience of oppression and inequality has shaped Engineer's entire discourse on religion. Like Esack, he approaches Islam and the Qur'an in particular as a revolutionary resource that can be drawn upon to combat states of oppression.[60] Justice, he argues, is a core component of the Qur'anic call, with God commanding the believers to firmly uphold justice (Q. 7:29; 49:9) and even wedding it to *taqwa*, or piety (Q. 5:8)—a key scriptural term that will be explored in greater depth in the upcoming chapters on Wadud and Barlas.[61] Without social justice, then, piety is lacking, incomplete. Economic equality is an integral aspect of Engineer's understanding

---

[57] Ibid, 44–5.   [58] Ibid, 45–6.   [59] Ibid, 63–4.

[60] Engineer, *Islam and Liberation Theology*, v.

[61] Ibid, 5. The two words, as well as their linguistic derivatives, that are used in these verses—*'adl* and *qist*—are the main terms in the Qur'an for justice, the former literally meaning to divide something into exactly two equal parts and the latter referring to fair and equitable conduct. See Abdur Rashid Siddiqui, *Qur'anic Keywords: A Reference Guide* (Markfield, Leicestershire: The Islamic Foundation, 2008), 4.

of Qur'anic justice. Far from being a discourse of benevolence centred on goodwill and charity (*sadaqa*), he writes that the text speaks to the fundamental right of the poor in the possessions of the affluent.[62] And it is this radical language of economic rights, as opposed to simply that of charity, which can confront the sin of structural poverty. Citing God's commandment to Prophet Muhammad—'They ask thee what they ought to spend. Say: That which is superfluous.' (Q. 2:219)—Engineer comments that the faithful should keep only that which will fulfil their basic needs, distributing 'that which is superfluous' to the poor and needy.[63] Paralleling Esack, he argues that the Qur'an reflects a deity who not only demands egalitarian conduct, but also stands in solidarity with the powerless against the powerful.[64] Engineer passionately quotes the following Qur'anic passage, referring to the ancient Children of Israel suffering under the despotic rule of Pharaoh's regime:

It is Our Will to bestow Our grace upon the downtrodden of the Earth, and to make them the leaders and to make them the inheritors of the Earth. And to establish them securely on the Earth, and to let Pharaoh and Haman and their hosts experience through them (the Children of Israel) the very thing against which they sought to protect themselves. (Q. 28:5–6)

That Engineer, in making a theological case for a just deity who intervenes in history to stand alongside the oppressed, cites precisely the same verses as Esack is hermeneutically significant, suggesting the centrality of this passage in Islamic liberation theology.

But in order for the Qur'an to function as a liberating text, it must first become a *liberated* text. A core critique that Engineer levels against mainstream Islamic thought is that it has taken a radical Qur'anic message of social liberation and reduced it to mere, metaphysical and spiritual abstractions wholly divorced from lived realities. This discursive move, moreover, is an inevitable consequence of Islamic theology's alliance with the status quo. In fact, the argument could be made, Engineer adds provocatively, that the more abstract the theology, the deeper the political complicity.[65] This historic,

---

[62] Engineer, *Islam and Liberation Theology*, 82.
[63] Ibid. This verse has been quoted directly from Engineer's writings.
[64] Engineer Interview, 2010.
[65] Engineer, *Islam and Liberation Theology*, 1–2.

hermeneutical shift within Islam from social to solely spiritual liberation is a compelling observation that Engineer makes. The Islamic
scholar Abdullah Saeed has noted that with the emergence of the
shari'a in the first three centuries of Islam, Muslims increasingly
approached the Qur'an—the substance of which was broadly ethical
in nature, espousing values and principles—as a strictly legal document.[66] Because of losing sight of the socially egalitarian vision of the
Qur'an, Engineer continues, what has taken centre-stage in Muslim
life has not been a commitment to creating a world characterized by
justice and compassion, but an obsession with dogmas and rituals.
The Islamic revival that has swept through Muslim-majority societies
since the 1970s is a contemporary example of a highly ritualized
Islam, writes Engineer, pointing to its heavy emphasis on piety and
worship,[67] such as praying five times a day, wearing the veil and
fasting in the month of Ramadan. An uncritical accent on rites
and rituals only serves to entrench further the trappings of religious
authority, for 'rituals require a priestcraft',[68] thus allowing the *'ulama*
to strengthen their already privileged positions as the custodians of
Islam. This is not to suggest that Engineer rejects the rituals—on the
contrary, I recall seeing him at the Friday Prayer when he spoke at the
University of Oxford—but rather that he seeks to problematize
understandings and practices of Islam that are blind to human
suffering, that are not grounded in historical projects. In order for
Islam to become a truly liberating faith, therefore, it needs to be
stripped of those accumulated accretions, from 'soulless rituals' to
'sheer metaphysical abstractions', that have been introduced to per-
petuate the status quo instead of subverting it.[69] To put it another
way: Engineer's liberation theology must first entail the 'liberation of
theology'.[70]

---

[66] Abdullah Saeed, *The Qur'an: An Introduction* (London: Routledge, 2008), 13.
A legal document can, of course, be ethical. The point that I am trying to make here is
that over the course of Muslim history the Qur'an was engaged progressively as a book
of law, as a predominantly legal text. Yet even a casual perusal of the Qur'an would
reveal that questions of law are not a prominent feature. Rather, the Qur'an is a book
of guidance for humankind, in which moral and ethical commitments to society play a
crucial role.
[67] Engineer, *Islam and Liberation Theology*, 107.
[68] Engineer, *On Developing Theology of Peace in Islam*, 183.
[69] Engineer, *Islam and Liberation Theology*, 22.
[70] Ibid, 21. Though Engineer does not cite anyone when making this argument, it is
important to note that the Uruguayan liberation theologian and Jesuit priest Juan Luis

And it is struggle that effects this liberation of theology, transforming the Qur'an into a liberated and liberating scripture. Engineer moves beyond a simplistic, sweeping call for social change, for the key question that he raises—in a strikingly similar manner to Esack— is change for *whom*? That is, change to what ends? According to Engineer, societal transformation, of which religious reform is part and parcel, must be undertaken to benefit the weak and disenfranchised.[71] However, liberating exegesis cannot come into being through the work of a detached commentator, but rather an engaged interpreter who actively struggles with the weak against the powerful, and thus partakes in *praxis*—the hermeneutical hallmark of liberation theology that was discussed in the second chapter. Citing Q. 4:95, Engineer argues that the Qur'an endorses a *praxis*-based approach, explicitly singling out the *mujahid*, or one who partakes in *jihad*.[72] The passage reads:

> The faithful who sit idle, other than those who are disabled, are not equal to those who fight in the way of God with their wealth and lives. God has exalted those in rank who fight for the faith with their wealth and lives over those who sit idle. Though God's promise of good is for all, He has granted His favour of the highest reward to those who struggle in preference to those who sit at home.

The text, therefore, has a heavy emphasis on action, and it is this commitment to act that ought to form the hermeneutical key with which to unlock scripture, making it speak to lived realities of suffering and, in so doing, transforming the Qur'an into an empowering text. It is important to note, moreover, that this reading strategy is at epistemic loggerheads with conservative notions of religious hierarchy. The Christian scholar Christopher Rowland sums up the relationship between authority and liberation theology:

> The primary text of oppression, poverty and dehumanizing attitudes and circumstances as a result makes theologians out of all God's people. The experts do not have a privileged position in the understanding of God as there is emphasis on the insight of the poor as interpreters of the word of God.[73]

Segundo (d. 1996) authored a study with the same title. See Juan Luis Segundo, *Liberation of Theology* (Maryknoll, NY: Orbis Books, 1976).

[71] Engineer, *Islam and Liberation Theology*, 16.   [72] Ibid, 6.
[73] Rowland, 11.

A characteristic feature of liberation theology, then, is the idea of twin texts. For the Qur'an (or the Bible or the Torah) is not the only text that is to be read and reflected upon. *Life*—referring to the experience of oppression and the ensuing struggle to combat such injustice—is as central a text that is to be interpreted alongside the text of scripture, and it is at the critical interface between these two texts that a radical theology arises.

Engineer's hermeneutic is thus a pressing hermeneutic of the here and now, of this world and *then* the next. Most discussions of justice in Islam centre on the theme of divine judgement: a Day of Reckoning (*yawm al-din*) in which all human beings will be gathered before the Creator and shown each and every deed they have committed.[74] Upon judgement, the righteous will enter paradise while the sinful will be condemned to hellfire. The Day of Reckoning, therefore, reflects the promise of accountability in the Hereafter—a revolutionary concept for the Meccans of Muhammad's time, as they did not believe in resurrection.[75] Yet what is so provocative about Engineer's hermeneutic is that the next world is consigned to the very edges of his exegesis. It is this world that is foregrounded. And it is within this worldly context, and his underlying commitment to liberation, that Engineer reflects on the meaning and implications of belief. Interpreting for the present, he offers a novel reading of the Qur'anic phrase *iman bi-l ghayb* (Q. 2:3), or belief in the Unseen, customarily referring to the ever-present but invisible God:

> If properly interpreted, in keeping with the spirit of the Qur'an, it implies faith in the infinite potentialities which have not yet been actualised and are hence unseen. These potentialities are both within human beings and out there in the cosmos. One should therefore have deep faith in ever developing possibilities and creative powers residing within and hidden from immediate sight.[76]

This is not to imply, of course, that Engineer rejects God, but rather that he approaches Qur'anic meaning as being rooted in two worlds at precisely the same moment. For belief in the Unseen, in an interpretation that speaks to the problems of the present, must refer

---

[74] Sells, 35.
[75] Ingrid Mattson, *The Story of the Qur'an: Its History and Place in Muslim Life* (Oxford: Blackwell Publishing, 2008), 45.
[76] Engineer, *Islam and Liberation Theology*, 10.

not simply to faith in God but in the possibilities of building a qualitatively different society marked by compassion, love and equality, encountering God through this transformative process. Consider Engineer's exegesis of Q. 104:

> Woe to every scorner and mockerer, who collects wealth and counts it.
> He thinks that his wealth will make him immortal. No! He will surely be
> thrown into the Crusher. And what will show you what is the Crusher?
> It is the fire of God, set ablaze, which will spread over the hearts. Indeed,
> it will close in upon them in outstretched columns.

Whereas conventional commentaries of this short chapter would interpret the Crusher and its fiery punishment as a form of divine justice in the Hereafter, Engineer interprets otherwise. Judgement and retribution must be rendered for this world. The Crusher that will devour those who hoard wealth, he comments, refers to an impending social upheaval, fuelled by popular discontent with the glaring inequalities of wealth in Meccan society,[77] which will ultimately destroy the city elite. Sensing this imminent destruction, Prophet Muhammad's call was a prescient warning to the Meccan leadership of a grave punishment that will be meted out in this life—a divine will channelled through the insurrectionary violence of the downtrodden—unless they duly repent and reform their ways. Through reinterpreting this chapter, Engineer argues that all such Qur'anic passages that speak to divine retribution need to be revisited in light of both worlds, or what he calls a 'socio-theological approach'[78] to exegesis—the first term (socio) referring to the Here and Now and the second, and thus *secondary*, term (theological) to the Hereafter.

It is important to note that Engineer, like Esack, does not see his radical reading of Islam as a theological innovation or a rupture with past practices, but rather as a recovery of an established, prophetic precedent. Engineer points out that all the Qur'anic prophets, with the exceptions of David and Solomon, emerged from the weakest segments of society—a deliberate move on God's part to ensure that they would be sensitized to lived realities of inequality.[79] Indeed, he argues that the Meccan elite's principal grievance with Muhammad was not his religious doctrine, but rather the socioeconomic implications

---

[77] Ibid, 75. While Engineer translates the Arabic word *al-hutama* as 'the Consuming One', I prefer Ali Quli Qara'i's translation: 'the Crusher'. See Qara'i, 861.

[78] Engineer, *Islam and Liberation Theology*, 75.

[79] Engineer Interview, 2010.

of his preaching, which challenged their privilege and wealth accumulation.[80] Engineer does not confine his historical argument of an
egalitarian Islam to the prophets, referring to early Muslim figures
who were committed to justice. He cites, for example, the famous
letter that Ali—the first *imam* of Shi'a Muslims and fourth caliph of
Sunni Muslims—wrote to his governor in Egypt, Malik al-Ashtar,
instructing him to treat the Egyptians with justice and dignity. The
selected passage reads:

> So far as your own affairs or those of your relatives and friends are
> concerned, take care that you do not violate the duties laid down upon
> you by God and usurp the rights of mankind, be impartial and do
> justice, because if you give up equity and justice then you will certainly
> be a tyrant and oppressor. And whoever tyrannizes and oppresses
> creatures of God will earn the enmity of God along with the hatred of
> those whom he has oppressed.[81]

In addition to specific individuals, Engineer mentions social movements in Islamic history. For instance, he describes the Qaramita—a
tenth-century Shi'a Isma'ili group based in eastern Arabia—as having a
'revolutionary theology', noting that they were against private property,
sharing the wealth by organizing themselves into communes.[82]

Karbala: An Islamic Paradigm of Liberation

While Esack draws upon the Exodus as a model of struggle, Engineer
turns to the Battle of Karbala, reflecting his own religious background
as a Shi'a Muslim. Over the course of his writings, he invokes a number
of liberative paradigms. Like Wadud and Barlas—whose Qur'anic
hermeneutics we will explore in subsequent chapters—Engineer highlights the social implications of *tawhid*. For an understanding of
Islamic monotheism rooted in struggle, he argues, must entail not

---

[80] Asghar Ali Engineer ed., *Islam and Revolution* (Delhi: Ajanta Publications,
1984), 26.

[81] Ali ibn Abi Talib, as quoted in Engineer, *Islam: Misgivings and History*, 120. This
is an excerpt from Letter 53 of *Nahjul Balagha* (literally, the Peak of Eloquence), a
famous compilation of Ali's numerous sermons, sayings and letters. See Ali ibn Abi
Talib, *Peak of Eloquence: Nahjul Balagha, with Commentary by Ayatollah Murtada
Mutahhari*, ed. Yasin T. al-Jibouri (Elmhurst, New York: Tahrike Tarsile Qur'an,
2009), 791–802.

[82] Engineer ed., *Islam and Revolution*, 17.

only the unity of the Creator but also the unity of the creation, undivided by socioeconomic hierarchy.[83] The Battle of Karbala, however, is the most distinctive paradigm in Engineer's liberation theology, in which Husayn b. Ali (d. 680), the grandson of Prophet Muhammad and third *imam* of Shi'a Muslims, along with seventy-two of his followers, rebelled against the despotic caliph Yazid (d. 683) and were brutally massacred in the plains of Karbala, located in modern-day Iraq. Yazid's ascension to the caliphate following the death of his father, Mu'awiya (d. 680), represented the introduction of monarchy into Islamic governance, and therefore a radical departure from Qur'anic values of fellowship and egalitarianism.[84] This development was exacerbated by Yazid's politics, marked by nepotism and arbitrary rule, as well as his personality, taken to the sensual pleasures of courtly life and thus utterly divorced from the realities of the broader Muslim community. In fact, if Islam represented a sociopolitical revolution in seventh-century Arabia, the reign of Yazid, to quote Engineer, constituted a 'counter revolution'.[85] But the rebellion of Husayn was not simply against Yazid, Engineer continues, rather what this individual symbolized: namely, the degeneration of Islam into a religion of establishment.[86] This was a struggle, then, that sought to reclaim the revolutionary soul of the faith, to restore Muslim practices to the ethical teachings of the Prophet. Though Esack's and Engineer's paradigms of preference are clearly different in that the former looks towards an event within scripture— the Exodus—while the latter draws inspiration from an episode that transpired roughly five decades after the Qur'anic revelation, it is important to note that Engineer's hermeneutical emphasis on Karbala does not necessarily make it any less Qur'anic. For Husayn's martyrdom exemplifies core principles embedded in the text, such as justice, courage and self-sacrifice. It is in Husayn's commitment, therefore, to put the Word into practice in the face of overwhelming odds that the link between this historic event and scripture lies. The following Urdu couplet by Muhammad Iqbal (d. 1938), the distinguished South Asian poet and intellectual founder of Pakistan, evocatively captures

---

[83] Engineer, *Islam and Liberation Theology*, 56.
[84] Engineer Interview, 2010.
[85] Engineer, *Islam and Liberation Theology*, 230.
[86] Engineer Interview, 2010.

this relationship: 'I learned the lesson of the Qur'an from Hussain. In his fire, like a flame, I burn.'[87]

As this couplet suggests, Engineer is not the first Muslim thinker to have been inspired by the legacy of Husayn. Indeed, the Battle of Karbala has become a pervasive paradigm of struggle in contemporary Islam. During the 1978–9 Iranian Revolution, references to Husayn's martyrdom permeated revolutionary discourse, especially in the Islamic writings of Shari'ati—the exegete of *tawhid* whom we met in the previous chapter—discerning in Husayn an insurrectionary figure fighting for the cause of social liberation.[88] What makes the memory of Karbala so compelling, so subversive as a political language of resistance is the remarkable fluidity with which it can be applied to markedly different contexts. In contemporary Iraq, for instance, resistance fighters have called the American occupation forces the 'Army of Yazid', while before the invasion the same term was used to denote Saddam Hussein's regime.[89] The Battle of Karbala, then, not only acted as a powerful language of protest against domestic dictatorship but, once this regime was toppled by foreign powers, it was able to swiftly switch discursive gears and denounce imperialist invasion. It is important to note that while the memory of Karbala has inspirited Muslims of all sectarian stripes (recalling Iqbal's poetry) it has had a particularly formative impact on Shi'a Islamic thought. Because the Shi'a, as the devout followers of the Prophet's family, were marginalized from the very outset by the Sunni-dominated Muslim polity—a betrayal that would eventually culminate in the martyrdom of Husayn—Shi'a Islam has historically exhibited an acute awareness of power, cultivating a culture of protest. Speaking truth to power is a central teaching of Shi'a ethics for, by siding with the oppressed and downtrodden, the believer stands up not only for 'the historical Hossein but for all the Hosseins of the world.'[90] I do not mean to suggest, of course, that Shi'a Islam is *essentially* radical. As the Iranian scholar Hamid Dabashi has observed, Shi'a Islam remains a 'religion of protest' so long as it exists on the edges of society, but that once it attains power, thereby

[87] Muhammad Iqbal, as quoted in Syed Akbar Hyder, *Reliving Karbala: Martyrdom in South Asian Memory* (Oxford: Oxford University Press, 2006), 137.

[88] Keddie, 206.

[89] Hamid Dabashi, *Islamic Liberation Theology: Resisting the Empire* (London: Routledge, 2008), 178.

[90] Safi, *Memories of Muhammad*, 256.

transforming into a religion of establishment, it undoes its own social message.[91]

An All-Encompassing Justice? Class, Gender, and Pluralism

The problem of poverty, as we have already noted, is a major theme in Engineer's discourse. In fact, it is arguably the most important aspect of his liberation theology. For Engineer, greed constitutes the root source of human suffering. Yet greed should not be understood simply as a personal desire for riches, but as a structural expression of wealth accumulation: that is, economic systems like contemporary capitalism that systematically disenfranchise the many in order to enrich the few.[92] Referring to the Qur'anic narratives of Adam's expulsion from Paradise, Engineer argues that greed was the first cardinal sin committed by humankind. The following passage narrates the story:

> Certainly We had enjoined Adam earlier; but he forgot, and We did not find resoluteness in him. When We said to the angels, 'Prostrate before Adam,' they prostrated, except Iblis [the name of Satan before his expulsion from Paradise]: he refused. We said, 'O Adam! This is indeed an enemy of yours and your mate's. So do not let him expel you from Paradise, or you will be miserable. Indeed you will neither be hungry in it nor naked. Indeed you will neither be thirsty in it nor suffer from the sun.' Then Satan tempted him. He said, 'O Adam! Shall I show you the tree of immortality, and an imperishable kingdom?' So they both ate of it, and their nakedness became exposed to them, and they began to stitch over themselves with the leaves of paradise. Adam disobeyed his Sustainer, and went amiss. (Q. 20:115-121)

Adam and his partner, therefore, had everything that they *needed* in Paradise—a place of security in which they would be neither hungry nor naked, thirsty nor exposed to the sun—and it was precisely when they coveted what was beyond their basic needs, seeking to satisfy their greed and rebelling against their Creator in the process, that they were banished to the Earth.[93] As we have discussed earlier, Engineer argues that the Qur'an calls for a simple, even austere, style of living that is based on fulfilling one's immediate needs, spending all surplus wealth in the way of the poor and needy (Q. 2:219).[94] This is not to

---

[91] Dabashi, 67–8.   [92] Engineer Interview, 2010.   [93] Ibid.
[94] Engineer, *Islam: Misgivings and History*, 9.

imply that the text outlines a specific ideology, such as Marxist economics, but rather that an underlying commitment to socioeconomic equality, as mirrored by need-based living on both personal and structural levels, is a principle that the Qur'an upholds.[95] And it is because free-market capitalism is fundamentally at variance with such values, concludes Engineer, that this economic system must be squarely rejected.[96] Citing the reported proverb of Prophet Muhammad—'Wisdom is the lost property of the faithful; he should acquire it wherever he finds it'—Engineer continues that if other systems, such as socialism and state-controlled economies, are more congruent with Islamic commitments to economic justice, then Muslims should embrace them.[97] That Engineer cites a prophetic report in making this case is telling, demonstrating his openness to the *hadith* when its substantive content can be hermeneutically channelled to affirm Qur'anic principles.

His critique of economic hierarchy leads to a wider criticism of political injustice around the world. The global economy has divided the Earth, Engineer laments, and the powerful economies of Europe and North America have systematically exploited and impoverished those of the Third World.[98] Such stark economic inequality, in turn, has spawned political structures and international institutions that are highly undemocratic. The exclusive composition of the UN Security Council is an illustrative example. Comprising a handful of the most powerful nations in the world, which represent the council's permanent membership, this elite body has overridden time and again the majority decisions of the General Assembly.[99] He singles out the USA in particular as a principal source of global injustice. Despite the US's discourse of supporting (and in the case of the Bush administration *spreading*) democracy in Muslim-majority societies, the USA has consistently allied with repressive, dictatorial regimes whenever doing so has advanced American interests.[100] In terms of the Middle East, the Zionist state of Israel—which, Engineer adds, with the assistance of colonial powers was established on indigenous Palestinian land, dispossessing almost a million Palestinians in the

---

[95] Engineer, *Islam and Liberation Theology*, 52.   [96] Ibid.
[97] Ibid, 87.   [98] Ibid, 76.
[99] Asghar Ali Engineer, 'Israeli Aggression and the World', *Secular Perspective*, 1 August 2006, available at: http://www.csss-isla.com/wp-content/uploads/2015/06/August-1-15-06.pdf accessed 12 August 2016.
[100] Engineer, *Islam: Misgivings and History*, vii.

process—has been a critical ally of the USA.[101] Indeed, Israel is 'an American imperialist outpost', a geostrategic instrument through which the USA can ensure its own privileged access to the region's oil resources.[102] Engineer's critique of oppression, therefore, is acutely transnational.

As was shown in the methodology section, gender justice is a prominent feature in his writings. Any liberation struggle that does not include the rights of women, warns Engineer, is fundamentally lacking.[103] When I asked him when exactly he first began to *see* patriarchy, discerning the social inequalities that existed between women and men, he pointed to the division of labour in the family:

> The whole family structure and the distribution of power in the family, that itself convinced me that power lies with men, not with women ... the division of labour itself is political. I mean, it is the powerful who decide the division of labour. So the division of labour is coercive. It is not based on justice or fairness ... and once you internalise it, it becomes natural for you. But it is not natural.[104]

Politics is thus not confined to issues of economic inequality and imperial domination, but is present in every societal space wherein uneven relationships of power exist. In a similar fashion to Esack, Engineer shows an awareness of the complexity of oppression, calling for a generally comprehensive commitment to justice—I will explain shortly why I use the qualifier 'generally'—and in which women's equality constitutes a central component. It is in the sphere of gender justice, moreover, that Engineer's preference for the Qur'an over other Islamic texts like the *hadith* comes out most clearly. Consider the issue of women's leadership. When Benazir Bhutto (d. 2007) was first elected Prime Minister of Pakistan in 1988, the following prophetic report became widely circulated amongst conservative Muslims: 'a nation can never prosper which has assigned its rulership to a woman.'[105] Countering this misogynistic report, Engineer argued that not only did *hadith* scholars consider this report to be weak in terms of authenticity, but also, and far more significantly, that the Qur'an speaks highly of a female ruler, the Queen of Sheba,[106] portraying her as a capable

---

[101] Engineer, 'Israeli Aggression and the World'.   [102] Ibid.
[103] Engineer, *Islam and Liberation Theology*, vi.
[104] Engineer Interview, 2010.
[105] Engineer, *The Rights of Women in Islam*, 17.   [106] Ibid.

leader endowed with wisdom and political foresight (Q. 27:29–35). By
trumping this *hadith* with the Qur'an, he uses the vested authority of
scripture as an empowering tool with which to undercut patriarchal
religious discourses.[107] Though gender justice is clearly an integral
part of Engineer's discourse, it is important to point out the limits, the
boundaries of his understanding of gender justice. Unlike Esack and
Wadud, Engineer does not support queer rights through an Islamic
framework, stating that the Qur'an 'denounces homosexuality in no
uncertain terms' and that holding such 'radical positions' will only
weaken the cause of human rights in Muslim-majority countries.[108]
His statement about the Qur'an is erroneous, however, as the Islamic
scholar Scott Kugle has shown that the text itself does not explicitly
condemn homosexuality and that classical jurists read this understanding into the text.[109] In sum, Engineer's conceptualization of
gender justice does not include sexual justice, which is why I state
that he has a generally (as opposed to a fully) comprehensive commitment to justice.

Engineer's liberation theology, moreover, crosses religious boundaries, accepting pluralism and the diverse ways with which human
beings can respond to the divine call. At the heart of his conception of
pluralism lies the conviction that there is no singular, unanimous
understanding of God,[110] and it is this humble acknowledgment that
enables Engineer to embrace the religious Other. The Qur'an, he
continues, explicitly affirms religious pluralism, citing the following
verse by way of example:

> We have sent down to you the Book with the truth, confirming what
> was before it of the Book and as a guardian over it. So judge between
> them by what God has sent down, and do not follow their desires
> against the truth that has come to you. For each community among
> you We have appointed a law and a way of life, and had God wished He
> would have made you one community, but He wished to test you by

---

[107] To be sure, he also uses precedents in the early history of Islam to support
women's participation in public life, pointing to female figures such as 'Ayesha (d. 678),
who was active in political affairs and even led troops into battle. See Asghar Ali
Engineer, 'Women and Administration', in *Proceedings: National Seminar on the
Status of Woman in Islam* (New Delhi: Bait-al-Hikmat, 1983), 37.

[108] Engineer, *A Living Faith*, 197.

[109] Kugle, 50. For Kugle's close reading of the Lot story, see Chapter 2: 'Liberating
Qur'an: Islamic Scripture'.

[110] Engineer Interview, 2010.

that which He gave you. So take the lead in all good works (*al-khayrat*). To God shall be the return of you all, whereat He will inform you about that which you used to differ. (Q. 5:48)

This Qur'anic passage squarely rejects any notion of Muslim supremacy. For not only did God provide different laws and ways of life for different communities, Engineer observes, but plurality is actually a part of God's plan, as this all-powerful deity could easily have crafted one single community.[111] Indeed, as the Islamic scholar Carl Ernst has observed, the word *islam* (submission) is of relatively minor importance in the Qur'an, occurring only eight times, while broader and more inclusive concepts such as *iman* (faith) and *mu'min* (believer) receive greater attention.[112] Yet it is not even belief but action—*al-khayrat* ('good works'), to quote from the above verse— that will ultimately determine the fate of the faithful. According to the Qur'anic text, then, salvation is achieved not by virtue of accidental birth into the right religious community, but rather, as the progressive Islamic scholar Omid Safi notes, by coupling an abiding faith in God with an equally abiding commitment to righteous conduct (*ihsan*).[113]

Drawing upon the ideas of earlier Islamic mystics and thinkers, Engineer contrasts the famous Muslim belief found in the *hadith*, that God sent 124,000 prophets to humankind with the fact that the Qur'an—which selectively refers to the stories of past prophets to illustrate lessons to the reader, rejecting any claim to comprehensiveness— mentions only twenty-five prophets by name.[114] And it is in the disparity between these two numbers that Engineer carves out a theological space for the religious Other, since we do not know where numerous prophets were sent and, therefore, such historical figures as Raam and Krishna may well have been messengers of God.[115] This hermeneutical manoeuvre is indicative of Engineer's nuanced treatment of the *hadith*. For whereas in terms of gender justice we saw how he undermined a misogynistic *hadith* report through scripture, here he actually uses a *hadith* to flesh out a Qur'anic

---

[111] Asghar Ali Engineer, 'Islam and Pluralism', in *The Myth of Religious Superiority: A Multifaith Exploration*, ed. Paul F. Knitter (Maryknoll, New York: Orbis, 2005), 212–13.

[112] Ernst, 63.   [113] Safi, *Memories of Muhammad*, 200.

[114] Despite its popularity, *hadith* scholars consider the authenticity of this report to be weak (*da'if*). It can be found in the *musnad*—or a *hadith* collection that is arranged according to the chains of narration—of Ahmad ibn Hanbal (d. 855).

[115] Engineer Interview, 2010.

hermeneutic of religious pluralism. But Engineer does not only use
the idea of prophecy to reconcile theological differences between
Islam and other religions like Hinduism, but also, and perhaps
paradoxically, the very concept of monotheism itself. He describes
the Hindu faith as follows:

> the theory and practice of Hinduism are very different. In theory, Hin-
> duism is as monotheistic as Christianity or Judaism or Islam. Because
> what is the real concept of *ishwar* [Sanskrit: God] in the Hindu religion?
> *Ishwar* is conceived of as formless and without attributes. And if this is
> not monotheism then what is monotheism?[116]

As commendable as Engineer's pluralistic intentions may be, the
above passage raises some larger questions with regard to the meaning of religious diversity. Does this type of theological reasoning do
justice to the religious Other and the Hindu Other in particular? That
is, do I as a Muslim reconcile the express polytheism of Hinduism by
simply explaining it away as being a misunderstood, mispracticed
(Islamic) monotheism? In other words, they are *really* like us. Or do
I engage in the far more difficult and unsettling theological task of
actually embracing difference?

SECULARISM, MODERNISM, PEACE: THREE CRITIQUES

Communal Violence and the Secular Alternative

It is on the issue of the religious Other that we arrive at the primary,
contextual backdrop in which Engineer writes: namely, that of communal rioting between Hindus and Muslims in contemporary India.
The central argument that he puts forth concerning communal violence is that, contrary to the dominant discourse in Indian society,
not only is religion not the principal cause behind such conflict, but it
can act as a rich resource for peace-building between the two communities.[117] Instead, Engineer posits, elite politics is the main culprit
behind communal violence:

---

[116] Ibid.   [117] Ibid.

Communalism is not, as is often thought by some, a product of religion, but, rather, of the politics of the elite of a religious community. In other words religion per se does not give birth to communalism; a religious community does ... It is competitive politics between the elites of two or more communities, which give rise to communalism.[118]

The key argument here is that politicians play a vital role in stirring up discord between Hindus and Muslims to safeguard their own interests, to consolidate control over their respective communities. This thesis certainly holds true in the Hindu context, in which Hindu nationalist groups have consistently used the Dalits (literally, the Crushed People, denoting the so-called Untouchables), in addition to other disenfranchised Hindus of lower caste standing, to attack Muslims, especially during the Gujarat riots in 2002.[119] Playing the identity card so as to exploit the historic exclusion of lower caste Hindus from mainstream Indian society, these nationalist groups have called on poor Hindus to attack the Muslim Other in order to *prove* their Hinduness.[120]

Engineer's elite politics argument is unsound, however, when it comes to the Muslim community. Indeed, the quoted passage above gives the impression that Hindus and Muslims, in terms of socio-economic standing and political power, are roughly on a par with one another. Though there is undoubtedly a wide discrepancy in material standing amongst Hindus, Indian Muslims—as Engineer himself notes—are almost as economically impoverished as Dalits.[121] For instance, a survey conducted on childhood education (6–14 years) revealed that in the 1992–3 school year upper caste Hindus had an enrolment rate of 80.7 per cent for boys and 64.1 per cent for girls; lower caste Hindus an enrolment rate of 66.5 per cent and 44.9 per cent; and Muslims 66.5 per cent and 52.9 per cent.[122] Furthermore,

---

[118] Engineer, *The Gujarat Carnage*, 2.

[119] Asghar Ali Engineer, 'Dalit-Muslim Dialogue', *Secular Perspective*, 16 August 2004, available at: http://www.csss-isla.com/wp-content/uploads/2015/06/August-16-31-04.pdf accessed 12 August 2016.

[120] Ibid.   [121] Ibid.

[122] Sonia Bhalotra and Barnarda Zamora, 'Social Divisions in Education in India', in *Handbook of Muslims in India: Empirical and Policy Perspectives*, eds. Rakesh Basant and Abusaleh Shariff (Oxford: Oxford University Press, 2010), 191. This volume is a landmark contribution to our knowledge of Muslim poverty, documenting how Muslims have fared in fields like the labour market, education and child healthcare.

while the state has sought to rectify the plight of the Hindu poor, it has continued to turn a blind eye to their Muslim counterparts:

> The Government of India has put in place several policies to reverse the disadvantages suffered by two major groups—Dalits and adivasis [literally, the indigenous people]. These include scholarships and grants, reserved quota for admission to coveted educational programmes, and reserved quota for employment in government and public sectors. Many of these policies have been in place since independence in 1947, but have been implemented far more vigorously since 1990. Since the state plays an important role in Indian educational system and government employment forms about two-thirds of the jobs in the formal sector, one expects these policies to have a significant impact. There have been no such explicit policies and programmes favouring the largest minority religious group, Muslims, who too like Dalits and adivasis have been victims of social exclusion and marginalization from the mainstream Indian society.[123]

Communal violence in India, then, is not about two, roughly equal parties battling it out with each other, but rather of a far more powerful and established community besieging a vulnerable religious minority. To be sure, Engineer has been outspoken in condemning Hindu violence against Muslims in Gujarat, showing how this alleged riot was, in fact, a premeditated and meticulously executed massacre of Muslims.[124] Yet he is not so swift to point fingers at the Hindu community when it comes to other cases of communal rioting, resorting instead to a more generalized and less controversial language of criticizing politicians and elite politics, despite the fact that his own writings acknowledge the deep complicity of the Hindu-dominated Indian state, and of the police force in particular, during acts of communal violence against Muslims.[125]

Engineer calls for secularism as a lasting solution to communal discord. In 1993, he, along with a number of Hindu and Muslim academics and activists, established the 'Center for the Study of Society

[123] Sonalde Desai and Veenu Kulkarni, 'Unequal Playing Field: Socio-Religious Inequalities in Educational Attainment', in *Handbook of Muslims in India: Empirical and Policy Perspectives*, eds. Rakesh Basant and Abusaleh Shariff (Oxford: Oxford University Press, 2010), 285.

[124] Engineer, *The Gujarat Carnage*, 21.

[125] Asghar Ali Engineer, 'Secularism and its Problems in India', *Secular Perspective*, 1 December 2007, available at: http://www.csss-isla.com/wp-content/uploads/2015/06/December-1-15-07.pdf accessed 12 August 2016.

and Secularism'—a research organization committed to countering communal violence in India. The Center publishes two journals that clearly underscore its ideological commitments, titled *Secular Perspective* and the *Indian Journal of Secularism*, and through which Engineer disseminates his writings. Given the centrality of religion and spirituality in South Asian life, it is important to point out here that secularism as a discourse has a distinct meaning in the Indian context. As Engineer notes, secularism does not refer to an atheistic rejection of religion, but rather to a political philosophy conceived during India's independence to ensure that the country's multiple faith traditions would be treated with equality and respect.[126] Secular nationalism in India, then, was envisaged as a crucial counterweight to communal politics, for while the latter divided the nation, the former united it.[127] Because of its emphasis on inclusion, the call for a thoroughly secular state has long been a mutual rallying point for Indian progressives, including Leftists, feminists, and secular nationalist reformists.[128] Indeed, Indian Muslims like Engineer are not the only religious minorities to have picked up the banner of secularism. The Christian theologian and social activist M.M. Thomas (d. 1996) is a compelling case in point. Deeply influenced by the horrific communal violence that erupted during Partition between Hindus, Muslims, and Sikhs, Thomas became a staunch supporter of secularism, calling on fellow Christians and church leaders to partake in the creation of a socialist and democratic India, in which all religious communities would be welcomed and protected.[129] But the problem with Indian secularism, bemoans Engineer, is that it looks far better on paper than in practice. For while the Indian constitution upholds the principle of secularism, securing the rights of religious minorities,[130] successive governments—the majority of which, interestingly enough, have been led by the so-called secular Congress Party—have appeased the interests of Hindu lobbyists rather than abiding by constitutional dictates.[131]

[126] Ibid.
[127] Needham and Rajan, 13–14.
[128] Bastiaan Wielenga, 'Liberation Theology in Asia', in *The Cambridge Companion to Liberation Theology*, ed. Christopher Rowland (Cambridge: Cambridge University Press, 2007), 59.
[129] Ibid, 66.   [130] Engineer, 'How Secular is India Today?'
[131] Engineer, 'Secularism and its Problems in India'.

His sweeping accent on the secular is problematic, however, because of the *normativity* of Hinduism in contemporary India. Comprising the bulk of the population, the experiences of the Hindu community have effectively become institutionalized, constituting the default narrative of what it means to be Indian. As a result, religious minorities, and particularly Muslims, have become the Other of Indian nationalist modernity. The Bengali historian of Hindu-background, Dipesh Chakrabarty, recounts his experience growing up in the Indian schooling system:

> I am also very sadly aware of the historical gap between Hindu and Muslim Bengalis ... this forgetting of the Muslim was deeply embedded in the education and upbringing I received in independent India. Indian Bengali anticolonial nationalism implicitly normalized the 'Hindu.' Like many others in my situation, I look forward to the day when the default position in narratives of Bengali modernity will not sound exclusively or even primarily Hindu.[132]

It is precisely because of the universalization of Hindu discourses, such as in the national educational curriculum, that Hinduness has taken on an aura of neutrality. The field of law is another case in point. That Hindu nationalists, when countering Muslim demands for their own civil law system, have called for the implementation of a Uniform Civil Code,[133] as opposed to an *explicitly* Hindu civil code, reflects the close nexus between Hinduness and codified, secular law. The problem with Engineer's language of secularism, then, is that it fails to raise the following, critical question: secularism on whose terms? That is, who gets to define the secular?[134] Though religious minorities and political progressives have rallied around secularism, especially in the face of militant Hindu nationalism, it is the Hindu community that has nevertheless set the basis, the parameters of secular discourse in India. As Engineer himself notes, Hindus consistently portray themselves as being secular and liberal, while, conversely, presenting Muslims as being, at best, religiously conservative

---

[132] Chakrabarty, 21.   [133] Engineer, *The Rights of Women in Islam*, 166.
[134] The anthropologist Talal Asad has played a pioneering role in challenging the perceived neutrality, the ahistoricity of secularism, situating this discourse within a wider web of power relations. See Talal Asad, *Formations of the Secular: Christianity, Islam, Modernity* (Stanford: Stanford University Press, 2003) and David Scott and Charles Hirschkind eds., *Powers of the Secular Modern: Talal Asad and his Interlocutors* (Stanford: Stanford University Press, 2006).

and, at worst, raging fundamentalists.[135] Indeed, this deeply reductive discourse of contrasting the secular, modern Hindu with the fanatical, medieval Muslim is so entrenched within Indian society that even expressly Hindu supremacist groups like the Bharatiya Janata Party (BJP)—a major political movement built on the ideology of Hindu nationalism (*hindutva*)—have claimed that Hindus, by their very nature, are secular and that it is due to Hindu efforts that India is a secular state.[136] At what point, therefore, does Engineer's blanket espousal of secularism inadvertently play into this dichotomous discourse?

Reason and Literacy: A Modernist Hermeneutic

Engineer's liberation theology, moreover, reflects a distinctly modernist reading—an ideological tendency that comes out most acutely in his juxtaposition of rationalist thinking, on the one hand, with superstitious belief, on the other. Because the Bohra community in which he was raised was staunchly conservative, laying heavy emphasis on unquestioned obedience to age-old traditions, Engineer gravitated towards rationalist thought, particularly modern science and Western philosophy.[137] As a result, reason—that is, a process of judgement and comprehension centred on the use of logic—has come to play a prominent role in his exegesis.[138] Indeed, he points out, the Qur'an emphasizes the use of one's intellect, constantly exhorting humankind to ponder, to reflect and not to follow blindly the customs of their ancestors.[139] That being said, Engineer is careful to avoid

---

[135] Engineer, *The Gujarat Carnage*, 17. It is worthwhile noting that Hindu calls for a Uniform Civil Code have routinely been wrapped in a rhetoric of Muslim modernization: specifically, that the implementation of a universal legal system will enlighten the backward Muslim community and liberate their passive, agentless women from Islamic bondage, such as by abolishing polygamy. In doing so, it will facilitate the integration of Muslims into the nation. See Flavia Agnes, 'The Supreme Court, the Media, and the Uniform Civil Code Debate in India', in *The Crisis of Secularism in India*, eds. Anuradha D. Needham and Rajeswari S. Rajan (Durham, US: Duke University Press, 2007), 297–8.

[136] Engineer, *The Gujarat Carnage*, 17.   [137] Engineer Interview, 2010.

[138] To be sure, he clarifies that liberation theology is not synonymous with rational theology. That is, while (his) liberation theology is a rational theology, rational theology is not necessarily liberative and can serve the interests of the powerful. See Engineer ed., *Islam and Revolution*, 24.

[139] Asghar Ali Engineer, *Rational Approach to Islam* (New Delhi: Gyan Publishing House, 2001), 61.

partaking in *tafsir 'ilmi*, or the scientific interpretation of scripture. Fixated on reconciling recent scientific discoveries with the Qur'an, from the Big Bang to the formation of the fetus, *tafsir 'ilmi* has emerged as a major apologetic body of literature in contemporary Islam. Engineer is sceptical of such overtly modernist readings, arguing that the Qur'an is not 'a sourcebook for science' but a book of guidance and cautioning that in the fluid world of scientific knowledge what is considered as an empirical truth today may well be challenged tomorrow.[140] His emphasis on reason, in turn, leads to a scathing criticism of superstition, which comes to exemplify everything that is backward in Muslim societies. Commenting on Q. 17:90–5, Engineer maintains that Prophet Muhammad, as the bearer of a divine message based on reason, sought to cleanse the world of superstitious and supernatural beliefs, refusing to perform any miracles.[141] The passage reads:

> They say, 'We will not believe you [Muhammad] until you make a spring gush forth for us from the ground. Or until you have a garden of date palms and vines and you make streams gush through it. Or until you cause the sky to fall in fragments upon us, just as you would aver. Or until you bring God and the angels in front of us. Or until you have a house of gold, or you ascend into the sky. And we will not believe your ascension until you bring down for us a book that we may read.' Say [God commanding Muhammad]: 'Immaculate is my Sustainer! Am I anything but a human, a messenger?!' Nothing kept the people from believing when guidance came to them, but their saying, 'Has God sent a human as messenger?!' Say [God commanding Muhammad]: 'Had there been angels in the Earth, walking around and residing (in it like humans do), We would have sent down to them from the Heavens an angel as messenger.'

Engineer's conclusion that God's *refusal* to deliver any miracles in this particular context translates into a categorical *rejection* of miracles is incoherent not only because the Qur'an is full of the miraculous—from Prophet Moses' parting of the Red Sea to Prophet Jesus' raising of the dead to divine promises of the Resurrection—but also, and most significantly, because the very foundation of Islam (and of religion as a whole) is built on the supernatural, the illogical: namely, faith in an unseen and yet ever-present deity.

---

[140] Engineer, *Islam: Misgivings and History*, 102–3.
[141] Engineer, *Islam and Liberation Theology*, 32.

Just as Engineer privileges the rational over the superstitious so, too, does he elevate the literary over the oral. Muslims routinely refer to pre-Islamic Arabia as the Age of Ignorance (*jahiliyya*), alluding to the widespread practice of polytheism. Describing this period, Engineer writes: 'People were steeped in superstitions and there were no more than seventeen persons who could read or write.'[142] Here, he not only connects superstition with illiteracy, but also implicitly associates the ignorance of literacy with a wider ignorance of God. The mission of Muhammad, then, was not simply to bring knowledge of the Word, but of the written word in general. Reflecting upon Q. 96:1–5—the first verses that were revealed to the Prophet— Engineer claims that the call to literacy came packaged with the Qur'anic message of monotheism. The verses read:

> Recite! In the Name of your Sustainer who created; created the human being from a clot of blood. Recite! And your Sustainer is the most generous, who taught by the pen (*al-qalam*), taught the human being that which he knew not.

Literacy, expounds Engineer, is intrinsically linked to knowledge and thus guidance—a sacred relationship embodied in the above verse by the metaphor of the pen (*al-qalam*).[143] Engineer's exegetical emphasis on the literary is problematic not only because the first Muslims engaged the Qur'an primarily as an oral text, but also because he overlooks the complex ways in which knowledge was historically transmitted in pre-Islamic Arabia, reducing it, literally, to an age of ignorance. In fact, it was possible for the first Muslims to memorize lengthy Qur'anic passages precisely because mass memorization was how knowledge had been preserved—a reading practice facilitated by such poetic techniques as versification, and which the Qur'an itself would later adopt—in an oral society.[144] By elevating the written letter over the oral word, Engineer takes the richness and intellectual sophistication of *orality* and demotes it to *illiteracy*, and therefore as something that is necessarily negative, lacking. Engineer's literary biases stand in contrast to Esack, who is keenly aware of the value of orality, even devoting the first chapter of his textbook on the Qur'an to its popular reception and underscoring the fact that the

---

[142] Engineer, *Islam: Misgivings and History*, 41.
[143] Engineer, *Islam and Liberation Theology*, 31.
[144] Mattson, 45.

vast majority of Muslims continue, legitimately, to encounter the Qur'an as an oral text, especially in terms of its rhythmic recitation.[145] What makes Engineer's modernist bent towards the written letter even more problematic, particularly in the Indian context where illiteracy is high, is that the traditions and testimonies of the downtrodden are rarely written down, but rather rooted in the oral, the folkloric. Thus, the task of liberation theology, as a theology that is in critical conversation with the oppressed, is to unearth and safeguard these much maligned traditions. For example, a principal project of Dalit Theology, which seeks to empower the so-called Untouchables in an oppressive, caste-based society, is to reclaim Dalit culture and history, embedded in oral media like songs, folk stories, and myths.[146]

Is a Theology of Liberation Necessarily a Theology of Peace?

But perhaps the most pressing problem in Engineer's liberation theology is his sweeping discourse of peace, which he equates wholly with Islam. According to Engineer, the Qur'anic term *jihad* has nothing to do with violence (Q. 9:24; 22:78; 49:15),[147] pointing out that when the text does refer to fighting (*qital*), it is used in a decidedly defensive context (Q. 22:39).[148] Peace is a sacred theme that envelops the Qur'anic worldview, which describes God as *salam* ('peace') and Paradise as a celestial abode in which the faithful will enjoy 'peace and security'.[149] Muhammad—whom Engineer calls the

---

[145] Esack, *The Qur'an: A User's Guide*, 21. This popular engagement with the Qur'an falls under what Esack classifies (descriptively, he is not setting up a normative order) as the first level of Muslim interaction with the text, which is not intellectual, let alone critical. Confessional Muslim scholarship is the next level, entailing a scholarly elucidation of the Qur'an to the rest of the world, though in an idealized and apologetic fashion. Critical Muslim scholarship—Esack's own exegetical terrain— falls under the third level of interaction, asking more difficult questions about the text's language, nature and origins. See Farid Esack, 'The Territory of the Qur'an: "Citizens," "Foreigners," and "Invaders"', in Mumtaz Ahmad, Zahid Bukhari and Sulayman Nyang eds., *Observing the Observer: The State of Islamic Studies in American Universities* (Herndon, VA: International Institute of Islamic Thought, 2012), 54–6.
[146] Wielenga, 68.
[147] Engineer, *On Developing Theology of Peace in Islam*, 27.
[148] Ibid, 31.   [149] Engineer, *Islam: Misgivings and History*, 6.

'Prophet of Non-Violence'[150]—embodied these teachings of peace. The Prophet refrained from wars of aggression and, whenever possible, would opt for a non-violent resolution to conflict. That is, whatever battles the Prophet waged, Engineer maintains, were defensive in nature, necessitated by contextual circumstances.[151] While Engineer's emphasis on peace is clearly meant to counter popular perceptions of the faith as inherently violent, particularly within the Indian context, this idea of Islam as being a religion of peace has become, as we have already seen in this book, a powerful, apologetic discourse amongst Muslims since 9/11.[152] Indeed, the similarities between the language of liberal Muslims in the USA and that of Engineer in India are striking. The debate over the meaning of *islam* is a compelling case in point. This term, Engineer writes, is drawn from the three-letter Arabic root *s-l-m* and means *salam* (peace), thus proving that Islam is a religion of peace.[153] As Esack has shown, precisely the same linguistic argument was circulated widely within liberal American Muslim circles following 9/11.[154] This theological discourse not only essentializes Islam as being a message of peace and only peace, dismissing militant interpretations as being outside the fold of the faith, but is also at odds with historic understandings of the term. The word *islam*, interjects Esack, has for centuries been understood by Muslims as submission—that is, submission to God—and though the word *salam* is derived from the same three-letter root, it is blatantly inaccurate to conclude that the two terms therefore share the same meaning, for in Arabic a host of distinct, even contradictory, words can be formed from the same root.[155] The larger point that Esack seeks to make here is that despite liberal Muslims' incessant claims to authenticity, their discourse was profoundly shaped by the context of 9/11.

Engineer's Islamic discourse of peace raises a crucial question concerning the very meaning of liberation theology: namely, is a

[150] Asghar Ali Engineer, *The Prophet of Non-Violence: Spirit of Peace, Compassion and Universality in Islam* (New Delhi: Vitasta Publishing, 2011), 3.
[151] Ibid, 13–15.
[152] Safi, *Progressive Muslims*, 24. This apologetic claim that Islam equates to peace has also been made by well-intentioned non-Muslims. See, for instance, Amitabh Pal, *'Islam' means Peace: Understanding the Muslim Principle of Nonviolence Today* (Santa Barbara, California: Praeger, 2011).
[153] Engineer, *Islam and Liberation Theology*, 150.
[154] Esack, 'In Search of Progressive Islam Beyond 9/11', 95.   [155] Ibid.

theology of liberation necessarily a theology of peace? He stresses that peace ought to be attained not by fighting, but by entering into political agreements with one's opponents.[156] With regard to Kashmir, for example, Engineer maintains that, notwithstanding the genuine grievances of the Kashmiri people living under Indian military rule, there is no justification for armed struggle and thus the use of violence.[157] He rehashes the same argument when discussing the Palestinian–Israeli conflict. Twinning violence and 'falsehood' on the one hand and non-violence and 'truth' on the other, Engineer implores Israelis and Palestinians to partake in peaceful dialogue in order to resolve the conflict.[158] What is missing in his analysis, therefore, is the critical acknowledgement that a simplistic language of peace is often propagated by the oppressive status quo as a tool of pacification, as a means of maintaining the way things are. In terms of the Israeli occupation, for instance, the Palestinian intellectual Edward Said (d. 2003) has deftly argued—in *Peace and its Discontents: Essays on Palestine in the Middle East Peace Process* (1995)—that the US-brokered peace plan in the early 1990s was a set of treaties conceived completely on Israel's terms, designed to quell indigenous resistance and to further divide and impoverish the Palestinian people.[159] Because the Palestinian national struggle in general and the First Intifada (1987–93) in particular constituted a threat to ongoing Zionist colonization, and because Israeli security was a cornerstone of American imperialism in the region, peace became policy. In contrast to Engineer, Esack, as was seen in the preceding chapter, exhibits an acute awareness of the collusion between the status quo and rhetorics of peace and stability—a discourse that was championed by the South African regime, portraying anti-apartheid activists as threats to the peace. To borrow Esack's own words:

> When peace comes to mean the absence of conflict on the one hand, and when conflict with an unjust and racist political order is a moral imperative on the other, then it is not difficult to understand that the

[156] Engineer, *On Developing Theology of Peace in Islam*, 33.
[157] Asghar Ali Engineer, 'Kashmiri Youth and Prospects of Peace', *Secular Perspective*, 1 September 2006, available at: http://www.csss-isla.com/wp-content/uploads/2015/06/Septe-1-15-06.pdf accessed 12 August 2016.
[158] Engineer, 'Israeli Aggression and the World'.
[159] Edward Said, *Peace and its Discontents: Essays on Palestine in the Middle East Peace Process* (New York: Vintage Books, 1995), 90.

better class of human beings are, in fact, deeply committed to disturbing the peace and creating conflict. Along with other progressive forces in South Africa, I affirmed the value of revolutionary insurrection against the apartheid state and conflict as a means to disturbing an unjust peace and a path to just peace.[160]

My point here is not that there is no legitimate role for peaceful protest, that languages of non-violence are the preserve of the privileged. On the contrary, expressly non-violent civil disobedience has historically been used—and continues to be used—as a robust moral argument on the part of the oppressed, most memorably in Ghandi's involvement in the Indian liberation movement and his guiding principles of *ahimsa* (non-violence) and *satyagraha* (passive resistance).[161] Nor, for that matter, do I wish to simplify, to idealize armed struggle. Rather, my argument is (a) that peaceful resistance is only possible in certain contexts, that it presupposes a set of circumstances and, conversely, in contexts of manifest injustice, of radical power asymmetry, armed struggle can become the only meaningful channel for resistance; and (b) that there is a fundamental difference between 'peace (as conflict *resolution*) and pacification (as, in effect, the victory of the stronger party).'[162] In the context of the latter, a theology of peace can actually act as a theology of suppression, silencing the marginalized by providing religious justification for the preservation of the status quo. The central question that the liberation theologian needs to raise, then, is whose peace—that of the powerful or the powerless? To put it another way: are we simply interested in categorical calls for ceasefire, thereby ignoring the significant power differentials that will continue to exist between oppressor and oppressed, or in a

---

[160] Esack, 'In Search of Progressive Islam Beyond 9/11', 85.

[161] The role of non-violence and its moral authority in liberative struggle has generated a considerable literature, inspired largely by Gandhi as well as Martin Luther King Jr's leadership of the American civil rights movement. See, among others: Adam Roberts and Timothy Garton Ash, *Civil Resistance and Power Politics: The Experience of Non-Violent Action from Gandhi to the Present* (Oxford: Oxford University Press, 2009); Gene Sharp, *The Politics of Nonviolent Action*, 3 vols. (Boston: Peter Sargent Publishers, 1973); James A. Colaiaco, *Martin Luther King Jr.: Apostle of Militant Nonviolence* (New York: St. Martin's Press, 1988); and M.K. Gandhi, *Non-Violent Resistance (Satyagraha)* (Mineola, New York: Dover Publications, 2001).

[162] James McDougall (in discussion with the author). McDougall, a postcolonial historian of North Africa, credits the Palestinian historian Abdel Razzaq Takriti for this insight.

truly just and lasting resolution to conflict, entailing a structural reconfiguration of the status quo?

CONCLUSIONS

Scripture lies at the heart of Engineer's liberation theology. He focuses on the Qur'an because in the Islamic worldview it reflects the living Speech of God, addressing the faithful in all times and places. But Engineer does not dismiss outright the *hadith* literature or the inherited, intellectual tradition. In fact, various prophetic reports and the statements of classical and medieval scholars surface throughout his writings. He makes sure, however, to engage these sources in a critical manner, approaching them through the framework of the Qur'an. For it is the values, the principles embedded within this authoritative text that ought to take precedence in Islamic thinking. The hermeneutical foregrounding of scripture, then, is a major methodological similarity between Engineer's and Esack's liberation theologies. That being said, there is also an important difference between these two exegetes. Whereas Esack is wary of idealizing the Qur'an, acknowledging that in spite of its otherwise subversive, social message it remains an androcentric text, Engineer resorts to apologetics, essentializing the text and, by extension, Islam as a whole. The Qur'an can only be read in one way, and that is as a liberating scripture. Furthermore, his accenting of the Qur'an is inextricably linked to an underlying critique of religious hierarchy. Growing up in a conservative community with an entrenched and exploitative clerical establishment, Engineer is deeply suspicious of sacred authority. Since accountability before God lies with the individual, he argues, authority is vested in that individual and not with Muslim scholars. The interpretive order of the Islamic texts in his liberation theology, therefore, also needs to be appreciated in terms of access: that it is precisely because the Qur'an, in addition to being the Word of God, is an accessible text available to all Muslims, whether in its original Arabic or through translation, that it takes centre-stage in his discourse.

The Qur'an is a liberating text that forcefully speaks to contexts of oppression. Not only does the Qur'an move beyond a patronizing discourse of charity, pointing to the fundamental right of the poor in the wealth of the affluent, but it also reflects a just deity who stands in solidarity with the oppressed against their oppressors. But in order for Islamic theology to become liberating, writes Engineer, it must be stripped of those discourses and practices that support the status quo, from philosophical abstractions to a blind obsession with rites and rituals. A truly liberating theology, then, must also be a liberated theology. Or, to put it another way: a theology of liberation must come packaged with a liberation of theology. Like Esack, Engineer highlights the immense value that the Qur'an places on action as opposed to solely belief, calling for a radical rereading of the text rooted in *praxis*, or the idea that the struggle for social justice ought to form the point of departure for religious reflection. And it is this firm exegetical emphasis on transforming the lived realities of the interpreter that makes Engineer's hermeneutic a pressing hermeneutic of the here and now: that is, a Qur'anic commentary of this world and then the next. Arguing for a 'socio-theological approach' to exegesis, he expounds scripture and, in particular, those passages that prophesy divine retribution in the Hereafter (the 'theological' aspect) through the prism of the present (the 'socio' aspect), and thus as events that are yet to unfold in this world. In a similar manner to Esack, he exhibits an awareness of the complexity of human suffering, calling for a generally comprehensive commitment to justice, incorporating questions of class, empire, pluralism, and gender justice (though not sexual justice) into his Islamic thinking. But whereas Esack draws upon the Exodus as a Qur'anic model of struggle, Engineer turns to the Battle of Karbala as an Islamic paradigm of liberation. Although this fateful rebellion took place several decades after the revelatory period, what makes Karbala so compelling for this exegete, what ties it so intimately to the text, is the way in which the martyrdom of Husayn and his followers captures core Qur'anic principles, such as courage, sacrifice, and, above all, an abiding commitment to justice. It is the underlying, ethical connection between this historic event and the sacred text, then, that makes Engineer's hermeneutical engagement with Karbala a distinctly Qur'anic one.

There are some larger differences between Esack's and Engineer's discourses, however. Addressing the communal violence that has plagued Hindu–Muslim relations in contemporary India, Engineer insists that it is not religion but rather competitive politics amongst the elite of both communities that is the root source of suffering—an interesting thesis but one that overlooks the considerable power differential that exists between these two communities. Secularism, understood not as an attack on religion but as a national philosophy with which to be inclusive of different faith traditions, is a key component of Engineer's discourse on communal violence. For it is due to a lack of commitment to secular values, as enshrined in the Indian constitution, that successive governments have failed to intervene and put a decisive end to communal rioting. Engineer's fixation on secularism is problematic because he fails to ask who gets to define the secular? Because of the universalization of Hinduism and Hindu experiences in independent India, secularism is anything but a neutral category and has been shaped by Hindus, even ardent Hindu nationalists, who have portrayed themselves as modern and secular, juxtaposed to a medieval and fanatical Muslim Other. Engineer's hermeneutic, moreover, is a markedly modernist one. While he critiques *tafsir 'ilmi*, or the scientific interpretation of the Qur'an, rationalism remains a major theme in his exegesis, maintaining that scripture was revealed to liberate humanity from belief in supernatural powers, thereby illuminating the darkness of superstition with the light of reason. Just as Engineer elevates the rational over the supernatural, so does he privilege the written letter over the oral word, twinning divine knowledge with literacy, ignorance with illiteracy—an untenable hermeneutical move given the centrality of orality in the classical period and the fact that the vast majority of Muslims today continue to encounter the Qur'an as a primarily oral text. The modernism of Engineer stands in contrast to Esack, who shows a keen appreciation for the value of oral culture and the rich, manifold ways in which scripture is embodied in popular Muslim practice. A far more significant difference between Esack's and Engineer's liberation theologies, however, lies in the latter's overwhelming emphasis on peace, raising a wider question concerning the relationship between peace and liberation. In line with his tendency towards apologia and essentialism, Engineer argues that violence has no place in the Qur'an and, by extension, Islam as a whole. Rather, it is the divine message of peace that reigns supreme. Resistance against oppression, such as that of Palestinians in the Middle East, can only be legitimate through peaceful and democratic means. What is absent in Engineer's thinking, then, is a critical awareness of the historic collusion between the unjust status quo and languages of peace and, conversely, the potentially liberating experience of militant struggle in deeply oppressive contexts wherein there is no space for democratic expression and non-violent protest. Indeed, in situations of manifest injustice, a theology of peace can devolve into a theology of accommodation, suppressing voices of dissent by using the authority of religion to reinforce the powers that be.

4

Gender Justice as a Way of Life

The Reading of Amina Wadud

INTRODUCTION

This chapter examines the gender egalitarian exegesis of the Black American scholar Amina Wadud. The first part of this chapter will address the question of interpretive method: namely, how exactly does she read scripture? Like Esack and Engineer, Wadud prioritizes the Qur'an over other Islamic texts and traditions, such as the *hadith* literature and the Islamic intellectual heritage. But whereas Esack's hermeneutic is built on *praxis*, or a dialectical interplay between action and reflection, Wadud's hermeneutic, I argue, is a more linear mode of reading, in which liberating interpretations of the text are applied to contemporary contexts of oppression. In this methodology section, I also analyse and critique her discourse on religious authority, which is influenced by Fazlur Rahman's 'double movement' theory. The chapter will then explore the relationship between Islam and gender justice. Specifically, how does Wadud (re)interpret the Qur'an in order to affirm the equality of women, to further the struggle against patriarchy? By unpacking the ways in which she expounds various aspects of scripture, from the Creation Story and depictions of the Hereafter to pressing women's issues like polygamy and female leadership, I underscore the centrality of two hermeneutical tools in her exegesis: namely, textual analysis and historical criticism, the former entailing a careful, holistic study of what exactly the Qur'an says and, just as significantly, does not say, and the latter seeking to understand the text in light of its immediate setting of revelation. While Esack and Engineer draw upon the Exodus and the Battle of

Karbala, respectively, as paradigms of struggle, Wadud fleshes out the sociopolitical implications of *tawhid* (the unity of God) and *khilafa* (human trusteeship). This chapter will conclude by unpacking the scope of her discourse on social justice. As a result of her formative experiences as a woman born into a poor, Black household, Wadud has a comprehensive approach to justice, making connections with other forms of oppression, in particular racism. Like Esack and Engineer, then, she has a keen sense of the complexity of human suffering—a layered experience that is most eloquently embodied, for Wadud, in the figure of Hagar. However, the most crucial aspect of her comprehensive approach to liberation, I argue, is the commitment to live out such progressive values in the private sphere, particularly within the family. Indeed, to stand for justice in the public sphere is meaningless, even hypocritical, unless this act is paralleled by a practice of egalitarianism in one's own home. As with the preceding chapters, I will set the context for discussion by providing some historical and biographical background. Before doing so, however, it is necessary to say a few words about terminology.

Language and its Discontents

The reader will notice that I refer to the hermeneutics of Wadud and Barlas as 'women's gender egalitarian readings' of the Qur'an. I am uncomfortable classifying these exegetes as feminists, even as Islamic feminists, because—as this and the following chapter will show—they both explicitly reject identifying as feminists, citing various reasons. These include critiques of the racial dominance of White women within feminist circles as well as feminism's secular biases. It is precisely for these reasons that Wadud, though willing to use feminist as an *adjective* to describe her work, prefers to position herself as 'pro-faith, pro-feminist'.[1] In light of her refusal to identify as feminist, it can be argued that she views the signifier 'pro-faith, pro-feminist' as an alternative to feminism rather than an alternative feminism, that is, an approach that is critical of dominant practices of feminism but nonetheless identifies as feminist. At the same time, I also find the term 'women's readings' of the Qur'an problematic. While the term effectively conveys the centrality of women's agency in the exegetical

---

[1] Wadud, *Inside the Gender Jihad*, 79–80.

task, producing readings based on their own experiences (as opposed to male readings about women, whether patriarchal or egalitarian), it falls into the trap of essentializing the type of readings that women produce. That is, the term 'women's readings' of the Qur'an presumes that these readings will necessarily be progressive, liberative, radical. But cannot a woman's reading—or, for that matter, a reading of any marginalized group—accept, even embrace, unequal power structures? And, if so, are these readings to be hastily dismissed as expressions of false consciousness? In other words: are they *really* women's readings? To avoid such essentialism, I have added the qualifier 'gender egalitarian' when referring to Wadud's and Barlas' work and to justice-based readings produced by women in general.

Historical Context

Islam has deep roots in American history. Though it is widely assumed that Africans who were enslaved and shipped across the Atlantic practiced traditional African religions, a significant number of them were in fact Muslims, as the areas of West Africa that had been raided for slaves had housed large Muslim communities for over 600 years.[2] The following autobiographical account from Omar ibn Seid (d. 1864)—a West African Muslim captured in the early 1800s and shipped to Charleston, South Carolina—is an illustrative example of the Islamic backgrounds of the African slaves:

> My name is Omar ibn Seid. My birthplace was Fut Tur [that is, the Futa Tooro region, located in southern Mauritania and northern Senegal], between the two rivers. I sought knowledge under the instruction of a Sheikh called Mohammed Seid, my own brother, and Sheikh Soleiman Kembeh, and Sheikh Gabriel Abdal. I continued my studies twenty-five years, and then returned to my home where I remained six years. Then there came to our place a large army, who killed many men, and took me, and brought me to the great sea, and sold me into the hands of the Christians, who bound me and set me on board a great ship and we

---

[2] Amina Beverly McCloud, *African American Islam* (London: Routledge, 1995), 1. Also, see Allan D. Austin, *African Muslims in Antebellum America: Transatlantic Stories and Spiritual Struggles* (London: Routledge, 1997) and Sylviane Diouf, *Servants of Allah: African Muslims Enslaved in the Americas* (New York: New York University Press, 1998).

sailed upon the great sea a month and a half, when we came to a place called Charleston in the Christian language.[3]

This Muslim heritage, however, would be largely wiped out with the passage of time. Indeed, it would not be until the formation of the Nation of Islam in the early twentieth century that Islam would resurface in the USA. Established by Wallace D. Fard and his disciple, Elijah Muhammad, in Detroit in the 1930s, the Nation of Islam was committed to the liberation of Blacks in a White supremacist society. The organization called for the political self-determination and economic independence of the African American community, urging their brothers and sisters to set up their own associations and businesses.[4] Malcolm X (d. 1965), arguably the most charismatic minister of the Nation, played a crucial role in expanding the movement's following, reaching a formal membership of approximately 20,000 by the early 1960s and gaining widespread support among non-Muslim African Americans.[5] Shortly after Elijah Muhammad's death in 1975, the Nation split into two offshoot organizations. His oldest son, Warith Deen Muhammad, took over the reins of leadership, steering the movement towards mainstream Sunni Islam and renaming it as the 'World Community of Islam in the West.'[6] Countering this ideological shift, Louis Farrakhan—an influential minister and protégé of Elijah Muhammad—re-established the Nation and its original teachings.[7] A more significant development, however, would fundamentally change the face of Islam in America. In October 1965, a new immigration law was passed that removed the racist quotas of earlier legislations, which had largely restricted immigration to predominantly White countries.[8] As a result, immigrants from Africa and Asia—a considerable number of whom were Muslim—poured into the USA. Yet despite this massive influx of Muslims, particularly from the Middle East and South Asia, Black Muslims continue to constitute the single largest ethnic community, comprising over 40 per cent of the American Muslim population.[9] As shall be shown later on in

[3] Omar ibn Seid, as cited in Edward E. Curtis IV, *Muslims in America: A Short History* (Oxford: Oxford University Press, 2009), 23–4.
[4] Curtis, 39.
[5] Carolyn Moxley Rouse, *Engaged Surrender: African American Women and Islam* (Berkeley: University of California Press, 2004), 95.
[6] Ibid, 97–8.   [7] Ibid, 98.   [8] Curtis, 72.
[9] Wadud, *Inside the Gender Jihad*, 103.

the chapter, a communal rift has emerged between immigrant and Black Muslims, as reflected in separate institutional structures, community publications, and religious gatherings.[10]

An African American convert to Islam, Wadud has become an influential Islamic scholar and social activist, focusing her efforts on achieving gender justice within the Muslim community. Born as Mary Teasley on 25 September 1952 in Bethesda—a small town in Maryland—she grew up in a devout Christian family. Wadud's early years were marred by poverty. While she was still a child, her family was evicted from their house, as they were unable to pay the mortgage.[11] Rendered homeless, the family was forced to sleep in their car, later shifting to a trailer, and, eventually, relocating to Washington, DC, where Wadud's father had rented a couple of rooms in someone else's house.[12] At the age of fourteen, Wadud left her family to finish her final three years of high schooling at an all-White, public institution in Boston, living with various families.[13] Upon completing high school, she attended the University of Pennsylvania. It was during her college years that Wadud converted to Islam, proclaiming the *shahada* (the testimony of the Muslim faith) on Thanksgiving Day, 1972. She graduated with a bachelor's degree in education, concentrating in English, and worked as a teacher for several years after college.[14] She later decided to pursue graduate work in Islamic studies at the University of Michigan, writing her doctoral dissertation on portrayals of women in the Qur'an. In other words, while Esack had a hybrid education marked by both modern university schooling and traditional training in a *madrasa*, Wadud has no formal traditional background. That Barlas, whose exegesis we will explore in the next chapter, also has no traditional training is telling, suggesting that the so-called secular university has become an important institutional space in which Muslim women, who would have otherwise been excluded from the male-dominated world of the *madrasa*, can partake in Islamic scholarship. After completing her Ph.D. in Islamic studies in 1988, Wadud moved to Kuala Lampur, where she taught for three years (1989–92) at the Department of Revealed Knowledge and Heritage at

---

[10] McCloud, 169.
[11] Amina Wadud, 'On Belonging as a Muslim Woman', in *My Soul is a Witness: African-American Women's Spirituality*, ed. Gloria Wade-Gayles (Boston: Beacon Press, 1995), 255.
[12] Ibid, 255–6.   [13] Wadud, Interview 2009.   [14] Ibid.

the International Islamic University.[15] It was here, in Malaysia, that she became a founding member of Sisters in Islam (SIS)—an organization that advocated women's rights through an Islamic framework. Acting as the movement's resident specialist in Islam, she became intimately involved with SIS and would continue to work with them well after her contract at the university expired in 1992, flying back and forth to Malaysia every year and a half.[16] Following this stint at the International Islamic University, Wadud returned to the USA, taking up a post as a professor of Islamic studies at Virginia Commonwealth University, which she held until her retirement in 2008.

HERMENEUTICAL APPROACH

A Qur'anic Discourse

As it is for Esack and Engineer, the Qur'an is the primary textual source in Wadud's Islamic writings. Surprisingly, the person who would become renowned for her work on the Qur'an only came across the text several months after her conversion to Islam, when she acquired a copy in March 1973.[17] Once she began to read the Qur'an, however, she became instantly drawn to the book, describing her deep, spiritual attachment to it as a 'love affair'.[18] Because of its undisputed status among Muslims as the Word of God, writes Wadud, the Qur'an is the most authoritative source in Islam.[19] Moreover, a critical distinction needs to be made between the Qur'anic text and its exegesis—a difference that is often glossed

---

[15] Mehran Kamrava ed., *The New Voices of Islam: Rethinking Politics and Modernity: A Reader* (Berkeley: University of California Press, 2006), 201.

[16] Wadud, Interview 2009. In order to avoid jeopardizing the reputation of SIS following her leading of the Friday Prayers in New York City in 2005—a highly controversial event within the mainstream Muslim community and which will be discussed at length later on in the chapter—Wadud renounced her membership with the organization in 2006.

[17] Ibid. See also: Amina Wadud, 'Qur'an, Gender and Interpretive Possibilities' *Hawwa* 2:3 (2004): 316. In our interview, Wadud recounted that at the time of her conversion, the *da'wa* (Muslim proselytization) group that had given her information on Islam had, like most mainstream Muslims, failed to present any sort of hierarchy with regard to the textual sources of the faith. At the time of her conversion, then, the Qur'an was not the central source in her Islamic thinking.

[18] Wadud, Interview 2009.   [19] Wadud, *Qur'an and Woman*, ix.

over by Muslims. For while the Qur'an reflects 'the articulation of the divine will', exegesis is a thoroughly human exercise limited to the contextual baggage of the exegete,[20] reflecting assumptions and worldviews rooted in time, place, gender, race, and class, among other factors. While Wadud hermeneutically foregrounds the Qur'an, it is important to note that she does not approach the text as the *only* articulation of the divine will. Citing Q. 31:27, she observes that the Qur'an itself acknowledges that God cannot be reduced to a text, as if a single scripture could exhaust the infinite possibilities of divine disclosure.[21] The verse reads:

> If all the trees on the Earth were pens and the seas were ink, with seven more seas added to it, the words of God would never be exhausted, for truly God is All-Mighty, All-Wise.

Indeed, the Qur'an's very revelation in the Arabic language, Wadud points out, is testament to the contextually conditioned nature of the text, as it addresses a specific historical community. The Qur'an even professes its own rootedness in a particular setting, stating that it was revealed in 'plain Arabic' (Q. 26:195), thereby underscoring its intention of communicating to the seventh-century Arabs in their own tongue.[22] In other words, at precisely the same time that the Qur'an, as the living Word of God, is a transcendent text, or one that can speak to multiple contexts, to generations of Muslims in different times and places, it is also a historical text, and therefore cannot possibly encapsulate all of God's speech. And the crucial source that stands next to the Qur'an, further articulating the divine will to the believer, is one's *context*: that is, one's own reality and lived experience. As Wadud put it in our interview:

> we're locking Allah into a time capsule, and by that imprisonment we are making Allah obsolete. I really don't think that Allah is limited to the Qur'an. I think there is some self-disclosure in the Qur'an that Allah does self-disclose, but not in isolation to the rest of the reality that Allah has given us. Our own bodies, our environment, we have so many *ayat* [literally, signs] and if we don't have the ability to put them

[20] Amina Wadud, 'Alternative Qur'anic Interpretation and the Status of Muslim Women', in *Windows of Faith: Muslim Women Scholar-Activists in North America*, ed. Gisela Webb (Syracuse, New York: Syracuse University Press, 2000), 11.

[21] Wadud, *Inside the Gender Jihad*, 212.

[22] Ibid. While I have used Wadud's translation, the Arabic phrase—'*arabiyyin mubin*—can also be rendered as 'clear Arabic'.

together then we are going to actually destroy the gift that the Qur'an is to us.[23]

In her emphasis on understanding the divine will through both the *word* and the *world*, encountering God through these twin revelations, Wadud's hermeneutic parallels that of liberation theology, which approaches lived experience, in particular the experience of oppression, as a text that is to be read alongside scripture.[24] I use the word 'parallel' here because, while Esack explicitly draws upon the hermeneutics of liberation theology when emphasizing the significance of one's context, Wadud does not situate herself within this literature, thus arriving at her understanding independently.

The *hadith* literature is the second most important textual source in her Islamic discourse. While she underscores the Qur'an's unique place in Islamic theology as the Word of God, she clarifies that her interest in scripture is also a disciplinary one, reflecting her choice to specialize in the study of the Qur'an.[25] Her hermeneutical emphasis on the Qur'an, then, should not be read as a categorical dismissal of other Islamic texts. In fact, Wadud considers the *sunna* to be one of 'the two primary sources' of Islam, alongside the Qur'an.[26] That being said, the *sunna* is not on a par with the Qur'an, for the value of the *sunna* (and, by extension, the *hadith* literature) lies in its ability to capture and flesh out wider Qur'anic principles. Indeed, she describes the *sunna* as the 'living embodiment' of the Qur'an,[27] thereby connecting the two and conferring legitimacy on the former vis-à-vis the latter. Wadud does not hesitate to include *hadith* reports that uphold Qur'anic values like compassion and justice. For instance, when discussing gender relations in the household, she cites the prophetic saying 'The best of you is he who is best to his family',[28] and, whilst calling for a culture of egalitarianism and reciprocity amongst Muslims, refers to the following report: 'One of you does not believe until he/she loves for the other what is loved for oneself.'[29] But just like Esack and Engineer, Wadud is sceptical of the

---

[23] Wadud, Interview 2009.   [24] Rowland, 8.

[25] Wadud, *Qur'an and Woman*, xvii.

[26] Wadud, 'Alternative Qur'anic Interpretation and the Status of Muslim Women', 4.

[27] Ibid.   [28] Wadud, *Qur'an and Woman*, 91.

[29] Wadud, *Inside the Gender Jihad*, 29. After citing this report, Wadud adds that while the original Arabic presumes a male subject—'one of you does not believe until *he* loves for his brother'—her translation, in order to be gender inclusive, incorporates both male and female subjects. See fn. 23 in ibid, 265–6. This specific report can be found in the celebrated *hadith* collection of Imam al-Nawawi (d. 1277). See Hadith

veracity of the *hadith* literature, even those reports that are considered *sahih* (authentic).[30] And it is precisely because of the disputed authenticity of the *hadith* that she is able to engage this corpus in a highly selective manner, drawing inspiration from those reports that affirm Qur'anic values while not feeling bound by problematic reports that violate such principles.[31] For example, a significant number of misogynistic *hadith* reports, Wadud noted during our interview, can be traced back to one individual: namely, the companion Abu Hurayra (d. 681).[32] This raises the larger, hermeneutical question, then, as to whether such reports are a genuine reflection of the Prophet himself or of the people who surrounded him. This is an especially salient question given that Abu Hurayra, as the Moroccan scholar Fatima Mernissi has pointed out, fulfilled the rather unlikely task of recounting roughly 5,300 prophetic reports—far more than any other *hadith* narrator—whilst being in the company of the Prophet for only three years.[33]

Unlike the Qur'an and the *hadith* literature, Wadud does not consider the *shari'a* to be a primary source of the faith. A major problem that she has with the inherited, intellectual tradition, of which the *shari'a* is part and parcel, is that it has overshadowed the Qur'an, with Muslims equating these later, human-made texts with the Word of God.[34] As shall be shown in the next chapter on Barlas, this conflation of the texts is a key critique that gender egalitarian female exegetes have levelled against traditional Islamic thought. Furthermore, Wadud continues, because men have almost single-handedly produced the *shari'a*, women have been reduced to mere, material objects. For instance, in Pakistan's rape laws, which are based on the *shari'a*, the crime is actually treated as an act of theft, as rape is understood as stealing another man's private property—that is, access to the sexual organs of his wife—rather than a brutal act of violence against the woman.[35] Yet despite Wadud's deep-seated grievances with the *shari'a*,

---

#13 in Yahya ibn Sharaf al-Nawawi, *The Complete Forty Hadith of Imam al-Nawawi*, translated by Abdassamad Clarke (London: Ta-Ha Publishers, 2009), 66.

[30] Within the *hadith* sciences, scholars have established a scale of ratings to gauge the authenticity of various reports, such as *da'if* (weak), *hasan* (good), and *sahih* (authentic).

[31] Wadud, Interview 2009.   [32] Ibid.

[33] Fatima Mernissi, *The Veil and the Male Elite: A Feminist Interpretation of Women's Rights in Islam* (New York: Basic Books, 1991), 80.

[34] Wadud, *Qur'an and Woman*, xx–xxi.

[35] Amina Wadud, 'Aisha's Legacy: The Struggle for Women's Rights within Islam', in *The New Voices of Islam: Rethinking Politics and Modernity: A Reader*, ed. Mehran Kamrava (Berkeley: University of California Press, 2006), 203.

she argues that it is still necessary to engage this body of literature. When I asked her why she did not simply dismiss secondary source traditions like the *shariʿa* altogether, she replied:

> I engage them because religion is a human construct and the Islamic religion consists of all the sources that we have legitimated as representing what it means to be Muslim: Qur'an, *sunna*, *hadith*, *fiqh* [Islamic jurisprudence]. And I engage *shariʿa* because within the history of our tradition we have developed it, codified it, lived by it, and now we are being slapped in the face by people who think we can sort of like slap it back onto the modern nation-state. So I engage it as part of the reality of the history of Muslims. Islam is nothing if not lived by people and those people would be Muslims.[36]

Wadud's engagement with the *shariʿa*, then, is a thoroughly pragmatic one. Because the legal tradition has been an important part of Muslim history and continues to exercise considerable influence on the lives of Muslims today, especially women, Islamic reformists have no choice but to tackle the *shariʿa*. There are two principal tasks, moreover, within this reformist project: firstly, to rewrite an essentially medieval tradition in the light of lived realities, thereby creating a system of law that is applicable to the present time (*fiqh al-waqiʿa*); and, secondly, to ground this new judicial system firmly on broader Qur'anic principles of social justice and moral conduct.[37] This is a dual critique of Islamic law that, as we have seen in the previous chapter, is shared by Engineer. In other words, for Wadud the underlying 'ethical foundation' of the *shariʿa* needs to be forcefully foregrounded and, if women's rights are to be taken seriously, gender, as a category of thought, has to be integrated within Islamic ethical theory.[38]

An Exegesis for the Present (and who has the authority to do it)

Making Islam relevant to the contemporary world is a prime objective of Wadud's scholarship. As she put it in her pioneering work, *Qur'an and Woman: Rereading the Sacred Text from a Woman's Perspective* (1999):

> despite fourteen centuries of existence, the Qur'an must be kept alive. Otherwise, it will suffer the fate of other 'dead texts' and defeat its stated purpose: to guide humankind—unconstrained by time and place.[39]

---

[36] Wadud, Interview 2009.   [37] Wadud, *Inside the Gender Jihad*, 205.
[38] Ibid, 48.   [39] Wadud, *Qur'an and Woman*, xxiii.

But how exactly can the Qur'an become alive, escaping the fate of other 'dead texts' and addressing the complex realities of the present? In answering this pressing, hermeneutical question, Wadud draws upon Rahman's double movement theory. As discussed earlier in this book, Rahman's proposed methodology of interpreting the Qur'an consisted of two movements. The first movement entailed an in-depth study of the immediate setting of revelation in seventh-century Arabia, examining how the Qur'an spoke to this specific context. Broader ethical principles would then be 'distilled' from this classical setting.[40] While the first movement focussed primarily on the past, moving from the particular to the universal, the second movement concerned itself with the present, applying these timeless principles to a radically different set of historical circumstances. And just as an in-depth examination of the classical context was necessary to arrive at wider Qur'anic principles, the contemporary context, too, required careful study in order to translate faithfully these universal principles (back) into concrete realities.[41] Like Esack and Engineer, Wadud's exegesis is thus marked by a deep desire to move beyond the literal letter of the text, seeking to uncover its underlying *spirit*, as embodied in such principles as 'justice, equity, harmony, moral responsibility, spiritual awareness, and development.'[42] Furthermore, she notes, this scholarly project of discerning the socio-moral objectives of the Qur'an can be facilitated further by a linguistic study of the text, exploring its grammatical composition.[43] This commitment to interpreting the faith through the prism of the present, then, enables Islam to transform from a static religion, bound to the historical constraints of seventh-century Arabia and one that is to be blindly imitated, into a 'dynamic process',[44] wherein the Qur'an's wider, ethical principles must be continuously understood and re-understood by each people, as they apply these principles in light of their own lived experiences and contextual realities.

Wadud's adoption of the double movement theory is problematic, however, in terms of religious authority. To be sure, she is critical of interpretive hierarchy, calling for a 'shared privilege' in which Qur'anic exegesis is a truly gender inclusive enterprise, welcoming

---

[40] Rahman, *Islam and Modernity*, 6.   [41] Ibid, 7.
[42] Wadud, *Qur'an and Woman*, 3.   [43] Ibid.
[44] Wadud, 'Alternative Qur'anic Interpretation and the Status of Muslim Women', 10.

the insights and experiences of both women and men.[45] Indeed, the very fact that Wadud is a female commentator puts her at odds with clerical Islam, as the *'ulama* have historically been, and continue to be, men.[46] In a 2012 keynote address—entitled 'The Authority of Experience'—at a conference on Muslim women and sacred authority at Boston University, she fleshed out her ideas on what is authoritative.[47] Challenging the traditionalist assumption that authority is based on the accumulated knowledge of Islamic texts alone ('received knowledge'), Wadud calls for a broader understanding of knowledge that, in turn, will lead to new understandings of authority derived from this knowledge.[48] Specifically, women's lived experiences—as 'represented by the ones who have the experiences, namely women'—ought to be considered an authoritative form of knowledge, and therefore Islamic scholars (including not only men but also women who have begun to reinterpret the faith) must consult specialists in women's issues, such as social workers and psychologists.[49] Essentially, what is needed is a cooperative relationship between Muslim thinkers and 'lay' Muslims,[50] for in order to command authority, knowledge of Islamic texts is necessary but insufficient. Wadud's critique of religious authority, moreover, is not confined to gender. According to her, every Muslim has the right to interpret the texts and, in so doing, to partake in defining Islam—an egalitarian interpretive practice that will only be possible when Muslims

[45] Amina Wadud, 'Towards a Qur'anic Hermeneutics of Social Justice: Race, Class and Gender', *Journal of Law and Religion* 12 (1995–6): 49.

[46] To be precise, this gender imbalance is most acute in the fields of jurisprudence and exegesis. However, in other spheres, in particular Sufism, women have made historical inroads, even acquiring influential and lasting leadership roles. The following text by the Persian Sufi scholar Abu 'Abd al-Rahman al-Sulami (d. 1021), for example, provides biographical sketches of eighty women in the classical period who became leading teachers and guides in the Islamic mystical tradition: Abu 'Abd al-Rahman al-Sulami, *Early Pious Women: Dhikr an-niswa al-muta'abbidat as-sufiyyat*, edited and translated from the Riyadh manuscript with introduction and notes by Rkia E. Cornell (Louisville, Kentucky: Fons Vitae, 1999).

[47] Amina Wadud, 'The Authority of Experience' (keynote address at the conference 'Muslim Women and the Challenge of Authority', Boston University, Boston, 31 March 2012). I am grateful to Wadud for sharing a copy of the speech with me.

[48] Ibid. [49] Ibid.

[50] Amina Wadud, 'Beyond Interpretation', in *The Place of Tolerance in Islam*, Khaled Abou El Fadl with Joshua Cohen and Ian Lague eds. (Boston: Beacon Press, 2002), 59–60.

come to respect and value the inherent ability of each believer to make a contribution to Islamic thought.[51]

Yet Wadud's otherwise inclusive discourse towards religious authority is at variance with her adoption of the double movement theory as a mode of Qur'anic exegesis. In order to get a sense of the elitism of this interpretive method, it is worthwhile providing here Rahman's own description. Referring to the first movement, which centres on the classical period, he writes:

> one must understand the import or meaning of a given statement by studying the historical situation or problem to which it [the Qur'an] was the answer. Of course, before coming to the study of specific texts in light of specific situations, a general study of the macrosituation in terms of society, religion, customs, and institutions, indeed, of life as a whole in Arabia on the eve of Islam and particularly in and around Mecca—not excluding the Perso-Byzantine Wars—will have to be made.[52]

Clearly, such a scholarly undertaking is one in which very few Muslims can participate. Furthermore, while the second movement is relatively more inclusive, entailing a comprehensive study of contemporary circumstances and thus requiring Muslim expertise in all fields of knowledge—recalling Wadud's emphasis on specialists in women's issues—this movement, too, is hierarchal. The discourse of the Islamic scholar Tariq Ramadan, who has also espoused the double movement theory, is a compelling case in point. Inspired by Rahman's method, Ramadan—as noted in the second chapter—has differentiated between two types of scholars who need to work together in order to see the second movement through: namely, 'text scholars' (*'ulama an-nusus*), or specialists in Islamic sciences like jurisprudence, and 'context scholars' (*'ulama al-waqi'*), or experts in contemporary fields of knowledge, such as the natural sciences.[53] Upon making this distinction, however, Ramadan hastily qualifies that 'the fundamentals of belief (*'aqidah*) and worship (*'ibadat*) obviously remain the prerogative of the *fuqaha*',[54] or Islamic jurists. The problem with the second movement, then, is that it is not only classist, excluding poor, non-skilled Muslim labourers who do not

---

[51] Wadud, Interview 2009.   [52] Rahman, *Islam and Modernity*, 6.
[53] Ramadan, *Radical Reform*, 121.   [54] Ibid.

boast expertise in a specific field,[55] but, even in terms of those who are skilled, it is squarely functional: Muslims who are not religious scholars are welcomed to contribute vis-à-vis their expertise in their respective professions, whether that be in social work, economics, or healthcare, but not as believers who could actually make a lasting, theological contribution to Islamic thought. The elitism of the double movement theory, therefore, stands in contrast to the radical inclusivity of liberation theology, in which religious authority and interpretive insight is derived not from acquired knowledge but rather through everyday experiences of marginalization and suffering, making '*theologians* out of all God's people'.[56]

Let me further illustrate my critique of Rahman's double movement theory by discussing a rather different approach to women's authority and Qur'anic exegesis. In an illuminating article—'A *Tafsir* of Praxis: Gender, Marital Violence, and Resistance in a South African Community' (2007)—the Islamic scholar Sa'diyya Shaikh conducts in-depth interviews with eight battered Muslim women in Cape Town to discern how they have ethically wrestled with the Qur'an in light of their own experiences of physical abuse by their (ex)husbands. That is, how do ordinary Muslim women 'engage, interpret, contest, and redefine dominant understandings of Islam'[57] through realities of pain and suffering—an experiential hermeneutic that Shaikh terms an 'embodied *tafsir*' or a '*tafsir* through praxis'.[58] Her research demonstrates that, despite being untrained in the Qur'an or interpretative methods, these women challenged patriarchal understandings of Islam, foregrounding their deep-seated belief that God is a just deity and, therefore, cannot condone domestic violence.[59] The just nature of God, in turn, requires that human relationships be just, and transgressors will be held accountable to God.[60] In other words, theological arguments drawn from experience—as opposed to *textual* arguments drawn from experience, which still require some degree of scholarly

---

[55] It should be noted that Wadud has a more nuanced approach to expertise than Ramadan, as she includes 'activists' alongside professionals like psychologists. See Wadud, 'The Authority of Experience'.

[56] Rowland, 11. My italics.

[57] Sa'diyya Shaikh, 'A *Tafsir* of Praxis: Gender, Marital Violence, and Resistance in a South African Community', in *Violence Against Women in Contemporary World Religions: Roots and Cures*, eds. Daniel Maguire and Sa'diyya Shaikh (Cleveland, OH: Pilgrim Press, 2007), 70.

[58] Ibid, 75.   [59] Ibid, 79.   [60] Ibid.

immersion—shaped these women's understanding of Qur'anic ethics. My purpose in highlighting this study is not to suggest that textual scholarship is not important. It is extremely important, and Shaikh herself has written extensively on gender and premodern Islamic texts, especially the mystical tradition.[61] Rather, I point to this article because it takes as authoritative not only the experiences of the oppressed, of how they endure and resist injustices on a daily basis, but also the profound religious insights that emerge from these experiences and which do not require knowledge of religious texts.

Between *Praxis* and Application

Action is a central aspect of Wadud's Qur'anic hermeneutic, for liberating ideas can only truly be liberating if they are translated into concrete realities. As she puts it:

> theory alone is insufficient to bring an end to patriarchy and gender asymmetry. There is a crucial interplay between belief in certain ideas and the practical implementation of gender justice in the context of present global circumstances.[62]

The pursuit of knowledge, then, is not some pristine, scholarly endeavour detached from the rest of the world, but rather one in which new insights are used to create a new world built on social justice. Wadud refers to this wedding of theological study and transformative struggle, whether that struggle takes place in the university classroom or in community affairs, as 'spiritual activism'.[63] Indeed, the twinning of study and struggle—a liberating practice that has also been termed 'scholarship activism'—is a significant contribution that gender egalitarian female interpreters have made to contemporary Islamic thought, challenging patriarchy within the Muslim

---

[61] See Sa'diyya Shaikh, 'Exegetical Violence: *Nushuz* in Qur'anic Gender Ideology', *Journal for Islamic Studies* 17 (1997): 49–73; 'In Search of *al-Insan*: Sufism, Islamic Law, and Gender', *Journal of the American Academy of Religion* 77:4 (2009): 781–822; 'Knowledge, Women and Gender in the Hadith: A Feminist Approach', *Islam and Christian-Muslim Relations* 15 (2004): 99–108; and *Sufi Narratives of Intimacy: Ibn 'Arabi, Gender, and Sexuality* (Chapel Hill: University of North Carolina Press, 2012).

[62] Wadud, *Inside the Gender Jihad*, 42.

[63] Amina Wadud, 'Teaching Afrocentric Islam in the White Christian South', in *Black Women in the Academy: Promises and Perils*, ed. Lois Benjamin (Gainesville: University Press of Florida, 2007), 142.

community through their research on Islam.[64] While this accent on
the practical implementation of one's research may seem novel in the
context of the academy, it is important to note that this is actually a
recognized form of scholarship. In his now classic study—*Scholarship
Reconsidered: Priorities of the Professoriate* (1990)—Ernest Boyer
challenges the reduction of scholarship to research and publication
alone, or what he calls 'the scholarship of discovery'.[65] He outlines
three additional interrelated paradigms that are equally significant:
namely, drawing critical linkages between disciplines and, in so
doing, making one's research accessible to non-specialists ('the scholarship of integration'); implementing one's research to address societal needs and problems, thereby serving the larger community ('the
scholarship of application'); and transforming—not simply *transmitting*—one's research through the process of teaching (hence, 'the
scholarship of teaching').[66]

Wadud's encounter with SIS played a formative role in her discourse on action, allowing her to see how purely theoretical concepts
could be translated into practical reforms. In our interview, she
described the impact of SIS on her thinking as follows:

> I didn't realize until after those three years of being in Malaysia that all
> the work I had done, which was basically theory, had very pragmatic
> application. So if I were to say there was a turning point, it would be
> between 1989 and 1992, working with Sisters in Islam . . . I think the
> result of reading for gender in the Qur'an is social justice, and that's
> what happened with the Sisters. The results of my research computed
> into strategic, meaningful, practical changes in terms of lived reality.[67]

The Malaysian experience shaped Wadud's Islamic discourse, then,
by shifting it from the 'devotional act'[68] of an individual—that of a
Muslim woman reading the Qur'an through the lens of gender
justice—to a collective act that is explicitly political, coming together
with likeminded Muslim women and using the results of this research
to address everyday problems faced by women. As SIS organized one
outreach activity after another, from public lectures and open forums
to the publication of newspaper editorials and pamphlets on pressing

[64] Gisela Webb ed., *Windows of Faith: Muslim Women Scholar-Activists in North
America* (Syracuse, New York: Syracuse University Press, 2000), xi.
[65] Ernest Boyer, *Scholarship Reconsidered: Priorities of the Professoriate* (San
Francisco: Carnegie Foundation for the Advancement of Learning, 1990), 17.
[66] Ibid, 18–24.   [67] Wadud, Interview 2009.   [68] Ibid.

issues like domestic violence and the equality of men and women in Islam,[69] Wadud witnessed the myriad ways in which an idea, through action, could transform a society. That being said, at the same time as SIS showed Wadud the political potential of scholarship, she also had a tremendous impact on the movement's thinking. Before her arrival on the Malaysian scene, SIS had little interest in the Qur'an and focussed far more on questions of *shari'a*. By the time Wadud left Malaysia in 1992, the organization's discourse had squarely shifted from secondary sources to the scriptural source of Islam, foregrounding the Qur'an and using this text as a tool to fight for Muslim women's rights.[70]

It is in Wadud's accent on action, moreover, that a critical difference emerges between her hermeneutic and that of Esack, for while Esack's is a hermeneutic of *praxis*, Wadud's is a hermeneutic of *application*. According to Wadud, actions are 'a necessary extension of faith.'[71] Her liberating exegesis is marked by a generally linear mode of reading, in which radical reinterpretations of the text are practically applied to real world contexts. To be sure, she clarifies that there cannot be one universal model of implementation, since any effective implementation 'reflects time, place, gender, level of knowledge, circumstances of history and culture'.[72] But what about the reverse direction? Can the insights and perspectives gained through action not lead to a renewed, reinvigorated reflection? The largely unidirectional character of Wadud's exegesis stands in contrast to that of Esack. As was shown in the second chapter, according to Esack a liberating exegesis is based on *praxis*, or the idea that religious reflection ought to take shape in the very midst of struggle. As a result, not only does reflection lead to action but this action, too, has a constitutive effect, creating new insights and revelations into the text.[73] To put it simply: while Wadud's exegesis is more linear, Esack's

---

[69] Amina Wadud, 'Sisters in Islam: Effective against all Odds', in *Silent Voices*, eds. Doug A. Newsom and Bob J. Carrell (Lanham, Maryland: University Press of America, 1995), 123–4. For the pamphlet publications, see: Sisters in Islam, *Are Women and Men Equal before God?* (Kuala Lampur: Sisters in Islam, 1991) and *Are Muslim Men Allowed to Beat their Wives?* (Kuala Lampur: Sisters in Islam, 1991).

[70] Wadud, 'Sisters in Islam', 120.   [71] Wadud, *Inside the Gender Jihad*, 98.

[72] Amina Wadud, 'What's Interpretation Got to Do With It: The Relationship between Theory and Practice in Islamic Gender Reform', in *Islamic Family Law and Justice for Muslim Women*, ed. Hjh Nik Noriani Nik Badlishah (Kuala Lampur: Sisters in Islam, 2003), 93.

[73] Esack, *Qur'an, Liberation, and Pluralism*, 13.

is more dialectical, characterized by a continuous interplay between action and reflection.[74] It is precisely because liberation theology, as a theology of *praxis*, is forged in the heat of struggle that it makes no claim to objectivity, neutrality, and the truth. Rather, it reclaims the value of subjectivity, privileging the experiences, the perspectives, the truths of the oppressed. Yet Wadud's generally linear hermeneutic, based on extracting broader principles from the Qur'anic text (theory) and then pragmatically implementing these principles in the present (practice), subscribes, at least to some extent, to notions of objectivity.[75] For example, in *Qur'an and Woman* she differentiates between reading and exegesis, arguing that while reading is a subjective enterprise, conditioned by 'the attitudes, experiences, memory, and perspectives on language of each reader', exegesis is a different creature, attaining a measure of objectivity by employing hermeneutical methods.[76] As the next chapter will show, Barlas criticizes Wadud's distinction between reading and exegesis, pointing out that it is impossible to split these two language acts into separate, hermetically sealed categories, as any textual engagement is inescapably shaped by the contextual baggage of the reader.[77]

QUR'AN AND GENDER JUSTICE

Women Reading as Women

The entry of women into the field of exegesis—a discipline that has historically been, and that continues to be, dominated by men—is the

[74] Indeed, in reality linear readings are a hermeneutical impossibility, for one does not simply pick up a text, read it once, and then spend the rest of one's life *implementing* its teachings. Rather, there is a constant, even if unintentional, dialectic between the text and life. I am grateful to Christopher Rowland for this insight. All readings, therefore, are necessarily dialectical, and what differentiates Esack's hermeneutic (and that of liberation theology as a whole) is that he consciously foregrounds this cyclical aspect of interpretation.

[75] As discussed in the second chapter, this is a key problem that Esack has with Rahman's double movement theory, arguing that the very idea of extracting perennial principles from the text is premised on objectivist notions of discovering and accessing the real truth, and thus failing to consider crucial questions of reader subjectivity, interpretive pluralism, and who gets to define truth. See ibid, 68.

[76] Wadud, *Qur'an and Woman*, 94.

[77] Barlas, *'Believing Women' in Islam*, 118.

first, critical step in moving towards a truly gender inclusive approach to the text. This is a seminal point that resurfaces time and again in Wadud's writings. An inevitable consequence of the monopoly that men have exercised in interpreting Islamic texts, she observes, is that God has been reduced to the limitations of male experiences and understandings.[78] Drawing upon wider feminist critiques of patriarchy, she argues that just as God has been restricted to the experiences of men so, too, has the normative human being.[79] That is, humankind and human experience have become little more than synonyms for mankind and male experience. It is crucial, therefore, that women become producers of Islamic knowledge, challenging its androcentrism by bringing their own experiences, subjectivities, and insights to the interpretive task. The Islamic scholar Hibba Abugideiri succinctly sums up the significance of Wadud's argument:

> It is not enough for modern Qur'anic commentators to simply 'add women and stir,' or integrate the subject of woman into the interpretive process while ignoring her agency. Wadud shows that a hermeneutical approach to interpreting woman in the Qur'an must include women as active agents.[80]

Gender egalitarian exegesis is thus not about male commentators now writing on the timely topic of women in Islam, thereby reducing women to objects that are to be reflected upon, but rather about women becoming the subjects of the interpretive process, approaching the text *as* women. And it is precisely when Muslim women read the Qur'an unfettered by layers of patriarchal commentary, Wadud argues, that they will find a compassionate and liberating scripture that speaks to their suffering and marginalization.[81] What follows is a thematic survey and analysis of Wadud's own empowering encounter with the Qur'an.

The Origins of Humankind

Wadud commences her exegesis by revisiting the Creation Story. Due to a lack of detailed discussion in the Qur'an with regard to the

---

[78] Wadud, 'Towards a Qur'anic Hermeneutics of Social Justice', 48.

[79] Wadud, *Qur'an and Woman*, ix.

[80] Hibba Abugideiri, 'Hagar: A Historical Model for "Gender Jihad"', in *Daughters of Abraham: Feminist Thought in Judaism, Christianity, and Islam*, eds. Yvonne Y. Haddad and John L. Esposito (Gainesville: University Press of Florida, 2001), 92.

[81] Wadud, *Qur'an and Woman*, xxi–xxii.

creation of Adam and Eve, she notes, early commentators drew extensively upon biblical accounts.[82] As a result, the distinctly biblical notion of Eve as being created from Adam's rib became mainstreamed in Islamic thought. The precise passage, found in the Book of Genesis, reads:

> So the Lord God caused a deep sleep to fall upon man, and while he slept took one of his ribs and closed up its place with flesh. And the rib that the Lord God had taken from the man he made into a woman and brought her to the man. Then the man said, 'This at last is bone of my bones and flesh of my flesh; she shall be called Woman, because she was taken out of Man.'[83] (Genesis 2:21–3)

Women's gender egalitarian readings have shown how the *hadith* literature, which was heavily influenced by biblical lore, acted as an important literary medium through which such ideas entered Qur'anic exegesis, for it was common practice for exegetes to refer to *hadith* reports while interpreting the text. The Pakistani scholar Riffat Hassan gives the following *hadith* report, narrated by the controversial companion Abu Hurayra, as an example of the striking convergence between the *hadith* and the Bible on the origins of woman:

> Treat women nicely, for a woman is created from a rib, and the most curved portion of the rib is its upper portion, so if you should try to straighten it, it will break, but if you leave it as it is, it will remain crooked. So treat women nicely.[84]

It is important to note, moreover, that Qur'anic commentators were well aware that such *hadith* reports drew upon biblical accounts. For instance, the great exegete Abu Ja'far al-Tabari (d. 923) openly acknowledged in his *hadith*-based commentary of the Qur'an that such accounts had been 'learned from the people of the Torah', adding that 'God knows best' (*wallahu 'a'lam*) regarding the reliability of these accounts.[85]

---

[82] Ibid, 20.

[83] In this book, all translations of biblical passages have been taken from *Holy Bible: English Standard Version, Anglicized Edition* (London: Collins, 2007).

[84] As cited in Hassan, 'An Islamic Perspective', in *Women, Religion and Sexuality: Studies on the Impact of Religious Teachings on Women*, ed. Jeanne Becher (Philadelphia: Trinity Press International, 1990), 102.

[85] Abu Ja'far al-Tabari, as cited in Barbara F. Stowasser, *Women in the Qur'an, Traditions, and Interpretation* (Oxford: Oxford University Press, 1994), 28. It is

After pointing out the lack of any Qur'anic basis behind this idea of woman as being created from man's rib—that is, highlighting what the text does *not* say—Wadud discusses the Qur'an's portrayal of the origins of humankind. Paralleling the earlier work of Hassan,[86] she underlines that in the Qur'an woman and man were created from a 'single soul'. The verse reads:

> O humankind, be conscious of your Sustainer, who has created you from a single soul (*nafsin wahidatin*), and from it created its mate (*zawjaha*), and from the two of them dispersed men and women in multitudes.[87] (Q. 4:1)

There is clearly no mention here of woman being created from the flesh, or even soul, of man. In fact, in a strictly grammatical sense, notes Wadud, the feminine was created first and it is the masculine that is derived, for the Arabic word for soul (*nafs*) is a feminine noun while that of mate (*zawj*) is a masculine one.[88] But conceptually speaking, she clarifies, this verse moves beyond gender distinctions,[89] thereby establishing the ontological equality of women and men. Reflecting upon this verse, as well as others like Q. 51:49—'And of all things We have created pairs (*zawjayn*), perhaps you will then reflect'—she concludes that *duality* is a defining feature of the creation,[90] with each partner existing in a symbiotic relationship of harmony with the other.

In addition to rereading the Creation Story, Wadud critically analyses the Events of the Garden. Just as Qur'anic commentators were deeply influenced by biblical accounts (or what are referred to as the *isra'iliyat* literature in Islamic scholarship) when it came to explaining the origins of humankind so, too, were they informed by this earlier literature while interpreting Satan's temptation of Adam and Eve. According to the Old Testament, Satan first whispered into

interesting to note here that the Arabic name used by Muslims to refer to Eve— *Hawwa'*—is also drawn from the *hadith* literature and not found anywhere in the Qur'an. Indeed, as the following *hadith* excerpt from Tabari's commentary shows, the name *Hawwa'* is itself based on the entrenched idea of woman as being created from man's rib: 'The angels said: Why was she named *Hawwa'*? He [Adam] said: Because she was created from a living (*hayy*) thing.' See ibid, 29.

[86] Hassan, 'An Islamic Perspective', 98.
[87] The origins of humankind are also described, as Wadud notes, in Q. 6:98, 7:189, and 39:6.
[88] Wadud, *Qur'an and Woman*, 19–20.
[89] Ibid.   [90] Ibid, 20–1.

the ear of Eve, who then, enticed by his words, approached Adam. The biblical account, found in Genesis 3:1–7, reads:

> Now the serpent was more crafty than any other beast of the field that the Lord God had made. He said to the woman, 'Did God actually say, "You shall not eat of any tree in the garden?"' And the woman said to the serpent, 'We may eat of the fruit of the trees in the garden, but God said, "You shall not eat of the fruit of the tree that is in the midst of the garden, neither shall you touch it, lest you die."' But the serpent said to the woman, 'You will surely not die. For God knows that when you eat of it your eyes will be opened, and you will be like God, knowing good and evil.' So when the woman saw that the tree was good for food, and that it was a delight to the eyes, and that the tree was desired to make one wise, she took of its fruit and ate, and she also gave some to her husband who was with her, and he ate. Then the eyes of both were opened, and they knew that they were naked. And they sewed fig leaves together and made themselves loincloths.

Indeed, by the time of al-Tabari in the tenth century, the majority of Muslim scholars believed that it was through the inherent weakness of Eve that Satan was successfully able to tempt Adam.[91] In stark contrast to the biblical account, Wadud points out that the Qur'an does not blame the woman, as it uses the Arabic dual form when describing Satan's temptation.[92] Q. 7:20–2 is a compelling case in point:

> But Satan whispered to both of them, in order to reveal their hidden parts of which they were not aware (till then), and said: 'Your Sustainer has forbidden you to go near this tree lest you become angels or immortal.' Then he swore to both of them an oath: 'I am your sincere friend;' And led them both (to the tree) by deceit. When they both tasted the tree their disgrace became exposed to them, and they patched the leaves of the Garden to hide it. And the Sustainer said to both of them: 'Did I not forbid you this tree and tell you that Satan is your open enemy?'

It is important to note here that Wadud is not the first Muslim scholar to offer such a gender-sensitive reading of this fateful event. Hassan has also underlined the Qur'an's usage of the Arabic dual form, thereby showing that what transpired in the Garden was a collective act of disobedience in which Adam and Eve were equally responsible.[93]

[91] Stowasser, 29.   [92] Wadud, *Qur'an and Woman*, 25.
[93] Hassan, 'An Islamic Perspective', 104.

Furthermore, not only is the woman never singled out in the Qur'an's treatment of the narrative, but, Wadud observes (paralleling Hassan again),[94] in the sole exception to the text's usage of the Arabic dual form it is the pronoun 'him' that is employed.[95] The passage, which we have already discussed in the preceding chapter on Engineer who reinterpreted it through the lens of economic justice, reads:

> Certainly We had enjoined Adam earlier; but he forgot, and We did not find resoluteness in him. When We said to the angels, 'Prostrate before Adam,' they prostrated, except Iblis [Satan]: he refused. We said, 'O Adam! This is indeed an enemy of yours and your mate's. So do not let him expel you from Paradise, or you will be miserable. Indeed you will neither be hungry in it nor naked. Indeed you will neither be thirsty in it nor suffer from the sun.' Then Satan tempted him [*fawaswasa ilayhi al-shaytanu*]. He said, 'O Adam! Shall I show you the tree of immortality, and an imperishable kingdom?' So they both ate of it, and their nakedness became exposed to them, and they began to stitch over themselves with the leaves of paradise. Adam disobeyed his Sustainer, and went amiss. (Q. 20:115–21)

Yet how can this account that clearly blames Adam—'Then Satan tempted him'—be reconciled with other Qur'anic verses that use the dual form exclusively? Wadud explains this inconsistency by placing this passage in its wider, textual context. In particular, she looks at the verse that immediately precedes it (Q. 20:114), which reads: 'So exalted is God, the True Sovereign. Do not hasten [O Muhammad] with the Qur'an before its revelation is completed to you, and say, "My Sustainer! Increase me in knowledge."' Fearing that he would forget the Qur'anic revelations relayed to him by Gabriel, Prophet Muhammad was hastily repeating the revelations in order to memorize them. A prime function of this specific retelling of the Garden story, comments Wadud, is thus to illustrate to the Prophet that it is Satan who instils forgetfulness in humankind, as exemplified by Adam forgetting to stay away from the forbidden tree.[96] The implication being made here is that the Prophet need not worry about forgetting the revelations, for God will ensure that the Prophet memorizes the entire scripture.[97]

---

[94] Ibid.   [95] Wadud, *Qur'an and Woman*, 25.   [96] Ibid.
[97] This interpretive conclusion is corroborated further by Q. 75:16–19, which reassures the Prophet that, through divine assistance, he will indeed be able to memorize the Word correctly.

The Justice of Divine Judgement

Wadud also explores the Qur'an's apocalyptic depictions of the world to come. While she challenges classical and medieval commentators on the origins of humankind and the events of the Garden, she actually affirms their readings when it comes to the Day of Judgement, observing that there is 'an unusual consensus among the commentators with regard to the absence of male/female distinctions in the Qur'anic accounts of Judgement and recompense'.[98] This is a telling example of how her criticism of the exegetical tradition is hardly a sweeping one, categorically dismissing all prior reflections on the Qur'an, but rather a nuanced critique, problematizing those interpretations that undermine the full humanity of women. As Wadud notes, because the Qur'anic text is so explicit that equal recompense will be given to men and women—such as Q. 3:195: 'Lo! I suffer not the work of any worker, male or female, to be lost. You proceed one from another'[99]—it is, in fact, quite difficult to privilege men over women when discussing the Day of Judgement.[100] Significantly, the key term that the Qur'an uses with reference to death and the Hereafter, she points out, is that of the gender-neutral soul (*nafs*), which will be brought before its Creator to stand judgement, thereby transcending the sexual distinctions associated with the human body.[101] She cites Q. 21:47, among others,[102] to illustrate the text's emphasis on the soul when describing the world to come. The verse reads:

> We shall fix the scales of justice on the Day of Resurrection, and no soul will be wronged in the least; and even if it were equal to the weight of a mustard seed, We shall take it (into account). We suffice as reckoners.

So not only does the Final Day reflect the absolute justice of God, who will take every action into account 'even if it were equal to the weight of a mustard seed', but by focussing on the soul over the body, this verse also implicitly underscores this deity's refusal to differentiate between men and women, elevating the former over the latter.

---

[98] Ibid, 51.
[99] Q. 40:40 is another example of how divine justice will be meted out equally to the sexes on the Day of Judgement, explicitly mentioning women alongside men.
[100] Ibid.   [101] Ibid, 46.
[102] These include Q. 3:185–6, 39:42, and 81:1–7.

Like Esack and Engineer, a deep-seated conviction in the inherent justice of the Creator lies at the heart of Wadud's Islamic discourse. Citing verses like Q. 10:44—'Surely God does not wrong anyone; they wrong themselves'—she argues that God does not commit acts of injustice, but rather it is humankind who perpetrates oppression.[103] In fact, her very choice of 'Wadud'—one of the ninety-nine names of God and which she defines as 'the Loving God of Justice'[104]—as a family name upon converting to Islam reflects her abiding belief in God's endless compassion and commitment to justice. And it is precisely because God is just, concludes Wadud, that divine judgement is based solely on *taqwa* (literally, piety), denoting one's level of God-consciousness and how this spiritual consciousness, in turn, translates into ethical action.[105] Referring to Q. 49:13, she writes that *taqwa* is the chief criterion that differentiates one human being from another.[106] This verse, which has become a seminal passage in women's gender egalitarian readings of Islamic texts, is provided below:

> O humankind! We created you from a male and a female, and made you into nations and tribes, that you may know one another. The noblest among you in the eyes of God are the most pious among you. Indeed, God is all-Knowing, all-Aware.

Furthermore, God alone has the ability to gauge one's level of *taqwa* and thus to render judgement, cautions Wadud, and not other human beings.[107] Given the centrality of *taqwa* in the Qur'an, her usage of this concept as an organizing principle of gender-just exegesis is a persuasive interpretive move. Indeed, Rahman, in his pioneering study of the text, entitled *Major Themes of the Qur'an* (1980), noted that *taqwa* is arguably the single most important term in the entire scripture.[108] In her emphasis on *taqwa*, Wadud shares common

[103] Wadud, 'Towards a Qur'anic Hermeneutics of Social Justice', 46. She also cites Q. 9:70, 29:40, and 30:9.
[104] Wadud, *Inside the Gender Jihad*, 2. The famous ninety-nine names of God can be found in the Qur'an and denote various divine attributes, such as *al-Rahim* (the Compassionate), *al-Ghafur* (the Forgiving), and *al-Malik* (the King). The name *al-Wadud*, conventionally defined as the Loving, appears twice in the text (Q. 11:90, 85:14).
[105] Wadud, *Qur'an and Woman*, 36–7.   [106] Ibid.
[107] Wadud, *Inside the Gender Jihad*, 185.
[108] Rahman, *Major Themes of the Qur'an*, 28–9. The first edition of this book was published in 1980.

ground with Esack who, as already seen in the second chapter, also uses *taqwa*—which he defines as 'integrity and awareness in relation to the presence of God'—as a hermeneutical key in his liberationist exegesis.[109]

The Final Abodes

After reading Qur'anic depictions of the Day of Judgement through the eyes of gender justice, Wadud moves on to the two, final destinations of humankind: namely, Heaven and Hell. Like the Final Day, she comments, portrayals of Hell in the Qur'an are remarkably gender neutral, as it is described in very general terms as being a place of severe punishment and utter despair.[110] As a result, her hermeneutical engagement with Hell is minimal. While Wadud does not compare the Qur'an's portrayal of Hell with other Islamic texts—an understandable omission given her express disciplinary interest in scripture—it is important to note that the Qur'an's gender-neutral discourse on Hell is at loggerheads with the *hadith* literature, in which descriptions of divine punishment are acutely gendered. The following prophetic report, found in the *hadith* collection of Sahih Bukhari, relates the story of Prophet Muhammad having a vision of Hell and seeing that it was filled mostly with women:

> The Prophet said: 'Hell was revealed to me, and I perceived that the majority of its occupants are women who are ungrateful.' He was asked: 'Are they ungrateful to God?' 'They are ungrateful to their husbands,' he replied. 'And they are ungrateful for any kindness shown them and if you have been kind to any one of them for a time and then she sees something that she does not like in you, she will then say, "I have never received anything from you!"'[111]

The authenticity of such *hadith* reports are, of course, hotly disputed amongst Muslims, and female scholars have problematized the reliability of numerous, misogynistic *hadith* reports. The Moroccan feminist Fatima Mernissi, for example, has shown how the

---

[109] Esack, *Qur'an, Liberation, and Pluralism*, 82–3.

[110] Wadud, *Qur'an and Woman*, 52.

[111] Nicholas Awde ed., *Women in Islam: An Anthology from the Qur'an and Hadiths* (New York: Hippocrene Books, 2005), 36.

companion Abu Hurayra—a key transmitter of anti-women *hadith* reports and who was introduced earlier on in this chapter—was considered a highly unreliable source by the first Muslims, in particular Ayesha, a wife of the Prophet.[112]

In her treatment of the final abodes, Wadud directs far more attention to Heaven, which, unlike Hell, is portrayed in scripture in starkly gendered terms. She commences her analysis by arguing that, because the Qur'an was revealed in a specific historical context, we need to make sense of its depictions of heavenly pleasure in light of this time and place. For instance, the recurring description of Paradise as a place of 'gardens with rivers flowing beneath' should not be taken literally, as such a portrayal is much more meaningful, as Wadud puts it, for 'someone living in an arid desert environment than, perhaps, for someone living in the tropics of Malaysia.'[113] What is necessary, then, is to extract the underlying message embedded within this metaphorical language: essentially, that Paradise is a place of unbound pleasure and eternal comfort. In a similar vein, descriptions of sexual pleasure, too, need to be interpreted through the framework of historical criticism. The *huri*, referring to an erotic, light-skinned virgin woman with a vigorous sex-drive, has become a pervasive image of Paradise amongst Muslim men and is mentioned four times in the text,[114] specifically in Q. 44:54, 52:20, 55:70–6, and 56:17–24. But this portrayal of the *huri*, argues Wadud, should not be taken literally. Rather, it ought to be read in terms of the prevailing understandings of beauty at the time:

> The specific depiction here of the companions of Paradise demonstrates the Qur'an's familiarity with the dreams and desires of those Arabs. The Qur'an offers the *huri* as an incentive to aspire after truth. It is impossible to believe that the Qur'an intends white women with large eyes to represent a single universal description of beauty for all humankind.[115]

More significantly, she observes, references to the *huri* only appear in the Meccan chapters,[116] or those chapters that were revealed in the earliest days of Islam before the Muslims fled to Medina (622) in order to escape persecution. There was a direct, hermeneutical link, therefore, between the androcentric sexuality of the Meccan chapters

---

[112] Mernissi, 78.   [113] Wadud, *Qur'an and Woman*, 52.
[114] Esack, *The Qur'an: A User's Guide*, 164.
[115] Wadud, *Qur'an and Woman*, 55.   [116] Ibid, 54–5.

and the dire state of gender relations in Meccan society, which was overwhelmingly patriarchal.[117] However, with the creation of a new society in Medina marked by relatively more egalitarian relations between women and men, continues Wadud, the Qur'an made a critical shift in its portrayals of pleasure in the Hereafter, abandoning the term *huri* altogether and adopting the gender-neutral *azwaj* (the plural of *zawj*, meaning partner or spouse).[118] She gives the following Medinan verse by way of example:

> Say: 'Shall I tell you of (things) even better (than the pleasures of this world)? With the Sustainer are gardens with rivers flowing beneath for those who keep from evil and follow the straight path, where they will remain forever with purified spouses (*azwajun mutahharatun*) and blessings of God.'[119] (Q. 3:15)

Countering patriarchal readings of this verse, in particular the interpretation that *azwaj* (spouses) refers to the pleasures of polygamy awaiting righteous men, Wadud underscores the grammatical fact that the usage of the plural *azwaj* here corresponds to the plural noun that precedes it—'those who keep from evil'—and, therefore, hardly constitutes textual proof of polygamy in Paradise.[120] To put it another way: just as the beginning of humankind's journey, in which man and woman were created from a single soul, was marked by a relationship of *duality*, so too will its end, when the righteous believer will be paired with her/his companion.

Polygamy, Veiling, and Seclusion

Indeed, by using hermeneutical tools like textual analysis and historical criticism, Wadud is able to make a convincing case against polygamous readings of the Qur'an. Most Muslims believe that polygamy—or, to be more precise: polygyny, in which only men

---

[117] Ibid.   [118] Ibid, 55.

[119] Wadud also cites a number of other passages, such as Q. 2:25, 4:57, and 36:54–6. Though this does not problematize Wadud's argument of a general shift from the Qur'anic usage of *huri* to *azwaj* with the Muslim migration to Medina, especially given the number of Medinan verses that corroborate this claim, it is worthwhile noting that the chapter in which the last citation is listed here—*Surat Yasin* (Chapter 36)—was actually revealed in the Meccan period.

[120] Ibid, 57.

have more than one partner[121]—is upheld in Islam, arguing that the Qur'an allows men to take up to four wives. Challenging this argument, Wadud writes that we need to examine the exact wording of the Qur'anic text with regard to this practice. The polygamy verse, in its entirety, reads:

> If you fear that you will not deal justly with the orphans, then marry women that you like, two, three, or four. But if you fear that you will not be able to deal justly with them, then only one, or what your right hands possess. That makes it likelier that you will not be unjust. (Q. 4:3)

Far from being an open license for polygamy, she comments, this passage deals with a specific social crisis that emerged in the early Muslim community, in particular that of the unjust treatment of orphans—a historical context evidenced further by the Qur'anic verse immediately preceding this one, which warns male guardians of orphans not to mismanage their wealth and mix it with their own.[122] The verse reads:

> Give the orphans their property, and do not replace the good with the bad, and do not eat up their property (by mingling it) with your own property, for that is indeed a grievous crime. (Q. 4:2)

A practical solution that the Qur'an put forth, then, to counter such exploitation was that of marriage to female orphans who had come of age,[123] thereby protecting them through the legal responsibilities that came packaged with the institution of marriage. Yet what historical circumstances led to this mismanagement of orphans' wealth? While Wadud does not engage this question, the Islamic historian Amira Sonbol has pointed out that the Chapter of Women (*Surat al-Nisa'*)—the Qur'anic chapter in which Q. 4:3 is located—was revealed shortly after the Muslim defeat at the Battle of Uhud (625),[124] and this explains the large number of orphans and widows.

---

[121] Whereas polygamy, strictly speaking, is a gender neutral term referring to either a man or woman having multiple partners, in reality most polygamous relationships have been based on the patriarchal practice of polygyny, in which only men have multiple partners. Polyandry, which is much rarer but not without historical precedent, refers to women having multiple partners.

[122] Ibid, 83.   [123] Ibid.

[124] Amira E. Sonbol, 'Rethinking Women and Islam', in *Daughters of Abraham: Feminist Thought in Judaism, Christianity, and Islam*, eds. Yvonne Y. Haddad and John L. Esposito (Gainesville: University Press of Florida, 2001), 133. Here, Sonbol cites the Qur'anic translator Yusuf Ali and his introductory notes for *Surat al-Nisa'*.

In addition to pointing out that Q. 4:3 speaks to a particular context, Wadud underscores a key condition that Q. 4:3 lays down for polygamous relationships: specifically, that such an arrangement is only possible *if* the husband is able to deal justly with all his wives.[125] The Qur'an reiterates the centrality of just conduct, observes Wadud, in a later verse in the same chapter, which reads: 'You will not be able to treat your wives with justice' (Q. 4:129)—a statement that has led numerous commentators to conclude that monogamy is, in fact, the preferred form of marriage.[126] And it is precisely because the text has this overwhelming emphasis on justice that the absence of this condition in the lived experiences of women in polygamous relationships today ought to constitute sufficient grounds for the abolition of this practice. As Wadud put it in our interview:

> Now what we need are specialists in social work who can provide evidence of the full effects of polygamy and they are, you know, interviewing children, men and women … and they are showing, this is the result. So if the Qur'an uses the term justice three times in the verse on polygamy, and then you show that obviously there is a travesty of justice in the experience, whatever it was that the Qur'an intended and however it may have been practiced at the time of the Prophet, what we are seeing now is the injustice of it.[127]

Furthermore, she continues, contemporary Muslims have rightly criticized and abandoned the practice of slavery—an institution that is never explicitly prohibited in the Qur'an, though the text does emphasize the just treatment of slaves and their freeing as a form of atonement for specific sins.[128] So if today Muslims, without much hesitation, are able to condemn slavery on the basis of it being an affront to human dignity and without any Qur'anic mandate,[129] then why not oppressive practices against women like polygamy?

[125] Asma Barlas, 'Amina Wadud's Hermeneutics of the Qur'an: Women Rereading Sacred Texts', in *Modern Muslim Intellectuals and the Qur'an*, ed. Suha Taji-Faruqi (Oxford: Oxford University Press, 2004), 115.
[126] Wadud, *Qur'an and Woman*, 83.   [127] Wadud, Interview 2009.
[128] Wadud, 'Alternative Qur'anic Interpretation and the Status of Muslim Women', 14–15.
[129] For the history of slavery in the Muslim world and its long road towards abolition, see, among others: Alan G.B. Fisher and Humphrey J. Fisher, *Slavery in the History of Black Muslim Africa* (London: Hurst and Company, 2001) and William G. Clarence-Smith, *Islam and the Abolition of Slavery* (Oxford: Oxford University Press, 2006).

Wadud also uses the Qur'an to critique such established Muslim practices as veiling and female seclusion. While she has chosen to observe the headscarf, she clarifies that she does 'not consider it a religious obligation, nor ascribe to it any religious value per se.'[130] In fact, it was not questions of religion but rather race—specifically, as a Black woman living in a White supremacist society—that compelled her to don the veil, even *before* her conversion to the Muslim faith. To put it in her own words:

> The actual impetus behind my dress was in contradistinction to the experiences of African slave women who were stripped of their garments of piety before the lecherous eyes of slave auctioneers and masters. In fact, I covered my hair and wore long dresses before I accepted Islam.[131]

Citing Q. 7:26—'the best dress is the dress of *taqwa* [piety]'—Wadud argues that modesty cannot be reduced to mere physical attire, subject to the approval or disapproval of men and male-dominated communities, but rather is an ethical principle embodied in one's relations with others.[132] Indeed, such social practices as veiling and female seclusion were introduced into the early Muslim community, as the historian Leila Ahmed has shown in her pioneering study *Women and Gender in Islam* (1992), by Sassanian society, which was heavily segregated, as well as Christian communities in the Mediterranean and Middle East.[133] In addition to foregrounding the Qur'anic text's emphasis on modesty as a principle, Wadud highlights this historicity of the veil—that is, its emergence in a particular context in Muslim history—and how it initially symbolized protection, worn by women of wealth and power.[134] With regard to female seclusion, Q. 33:33 has become a popular passage amongst conservative men who believe that women should not leave their homes. The verse, written in the Arabic feminine plural, reads:

> Stay in your houses and do not deck yourselves with wanton display (*tabarruj*) as in the former Days of Ignorance. Maintain the prayer and pay the mandatory almsgiving, and obey God and His Apostle.

---

[130] Wadud, *Inside the Gender Jihad*, 176.
[131] Wadud, 'Teaching Afrocentric Islam in the White Christian South', 140.
[132] Wadud, *Inside the Gender Jihad*, 219.
[133] Leila Ahmed, *Women and Gender in Islam* (New Haven: Yale University Press, 1992), 5.
[134] Wadud, *Qur'an and Woman*, 9–10.

Wadud tackles this tricky verse with two, principal hermeneutical moves. Firstly, she places it within its wider textual context, citing it along with the verse that immediately precedes it (Q. 33:32),[135] which begins with the phrase, 'O wives of the Prophet', thereby clarifying that a specific group of people is being addressed. But even if women happen to be the immediate audience, she continues, why should this verse only be applicable to women? Can women not be used to illustrate larger lessons for the community? Far from being a categorical command to remain in the home, Wadud argues that there is a larger ethical principle underlying this verse and one that is equally applicable to men and women: namely, to observe modesty and humility by staying away from 'wanton display' (*tabarruj*) and ostentatious behaviour in front of others, as practiced in 'the former Days of Ignorance', referring to pre-Islamic Arabia.[136]

The Family: Then and Now

Wadud wrestles with problematic verses elevating men by highlighting the historical attitudes held towards the family at the time of revelation—a reality that inevitably shaped the text's discourse. The first part of Q. 4:34 is a passage commonly cited to *prove* God's preference for men over women. It reads: 'Men are the guardians (*qawwamun*) of women, because of the advantage God has granted some of them over others and by virtue of their spending out of their wealth.' Reflecting on this verse, she notes that a critical connection is being made here between privilege—that is, men's role as guardians—on the one hand, and responsibility, or the financial provision for women's needs, on the other.[137] Addressing a specific historical context, this verse presupposes, indeed is conditional upon, a specific type of familial arrangement: namely, one in which the husband earns, spending out of his wealth, and the wife stays at home. With regard to 'the advantage God has granted some of them over others', Wadud argues that this statement—rather than being a categorical expression of male preference—refers to the fact that men are given twice the share of inheritance (Q. 4:11).[138] And this preference in

---

[135] Ibid, 97–8.   [136] Ibid.   [137] Ibid, 70–1.
[138] Ibid, 70. The verse is incorrectly cited in Wadud's work as Q. 4:7. She adds that the phrase in Q. 4:34—'some of them over others' (*ba'dahum 'ala ba'din*)—

inheritance, she continues, is precisely due to the solemn financial responsibility that lay solely upon men's shoulders in that time.[139] But what if the present time is radically different, in which large numbers of Muslim women have become breadwinners alongside men or even the sole breadwinners? This question is particularly acute in the African American context. As Wadud points out, slavery 'precluded the idea of [Black] men serving as protectors and maintainers' and, due to enduring racism within American society, even after the abolition of slavery Black women—viewed as being less threatening than Black men—were more likely to gain employment, however poorly paid, becoming the providers of the family.[140] Because Q. 4:34 squarely bases men's authority on the assumption that they are the primary providers of the family, gender egalitarian female readers have argued that in a new context wherein both spouses are economically productive (including, of course, arrangements in which the wife is the sole earner) the husband would cease to function as guardian.[141] Passages like Q. 4:11 and 4:34, then, need to be interpreted in light of contemporary circumstances, in which understandings of the family have shifted significantly.

Furthermore, the fact that the Qur'an speaks to the sensibilities of a given society does not mean that it endorses such social norms, upholding them as timeless models that are to be emulated by subsequent generations of Muslims. As Wadud puts it:

> The Qur'an does not attempt to annihilate the differences between men and women or to erase the significance of functional gender distinctions which help every society to run smoothly and fulfil its needs . . . However, the Qur'an does not propose or support a singular role or a single definition of a set of roles, exclusively, for each gender across every culture . . . Such a specification would be an imposition that would reduce the Qur'an from a universal text to a culturally specific text.[142]

This is not to imply, however, that everything about gender dynamics in seventh-century Arabia was problematic and to assume, rather

---

complicates this (conditional) preference even further, since some men, rather than *all* men, are advantaged over 'others', including men and women. See ibid, 71.

[139] Ibid.

[140] Amina Wadud, 'The Ethics of *Tawhid* over the Ethics of *Qiwamah*', in *Men in Charge? Rethinking Authority in Muslim Legal Tradition*, eds. Ziba Mir-Hosseini, Mulki Al-Sharmani, and Jana Rumminger (London: Oneworld, 2015), 258–9.

[141] Ali, *Sexual Ethics and Islam*, 119.   [142] Wadud, *Qur'an and Woman*, 8–9.

arrogantly, that we in the twenty-first century have finally gotten it *right*. On the contrary, there are aspects of family relations in the classical period that can be reclaimed by Muslim progressives in their struggle for social justice. In an illuminating discussion on mothering, Wadud points out that at the time of the Prophet, delivery and nursing were seen as completely unrelated tasks, for the mother was understood simply as being the one who gave birth, while it was the responsibility of the father's tribe to nurture and raise the child.[143] This is why, Wadud observes, in the prophetic biographical sources there is no negative stigma associated with Amina, the biological mother of Muhammad, despite the fact that she sent him off to live with a wet-nurse, Halima, shortly after his birth.[144] In other words, in the world of the first Muslims, a societal distinction was drawn between bearing and rearing—a very different approach to motherhood that is at odds with understandings of the term today, in which the two acts are conflated. By using the formative Islamic period to historicize the role of mother, Wadud undermines any essentialist claims about motherhood—that there is something *natural* about this social function—and which are invariably invoked to legitimate, and thus to ignore, the burdens of care that mothers in general and single mothers in particular are expected to endure, as well as to exempt men from responsibility for familial care and housework.[145]

Saying No to (the Literal Letter of) the Text

But unlike Engineer, Wadud's liberationist exegesis is not an apologetic one, acknowledging certain problems with the literal wordings of the text. As discussed in the previous chapter, Engineer simplistically portrays the Qur'an as a 'charter of rights for women',[146] upholding complete gender parity. Indeed, he even goes so far as to claim that the Qur'an is 'the first revealed book that accords equal rights to women.'[147] While Wadud interprets the text through the eyes of justice, she is wary of falling into this apologetic trap. Her reading of Q. 4:34—the first part of which was discussed in the preceding

---

[143] Wadud, *Inside the Gender Jihad*, 127–8.   [144] Ibid, 128.
[145] Ibid, 128–9.   [146] Engineer, *Islam and Liberation Theology*, 33.
[147] Engineer, *Islam: Misgivings and History*, 98.

section—is an illustrative example of her refusal to explain away overtly problematic passages. The entire verse reads:

> Men are the guardians of women, because of the advantage God has granted some of them over others and by virtue of their spending out of their wealth. So righteous women are obedient,[148] safeguarding what is unseen of what God has enjoined them to guard. As for those wives whose misconduct you fear, (first) advise them, and (if ineffective) keep away from them in the bed, and (as a last resort) beat them. Then if they obey you, do not seek any course (of action) against them. Indeed, God is all-Exalted, all-Great.

In line with her hermeneutical emphasis on historical contextualization, Wadud argues that this verse, referring to beating as a last resort, ought to be understood as a 'severe restriction' on violence against women, as the biographies of the Companions and the pre-existing custom of female infanticide—a practice severely condemned in the Qur'an—suggest that violence against women was widespread in seventh-century Arabia.[149] This reading draws upon Wadud's belief in 'Qur'anic trajectories', or the idea that the text set into motion a 'radical momentum towards continual reforms in gender relations', challenging patriarchy to the extent that it could within the restricted circumstances of seventh-century Arabian society.[150] If this line of trajectory is faithfully followed, then, a restriction of an oppressive act in *that* time could cogently be read as a prohibition of that very act in *our* time. But despite forwarding this initial argument in *Qur'an and Woman*—that violence against women is presented as a last resort— Wadud retains deep reservations about this verse:

> There is no getting around this one, even though I have tried through different methods for two decades. I simply do not and cannot condone permission for a man to 'scourge' or apply *any kind* of strike to a woman . . . This leads me to clarify how I have finally come to say 'no' outright to the literal implementation of this passage.[151]

In other words, just as approaches to the family have dramatically changed since the time of the first Muslims so, too, have our

[148] Since my specific interest here is in Wadud's treatment of the last part of Q. 4:34, I have provided a discussion of how she and Barlas approach women's obedience in Q. 4:34 in the next chapter.
[149] Wadud, *Qur'an and Woman*, 76.
[150] Wadud, 'Qur'an, Gender and Interpretive Possibilities', 334.
[151] Wadud, *Inside the Gender Jihad*, 200.

understandings of social justice and sexual ethics, especially in terms of acknowledging the evils of domestic abuse.[152] Wadud's exegesis is thus closer to that of Esack who, as was shown in the second chapter, is critical of apologia, pointing out that men are the primary audience of the Qur'an.[153] Wadud also acknowledges the text's androcentrism. For instance, referring to Q. 2:223—'Your women are a tillage (*harth*) for you, so come to your tillage whenever you like'—she concedes that the Qur'an speaks to male desire, affirming the sexuality of men while treating women's sexuality as passive.[154] Paralleling Esack's emphasis on the egalitarian spirit of the Qur'an over its literal wording,[155] Wadud grapples with passages like Q. 4:34 by prioritizing the text's principles over its particulars, arguing that a literal reading of this verse violates wider Qur'anic commitments to 'justice' and 'human dignity'—the understandings of which have radically changed since late antiquity.[156] In so doing, she is able to say 'no' to the contextually bound letter of the Qur'an while, at the same time, upholding its underlying spirit.

On Gender Mainstreaming and Male Solidarity

An important component of Wadud's Qur'anic exegesis is gender mainstreaming: that is, approaching female figures discussed in the text as paradigms of piety for *all* Muslims, men and women. As Muslim progressives have noted, a pressing problem in Muslim women's leadership is not that it does not exist, but rather that it is largely restricted to women's issues and thus the leadership of other women.[157] The confinement of female participation to women's committees in the mosque, as opposed to wider leadership roles concerning the whole community, is an everyday example that immediately comes to mind. Yet the Qur'an, Wadud interjects, discusses a

---

[152] Ibid, 203. For an exhaustive study of the interpretive history of Q. 4:34, encompassing both the classical and contemporary periods, see Ayesha S. Chaudry, *Domestic Violence and the Islamic Tradition: Ethics, Law and the Muslim Discourse on Gender* (Oxford: Oxford University Press, 2013).

[153] Esack, 'Islam and Gender Justice', 195.

[154] Wadud, *Inside the Gender Jihad*, 193.

[155] Esack, 'Islam and Gender Justice', 203.

[156] Wadud, *Inside the Gender Jihad*, 203.   [157] Abugideiri, 89.

number of female figures in starkly universal terms. Q. 66:10–12 is a
compelling case in point:

> God draws an example for those who are faithless (*lilladhina kafaru*):
> the wife of Noah and the wife of Lot. They were under two of our
> righteous servants, yet they betrayed them, and even they [Noah and
> Lot] could not avail them in the least against God, and it was said to
> them: 'Enter the Fire, along with the incomers.' God draws another
> example for those who have faith (*lilladhina amanu*): the wife of
> Pharaoh, when she said, 'My Sustainer! Build me a home near You in
> Paradise, and save me from Pharaoh and his deeds, and save me from a
> wicked people.' And Mary, daughter of Imran, who guarded the chastity
> of her womb, so We breathed into it of Our spirit. She confirmed the
> words of her Sustainer and His Books, and she was one of the obedient
> ones (*qanitin*).

Highlighting the Arabic usage of the masculine plural, which grammatically includes both men and women, as opposed to the feminine
plural, which denotes only women, Wadud comments that this passage is usually interpreted as being applicable to women alone—a
problematic reading given that the above wording is gender neutral,
referring to 'those who are faithless', 'those who have faith', and 'the
obedient ones'.[158] These women, therefore, are being used as parables
for both men and women to reflect upon. Whereas figures like the
wife of Pharaoh and Mary are presented as paradigms of spiritual
leadership, the Qur'an also speaks of a woman who embodied the
qualities of political leadership. Like Engineer,[159] Wadud points out
that the Qur'an not only praises the personality of the Queen of
Sheba, singling out her political wisdom and diplomatic skill
(Q. 27:29–35),[160] but that she is also the only ruler, other than the
prophets, who is portrayed in a favourable light.[161] Yet despite the
text's celebration of this sovereign, she has curiously not become a
paradigmatic figure in Islamic political thought. As the Qur'anic
scholar Barbara Stowasser has shown, classical and medieval commentators, while ascribing various legendary tales to the Queen,
showed little interest in fleshing out wider lessons from her example,
examining how the queen's astute leadership skills could contribute

---

[158] Wadud, *Qur'an and Woman*, 33–4.
[159] Engineer, *The Rights of Women in Islam*, 17.
[160] Wadud, *Qur'an and Woman*, 40–1.   [161] Ibid, 89.

to Muslim thinking,[162] such as in the field of political theory. Indeed, in direct contradistinction to the Qur'an's positive portrayal of the Queen, as well as the fact that the text never presents men as natural leaders,[163] many Muslim men continue to approach leadership—political, social, religious, or otherwise—as a male prerogative, dismissing women as being inherently incompetent for the task of leadership.[164]

Women's leadership in ritual worship is a crucial aspect of gender mainstreaming. The struggle for gender justice, or what Wadud calls the 'gender jihad', is therefore a thoroughly comprehensive struggle, calling for the full and equal participation of women in every aspect of Muslim life.[165] While Wadud has popularized the term gender jihad, especially through the publication of her second book—*Inside the Gender Jihad: Women's Reform in Islam* (2006)—the origins of this phrase can be traced back, as she herself notes, to radical Muslim discourse in Apartheid South Africa. Here, the term was first used by Imam Rashied Omar,[166] the spiritual guide of the Claremont Main Road Mosque in Cape Town, and Esack, who actually has a section titled 'The Gender Jihad' in his book on Islamic liberation theology, published in 1997.[167] In fact, the first time that Wadud seriously considered the idea of a woman delivering the Friday sermon (*khutba*) and leading the prayers was whilst undertaking a speaking tour in South Africa in 1994, in which audience members asked her

---

[162] Stowasser, 65.   [163] Wadud, *Qur'an and Woman*, 89.

[164] In the previous chapter on Engineer it was shown that the *hadith* literature has been used to justify women's exclusion from leadership roles.

[165] Wadud, *Inside the Gender Jihad*, 10. As noted earlier, although the Arabic word *jihad* is commonly understood as holy war, it literally means to struggle or to exert effort and, therefore, includes all forms of strivings: individual or communal, peaceful or militant, expressly political or 'purely' spiritual.

[166] Ibid, 264. Omar (b. 1959) is a well-known progressive Muslim figure in South Africa. Like Esack, he has a traditional Islamic education—studying in South Africa, Pakistan, Sudan, and Malaysia—as well as a 'secular' academic one. Omar received his Ph.D. in Religious Studies from the University of Cape Town and is currently Research Scholar of Islamic Studies and Peacebuilding at the Kroc Institute for International Peace Studies at the University of Notre Dame in the USA. He spends two-thirds of the year in Cape Town serving as the coordinating *imam* of the Claremont Main Road Mosque. See Rashied Omar, faculty website, available at: http://kroc.nd.edu/facultystaff/Faculty/rashied-omar, accessed 13 August 2016.

[167] Esack, *Qur'an, Liberation, and Pluralism*, 239. An earlier reference by Esack to 'Gender Jihad', describing the 1994 Friday sermon in South Africa (which will be discussed next), can be found in Farid Esack, "Between Mandela and Man Dalla, Kafirs and Kaffirs: Post Modernist Islamic Reflections in a Post Apartheid South Africa," *Reviews in Religion and Theology* 2:3 (1995): 25.

about the possibility of women's leadership in ritual worship.[168] As it turned out, she delivered the Friday sermon during that very tour, speaking at the Claremont Main Road Mosque on the timely subject of Muslim women and 'engaged surrender', or the act of wilfully submitting to God through personal and social struggle.[169] As Esack recounts, despite the fact that the prayer organizers (of whom he was one) had diplomatically advertised Wadud's sermon as a 'pre-sermon lecture', this initiative was met with intense hostility by mainstream South African Muslims, who marched on the mosque in an ultimately unsuccessful attempt to shut down the programme.[170] This impassioned condemnation of woman-led prayer, spearheaded by conservative men, became internationalized in 2005 when Wadud led the Friday Prayer in New York City, speaking on the Unity of God and the nature of divine disclosure.[171] Traditional Islamic scholars from around the world vehemently voiced their disapproval, contending that a female prayer leader would only distract the male worshippers sexually, hampering their ability to concentrate.[172]

But despite all these heated responses to woman-led prayers, a significant number of which were personal attacks levelled against Wadud's character, what bothered her the most was the problematic attitude of progressive Muslim men who supported her leadership of the prayers. For far more attention was being paid, she laments, to the wonderful fact that a woman was finally giving the sermon (the form) rather than what that human being was actually saying at the pulpit (the substance).[173] Reflecting on the South African sermon, Wadud recounts that she was informed that she would speak less than an hour before the prayer and that flyers, as she would later find out, had been circulated before her arrival in Cape Town.[174] The substantive message of the lecture, then, was clearly not a priority for the organizers. She sums up her grievances as follows:

> the planners were thinking and acting like men in exclusion of women's full humanity, while yet pretending to employ a woman as an agent of gender transformation. They were thinking *for* the woman, rendering

[168] Wadud, *Inside the Gender Jihad*, 166.
[169] For the full text of the Cape Town sermon, see ibid, 158–62.
[170] Esack, *Qur'an, Liberation, and Pluralism*, 246.
[171] For the full text of the New York City sermon, see Wadud, *Inside the Gender Jihad*, 249–52.
[172] Ibid, 222.   [173] Wadud, Interview 2009.
[174] Wadud, *Inside the Gender Jihad*, 167–8.

her a mere object of their privileged agency. How can a woman be a full
and equal human being when the details of her public role are orches-
trated without her consultation? . . . informing me at the last minute
also indicates that very little value was attributed to the content of my
actual *khutba* [sermon]. This event was about form.[175]

In other words, in order for women to become meaningful leaders in
ritual worship—rather than simply being tokens pushed to the fore by
progressive men—not only must the substance of their religious
discourses be taken as seriously as the form (or the fact that a female
is delivering the sermon and leading the prayer) but women themselves need to play the chief role in planning and executing these
gender-inclusive activities.[176]

This brings us to the complex question of male solidarity: that is,
how can progressive men stand alongside women and partake in the
struggle against patriarchy? When I posed this question to Wadud in
our interview, she responded:

> The thing is that women have to be able to speak for themselves, even if
> they don't speak sufficiently at first. I mean they have to. So what
> happens? What's the role of men? The role of men is to inform
> themselves and then to advocate on behalf of gender justice with *other
> men*. That's the biggest role that they can do. . . . If men are together and
> other men make condescending statements about women, that's what
> men can do. But it's not that you speak for women.[177] [My italics]

So in order to avoid (mis)representing women and reproducing
gender inequality in the very struggle against patriarchy—such as
that of progressive men speaking over the voices of women, whether
these women are progressive, conservative, or otherwise—men need
to combat gender asymmetry within specifically male spaces. In
forwarding this argument, Wadud draws upon the ideas of the

---

[175] Ibid, 172. It is perhaps precisely because of the effective silencing of her voice at, ironically, the very moment that she spoke that Wadud includes the full texts of the South African and New York City sermons in her second book, *Inside the Gender Jihad*.

[176] For a critical feminist perspective on woman-led prayer in Islam, arguing that simply placing women at the helm of a hierarchal and exclusionary liturgical structure is insufficient, especially in terms of fostering inclusivity and community, see: Shadaab Rahemtulla, 'Toward a Genuine Congregation: The Form of the Muslim Friday Prayer, Revisited', in *Only One is Holy: Liturgy in Postcolonial Perspectives,* ed. Cláudio Carvalhaes (New York: Palgrave Macmillan, 2015).

[177] Wadud, Interview 2009.

Black American revolutionary Malcolm X and his stance on White solidarity,[178] summed up in his famous autobiography as follows:

What *can* a sincere white person do? When I say that here now, it makes me think about that [White] little co-ed [college student] I told you about, the one who flew from her New England college down to New York and came up to me in the Nation of Islam's restaurant in Harlem [asking how can a White person contribute to the struggle against racism?], and I told her that there was 'nothing' she could do. I regret that I told her that.... The first thing I tell them [White people] is that at least where my own particular Black nationalist organization, the Organization of Afro-American Unity, is concerned, they can't *join* us.... Where the really sincere white people have got to do their 'proving' of themselves is not among the black *victims*, but out on the battle lines of where America's racism really *is*—and that's in their own home communities. American racism is among their own fellow whites. That's where the sincere whites who really mean to accomplish something have got to work.[179]

Wadud's discourse on gender segregation, then, is a nuanced one. Whereas earlier on this chapter showed how she used the Qur'an to critique forced female seclusion, here she embraces segregation as not only a strategy to pre-empt the formation of patriarchal hierarchies that typify mixed gender spaces, but also as a means of enabling women to meet and work with other women, exchanging one another's experiences and struggles.[180] This is not to suggest, however, that she is dismissive of the commitments of progressive men. In fact, Wadud attributes the origins of her decades-long work on Islam and gender justice to the inspirational figure of her late father: a poor,

---

[178] Ibid.
[179] Malcolm X and Alex Haley, *The Autobiography of Malcolm X* (London: Penguin, 2001), 494–5.
[180] Wadud, Interview 2009. Although Wadud does not explicitly situate herself within a wider theoretical discourse here, it is important to note that separatism has a long history in feminist thought, particularly as a political strategy, as a short-term move in order for women to empower themselves collectively before re-entering patriarchal, gender-mixed spaces. On feminist separatism, see Dana R. Shugar, *Separatism and Women's Community* (Lincoln, Nebraska: University of Nebraska Press, 1995) and Marilyn Frye, 'Some Reflections on Separatism and Power', in *Feminist Social Thought: A Reader*, ed. Diana T. Meyers (London: Routledge, 1997). As the above quotation from Malcolm X suggests, separatism as a tool of empowerment also has deep roots in African American intellectual and social history. For an excellent, though admittedly dated, reference work on this body of literature, see Betty C. Jenkins and Susan Phillis, *Black Separatism: A Bibliography* (Westport, Connecticut: Greenwood Press, 1976).

Black Methodist minister who, despite overwhelming odds, strove tirelessly to provide for his family.[181] Moreover, it is important to note that while she sharply criticizes the gender dynamics of the South African sermon, she also salutes the courage of the male organizers, acknowledging that this event would not have been possible without their support.[182] Rather, the point that Wadud is driving home here is that social struggle requires the self-representation of the oppressed and because women alone are the owners of their experiences—lived realities that can only be understood and explained by women—it is paramount that they speak for themselves.[183]

Paradigms of Struggle: Tawhid and Khilafa

The conceptualization and development of theological paradigms that address women's suffering is an integral component of such self-representation. While Esack and Engineer focus on the Exodus and the Battle of Karbala, respectively, as hermeneutical models of liberation, Wadud reflects upon the Qur'anic concept of *tawhid*: the centrepiece of Islamic theology, referring to the absolute Oneness and Unity of God. Echoing Shari'ati, whose liberating exegesis of *tawhid* was discussed earlier in this book, Wadud argues that *tawhid* is not simply faith in a single, undivided deity, but also an ethical commitment to translating this monotheistic belief into the mundane realm, creating a single, undivided society. To quote her words:

> As an ethical term, *tawhid* relates to relationships and developments within the social and political realm, emphasizing the unity of all human creatures beneath one Creator. If experienced as a reality in everyday Islamic terms, humanity would be a single global community without distinction for reasons of race, class, gender, religious tradition, national origin, sexual orientation or other arbitrary, voluntary, and involuntary aspects of human distinction. Their only distinction would be on the basis of *taqwa*.[184]

---

[181] Wadud, *Inside the Gender Jihad*, 4.   [182] Ibid, 179.
[183] Wadud, 'Sisters in Islam', 131.
[184] Wadud, *Inside the Gender Jihad*, 28. While this text was published in 2006, it is worthwhile noting that an earlier articulation of *tawhid* as a socially liberating paradigm can be found in Amina Wadud, "An Islamic Perspective on Civil Rights Issues," in *Religion, Race, and Justice in a Changing America*, eds. Gary Orfield and Holly Lebowitz (New York: Century Foundation Press, 1999), 155–6.

The unity of God, then, has direct sociopolitical, economic, and gendered implications. To put it another way: divine unity is more than a state, a stable noun but also a dynamic verb with lasting social effects, for God is not only 'united', but *unites all things*.[185] Furthermore, in this radically revamped society built on the unity of the creation, one's worth is not determined by socioeconomic standing, gender affiliation, or racial identity, but rather solely by *taqwa* (piety). Yet although the unity of God is a divine characteristic that Muslims ought to emulate, this deity is also, at the same time, utterly unique. Citing Q. 42:11—'Nothing is like Him'—Wadud juxtaposes this *singularity* of the Creator with the *duality* of the creation (discussed earlier in this chapter), arguing that God is beyond any partner and thus forever unpaired: One.[186] And it is precisely when men seek to pair themselves and their experiences with God, such as by portraying God as a male being exhibiting masculine qualities, that the tenet of *tawhid* is effectively violated.[187] It is difficult to overemphasize the centrality of *tawhid* in Wadud's Islamic discourse. In fact, she even describes the interpretive method of her gendered exegesis—that is, of reading the Qur'an as a coherent whole, extracting wider principles from the text—through this very language of divine unity, calling her holistic approach a 'hermeneutics of *tawhid*'.[188] So the unity of God is reflected, too, in the unity of the Word. Thus, Muslims throughout the world, from Iran to South Africa to America, have drawn upon *tawhid* in multiple contexts of oppression.[189] But in terms of its

[185] Amina Wadud, 'Foreword: Engaging *Tawhid* in Islams and Feminisms', *International Feminist Journal of Politics* 10:4 (2008): 437. My italics.

[186] Wadud, *Qur'an and Woman*, 25–6; Wadud, 'The Ethics of *Tawhid* over the Ethics of *Qiwamah*', 266.

[187] Wadud, *Inside the Gender Jihad*, 81.

[188] Wadud, *Qur'an and Woman*, xii.

[189] It is interesting to note that Malcolm X also saw society through the prism of *tawhid*. In 1964, he undertook his famous pilgrimage to Mecca. Deeply moved by the camaraderie shared between Muslims of different racial backgrounds, Malcolm began to make links between the political implications of *tawhid* and his own struggle against White racism. Consider the following excerpts from his autobiography: 'All ate as One, and slept as One. Everything about the pilgrimage atmosphere accented the Oneness of Man under One God'; 'I could see from this [pilgrimage experience], that perhaps if white Americans could accept the Oneness of God, then perhaps, too, they could accept *in reality* the Oneness of Man—and cease to measure, and hinder, and harm others in terms of their "differences" in color; 'About twenty of us Muslims who had finished the Hajj were sitting in a huge tent on Mount Arafat. As a Muslim from America, I was the center of attention . . . They asked me what about the Hajj had impressed me the most . . . I said, "The *brotherhood*! The people of all races,

systematic, scholarly exposition, gender activists have been at the forefront of this hermeneutical project. Like Wadud, Barlas, as will be seen in the next chapter, has reflected extensively upon this key Islamic tenet. Paralleling Wadud's critique of mainstream, masculine projections of the divine, Barlas argues that because God's 'sovereignty' is indivisible and thus God's domain alone, attempts by men to impinge on this sovereignty, such as by acting as mediators between the divine and the rest of humanity, undermines *tawhid*.[190]

In addition to Islamic monotheism, Wadud also reinterprets the Islamic concept of *khilafa*, or trusteeship. Whereas Engineer's interest in the Battle of Karbala reflects his religious background as a Shi'a Muslim, her hermeneutical emphasis on *khilafa* (though not necessarily as a conscious move) speaks to her own sectarian affiliation as a Sunni Muslim. Historically understood as caliphate, *khilafa* became an enduring Sunni institution of political leadership following the Prophet's death. Referring to Q. 2:30, she brings this term back to its scriptural origins.[191] The verse, alluding to a primordial time before humankind's creation, reads:

> When your Sustainer said to the angels, 'Indeed, I am going to create a trustee (*khalifatun*) on the earth,' they said, 'Will You set in it one who will create corruption, and shed blood, while we celebrate Your praise and proclaim Your sanctity?' He said, 'Indeed, I know what you do not know.'

The purpose of humanity, Wadud concludes, is thus to function as a trustee, a vicegerent of the Creator on the Earth.[192] This duty is first and foremost an ethical one, in which the trustee—or, to use another definition that she forwards, 'moral agent'[193]—has the solemn responsibility to uphold divine justice,[194] to ensure that the unity of God, with all its sociopolitical ramifications, remains intact. She further argues that in the context of the contemporary world, characterized by the emergence of the nation-state as the hegemonic form of societal organization, a parallel can be drawn between *khilafa* and

colors, from all over the world coming together as *one!* It has proved to me the power of the One God."' See Malcolm X and Haley, 443; 455; and 452, respectively.

[190] Barlas, *'Believing Women' in Islam*, 13–14.
[191] This verse on *khilafa* is incorrectly cited as Q. 2:38 in Wadud, 'Towards a Qur'anic Hermeneutics of Social Justice', 48.
[192] Ibid.
[193] Wadud, *Inside the Gender Jihad*, 33.   [194] Ibid, 35.

an active, engaged citizenship.[195] In order to carry out one's role as
moral agent, therefore, one needs, as a citizen, to make use of all the
resources and avenues that civil society has to offer.[196] Citing
Q. 33:72, Wadud points out that humankind wilfully accepted this
role as trustee, thereby entering into a sacred covenant with their
Creator.[197] The verse reads:

> Indeed, We presented the Trust to the heavens and the earth and the
> mountains, but they refused to bear it, and were apprehensive of it; but
> the human being undertook it. Indeed, he has been an oppressor and
> ignorant.

Yet humankind has not only failed to live up to its role as trustee by
spreading suffering on the Earth, but also by hampering the ability of
fellow human beings to fulfil this divinely sanctioned purpose, such as
when men silence women's voices by claiming that women's voices
are taboo (*'awra*), and thus not to be heard.[198] In emphasizing
humankind's role as *khalifa*, Wadud echoes the earlier exegetical
work of Hassan, who has shown that biblical concepts like the Fall
and original sin—and, by extension, the idea of being redeemed and
saved—are non-existent in the Qur'an, as the Earth was understood
right from the very beginning as being the principal abode in which
the human being, as trustee of God, would dwell.[199]

JUSTICE FOR ALL

Liberation for Whom?

While the struggle for gender justice clearly lies at the core of
Wadud's liberationist discourse, she acknowledges the complexity
of human suffering, calling for a comprehensive approach to justice.
Because women are marginalized, if not excluded altogether, from
most articulations of social justice and of what constitutes a normative, egalitarian order,[200] she is acutely aware of the importance of

[195] Amina Wadud, 'Citizenship and Faith', in *Women and Citizenship*, ed. Marilyn
Friedman (Oxford: Oxford University Press, 2005), 170.
[196] Ibid, 186–7.   [197] Wadud, *Inside the Gender Jihad*, 35.
[198] Barlas, 'Amina Wadud's Hermeneutics of the Qur'an', 105.
[199] Hassan, 'An Islamic Perspective', 106–7.
[200] Wadud, 'Towards a Qur'anic Hermeneutics of Social Justice', 37.

making connections between different forms of oppression. She notes, for example, that even Qur'anic commentators who argue that the text seeks to establish justice have continued, rather paradoxically, to issue highly patriarchal interpretations of verses dealing with women, reflecting the striking absence of gender in their understandings of justice.[201] Liberation, then, has to be a genuinely inclusive commitment, embracing everyone's experiences. But just as Wadud has been left out of androcentric constructions of justice, she has also felt excluded, as a poor Black woman, from feminist discourses headed by wealthy White women.[202] Indeed, because the lives of African American women have been shaped primarily by the realities of racism, they have sharply criticized the feminist movement for failing to take their experiences into account.[203] Fleshing out this critique, Black women pioneered womanism and womanist theology as alternative liberationist discourses that acknowledged the key differences that exist between women, thinking holistically through questions of race, class, and gender.[204] Indeed, it is precisely because of the historic exclusion of Black women, as well as women based in the Third World, from the predominantly secular project of Western feminism that Wadud is wary of identifying as a feminist, situating herself instead as 'pro-faith, pro-feminist'.[205] This emphasis on the 'pro-faith agenda'[206] of her work, moreover, underscores her conviction in the compatibility of Islam and women's rights, thereby transcending the polarized positions of secular Muslim feminists and Islamist women: the former claiming that religion is an obstacle to women's liberation and the latter maintaining that Western discourses of human rights are alien to the faith and, thus, un-Islamic.[207]

Before embarking on an exploration of Wadud's perspectives on justice beyond gender, however, it is important to note that her treatment of gender *itself* reflects a comprehensive commitment to liberation. Unlike Engineer, Wadud does not restrict her gender discourse to the problems of (heterosexual) women alone, standing in solidarity with LGBTQ Muslims. Being heterosexual, she situates

---

[201] Wadud, *Qur'an and Woman*, 35–6.
[202] Wadud, *Inside the Gender Jihad*, 80.   [203] McCloud, 146.
[204] Mary Grey, 'Feminist Theology: A Critical Theology of Liberation', in *The Cambridge Companion to Liberation Theology*, ed. Christopher Rowland (Cambridge: Cambridge University Press, 2007), 111.
[205] Wadud, *Inside the Gender Jihad*, 79–80.
[206] Wadud, 'Sisters in Islam', 118.
[207] Wadud, 'The Ethics of *Tawhid* over the Ethics of *Qiwamah*', 262–3.

herself as an 'ally', drawing a parallel between how men can stand in solidarity with women—discussed earlier in this chapter—and how heterosexuals can be in solidarity with homosexuals.[208] For just as progressive men, in patriarchal contexts, need to challenge men who are sexist (as opposed to speaking for women) so must progressive heterosexuals, in heteronormative settings, confront fellow heterosexuals who are homophobic.[209] In our interview, Wadud pointed to her role as a teacher in the university classroom. In addition to addressing homophobic comments, she makes a concerted effort to integrate examples relating to homosexuality into her teaching, thereby undercutting heteronormativity.[210] But being an ally does not mean that one is uncritical. Wadud criticizes the discourse of homosexual Muslims for being androcentric, foregrounding the diverse sexualities of men.[211] As a result, the lived experiences and subjectivities of lesbian Muslims remain marginalized.

On Race and Religious Pluralism

As has been shown at numerous points in this chapter, issues of race permeate Wadud's writings. In fact, race is arguably the most crucial aspect of her analysis after gender. Looking back at her early life, she records how Blackness became an inseparable part of her identity, especially during the final three years of high school. Recall that at the age of fourteen, Wadud left Washington, DC, to attend a reputed high school in an all-White suburb of Boston, living with different families.[212] She vividly recounts her conflicted experience at this institution, being one of only two Black students:

> I was a black female. During those years I was never for a moment allowed to let my Blackness escape me. Aspects of my color and ethnicity were the points of entry and exit into many facets of my high school life. Privileges were given to me or withheld from me because of my race. In my first semester, I refused to stand for the pledge of allegiance. I was permitted to make my protest, but not to enter the classroom. So, for three years, I spent homeroom period wandering the halls. I was allowed to do this—although no one else

---

[208] Wadud, Interview 2009.   [209] Ibid.   [210] Ibid.
[211] Wadud, *Inside the Gender Jihad*, 86.
[212] Wadud, Interview 2009.

ever was. . . . I was even excused from dissecting a frog on the day that Martin Luther King was shot. None of these favors were permitted to white students. In each case the affirmation was only that one set of rules applied for the whites and another set applied for me. No one ever knew that I simply didn't want to dissect the frog. . . . Being Black was a special prize and a unique curse. My first highschool crush told me he couldn't kiss me because I was Black. I had no boyfriends because I was Black, or I had them out of curiosity or pity because I was Black. In short, at no juncture was I to forget that I was Black. So I never forgot.[213]

Though she had grown up in mostly Coloured spaces, it was, interestingly, with her entry into a predominantly White setting that her racial consciousness heightened.[214] This emerging sense of ethnic identity was intensified, moreover, by the wider American context: namely, the civil rights struggle—as the above passage notes, Martin Luther King Jr was assassinated during her senior years—and, more significantly, the rise of the Black Power movement.[215]

And just as with gender, Wadud brings her racial background to the interpretation of the Qur'an. Reflecting upon Q. 49:11–13, she argues that while the text acknowledges the differences that exist between various communities, it never uses these differences as a measure of human worth.[216] The passage reads:

O you who believe! Let not any people deride another people: it may be that they are better than they are; nor let women (deride) other women: it may be that they are better than they are . . . O humankind! We created you from a male and a female, and made you into nations and tribes that you may know one another. The noblest among you in the eyes of God are the most pious (*atqakum*) among you.

So whereas she drew upon the first part of Q. 49:13 when reading through the lens of gender justice—'We created you from a male and a female'—here she focuses on the latter part of this verse, referring to God creating 'nations and tribes' so that they may recognize one another. Furthermore, just as with the case of gender, it is *taqwa*, appearing in this passage in the superlative form (*atqakum*: literally, the most God-conscious among you), that becomes the central

[213] Wadud, 'On Belonging as a Muslim Woman', 259.
[214] Ibid.   [215] Wadud, Interview 2009.
[216] Amina Wadud, 'American Muslim Identity: Race and Ethnicity in Progressive Islam', in *Progressive Muslims: On Justice, Gender, and Pluralism*, ed. Omid Safi (Oxford: Oneworld, 2003), 274.

criterion with which God will render judgement.[217] But while White racism has undoubtedly played a formative role on Wadud's hermeneutic, it is important to note that the brunt of her critiques, at least insofar as race relations *within* the American Muslim community are concerned, centre on Arab and South Asian Muslim immigrants who, due to their superior socioeconomic standing in comparison to their African American coreligionists, have monopolized leadership and public representation roles within the American Muslim community.[218] Indeed, Wadud laments that the attacks of 9/11 have reinforced the misled notion that 'Islam in America is only the Islam of foreigners',[219] thereby rendering Black Muslims even more invisible.

Wadud also embraces questions of religious pluralism. Like Esack and Engineer, she is wary of exclusivist Islamic discourses that claim to *own* God, countering that Muslims constitute one of numerous faith communities that have been recipients of divine revelation.[220] As she put it in her Friday sermon in New York City in 2005:

> There is no chosen people, exclusive members of one of the world's many religions—some no longer in existence—some so widespread by numbers and powers that they look upon themselves as exclusively 'the chosen.' The 'chosen' are all of humanity.[221]

There can be little doubt that her emphasis on the transcendence of God, underscoring the chosen-ness of all people as opposed to solely Muslims, is a direct result of her own diverse religious background, being born into a devoutly Christian household, living for a year as a Buddhist, and, finally, converting to Islam.[222] This deeply enriching experience enabled her to appreciate the intrinsic value of different faiths, to acknowledge the plurality of divine disclosure. Wadud's

---

[217] Ibid.   [218] Ibid, 271–2.
[219] Amina Wadud, 'American by Force, Muslim by Choice', *Political Theology* 12:5 (2011): 701.
[220] Wadud, *Inside the Gender Jihad*, 207. For an innovative work that engages the religious Other by drawing on the hermeneutical insights of women's gender egalitarian Qur'anic readings, see Jerusha T. Lamptey, *Never Wholly Other: A Muslima Theology of Religious Pluralism* (Oxford: Oxford University Press, 2014). The Islamic scholar Adis Duderija has also analysed gender and religious difference in contemporary Islam, focussing on how one's interpretive methodology can lead to radically different understandings of a paradigmatic believer and woman. See Adis Duderija, *Constructing a Religiously Ideal 'Believer' and 'Woman' in Islam: Neo-traditional Salafi and Progressive Muslims' Methods of Interpretation* (New York: Palgrave Macmillan, 2011).
[221] Wadud, *Inside the Gender Jihad*, 207.   [222] Ibid, 62.

writings on religious pluralism also delve into apologetics, however. Her commentary on polytheism is an illustrative example:

> ... polytheism in Qur'anic discourse did not include any direct references to Hindu or African traditional religious polytheism, which have both the concept of numerous gods as well as the concept of the sacred as Ultimate.... There are no animists, believers in the sacred manifestations throughout creation, as in many indigenous traditions, like native African, Australian, and North and South American pre- and post-Qur'anic traditions. These are not directly spoken to in the Qur'an. Furthermore, all forms of Buddhism, Taoism, and Confucianism, with unembodied or non-personified concepts of the sacred, were excluded from Qur'anic discussions of faith or religion, despite their existence prior to the seventh century in other parts of the globe.[223]

But since the Qur'an spoke to a specific context, addressing the religious communities and practices that were immediately present in that time and place—precisely the reason why Jews and Christians, in addition to polytheists, are mentioned—is it persuasive to reason that just because other faith traditions are not discussed that they are, therefore, outside the fold of the text's discourse on monotheism? For the Qur'an puts forth a *principle* with regard to belief: namely, that of not associating any partners with God, thereby undermining the unity of the Creator. Particular manifestations of such divine association, then, are contingent upon different historical contexts. Given Wadud's hermeneutical emphasis on principles over particulars, it is surprising that here she focuses on particulars, shying away from making broader generalizations on polytheism.

With regard to Wadud's approach to religious pluralism, two points of clarification are in order. Firstly, although religious pluralism plays a role in Wadud's thinking, it is squarely secondary to that of racial justice. If the two are in conflict, the latter takes precedence. This prioritization of race is vividly illustrated in a roundtable discussion in which Wadud participated, entitled 'Feminist Theology and Religious Diversity'.[224] The roundtable addressed the Christian-centricness of feminist theology and included respondents from Jewish, Buddhist, and Muslim backgrounds. Rita Gross—a White American Buddhist theologian—set the stage for discussion by contributing

---

[223] Ibid, 194–5.
[224] Rita Gross ed., 'Roundtable Discussion: Feminist Theology and Religious Diversity', *Journal of Feminist Studies in Religion* 16:2 (2000): 73–131.

the opening article, reflecting on her own experiences as a non-Christian scholar in feminist theological circles. For Gross, a key problem is that discussions of diversity have largely revolved around diversity within Christianity:

> When I have pointed out that some of us are not Christians and that religious diversity, not just intra-Christian diversity, needs to be on the agenda, my comments have been repeatedly ignored. As soon as I would finish speaking, people would return to the topic of intra-Christian diversity and complain that not enough non-white Christian feminist theologians were in the group.[225]

Wadud responds with a pointed criticism of how 'diversity' is being framed, unearthing the racial privilege that underlies Gross' grievances:

> For anyone to espouse an enlightened expression about the use of the term diversity, she must first accept the necessity to annihilate all forms of white supremacy. I will not accept to coordinate my efforts with any white feminist—for whatever reasons of her own personal experiences of marginalization—who chooses to ignore this reality of race.[226]

In other words, why should the inclusion of non-Christians, in particular White non-Christians, into Christian feminist circles be privileged over the inclusion of Black and other Coloured Christians into these very circles? Is racial diversity, even within Christian contexts, less significant than interreligious diversity? Indeed, in this roundtable Wadud (despite her non-Christian faith) sides with her excluded Christian sisters of colour,[227] that is, she privileges racial diversity over interreligious diversity. Yet, as she herself observes, Christian-centricness *is* a problem in feminist theology.[228] So how can this be addressed while still paying due attention to pressing questions of race? She resolves this puzzle by switching her interlocutor altogether, speaking to *Coloured* Christian feminist theologians. Here, Wadud challenges the hegemony of Black Christian feminist thought and experience over womanist theology and how, for example, Islam's historic role in Black religion is routinely ignored.[229] What is necessary, then, is greater interreligious diversity within

[225] Rita Gross, 'Feminist Theology: Religiously Diverse Neighbourhood or Christian Ghetto?', *Journal of Feminist Studies in Religion* 16:2 (2000): 73.
[226] Amina Wadud, 'Roundtable Discussion: Feminist Theology and Religious Diversity', *Journal of Feminist Studies in Religion* 16:2 (2000): 92.
[227] Ibid.   [228] Ibid, 90.   [229] Ibid, 95–6.

feminist theologies of colour, which hitherto have been Christian dominated.

The second point of clarification is that, in terms of religious pluralism, Wadud's primary interest is not in Muslim/non-Muslim relations—interreligious pluralism—but rather in the interfaith dynamics that exist within the Muslim community, that is, intrareligious pluralism. Referring to Q. 2:256, 'There is no compulsion in religion', she argues that not only is entry into Islam a purely personal decision that cannot be forced upon anyone but so, too, is a Muslim's decision to leave the faith—a right that is severely undermined by the punishment of death for apostasy, as outlined in the *shari'a*.[230] This accusation of apostasy, of being outside the pale of Islam, is used not only to ensure that Muslims remain Muslims but also as a powerful tool to silence alternative religious voices within the community.[231] Indeed, Wadud herself, as a highly controversial figure amongst mainstream Muslims, has been constantly accused of being non-Muslim, even an enemy of Islam. A YouTube video that covered aspects of the 2005 Friday Prayer in New York City captures the deeply controversial (and marginal) nature of this event within the wider Muslim community, showing an angry group of Muslims protesting outside the prayer venue—a church, the Episcopal Cathedral of St. John the Divine—amongst them a man holding a placard that read: 'Ameena Wadud [*sic*] is not a Muslim according to the Qur'an and Sunnah.'[232] Fostering an inclusive atmosphere of interpretive pluralism within the community is crucial, therefore, in order to mainstream egalitarian interpretations of Islam, especially in terms of gender justice.

Class and Global Politics: A Problematic Analysis

Along with race and religious pluralism, Wadud incorporates class into her thinking. As was already noted in the biographical sketch at the beginning of this chapter, her early life was marred by poverty.

---

[230] Wadud, *Inside the Gender Jihad*, 81–2. She incorrectly cites the verse as Q. 3:256—an obvious typographical error given that there are only two hundred verses in the third chapter.

[231] Ibid, 55–6.

[232] 'Female Imams—Morocco', *YouTube*, http://www.youtube.com/watch?v=Qgk5JFGUkRw accessed 22 September 2011.

Because her father was unable to pay the mortgage for their house in semirural Maryland—a home that he himself had built—the family was forced into homelessness.[233] She recounts this painful episode:

> For the next 2 weeks, we must have slept in my father's car . . . When school was out, my father built a trailer for us to stay in . . . Since we did not remain at any one place for more than a month, I suppose I knew that we did not belong . . . By the time the school year started [that is, when Wadud entered the sixth grade] my father had rented 2 rooms on the 3rd floor of someone else's house. But this time, we were in the city: Washington, DC. We lived in these 2 rooms for 1 year.[234]

This formative experience has had a lasting impact on the way in which Wadud interprets scripture. Referring again to Q. 49:13—'O humankind! We created you from a male and a female, and made you into nations and tribes that you may know one another. The noblest among you in the eyes of God are the most pious among you'—she argues that by looking solely at piety (*taqwa*), God refuses to differentiate between human beings on the basis of wealth.[235] The affluent and the poor, then, are to be treated the same. And it is here that a notable difference emerges between Wadud's and Esack's readings, as the former is less radical than the latter. Esack, referring to the Exodus, maintains that God makes a 'preferential option' for the marginalized. He cites (among other verses) Q. 28:5,[236] which reads: 'It is Our Will to bestow Our grace upon the downtrodden of the Earth, and to make them the leaders and to make them the inheritors of the Earth.' In other words, this is a divine being that *does* take material realities into account. To put it another way: the affluent and the poor are not to be treated the same. According to the preferential option for the oppressed—a hallmark of liberation theology—a just deity, in a context of manifest inequality, cannot remain a neutral broker but rather must take sides, standing in solidarity with the poor against the wealthy. Indeed, in our interview Wadud explicitly refused to identify as a liberation theologian, underscoring two points: firstly, that while liberation theology has great value to the extent that it addresses oppression—that is, as a means to transition out of states of injustice—it has little to say beyond these oppressive contexts, and,

---

[233] Wadud, 'On Belonging as a Muslim Woman', 255.
[234] Ibid, 255-6.   [235] Wadud, *Qur'an and Woman*, 36-7.
[236] Esack, *Qur'an, Liberation, and Pluralism*, 98-9. Esack also cites Q. 7:136-7.

secondly, that she wants to situate herself within a more organic Qur'anic framework (as opposed to adopting an approach that emerged external to the text and Islam in general) and, thus, prefers to identify as a 'tawhidist'.[237]

It is in the realm of global politics, however, that Wadud's discourse on poverty is problematic. She is explicit about the evils of capitalism and consumerism, which she refers to as capitalism's 'bastard child', criticizing a cruel economy whereby massive numbers of people are being impoverished, particularly women and children.[238] At the same time, a tiny fraction of the world's population is enjoying increasingly lavish and wasteful lifestyles, driven by the market and fuelled by mass consumption.[239] To evidence her argument, Wadud provides statistics from the 1998 U.N.D.P. Human Development Report, showing that the wealthiest 20 per cent of the world's population consume a whopping 86 per cent of private consumption expenditure while the poorest fifth account for a meagre 1.3 per cent.[240] Yet after suggesting a critical linkage between the affluence of the few and the deprivation of the many—the implication clearly being that the sin of structural poverty can only be alleviated through a far-reaching, systematic redistribution of global wealth—she makes the following conclusion: 'We have the means to not only eradicate poverty but also to do so without depriving the well to do from experiencing extreme luxury and privilege.'[241] Constituting a glaring contradiction in an otherwise politically progressive discourse, this statement betrays wider inconsistencies in Wadud's approach to global politics.

Her writings on 9/11 are a compelling case in point. Radical Muslims like Esack have highlighted the political economy of 9/11, arguing that this event cannot be disentangled from the oppressive web of global inequalities sustained by American imperialism, as shown, for instance, by the rejoicing of people not only in the Muslim world but also in other parts of the South like Brazil and China.[242] To be sure, Wadud notes that 9/11 has forced Americans to wake up, to

[237] Wadud, Interview 2009.   [238] Wadud, *Inside the Gender Jihad*, 136–7.
[239] Ibid, 137.
[240] Ibid, 267. For the original report, see 'Human Development Report 1998', *United Nations Development Program*, available at: http://hdr.undp.org/en/reports/global/hdr1998/ accessed 23 September 2012.
[241] Wadud, *Inside the Gender Jihad*, 267.
[242] Esack, 'In Search of Progressive Islam Beyond 9/11', 94.

acknowledge the dire consequences of their quest for world dominance.[243] Yet despite her critique of US hegemony, she plays into
ideologically loaded language surrounding 9/11: namely, the juxtaposition of the good Muslim, who is peaceful, loving, and acquiescent,
with the bad Muslim, who is angry, violent, and virulently anti-
American.[244] The following passage reveals this dichotomous construction in her writings:

> Islam is not a monolith. It has a plethora of meanings and experiences . . .
> Indeed, just as Americans were presented with a horrible affront to their
> sense of integrity and security by the event of Sept. 11, 2001, when a dozen
> or so Muslim men laid claim to "Islam" as justification for their vehemence
> and violence, so too are babies born and women and men surrender in
> peace and harmony to a claim of 'Islam.' Which is the truer picture, the face
> of evil and destruction or the face of love and life? . . . while I do not identify
> with suicide bombers or acts of violence, I cannot ignore that they occur
> within the ranks of that vast community of Islam.[245]

While Wadud avoids the liberal Muslim trap of essentializing Islam—
one that, as was seen in the third chapter, Engineer falls into—
acknowledging that there are both peaceful and militant interpretations
of the faith, she reduces a highly politicized and symbolic event to
mere religious fanaticism, contrasting 'the face of evil and destruction'
(the bad Muslim) with 'the face of love and life' (the good Muslim). She
even uses the sweeping term 'the terrorists' to refer to the attackers,
arguing that so long as Americans continue to live in a state of fear and
alarm, as exhibited, for example, by increased security measures at
airports, 'the terrorists have won'.[246]
   A particularly curious aspect of Wadud's discourse on 9/11 is her
portrayal of this event as an expression of patriarchy in Muslim
societies. She states that 'men perpetrated these events in response
to actions men exclusively had decided upon, planned and orches-
trated', concluding that 'men make war while women and children
are victims as well as other men.'[247] Such statements problematically

<hr>

[243] Wadud, *Inside the Gender Jihad*, 224.
[244] For a seminal study of the emergence of this 'Good Muslim/Bad Muslim'
paradigm and its usage in American foreign policy, see Mahmood Mamdani, *Good
Muslim, Bad Muslim: America, the Cold War, and the Roots of Terror* (New York:
Pantheon Books, 2004).
[245] Wadud, *Inside the Gender Jihad*, 5.
[246] Wadud, 'American by Force, Muslim by Choice', 701.
[247] Wadud, *Inside the Gender Jihad*, 228.

presuppose that women themselves do not partake in violence, whether it be through imperialist wars waged by women in the global North to purportedly save Muslim women in the South or militant resistance in which women take up arms alongside men in order to defend their lands and families. Indeed, women have historically been, and continue to be, active participants in militant struggle, especially in nationalist resistance against occupation. The Palestinian medical worker Wafa Idris (d. 2002) is a noteworthy example. During the Second Intifada, she became the first female suicide bomber, and was followed in the same year by three other Palestinian women: namely, Dareen Abu Aisheh, Ayat Akhras, and Andaleeb Takatkeh.[248]

In order to appreciate my critique of Wadud's discourse on 9/11, it is essential to examine the wider global context in which 9/11 occurred. *Messages to the World: The Statements of Osama bin Laden* (2005), edited by Bruce Lawrence and translated by James Howarth, is a collection of letters, transcribed speeches, interviews, and video recordings of Bin Laden between 1994 and 2004. Collectively, these texts demonstrate that the 9/11 attacks, while certainly being cloaked in the language of a militant Islam, were far from simply being religiously motivated. Rather, Bin Laden's grievances were primarily political. The US military's stationing in Saudi Arabia during the 1991 Gulf War—and thus being in close proximity to the two holy cities of Mecca and Medina—and the US-backed Israeli occupation of Palestine are two recurring themes in Bin Laden's discourse.[249] He condemns not only the 'aggressive Crusader–Jewish alliance', but also 'traitorous and cowardly Arab tyrants' for collaborating with this alliance.[250] Furthermore, Bin Laden laments the deaths of countless children in Iraq[251]—an outcome of UN-imposed sanctions—as well as atrocities committed against Muslims in general, including in Kashmir, the Philippines, Somalia, Chechnya, and Bosnia-Herzegovina.[252] Hence, confronting empire in the Muslim world, particularly American empire, lies at the heart of his militancy and it is within this broader framework that the attacks of 9/11 have

---

[248] For a perceptive study of these four female fighters and how they have represented themselves and been represented within the larger Arab world, see Frances S. Hasso, 'Discursive and Political Deployments by/of the 2002 Palestinian Suicide Bombers/Martyrs', *Feminist Review* 81 (2005): 23–51.

[249] Bruce Lawrence ed. and James Howarth trans. *Messages to the World: The Statements of Osama bin Laden* (London: Verso, 2005), 7–9.

[250] Ibid.   [251] Ibid, 104.   [252] Ibid, 25.

to be understood, symbolically targeting both the political and economic centres (Washington and New York City, respectively) of the present world order. Though Bin Laden does not take direct responsibility for the 9/11 attacks and emphasizes that his role was one of 'incitement',[253] that is, encouraging Muslims to engage in anti-American militancy, he points out that the USA has no moral authority to condemn the targeting of innocent civilians:

> It is very strange for Americans and other educated people to talk about the killing of innocent civilians. I mean, who said that our children and civilians are not innocents, and that the shedding of their blood is permissible? Whenever we kill their civilians, the whole world yells at us from east to west, and America starts putting pressure on its allies and puppets. Who said that our blood isn't blood and that their blood is blood? What about the people that have been killed in our lands for decades?[254]

Thus, it is deeply problematic and simplistic to portray the 9/11 attacks, with their manifestly political grievances and demands, as a 'face of evil and destruction' and to frame the attacks in gendered terms, as another expression of Muslim men's dominance over Muslim women.

Hagar: The Complexity of Oppression Embodied

Wadud's holistic approach to injustice is captured paradigmatically in the figure of Hagar. Indeed, Hagar has become a central, scriptural symbol for womanist theologians, who have discerned in the Black slave of Abraham a 'woman who is rejected on the grounds of race, sex and class, yet at the same time is the recipient of a divine revelation.'[255] In particular, Wadud sees in Hagar's abandonment in the desert and in her desperate efforts to locate water for her child the predicament of the 'homeless, single parent',[256] forced to provide for herself and her family in a classist, patriarchal society. In so doing, Wadud forges a direct hermeneutical link between Hagar's experiences and her own as a divorced, single mother.[257] Her focus on Hagar, moreover, is significant in terms of interpretive methodology. For while she privileges the Qur'an over other Islamic texts, Wadud's

253 Ibid, 108.   254 Ibid, 117.   255 Grey, 112.
256 Wadud, *Inside the Gender Jihad*, 143.
257 Wadud, Interview 2009.

writings on Hagar reveal her interest in engaging the *shari'a*. A key problem with Islamic law, she argues, is that it is 'premised upon an ideal of an extended family network',[258] thereby ignoring the lived realities of a growing number of Muslim women in general and of African American Muslim women in particular. The *shari'a*, then, needs to be reinterpreted in order to address the Hagar paradigm, to speak to situations in which women are the sole, financial providers of their families.[259] But Wadud's interest in Hagar not only reflects her willingness to engage the *shari'a*, but also the Qur'anic exegetical tradition. Whereas Hagar is discussed in the Old Testament (Genesis 16), she is actually never mentioned by name in the Qur'an. Rather, she is implicitly referred to in a supplication that Abraham makes shortly after leaving Hagar and Ishmael in the desert.[260] The prayer reads:

> When Abraham said, 'My Sustainer! Make this city [Mecca] a sanctuary, and save me and my children from worshipping idols. My Sustainer! Indeed they have misled many people. So whoever follows me indeed belongs to me, and as for someone who disobeys me, surely You are All-Forgiving, All-Merciful. Our Sustainer! I have settled part of my descendants in a barren valley by Your sacred house, our Sustainer, that they may maintain the prayer. So make the hearts of the people fond of them, and provide them with fruits, that they may give thanks. Our Sustainer! Indeed you know whatever we hide and whatever we disclose, and nothing in the earth or in the sky is hidden from God. All praise belongs to God, who, despite my old age, gave me Ishmael and Isaac. Indeed, my Sustainer hears all supplications. My Sustainer! Make me a maintainer of the prayer, and my descendents. Our Sustainer, accept my supplication. Our Sustainer! Forgive me, my parents and all the faithful on the day when the reckoning is done.' (Q. 14:35–41)

Hagar has made her way into Muslim memory, therefore, not through the Qur'an itself but rather through Qur'anic commentaries, which drew upon a number of unauthenticated prophetic reports and biblical traditions (*isra'iliyat*) in order to flesh out her story.[261] The following passage from the medieval commentator Isma'il ibn Kathir (d. 1373) is an illustrative example, depicting Hagar's deep, abiding faith in God:

> When he [Abraham] left the two of them there and turned his back on them, Hagar clung to his robes and said: 'Abraham, where are you

---

[258] Wadud, *Inside the Gender Jihad*, 144.
[259] Ibid, 144–5.   [260] Abugideiri, 83.   [261] Ibid.

going, leaving us here without means to stay alive?' He did not answer. When she insisted, he would still not answer. So she said: 'Did God command you to do this?' He said: 'Yes.' Then Hagar said: 'He will not let us perish.'[262]

So despite Wadud's critique of the Qur'anic exegetical tradition, her usage of the Hagar paradigm shows that she is prepared to draw upon this body of knowledge when doing so can further gender egalitarian understandings of Islam.

Walking the Walk: Justice as a Way of Life

The most crucial aspect of Wadud's comprehensive approach to justice, however, is the commitment to *live out* these principles in the private sphere. Citing Q. 61:2—'Why do you say that which you do not do?'—she writes that calling for equality in the public sphere is meaningless, even hypocritical, if such progressive discourses are not put into practice in one's personal life.[263] As she phrased it in our interview:

> it's like you live that consciousness. And in that sense that's where I think back to my father. I think my father lived his consciousness as much as you can for a poor, not very well educated man. I mean like sixth grade's top education for him. So to me it's the idea of walking the walk, not just talking the talk...Islam as *din* [literally, religion], as a way of life. Justice is a way of life. Justice is a relationship between yourself and between others inspired by your relationship with God, who created you. And so there's no public/private divide, where you can do all kinds of stuff in private as long as you look good in public.[264]

The organizational dynamics of SIS reflected this commitment to walk the walk, to harmonize progressive pronouncements in the public sphere with egalitarian practice in daily life. While numerous human rights organizations call for social justice and gender equality, their administrative structures, paradoxically, tend to be rigidly hierarchal. There is a critical disconnect, then, between the empowering public discourse of these movements and the unequal manner in which their members actually relate to one another. However, SIS,

[262] Isma'il ibn Kathir, as cited in Stowasser, 47.
[263] Wadud, *Inside the Gender Jihad*, 207.   [264] Wadud, Interview 2009.

at least during Wadud's time in Malaysia between 1989 and 1992, was acutely non-hierarchal in its organizational structure, operating without a chairperson, president, or executive committee—what Wadud describes as 'the standard male corporate lines'—as members, working purely as volunteers, interacted with each other as essentially equals.[265] In other words, SIS not only forwarded an inclusive discourse in the public sphere, supporting women's full participation in sociopolitical and religious life, but also strove to translate these egalitarian ideals into its everyday functioning, fostering a genuine culture of sisterhood between its members.

The family is the most important private space wherein professed commitments to social justice need to be lived out. The centrality of the family in Wadud's writings is captured in the acknowledgements of her second book, *Inside the Gender Jihad* (2006), in which she emphasizes the pivotal role that her children have played in her life. Despite her pioneering contributions to Islam and gender reform, or what she collectively refers to as 'work for Allah outside the home',[266] it is the efforts and sacrifices that she as a single mother has made for her family—work for Allah inside the home—that takes centre-stage, constituting the very 'foundation'[267] of her gender *jihad*. But it is precisely here, in contributing to familial tasks like housework and childcare, that Wadud discerns a disjuncture between the public discourses and private lives of progressively minded Muslim men. As she forcefully put it in our interview:

There's too much lip service. This is a disappointment that I had with actual persons who are considered reformist. And then you go [to his] home and the wife never comes out of the kitchen ... [or] ... they are married to traditional women or women who are not as well educated as themselves so they don't engage them intellectually at the same level that they do with other men or even women who are educated in the public space ... whatever it is, I'm not seeing, I'm not seeing families, where the progressive men are doing everything that they say that they are talking about in the public space. It's like, who are you talking for? Are you talking for your wife here? Are you saying that, oh yeah, well, I want it in the public space but at home, you know?[268]

---

[265] Wadud, *Inside the Gender Jihad*, 117–18. She notes, however, that SIS has since developed into a full-fledged NGO with an executive director and salaried workers and, thus, an institutionalized, hierarchal structure.

[266] Ibid, xvii.   [267] Ibid.

[268] Wadud, Interview 2009.

Simply put: just conduct is equally important in the public and private spheres.[269] In order to be truly committed to justice, men need to *value* housework, to appreciate the labour that women have historically undertaken inside the home. Men need to start seeing this work as being as valuable in the eyes of God as the work that is done outside the home—recalling Wadud's description of both as 'work for Allah'—and then to play an even share in that labour. The Qur'an, she points out, never describes domestic activities like child rearing as being an essential aspect of womanhood.[270] There is no scriptural mandate, then, for a gendered division of labour across public and private spaces, leaving the distribution of these tasks open to the possibilities of new contexts. Such an egalitarian arrangement within the family exemplifies what Wadud calls the principle of reciprocity (*mu'awadha*). For her, a reciprocal moral culture is the solution to patriarchy and its base assumption of a hierarchal relationship of domination between women and men, reconfiguring this relationship into one of 'partnership',[271] marked by equality, interdependence, and mutual responsibility.

CONCLUSIONS

Paralleling Esack's and Engineer's exegeses, Wadud focuses on the Qur'an as the principal, textual source of Islam. Because the text represents the Word of God, a clear distinction needs to be made between this Word and other Islamic sources like the exegetical tradition, which is often conflated with the Qur'an itself. This is particularly problematic given that men have dominated the field of Qur'anic commentary, inevitably leading to patriarchal understandings of the text. Women, therefore, need to partake in the exegetical enterprise, bringing their subjectivities, insights, and experiences to the task of interpretation. While Wadud treats the *hadith* literature as a primary source of Islam, she, like Esack and Engineer, is wary of the

---

[269] Amina Wadud, 'Islam beyond Patriarchy through Gender Inclusive Analysis', in *Wanted: Equality and Justice in the Muslim Family*, ed. Zainah Anwar (Petaling Jaya, Malaysia: Musawah, 2009), 98.

[270] Wadud, *Qur'an and Woman*, 22.

[271] Wadud, 'Islam beyond Patriarchy through Gender Inclusive Analysis', 101–2.

authenticity of numerous prophetic reports and warns that this highly disputed corpus needs to be approached through the framework of the Qur'an. She does not consider the *shari'a* to be a primary source of Islam. But despite this subordination of the *shari'a* to the Qur'anic Word, she argues that the legal tradition still needs to be engaged due to the legitimacy that it enjoys within Muslim societies, exerting an enormous influence on people's lives, especially women. In interpreting the Qur'an, Wadud draws upon Rahman's double movement theory, which seeks to extract ethical principles from the text and then apply these principles to contemporary contexts. However, as this interpretive method is based heavily on historical criticism, entailing an exhaustive and systematic study of the original context of revelation, it raises a larger question concerning religious authority: namely, how accessible is this mode of reading for everyday Muslims? It also raises questions about objectivity, for who gets to decide what constitutes a Qur'anic principle? Wadud's espousal of the double movement theory points to the importance of action in her Islamic discourse. For once timeless, ethical principles are derived from the text, they need to be practically applied to lived contexts of oppression. Wadud's involvement with SIS played a crucial role in allowing her to see how theoretical research could be meaningfully translated into concrete reforms through activism. Knowledge, then, must necessarily lead to action. And it is here that a key difference emerges between Wadud's and Esack's exegeses, for while the former's is a hermeneutic of application, the latter's is a hermeneutic of *praxis*. Because the experience of struggle sheds valuable insight into the Word of God, Esack argues, knowledge does not simply lead to action but action, too, effects new understandings. In other words, whereas Wadud's hermeneutic is more linear in nature, characterized by a general movement from knowledge *to* action, Esack's is more dialectical, marked by a continuous interplay *between* knowledge and action.

Wadud uses textual analysis and historical criticism extensively in her work, reflecting the centrality of these twin interpretive strategies in women's gender egalitarian exegesis, as they play less prominent a role in Esack's and Engineer's commentaries. Her emphasis on a careful, linguistic study of the Qur'an—showing exactly what the text says and, just as significantly, does not say—comes out most clearly in her reading of the beginning of time. Critiquing the entrenched notion among Muslims that Eve was created from

Adam's rib, she shows that this is actually a biblical narrative and that the Qur'anic text itself never mentions this story, describing man and woman as being created from a single soul. While she utilizes textual analysis when interpreting the origins of humankind, she employs historical criticism to grapple with androcentric descriptions of sexual pleasure in Paradise, arguing that such depictions spoke to understandings of beauty at the time of revelation and were thus shaped by the patriarchal realities of Meccan society. Moving into the here and now, Wadud uses textual analysis and historical criticism to tackle a number of women's issues, from polygamy and female seclusion to veiling and men's guardianship over women. Her interpretation of the opening of Q. 4:34 is a compelling example of the convergence of these two hermeneutical techniques. Examining the precise wording of the passage, she comments that it never makes any categorical claims of men's superiority over women, presupposing a marital arrangement in which the husband is the sole financial provider. Men's authority is thus conditional, presuming a societal context in which women are confined to the home. Therefore, in a radically different context wherein both partners are economically productive, such as in the present time, the husband would cease to function as guardian and authority would be shared equally between both partners. However, unlike Engineer, who portrays the Qur'an as a human rights document upholding complete gender equality, Wadud steers away from apologetics. For instance, she argues that however the last part of Q. 4:34 may be reinterpreted, such as it being a significant restriction on violence against women in seventh-century Arabia, she cannot accept any type of physical strike against women. In a similar move to Esack, who also acknowledges certain problems with the Qur'an, she negotiates this difficult verse by prioritizing the underlying, egalitarian spirit of the text over its literal letter.

A number of theological paradigms surface at various points in Wadud's writings. Whereas Esack and Engineer draw on the Exodus and the Battle of Karbala as models of struggle, respectively, she reflects upon the nature of Islamic monotheism. Echoing the earlier ideas of Shari'ati, she argues that *tawhid* has direct sociopolitical consequences. For the unity of God must translate into the unity of humanity, undivided by gender, race, and class. But while humanity is marked by duality, as expounded in Wadud's reading of the Creation Story, God is utterly unique, unpairable. Therefore, patriarchal portrayals of God as being masculine—that is, pairing God with men's experiences—undercuts the singularity of this deity. In order to uphold *tawhid*, Muslims must thus tirelessly work towards creating an egalitarian and just social order. And in this new society, the only marker of distinction is that of *taqwa*—a key Qur'anic principle and a theme that permeates Wadud's Islamic discourse. A truly just deity, she argues, is one who looks beyond mere material and physical differences, focussing on piety alone as a measure of human worth. In addition to *tawhid* and *taqwa*, she unpacks the Islamic concept of *khilafa*, historically understood as the Sunni political institution of the caliphate. Bringing the meaning of *khilafa* back to its original Qur'anic usage, in which it is defined as trusteeship, she argues that it is the solemn duty of every human being, as trustee of God, to establish social justice on the Earth, thereby fulfilling her/his divinely sanctioned purpose. Hagar is the final paradigm that Wadud elaborates upon. What makes this figure so compelling for Wadud, and for womanist theologians in general, is the way in which Hagar captures the complexity of suffering, marginalized on the basis of class, race, and gender. Drawing on her own experience as a single working mother, Wadud sees in the example of Hagar, who was abandoned in the desert and forced to provide for her child in the face of overwhelming odds, an inspirational model of struggle for Muslim women today, especially African American Muslim women.

Indeed, as the Hagar paradigm suggests, Wadud has a holistic commitment to justice. Because she has been excluded from liberationist discourses—whether as a woman in androcentric struggles based primarily on class and race or, conversely, as a poor Black woman in feminist struggles spearheaded by affluent White women—she has an acute sense of the multifaceted nature of oppression. In a strikingly similar fashion to Esack and Engineer, she integrates questions of race, class, and religious pluralism into her thinking. While Wadud's discourse on race draws upon her lived experiences as a Black woman growing up in a White supremacist society, she is also highly critical of race relations among American Muslims, criticizing the privilege of Arab and South Asian immigrant Muslims, whose superior socioeconomic standing has allowed them to monopolize leadership and representational roles within the community. Embracing religious pluralism, Wadud acknowledges the plurality of divine disclosure and argues that Muslims constitute one of numerous recipients of revelation. The bulk of her writings on pluralism, however, focus on internal Muslim dynamics, criticizing the marginalization of alternative, reformist voices and defending the right to religious freedom. Like gender and race, the experience of poverty, particularly during her childhood years, has had a lasting impact on her Qur'anic hermeneutic. Reiterating her emphasis on piety as the chief criterion of human worth, she argues that God, as a fundamentally just deity, does not differentiate between humankind on the basis of wealth. At a global level, however, Wadud's discourse on poverty is problematic, for at the same time as she condemns the devastating economic inequalities created by capitalism, she concludes that such disparity can somehow be dismantled without a systematic redistribution of global wealth, without 'depriving the well to do from experiencing extreme luxury and privilege.'[272] Here, she is at variance with Esack and Engineer, for whom global socio-economic justice must entail precisely such a far-reaching redistribution of resources. Her discourse on the attacks of 9/11 is also problematic, representing an overtly political act of militancy—seeking to challenge US dominance in the Muslim world—as a simplistic manifestation of evil, even patriarchy. The most crucial aspect of a comprehensive approach to justice, for Wadud, is walking the walk: that is, living out professed progressive values in one's personal life, thereby collapsing the public and private spheres. And the family is the most important space wherein such commitments need to be actualized. Indeed, it is hypocritical to support women's rights in public while being complicit in patriarchal practices in one's own household. A genuine commitment to justice, then, must transcend discourse, impacting one's most intimate relationships.

[272] Wadud, *Inside the Gender Jihad*, 267.

5

Against Patriarchy

The Reading of Asma Barlas

INTRODUCTION

This chapter is devoted to the Qur'anic exegesis of the Pakistani American intellectual Asma Barlas. The first section will explore her interpretive methodology. Like Esack, Engineer, and Wadud, she privileges the Qur'an over other Islamic texts, such as the *hadith* and the *shari'a*. Barlas reads scripture in multiple ways, and this section will systematically outline the hermeneutical strategies that she employs. In so doing, I will show a key similarity between Barlas' and Wadud's methodologies: namely, their usage of historical criticism and textual holism as liberating modes of reading. I will then unpack Barlas' exegesis. Like Wadud, she seeks to demonstrate how the Qur'an can be interpreted to further the struggle for gender justice. However, while the works of these exegetes tend to be conflated, as if they are simply doing the same thing, I argue that they are actually engaged in substantively different projects, for whereas Wadud undertakes a study of woman in the Qur'an, Barlas interrogates the relationship between the text and patriarchy. That is, while the former explores the Qur'an's representations of women, from the Creation Story to the Hereafter, the latter makes a case for the anti-patriarchal basis of Muslim scripture, claiming that it is at variance with both 'traditional' and 'modern' understandings of patriarchy. *Tawhid*, the unity of God, is the most important theological paradigm that Barlas draws upon in this exegetical endeavour. That Wadud, as seen in the preceding chapter, also expounds the social and political implications of Islamic monotheism is significant, reflecting the centrality of this paradigm in women's gender egalitarian readings of the Qur'an. But unlike Wadud (and Esack), Barlas at times delves into apologetics, trying to fully reconcile a seventh-century text with contemporary understandings of gender justice. Like Engineer, she essentializes the Qur'anic text, portraying it as being inherently liberatory, thereby rendering patriarchal readings as 'misreadings'. The final part of this chapter will show that Barlas, in a markedly similar fashion to all the commentators considered in this book, has a holistic stance towards justice, reflecting not only on gender but also on class and empire, race and religious pluralism. This comprehensive approach to liberation, I argue, stems from her engagement in 'double critique', or her commitment to speak truth to power in both Muslim and non-Muslim Western contexts. This chapter will first set the stage for discussion by providing a brief history of Pakistan (where Barlas was born and spent the first three decades of her life) as well as a biographical sketch of this exegete.

Historical Context

Conceived as a Muslim homeland in South Asia, Pakistan has been ruled by military regimes for most of its history. The entry of the English into India, as discussed in Chapter 3, was primarily an economic one, headed by the East India Company in the 1600s. The Indian Revolt of 1857, however, effected a critical shift in colonial policy from the indirect imperialism of the Company to the overt political rule of the Crown, lasting until independence in 1947. Over the course of the Indian liberation struggle, Muslim leaders such as Muhammad Ali Jinnah (d. 1948) and Muhammad Iqbal (d. 1938) became increasingly anxious about the future of the Muslim community in what would inevitably become a Hindu-dominated state.[1] This concern led them to call for the creation of a Muslim homeland. As a result, when the British were forced to pull out in 1947, two sibling states came into existence: India and Pakistan.[2] While a Muslim

---

[1] John L. Esposito, *The Islamic Threat: Myth or Reality?* (Oxford: Oxford University Press, 1999), 64.

[2] There is a vast literature on the origins of communal politics, the Pakistan movement, and Partition. See, among others: Akbar Ahmed, *Jinnah, Pakistan and Islamic Identity: The Search for Saladin* (London: Routledge, 1997); Ayesha Jalal, *The Sole Spokesman: Jinnah, the Muslim League and the Demand for Pakistan*

homeland had successfully been established, however, Pakistan did not last long as a functioning democratic society. Politically fragmented, the country was swept up in 1958 by a military coup headed by General Ayub Khan (r. 1958–69). The army has dominated the political scene ever since. Though civilian rule was restored for a brief spell under the socialist prime minister Zulfikar Ali Bhutto (r. 1973–7), another coup took place in 1977, bringing General Zia ul-Haq (r. 1977–88) to power. In addition to denationalizing and deregulating the economy, Zia called for the Islamization of the Pakistani state. Indeed, he revamped the national myth of Pakistan's creation from being a 'Muslim homeland' to an 'Islamic state',[3] reflecting his conservative religious sensibilities. The authoritarian process of state-sponsored Islamization, which adopted a Wahhabi and thus literalist approach to Islam, had a deeply divisive impact on Pakistan's heterogeneous religious landscape,[4] exacerbating sectarian tensions not only between Sunnis and Shi'as but also amongst Sunnis of different shades, especially between Sufi-oriented Barelvis and puritanical Deobandis.[5] Zia's policy of Islamization manifested itself not only in domestic politics but also on the international level, most notably in his support for the Afghan Mujahidin—a militant resistance movement that emerged in response to the Soviet invasion of Afghanistan in 1979. Zia's backing of the Mujahidin, moreover, reflects a close nexus between Pakistan and the USA, which bankrolled the Afghan struggle against Soviet communism. It is important to note, however, that the alliance between Pakistan and the USA is

---

(Cambridge: Cambridge University Press, 1994); and Yasmin Khan, *The Great Partition: The Making of India and Pakistan* (New Haven: Yale University Press, 2008).

[3] Ian Talbot, *Pakistan: A Modern History* (New York: St. Martin's Press, 1998), 5.

[4] This process of homogenization is one that continues today, particularly in the Talibanization of Pakistan's North-West Frontier Province (NWFP). For a rich ethnographic study of the great diversity of Muslim practices in NWFP, specifically in the city of Chitral, and the rising religious tensions between them, see Magnus Marsden, *Living Islam: Muslim Religious Experience in Pakistan's North-West Frontier* (Cambridge: Cambridge University Press, 2005).

[5] Talbot, 251. The Barelvis and Deobandis represent two opposite poles of the vast interpretive spectrum of Sunni Islam in South Asia. Taking their name from Sheikh Ahmed Barelvi (d. 1921)—an Islamic scholar who was a Sufi and an ardent critic of Wahhabism—the Barelvis adhere to a mystical practice of Islam. In contrast to the Barelvis, the Deobandis reflect a much more literalist approach. Taking their name from a *madrasa* founded in 1866, Dar al-'Ulum Deoband (based, as its name suggests, in a town called Deoband), they condemn Sufi and Shi'a practices as being un-Islamic, calling for a return to the Qur'an and *sunna*.

hardly distinct to Zia's regime and can, in fact, be traced all the way
back to the first coup in 1958. Following the takeover, Khan gave the
USA, in particular Harvard University and the Ford Foundation,
control over Pakistan's economic policies—a disastrous move that
has effectively 'concentrated 80% of the national wealth in the hands
of a mere twenty-two families.'[6] In Pakistan's history, therefore, there
has been an enduring relationship between domestic dictatorship and
the USA, and one that has continued through the 2000s, as evidenced
by American support for General Pervez Musharraf (r. 2001–8).

Raised in Pakistan, Barlas was forced to flee the country during
Zia's rule and has made the USA her home ever since, thus suggesting
the important (and rather paradoxical) role that the USA has played
both as a major force in domestic Pakistani politics and as a principal
point of emigration for the Pakistani diaspora. Barlas was born on
10 March 1950 in Lahore. Her early childhood coincided with the
transformation of Pakistan from a civilian government to a military
state: she was eight years old when Khan seized control.[7] Barlas'
parents were socially privileged, coming from military households
and studying in elite Western institutions. Her father attended For-
man Christian College (est. 1864) and her mother Kinnaird College
for Women (est. 1913), thereby becoming one of the first Pakistani
women to earn a graduate degree.[8] Barlas would follow in the footsteps of her mother by enrolling in Kinnaird, receiving a bachelor's
degree in English literature and philosophy and later a master's
degree in journalism.[9] Upon completing her studies, she joined the
Ministry of Foreign Affairs as a diplomat. By this time, Zia had taken
power and was aggressively implementing his Islamization pro-
grammes. Barlas became a staunch critic of the regime, openly voicing her grievances with its authoritarian policies. This led to Zia
terminating her career in the foreign service and persecuting her
family.[10] After a brief stint as an assistant editor of *The Muslim*—an
oppositional newspaper—she was eventually forced to leave Pakistan
in 1983, seeking political asylum in the USA. Although Barlas arrived
in America as an exile, and thus not in search of upward social
mobility, her example is representative of a wider migration of

---

[6] Asma Barlas, *Democracy, Nationalism and Communalism: The Colonial Legacy
in South Asia* (Boulder, Colorado: Westview Press, 1995), 13.
[7] Barlas Interview, 2009.   [8] Ibid.
[9] Ibid.   [10] Ibid.

Muslims from Asia, Africa, and the Middle East to the USA in the second half of the twentieth century—a mass movement made possible by the passage of the Hart-Cellar Act (1965), which lifted the racist quotas of earlier American legislation restricting immigration to predominantly White countries.[11] Barlas continued her graduate studies in the USA, receiving an M.A. and Ph.D. in International Studies at the University of Denver in Colorado. Clearly conditioned by her experiences in Pakistan, her doctoral dissertation was a Marxist analysis of Muslim and Hindu politics in late British India, seeking to understand why Pakistan and India had taken such different paths—the former becoming a military dictatorship, the latter a functioning democracy—despite their shared colonial past.[12] Upon completing her Ph.D., Barlas joined the Department of Politics at Ithaca College in New York State. She is currently a professor at Ithaca College, as well as the director of the college's Center for the Study of Culture, Race, and Ethnicity. Her educational and professional trajectory is significant for two reasons. Firstly, like Wadud and unlike Esack and Engineer, Barlas has no traditional background in Islamic studies. Paralleling the educational paths of numerous Muslim intellectuals in the contemporary period, particularly women, she has been schooled solely within the so-called secular university. However, unlike Wadud, who as described earlier received a doctorate in Islamic studies from the University of Michigan, Barlas never studied religion academically. Rather, her training lies in politics and postcolonial theory, journalism and English literature. She is thus representative of an entirely different wave of Muslim thinkers, trained in diverse fields like education, engineering, and medicine, who are shaping Islamic discourse and, in so doing, challenging the authority of the *'ulama*.[13]

METHODOLOGY

The Primacy of the Word

Just as for the other exegetes studied in this book, the Qur'an stands at the centre of Barlas' Islamic discourse. Because the Qur'an reflects the

---

[11] Curtis, 72.   [12] Barlas, *Democracy, Nationalism and Communalism*, 1.
[13] Eickelman and Piscatori, 131.

actual speech of God, it is, according to Barlas, 'inimitable, inviolate, inerrant, and incontrovertible.'[14] It is this text, therefore, that ought to act as the authoritative point of departure for all Islamic thought and practice. As she phrased it in our interview:

> I think the Qur'an is the starting point and the ending point. Just like the Names of God: God is the First and God is the Last. So if the Qur'an is God's Word, then it is the First and it is the Last. It has to provide the framework, the yardstick, the touchstone in terms of which we formulate law or norms or anything else.[15]

In her emphasis on the Qur'an as the 'framework' and 'yardstick' for (re)understanding Islam, Barlas echoes the text's own self-description. *Al-Furqan*—literally, the Criterion or the Distinguisher—is one of the many names that the Qur'an uses to refer to itself (Q. 25:1), underscoring its express purpose as a book of guidance that will allow the believers to discern right from wrong, truth from falsehood.[16] Like Wadud,[17] Barlas criticizes the common practice of conflating the Qur'an with its historical exegesis,[18] which elevates human—or, to be more precise, male—interpretation with scripture. So while the Qur'an, as the Word, is 'incontrovertible', its earthly exposition is not.[19] In fact, she observes, the Qur'an makes a critical distinction between itself and its interpretation, warning those 'who write the Book with their own hands and say: "This is from God"' (Q. 2:79).[20] To be sure, this verse is usually understood as addressing the *Ahl al-Kitab* (literally, the People of the Book, referring to earlier monotheistic communities, including Jews, Christians, and Sabians), who, as the verse goes on to state, would forge scripture in order to 'sell it for a small profit'. But on a conceptual level, comments Barlas, this verse can be interpreted as a severe criticism of those who collapse divine discourse with its fallible, human exposition.[21] Furthermore, the equation of human interpretation with the Word has deeply problematic theological implications, as it entails, to use her own

---

[14] Barlas, *'Believing Women' in Islam*, 33.   [15] Barlas Interview, 2009.
[16] Siddiqui, 63. As Siddiqui goes on to note, the term *furqan* is also used in the Qur'an to describe the Old and New Testaments (Q. 2:53, 21:48), suggesting that it is the function of revelation, irrespective of the specific scripture in question, to act as a standard of ethical conduct for the faithful.
[17] Wadud, *Qur'an and Woman*, xxi–xxii.
[18] Barlas, *'Believing Women' in Islam*, 38–9.
[19] Ibid, 33.   [20] Ibid, 17.   [21] Ibid.

words, 'erasing the distinction between God and humans.'[22] To conflate the texts, then, is also to conflate the *authors* of the texts— that is, to elevate humans to the level of God—thus impinging upon divine sovereignty.

Barlas is largely dismissive of the *hadith* literature, criticizing the elevation of prophetic practice alongside the Qur'an. As already discussed, in mainstream Islam the *sunna* is approached as being on a par with the Qur'an, as being a form of divine inspiration.[23] Barlas has deep-seated grievances with this understanding of the *sunna* not only because of the unique status of the Qur'an as the direct Word of God, but also due to the questionable reliability of the *hadith*, which began to be collected over a century after the Prophet's death.[24] Like Esack, Engineer, and Wadud, Barlas is there- fore highly sceptical about the authenticity of this body of knowledge. Moreover, she charges the *hadith* with misogyny, portraying women as being ethically and spiritually lacking; intellectually deficient; and constituting the majority of the inhabitants of Hell, as punishment for being ungrateful to their husbands.[25] Citing Q. 3:79, Barlas argues that the Qur'an squarely positions the authority of God's Word over those of the prophets.[26] The passage reads:

> It does not behove any human that God should give him the Book, judgement and prophecy, and then he should say to the people, 'Be my servants instead of God's.' Rather (he would say): 'Be a godly people, because of your teaching of the Book and because of your studying it.'

This verse is significant for two reasons. Firstly, it states clearly that God stands at the core of the Muslim faith and not God's messengers, themselves being devout servants commissioned with the solemn task of prophecy. Secondly, and by extension, it is God's words that take centre-stage, with the prophets calling on their people to become

---

[22] Ibid, 79.
[23] Von Denffer, 18–19. This conflation of the authority of the *sunna* with the Qur'an (discussed in Chapter 3 on Engineer) has deep roots in Islamic history, going back to the classical period. The jurist Muhammad ibn Idris al-Shafi'i (d. 820) is generally credited as being the principal architect behind this approach to the *sunna*.
[24] Barlas, *'Believing Women' in Islam*, 42.
[25] Ibid, 45. Barlas does not provide any citations (*hadith* collection and chapter) or authenticity rankings when mentioning these reports, indicating her lack of system- atic treatment of the *hadith* literature and extra-Qur'anic sources in general—an aspect of her writings that will be discussed later in this chapter.
[26] Ibid, 123.

'godly' by teaching and studying 'the Book', or God's speech rather than their own. That being said, it is important to note that while Barlas takes issue with the *hadith* literature, her critique is not a categorical one. For the problem is not with the *hadith per se*, but rather with the selective privileging and mass circulation of a handful of reports that are blatantly anti-women. Indeed, she notes that there are only six misogynistic reports that are deemed reliable (*sahih*) and, conversely, that there are markedly egalitarian sayings 'that emphasize women's full humanity; counsel husbands to deal kindly and justly with their wives; confirm the right of women to acquire knowledge; elevate mothers over fathers...and record that the Prophet accepted the evidence of one woman over that of a man.'[27] The underlying problem with the *hadith* literature, then, is not only that it is used to interpret the Qur'an rather than the other way around—that is, using the Qur'an as the definitive criterion by which to read and evaluate (reported) prophetic discourse[28]—but also that those reports that do uphold gender justice remain unknown to most Muslims.

Her treatment of the legal tradition is less nuanced, however. In the preceding chapter it was shown that Wadud, in the spirit of pragmatism, has become increasingly inclined towards engaging the *shari'a*, arguing that Islamic law needs to be reinterpreted in the present time and in accordance with Qur'anic values.[29] Barlas seems to have moved in the opposite direction. While her Commentary—*'Believing Women' in Islam: Unreading Patriarchal Interpretations of the Qur'an* (2002)—called for the necessity to rethink Islamic juristic principles in light of the Qur'an's teachings,[30] she has since become disenchanted with the prospects of reforming the *shari'a*. When I interviewed Barlas in 2009, she articulated her changed platform in sharp and unambiguous terms:

[27] Ibid, 46. Here, Barlas draws upon the scholarship of the Moroccan scholar Fatima Mernissi. For an important reappraisal of the Prophet's legacy through the lens of gender justice, see Mernissi, *The Veil and the Male Elite*. While Barlas consults Mernissi's work—and thus secondary literature on the *hadith*—she does not make any direct references to the *hadith* corpus itself. She fails to specify and cite which 'six misogynistic *ahadith*' (plural of *hadith*) are considered reliable or, for that matter, which gender-egalitarian reports are being alluded to in the quoted passage above.
[28] Barlas, *'Believing Women' in Islam*, 123.
[29] Wadud, *Inside the Gender Jihad*, 205.
[30] Barlas, *'Believing Women' in Islam*, 75.

But clearly as it [the *shariʿa*] exists: no, there's no point in salvaging it. What's the point of salvaging something that is not just patriarchal but downright misogynistic and un-Qur'anic? What's the point? I don't understand.[31]

I then raised the question of pragmatism, pointing out that several Islamic gender activists, acknowledging the legitimacy that the *shariʿa* wields amongst mainstream Muslims, have called for a critical engagement with it on strategic grounds. To this she replied:

I don't know what to say to that. I understand the importance of pragmatism, but for me things are not always about strategy. They are about principle. And principles and strategies may or may not always cohere.[32]

The legal tradition, therefore, is simply too sexist and unjust to sustain any serious, systematic attempts at reform. In addition to legalizing gender inequality, she laments, the *shariʿa* fails to differentiate between premarital sex, adultery, and rape, taking pregnancy as evidence of voluntary extramarital relations.[33] This has resulted in raped women being doubly wronged, first by the rapist and then by the court, as the *shariʿa* prescribes stoning to death for adultery—a capital punishment that, she notes, has no basis in scripture.[34] While Barlas' grievances with the *shariʿa* are well founded, she ultimately fails to distinguish between the theory of Islamic law and its practice. In many cases the latter has little to no relationship with the former. For example, the Maliki school of law is the only school that takes pregnancy in an unmarried woman as proof of voluntary extramarital relations, while the other schools find pregnancy to be insufficient as evidence.[35] It is important to note here that Barlas' criticism of the *shariʿa* should not be read as a sweeping dismissal of the entire intellectual tradition, which is often reduced to its *legal* expression. As we shall see later on in this chapter, when discussing religious pluralism she draws upon the writings of two towering figures in medieval Islamic theology and mysticism: the Persian theologian Abu

---

[31] Barlas Interview, 2009.   [32] Ibid.

[33] Asma Barlas, *Islam, Muslims, and the US: Essays on Religion and Politics* (New Delhi: Global Media Publications, 2004), 78–9.

[34] Ibid.

[35] Ali, *Sexual Ethics and Islam*, 63. For a wider discussion of *zina* (illicit sexual relations) in the legal tradition, see Chapter 4 in Ali's book: 'Prohibited Acts and Forbidden Partners: Illicit Sex in Islamic Jurisprudence.'

Hamid al-Ghazali (d. 1111) and the Andalusian Sufi Muhyiddin ibn
'Arabi (d. 1240), respectively.[36]

How to Read the Qur'an: Hermeneutical Strategies

According to Barlas, the task of interpretation is open to all. Indeed,
the Qur'an mandates each and every Muslim, irrespective of gender
affiliation or scholarly expertise, to read and reflect upon its words.
For just as Muhammad—an unlettered prophet—was commanded to
'Read!' (Q. 96:1–5) so, too, are all believers 'equal inheritors of his
legacy of reading.'[37] Despite the fact that the overwhelming majority
of Islamic scholars are men, such stark gender asymmetry in religious
learning has no scriptural basis, as the Qur'an does not ascribe to
males 'any sort of epistemic privilege'.[38] In fact, Barlas adds, the text
launches a scathing critique of religious officials who, blinded by
greed, have misled their people (Q. 9:31, 9:34).[39] Muslims, therefore,
have to rely upon their own *'aql* (insight and intelligence), rather than
on a sanctified class of interpreters, in making sense of the Qur'an.
Mastery of classical Arabic, moreover, is unnecessary to qualify a
believer to interpret scripture. Though the Qur'an was revealed in
Arabic, she argues, this language is not endowed with any type of
sacred status, for God's choice of Arabic was a purely practical one,
seeking to communicate clearly to the seventh-century Arabs by using
their own tongue.[40] It is worthwhile noting here that Barlas herself
does not know Arabic—which is unsurprising given her educational
background in politics, journalism, and English literature—and developed her understanding of the Qur'an through the study of English
translations, particularly those of Abdullah Yusuf Ali, Muhammad

---

[36] Asma Barlas, 'Reviving Islamic Universalism: East/s, West/s, and Coexistence',
in *Contemporary Islam: Dynamic, not Static*, eds. Abdul Aziz Said, Mohammad Abu-
Nimr, and Meena Sharify-Funk (London: Routledge, 2006), 247–8.
[37] Asma Barlas, 'The Qur'an and Hermeneutics: Reading the Qur'an's Opposition
to Patriarchy', *Journal of Qur'anic Studies* 3 (2001): 33.
[38] Barlas, *Islam, Muslims, and the US*, 130.
[39] Barlas, *'Believing Women' in Islam*, 121. Barlas comments that while these verses
explicitly refer to Christian and Jewish priests, there is a larger lesson to be learnt
here—specifically, the historic nexus between priesthood and corruption—suggesting
that it is precisely for this reason that the Qur'an refused to sanction a priestly class.
[40] Ibid, 17.

Dawud, and Muhammad Asad.[41] In her Qur'anic commentary, she relies almost entirely upon Ali's translation. So translations, notwithstanding their inability to capture the complexity, the richness of the Word in its totality, are a completely legitimate means with which to engage scripture. For not only does the Qur'an not sanctify Arabic, but it never suggests that it is 'the only language in which we can understand revelation'.[42] In fact, to claim that the translated Qur'an is not really the Qur'an is theologically unsound, Barlas maintains, because this claim links the ontological status of God's Speech with humankind—specifically, with the socially constructed language of Arabic—rather than with God.[43] Barlas, as the Islamic scholar Juliane Hammer has observed, thus stands apart from Wadud, for although Wadud also rejects the sacredness of Arabic, she is schooled in classical Arabic and draws upon these linguistic skills extensively when interpreting the text.[44] Barlas' lack of knowledge in Arabic also distinguishes her from Esack and Engineer, who received training in classical Arabic.

If the task of interpretation is the vocation of all Muslims, how exactly ought the Qur'an to be read? A hermeneutical commitment to scriptural *unity*—or reading the text in a thoroughly holistic manner—is a major interpretive strategy that Barlas employs. Paralleling Wadud, she argues that the Qur'an cannot be approached (as it often is) in a selective, piecemeal fashion but rather, treating the text as an interconnected and organic whole, must be read intratextually.[45] That is, any passage within the text ought to be approached as just that—a passage *within* the text—and, thus, must be interpreted in light of this wider text. An underlying problem with mainstream interpretations of scripture, Barlas writes, is that they fixate on a few scattered verses, even words, especially when making claims of male superiority over women.[46] As discussed in the previous chapter, this

---

[41] Barlas Interview, 2009. See Abdullah Yusuf Ali, *The Holy Qur'an: Text, Translation and Commentary*, 2nd US edition (New York: Tahrike Tarsile Qur'an, 1988); N.J. Dawood, *The Koran*, 7th revised edition (London: Penguin Books, 2000); and Asad, *The Message of the Qur'an*.

[42] Barlas, *'Believing Women' in Islam*, 17.

[43] Asma Barlas, 'Still Quarrelling over the Qur'an: Five Interventions', *International Institute for the Study of Islam in the Modern World (ISIM) Review* 20 (Autumn 2007): 32.

[44] Hammer, 452.

[45] Barlas, 'Amina Wadud's Hermeneutics of the Qur'an', 109.

[46] Asma Barlas, 'Women's Readings of the Qur'an', in *The Cambridge Companion to the Qur'an*, ed. Jane D. McAuliffe (Cambridge: Cambridge University Press, 2006),

was a key criticism that Rahman levelled against traditional exegesis, which provided a verse-by-verse, cover-to-cover commentary. Such 'atomistic' readings, Rahman argued, rendered the interpreter blind to the text's larger worldview.[47] And it is precisely this worldview that enables the exegete to discern the Qur'an's general principles from its particulars,[48] the former applicable to all times and places and the latter historically bound. Furthermore, Barlas locates this reading strategy within scripture itself, which castigates those who 'have made the Qur'an into shreds' (Q. 15:91)—a charge, incidentally, also made against the ancient Israelites, who reduced their scripture 'into separate sheets for show', hiding the bulk of its contents (Q. 6:91)— while praising those who proclaim: 'We believe in the Book; the whole of it is from our Lord' (Q. 3:7).[49] But the Qur'an is not the only source that she cites in making a case for holistic readings. At various places in her exegesis Barlas points to the hermeneutical writings of the French philosopher Paul Ricoeur (d. 2005).[50] According to Ricoeur, a text is by its very nature interconnected, exhibiting a worldview greater than the sum of its constituent parts:

> a text has to be construed because it is not a mere sequence of sentences, all on equal footing and separately understandable. A text is a whole, a totality... This intention [of the text] is something other than the sum of the individual meanings of the individual sentences. A text is more than a linear succession of sentences. It is a cumulative, holistic process.[51]

By utilizing the interpretive insights of Ricoeur, Barlas' approach to the Qur'an reflects a broader trend in contemporary Islamic thought, particularly within European and North American universities, wherein Muslim intellectuals have drawn increasingly upon modern theories of hermeneutics and literary criticism.[52]

262-3. Here, Barlas gives the example of Q. 4:34, which will be quoted and discussed at length later in the chapter.

[47] Rahman, *Islam and Modernity*, 2-3. The exact word that Rahman uses is *weltanschauung*, or a comprehensive view of the world and humankind's relationship to it.

[48] Barlas, *'Believing Women' in Islam*, 60.

[49] Barlas, 'The Qur'an and Hermeneutics', 24.

[50] Barlas, *'Believing Women' in Islam*, 18, 35, 169.

[51] Paul Ricoeur, *Hermeneutics and the Human Sciences: Essays on Language, Action and Interpretation*, ed. and trans. John B. Thompson (Cambridge: Cambridge University Press, 1998), 211-12.

[52] Taji-Farouki, 14.

In addition to intratextuality, she unpacks the Qur'an's extratextuality, or the place of the text in history. Scripture needs to be contextualized. Historical criticism—what Barlas calls reading *behind* the text—is a necessary interpretive strategy in any liberating commentary because although the Qur'an speaks to all times and places, it was revealed in a specific historical setting and, consequently, its language was shaped by this inescapable context. Reading behind the text, then, entails making 'visible the historical contexts in which it was revealed and interpreted as a way of explaining its patriarchal exegesis.'[53] Like textual holism, the hermeneutical task of discerning timeless principles from historically bound particulars lies at the heart of her historical criticism.[54] Here, again, Barlas' commentary bears remarkable resemblance to Rahman's. As we have already discussed in this book, historical criticism was an integral component of Rahman's double movement theory. For in order to extract 'general moral-social objectives' from the classical context, he argued, Muslims must undertake an exhaustive study of seventh-century Arabian society, including its culture, religion, politics, and economics.[55] Echoing Wadud,[56] Barlas laments that it is precisely the failure to use historical criticism as a tool of interpretation that Muslims, rather than historicizing the particular, have, instead, universalized the particular.[57] This problematic practice is, in large part, due to the tendency to idealize the world of the first Muslims. Indeed, this formative period, particularly the reign of the first four caliphs (r. 632–61)—referred to as the Rightly-Guided Caliphs (*al-Khulafa' al-Rashidun*)—has been sacralized in mainstream Muslim memory as a 'golden, paradigmatic age',[58] and thus one that is to be emulated by later generations of believers. This canonization of the classical period, and, by extension, the commentaries that were composed in this time, constitutes a curious paradox for Barlas, as it 'serves to draw

---

[53] Barlas, 'Women's Readings of the Qur'an', 268.
[54] Barlas, *'Believing Women' in Islam*, 60.
[55] Rahman, *Islam and Modernity*, 6.
[56] Wadud, *Qur'an and Woman*, xii–xiii.
[57] Asma Barlas, '"Holding Fast by the Best in the Precepts": the Qur'an and Method', in *New Directions in Islamic Thought: Exploring Reform and Tradition* eds. Kari Vogt et al. (London: I.B. Tauris, 2008), 18.
[58] Asma Afsaruddin, *The First Muslims: History and Memory* (Oxford: Oneworld, 2008), 54.

Muslims close to what is distant from us in real time and to distance us from that which, in real time, is close to us.'[59]

As this astute observation suggests, for Barlas the most important aspect of the Qur'an's extratextuality is not a distant past but rather the immediate present. Like all the commentators considered in this book, her abiding interest is in the contemporary world, the lived reality of the interpreter. Reading behind the text, then, is necessary but insufficient for interpretation, as it must be paralleled by a concomitant commitment to 'read in front of the text:' that is, to recontextualize the Qur'an's teachings in the here and now.[60] Yet again, we see Barlas' deep intellectual debts to Rahman, and whom she explicitly cites,[61] for while the first move in Rahman's double movement theory entailed a historical reading, the second sought to apply the Qur'an's teachings to the present—a complex process that required a comprehensive study of the contemporary context.[62] Drawing upon an earlier insight of Wadud,[63] Barlas writes that in order 'for divine disclosure to speak to us, we must also continue asking questions of it.'[64] Scripture, therefore, becomes meaningful only insofar as it can respond effectively to the needs of its reader. But since needs are not timeless but defined, and continuously redefined, by time and space, new readers rooted in new contexts must necessarily bring new questions to the text. To put it another way: so long as Muslims fail to raise such pertinent questions, the text will fail to answer them. Barlas' emphasis on reading 'in front' of the Qur'an is arguably the most subversive strategy in her exegetical toolbox, as it holds the greatest potential to fundamentally alter received understandings of Islam. As she puts it:

> The Qur'an tells us that everything will perish but the face of God (28:88, 55:26–7). Hence that is the only unchangeable in Islamic thought and practice—all else is changeable and will pass, whether we will it to or not. This certainty should free us from a 'fear of freedom' and allow us to embrace a universe of unthought possibilities.[65]

---

[59] Barlas, *'Believing Women' in Islam*, 24.   [60] Ibid, 23.
[61] Ibid.   [62] Rahman, *Islam and Modernity*, 7.
[63] Wadud, *Qur'an and Woman*, xx–xxi.
[64] Barlas, 'Women's Readings of the Qur'an', 256.
[65] Barlas, 'Holding Fast by the Best in the Precepts', 22. Barlas' usage of the phrase 'fear of freedom' is taken from the Brazilian educational theorist, Paulo Freire (d. 1997). See Paulo Freire, *Pedagogy of the Oppressed*, trans. Myra Bergman Ramos (London: Penguin Books, 1996).

In addition to opening up infinite hermeneutical horizons, reading in light of the present is also unsettling because it makes visible the politics of interpretation, showing that a dominant reading is deemed authentic, even natural, not because it represents Truth, but rather because its exegesis has been tailored to the needs of a privileged few, thereby answering certain questions and not others.

It is on this issue of asking new questions of the text that the first key paradigm emerges in Barlas' exegesis: namely, that of Umm Salama (d. 680), a wife of Prophet Muhammad. As discussed in the introductory chapter, the Qur'an was not revealed at one go, but came down in stages over a period of twenty-three years (*c.* 610–32), addressing various issues and problems that arose within the burgeoning Muslim community. Reflecting on the Qur'an, which was still in the process of being revealed, Umm Salama confronted her husband, stating: 'O Prophet of God, I see that God mentions men but omits women.'[66] It was at this point that the following verse—Q. 33:35—was revealed:

> Surely, men and women who have submitted themselves to God, men and women who are believers, men and women who are obedient, men and women who are true to their word, men and women who are patient in adversity, men and women who are modest, men and women who give charity, men and women who observe fasting, men and women who guard their private parts, and men and women who remember God unceasingly, for them God has prepared forgiveness and a great reward.

It is difficult to overstate the centrality of this verse in Barlas' hermeneutic. Indeed, the very title of her Commentary—*'Believing Women' in Islam*—is a tribute to this profound passage. That God responded to, rather than ignored, Umm Salama's grievances with the text represents, for Barlas, a crucial moment in 'divine pedagogy', demonstrating to subsequent generations of Muslims the necessity of questioning, of interrogating the Qur'an as a mode of reading.[67] Approaching the text in such an engaged manner is especially important for women because they have been historically denied the right to ask questions, reflecting their own experiences and subjectivities, and, as a result, the Qur'an 'appears to remain silent' on

---

[66] Esack, *The Qur'an: A User's Guide*, 53.
[67] Barlas, 'Holding Fast by the Best in the Precepts', 21. Barlas credits her husband, Ulises Ali Mejias, with this specific phrasing.

gender issues.[68] But just as scripture spoke to the anxiety of Umm
Salama 1,400 years ago so, too, will it speak to the needs of believing
women today. That Umm Salama had the space to interrogate the
Qur'an so bluntly, moreover, suggests that while Islamic knowledge
production has become a male-dominated enterprise, this was not
always the case. As the historian Leila Ahmed has shown, in the
Prophet's time women participated actively in religious and political
life, openly voicing their opinions with the expectation of being
heard.[69] The frankness of Umm Salama, therefore, was not the exception but the norm.

Though Barlas is alone, among the four exegetes examined in this
book, in focussing on Umm Salama and her spirit of enquiry as a
hermeneutical model of reading the Qur'an, this paradigm shares
similarities with Esack's and Wadud's approaches. As discussed in
Chapter 2, Esack underscored the dialectical nature of Qur'anic
revelation—or what he referred to as the 'principle of progressive
revelation'—reflecting a deity who 'manifests His will in terms of the
circumstances of His people, who speaks to them in terms of their
reality and whose word is shaped by those realities.'[70] While Esack
did not make explicit reference to Umm Salama when discussing this
principle, her critical reflection on the Qur'an is perhaps the most
eloquent example of such revelatory dialectics. Barlas' usage of Umm
Salama as paradigm also shares parallels with Wadud's hermeneutic,
which, as discussed earlier, drew deep inspiration from Hagar, who
embodied, for Wadud, the plight of the abandoned single mother.[71]
Central to women's gender egalitarian readings of the Qur'an, then,
has been the rediscovery, the reclaiming of earlier believing women,
whether in the time of Muhammad or the preceding prophets, as
models of faith.

At the same time as Barlas calls for interpreting the Qur'an in the
here and now, highlighting the multitude of meanings that can
emerge from such a contextual reading, she cautions that not all
readings are equally legitimate. Citing Q. 7:145 and 39:18—the latter
adorning the front-cover of her Commentary—she points out that
the Qur'an itself acknowledges that not all interpretations may be

---

[68] Ibid.   [69] Ahmed, 72.
[70] Esack, *Qur'an, Liberation, and Pluralism*, 60.
[71] Wadud, *Inside the Gender Jihad*, 144.

appropriate, instructing the faithful to seek out 'the best' meanings.[72] The verses read:

> And We wrote down on the Tablets admonitions and clear explanations of all things for Moses, and We said, 'Hold fast to them, and bid your people to hold on to what is best [*ahsaniha*] in them.' (Q. 7:145)

> Those who listen to the Word and follow the best [*ahsanahu*] in it, they are the ones whom God has guided, and it is they who possess intellect. (Q. 39:18)

When making a case for a particular hermeneutical strategy, whether it is textual unity, interpretation for the present, or arriving at the best meanings, Barlas thus consistently positions herself *within* the text, foregrounding the scriptural basis of her approach. As such, her exegesis seeks to unearth (to use her own wording) the Qur'an's 'auto-hermeneutics',[73] or the ways in which the text calls for its own interpretation. We will revisit this reading strategy in the concluding chapter of this book. While she argues that the task of the engaged commentator is to arrive at the best meanings, it is important to note that she, unlike Wadud, does not subscribe to notions of objectivity. In fact, as discussed in the previous chapter, this was a critique that Barlas levelled against Wadud, who problematically distinguished between exegesis and reading, claiming that the former was an objective undertaking based on scientific methods while the latter was subjective, conditioned by the biases of the reader.[74] Because all textual engagement is inescapably subjective, writes Barlas, it is up to the reader to decide which interpretation is the most suitable—'the best'—given her/his specific circumstances.[75] It is this project of discernment, of figuring out which understandings of Islam can speak forcefully to the world today—and only today; the realities of the future may be radically different—that she refers to as *ijtihad*,[76] traditionally defined as a legal convention in the *shari'a*, wherein the jurist exercises independent judgement. Though Barlas derives this hermeneutical strategy from scripture, it is worthwhile noting that she has also been influenced by Ricoeur who, as discussed, shaped her stance on textual unity. According to Ricoeur, a 'text is a limited field

---

[72] Barlas, 'Holding Fast by the Best in the Precepts', 20.
[73] Barlas, *'Believing Women' in Islam*, 205.
[74] Barlas, 'Amina Wadud's Hermeneutics of the Qur'an', 118.
[75] Barlas, 'Holding Fast by the Best in the Precepts', 20.
[76] Barlas, 'Reviving Islamic Universalism', 251.

of constructions' and, thus, while all texts are open to interpretation, some interpretations are 'more probable' than others.[77] Readings, then, need to be compared in order to determine which are the most persuasive. And it is social justice, argues Barlas, that ought to act as the chief criterion in evaluating competing interpretations. The best readings are those that work towards securing justice for God's creation.[78] But how does she substantiate, scripturally, her positioning of social justice as the framework, the point of departure for arriving at the best meanings? It is here that the chapter moves to the next section, which unpacks the theology of justice that lies at the core of her commentary.

QUR'AN AND GENDER I: TRADITIONAL PATRIARCHY

Reading for Justice: A Different Approach

Barlas reflects extensively on the nature of the divine, and it is this critical reflection that forms the epistemological groundwork for her liberating hermeneutic. The commentaries of Wadud and Barlas tend to be lumped together, the latter often portrayed as simply rehashing the insights of the former. However, as I will demonstrate in the following sections, they are involved in substantively different (though complementary) exegetical projects. The preceding chapter showed that Wadud focuses on the subject of woman in Muslim scripture, thematically exploring topics like the Creation Story, the Events of the Garden, the Day of Judgement, and the Hereafter, as well as explicitly gendered issues such as divorce, polygamy, and male authority. Barlas, on the other hand, is more interested in the concept of patriarchy and, specifically, its relationship to the Qur'an. And herein lies her original, lasting contribution to women's gender egalitarian readings of the Qur'an, as these readings have failed to expound, in a systematic and detailed fashion, what they mean by the term patriarchy and, therefore, have not been able to appreciate fully the Qur'an's stances on this complex system of male privilege.[79]

---

[77] Ricoeur, 213.   [78] Barlas, *'Believing Women' in Islam*, 16.
[79] Ibid.

Indeed, in *Qur'an and Woman* Wadud devotes a two-page subsection to patriarchy, discussing the patriarchal backdrop in which the text was revealed and noting that this historical context inevitably shaped its language.[80] Elsewhere, she briefly describes patriarchy as not simply being 'an affirmation of men and men's experiences', but also being 'a hegemonic presumption of male superiority',[81] as well as a culture of 'persistently privileging one way of doing things, one way of being and one way of knowing.'[82]

Before we begin to unpack Barlas' treatment of patriarchy and its relationship to the Qur'an, two points of clarification need to be made. Firstly, while she clearly believes in the significance of the Qur'an, and by extension textual reinterpretation, as a factor in bettering Muslim women's lives, she acknowledges that patriarchy in Muslim societies cannot be reduced to the religious alone, and thus other contextual realities that may have nothing to do with religion, such as political economy, culture, and the state, also play a role in sustaining this oppressive system.[83] Secondly, she is explicit that, by interrogating patriarchy in light of the Qur'an, she is not trying to unearth a *theory* of gender equality in the Qur'an, since such theories are intellectual products of the modern period and cannot be read into a premodern text.[84]

In her exegesis, Barlas puts forth two principal arguments: namely, that the Qur'an is at odds with both 'traditional' and 'modern' forms of patriarchy. She defines traditional patriarchy—its modern manifestation will be discussed shortly—as follows:

> When I ask whether the Qur'an is a patriarchal or misogynistic text, I am asking whether it represents God as Father/male or teaches that God has a special relationship with males or that males embody divine attributes and that women are by nature weak, unclean or sinful. Further, does it teach that rule by the father/husband is divinely

---

[80] Wadud, *Qur'an and Woman*, 80–1.

[81] Wadud, 'What's Interpretation Got To Do With It', 92.

[82] Wadud, 'Islam beyond Patriarchy through Gender Inclusive Analysis', 101.

[83] Asma Barlas, 'Muslim Women and Sexual Oppression: Reading Liberation from the Qur'an', *Macalester International* 10 (Spring 2001): 118.

[84] Asma Barlas, 'Does the Qur'an support gender equality? Or, do I have the autonomy to answer this question?', in *Negotiating Autonomy and Authority in Muslim Contexts*, eds. Monique Bernards and Marjo Buitelaar (Leuven, Belgium: Peeters, 2013), 3.

ordained and an earthly continuation of God's Rule, as religious and traditional patriarchies claim?[85]

Theology, or how one conceptualizes God, therefore plays a pivotal role in Barlas' anti-patriarchal exegesis. There is an unbreakable bond between the divine and divine speech, between the *theological* and the *textual*. And it is precisely because 'our understanding of God's word cannot be independent of our understanding of God', she concludes, that 'we must seek the hermeneutic keys for reading the Qur'an in the nature of divine self-disclosure.'[86] That is, how does God describe God's self? It is only after the exegete has addressed this crucial question that s/he can then begin to interpret scripture, for a sound reading of the Qur'an must commence with a sound, theological conception of its author.[87] Here, in her emphasis on the intimate, inseparable connection between author and authored, Barlas clearly departs from Ricoeur. For a text, according to Ricoeur, is wholly independent of its author and takes on a life of its own,[88] an irreversible rupture that transpires at the very moment of the text's composition. As we shall see, this linking of the theological (God) and the textual (God's Word) has a lasting payoff for Barlas' hermeneutic, enabling her to expound the text in light of a liberating theology.

The Infinite Justice of the One God

Justice is a key aspect of divine self-disclosure. Like all the commentators studied in this book, Barlas is deeply committed to the belief in a compassionate and just Creator, observing that the Qur'an persistently negates any association of *zulm* (oppression) with God.[89] As the Japanese Islamic scholar Toshihiko Izutsu has noted, Qur'anic descriptions of God, which present this deity's 'essentially ethical nature', are brought together in the scriptural trope of Divine Names, referring to God as the Benevolent (*al-Rahman*), the Merciful (*al-Rahim*), and the Forgiving (*al-Ghaffar*), among others.[90] Reading

[85] Barlas, *'Believing Women' in Islam*, 1.
[86] Barlas, 'Holding Fast by the Best in the Precepts', 19.
[87] Barlas, 'Women's Readings of the Qur'an', 261.   [88] Ricoeur, 211.
[89] Barlas, 'Holding Fast by the Best in the Precepts', 19. While Barlas does not provide any Qur'anic citations when making this claim, there are a number of verses that explicitly deny God's association with oppression, such as Q. 4:40, 11:117 and 40:17.
[90] Izutsu, 17.

the text for the best meanings must centre on recovering justice, then, because its author is utterly just.[91] Moreover, Barlas argues, the justice of God establishes the fundamental equality of men and women, as such a deity would never favour a specific sex. Citing Q. 33:35—the Believing Women verse, which was quoted earlier when discussing the Umm Salama paradigm—she argues that 'moral praxis' is the sole basis on which humankind will be judged, and that women and men are endowed equally with the ability to attain *taqwa*, or 'God-consciousness'.[92] Barlas thus echoes Wadud who, as we saw in the last chapter, drew upon *taqwa* as an organizing hermeneutical principle when arguing for the equality of the sexes (Q. 49:13).[93] But if God is inherently just, continues Barlas, then this has lasting implications in terms of how we approach scripture, for if 'God never does *zulm* to anyone, then God's speech (the Qur'an) also cannot teach *zulm* against anyone.'[94] Conversely, reading oppression into the text associates oppression with its divine author, who is expressly described as just. Indeed, this constitutes one of the great contradictions of Islamic history, she laments, for at the same time as Muslims have believed in the justice of God they have continued to read patriarchy into this deity's living words.[95]

It is here, in discussing Barlas' liberating theology, that we arrive at the single most important paradigm in her Islamic thinking: *tawhid*, the absolute unity of God. Monotheism, she comments, is a central theme running through the Qur'anic text, which states clearly and unequivocally that 'Your God is One God' (Q. 16:22), even dedicating an entire chapter to this belief.[96] *Surat al-Tawhid*, or the Chapter of Unity (Q. 112) is one of the shortest and most straightforward chapters in the text. It reads: 'Say: "He is God, the One. God is the Eternal. He neither gave birth, nor was He given birth, and there is none comparable to Him."' And it is this aspect of divine self-disclosure that functions as the principal, hermeneutical key in Barlas' anti-patriarchal exegesis. For *tawhid* reflects the indivisibility of God's sovereignty, and therefore any human attempts to partake in this

91 Barlas, *'Believing Women' in Islam*, 16.
92 Barlas, 'The Qur'an and Hermeneutics', 25–6.
93 Wadud, *Qur'an and Woman*, 36–7.
94 Barlas, *'Believing Women' in Islam*, 14.
95 Ibid, 204. 96 Ibid, 95.

sovereignty undermines Islamic monotheism.[97] In terms of gender relations, she continues, this means that patriarchy—as a system that upholds male privilege, giving men sovereignty over women and setting up men as intermediaries between women and God—is at odds with divine sovereignty, with *tawhid*, and thus must be dismantled on Qur'anic grounds.[98] In her theological exposition of the gendered implications of *tawhid*, Barlas shares common ground with Wadud. To be sure, these two exegetes differ (albeit slightly) in how they reinterpret Islamic monotheism. Though Wadud also emphasizes the sovereignty, the transcendence of God, thereby problematizing male portrayals of God as having masculine qualities,[99] she makes a second hermeneutical move. In addition to expounding on the unity of God, Wadud, echoing the writings of Shari'ati,[100] reflects upon the unity of *humanity*, arguing that the Oneness of God must necessarily translate into the Oneness of humankind, undivided by 'race, class, gender, religious tradition, national origin, sexual orientation or other arbitrary, voluntary, and involuntary aspects of human distinction.'[101] While Barlas may well support this interpretation, it is not one that explicitly figures in her hermeneutic; her primary interest with regard to *tawhid* is the indivisibility of God and the gendered ramifications of this sovereignty. That *tawhid* plays such a prominent role in both Wadud's and Barlas' thinking is significant, reflecting the centrality of this theological paradigm in women's gender egalitarian readings of the Qur'an. In fact, monotheism is so crucial to Islamic critiques of patriarchy that Muslim women focussing on other textual traditions have also reinterpreted this foundational belief. The Lebanese American legal scholar Azizah al-Hibri is a compelling case in point. Writing in the context of the *shari'a*, she argues that *tawhid* is 'the core principle of Islamic jurisprudence', establishing the supremacy of God and, by extension, 'the fundamental metaphysical sameness of all humans as creatures of God.'[102] In order for legal rulings to comply conceptually with *tawhid*, therefore, they must treat men and women as fully equal human beings.

[97] Ibid, 13.
[98] Ibid, 13–14.   [99] Wadud, *Inside the Gender Jihad*, 81.
[100] Shari'ati, 3.   [101] Wadud, *Inside the Gender Jihad*, 28.
[102] Al-Hibri, 'An Introduction to Muslim Women's Rights', 51–2.

Our Father who art in Heaven

If God is One, if no other being can partake in divine sovereignty, then God is unparalleled, unmatched, unique. And it is this unrepresentability of God—the inability to compare this deity with humans, to portray the divine in anthropomorphic terms—that constitutes the third hermeneutical key, alongside divine justice and unity, with which Barlas rereads scripture.[103] Indeed, as the Qur'anic scholar Abdur Rashid Siddiqui has noted, while *Allah* literally means the God (*al-ilah*) it also suggests the state of being hidden from vision, of lying beyond the boundaries of human comprehension (Q. 6:103; 42:11), forever perplexing and bewildering the believers.[104] Yet despite the Qur'an's description of God as being unrepresentable, Barlas bemoans, Muslims have drawn parallels between God and men, implying that God shares a special affinity with men, that God is, in effect, male. For example, the medieval Persian scholar Abu Ali Fadl al-Tabrisi (d. 1153) commanded wives to bow down to their husbands, claiming that God's dominion over humankind entailed men's dominion over women, while the South Asian scholar Ashraf Ali Thanawi (d. 1943) compared a wife's ingratitude to her husband with ungratefulness to God.[105] As the post-Christian feminist theologian Mary Daly has argued, the conceptualization of God as male, as exhibiting masculine characteristics, plays a seminal role in legitimizing such unholy equations, for if 'God is male, then the male is God.'[106] But the Qur'an, interjects Barlas, squarely rejects representations of God as male and, specifically, as Father—a theological staple of traditional patriarchies. Once again, she turns to the Chapter of Unity (*Surat al-Tawhid*): 'Say: "He is God, the One. God is the Eternal. He neither gave birth, and nor was He given birth, and there is none comparable to Him."' Not only does this Qur'anic chapter, Barlas comments, clearly establish God's unrepresentability ('there is none comparable to Him'), but it also defies portrayals of God as Father ('He neither gave birth') or Son ('nor was He given

---

[103] Barlas, *'Believing Women' in Islam*, 14–15.
[104] Siddiqui, 16–17.   [105] Barlas, 'The Qur'an and Hermeneutics', 22.
[106] Mary Daly, *Beyond God the Father: Toward a Philosophy of Women's Liberation* (Boston: Beacon Press, 1978), 19. The masculinization of God is an especially problematic practice in mainstream Christianity, given that the Old and New Testaments explicitly describe God as a father figure. See, among others: Isaiah 64:8; Psalms 89:26–7; Matthew 5:14–16; and Luke 23:34.

birth').[107] In fact, she continues, the Qur'an launched a scathing criticism of the Jews and Christians of seventh-century Arabia for portraying God as a father figure:[108]

> The Jews say, 'Ezra is the son of God,' and the Christians say, 'Christ is the son of God.' These are sayings that they utter with their mouths, following assertions made by unbelievers in earlier times. May God assail them! How perverted are their minds![109] (Q. 9:30)

While the text vigorously disassociates God from being Father, there remains the thorny question of why the text continuously refers to God with the male pronoun 'He' (*huwa*)? Does this not reflect a glaring contradiction in the text? Barlas tackles this question by drawing upon historical criticism, highlighting the societal context in which the Qur'an was revealed. In particular, she points out that there is no neuter in Arabic grammar and that even inanimate objects are classified as being either masculine or feminine.[110] This is a *linguistic* feature distinct to the Arabic language, then, and cannot be used to engender God, especially in light of the Qur'an's wider emphasis on divine unrepresentability.

But just as portraying God as paternalistic is problematic so, too, is the reverse representation: reclaiming God as a motherly figure. In the face of patriarchal projections of God the Father, feminists have sought to recover past theologies wherein God exhibits feminine qualities, as exemplified by the Mother-God or Goddess. The historian Leila Ahmed, for instance, has written that the ancient cultures of the Middle East prior to the Christian era, such as in Mesopotamia and Egypt, venerated goddesses, concluding that the 'decline in women's status was followed eventually by the decline of goddesses and the rise of supremacy of gods.'[111] Barlas takes issue with Ahmed's linkage of goddess worship with gender egalitarianism, countering that the public presence of goddesses and priestesses is not necessarily reflective of an equitable distribution of gendered power on the

---

[107] Barlas, 'The Qur'an and Hermeneutics', 27.   [108] Ibid.

[109] Indeed, the underlying theme in the Qur'an's discourse on Christianity and Jesus in particular is the denial that this prophet had any filial relationship to God, which is precisely why Jesus is routinely referred to as 'Jesus son of Mary' (*'isa ibn maryam*). See, for instance, Q. 4:171.

[110] Ibid, 35.   [111] Ahmed, 12.

ground.[112] She gives the example of the people of ancient Greece, who 'in spite of strong female goddesses in their pantheon, believed that women were just lesser men who lacked the ability to reason. On this basis, they excluded women from public and political life and the rights extended to men.'[113]

Ahmed's historical account, then, is representative of a broader, essentialist tendency amongst feminists to romanticize the goddess cult as inherently empowering for women. And insofar as the Qur'an is concerned, adds Barlas, not only is there no scriptural basis for God being a motherly or female figure—as has been seen, this is a deity that is beyond gender classification, literally or metaphorically—but the Qur'an also explicitly rejects ascriptions of either sons *or* daughters to God (Q. 6:100).[114] The text, therefore, rules out the possibility of this deity exhibiting any anthropomorphic qualities. As the Islamic scholars Kecia Ali and Oliver Leaman have noted, the Qur'an's denial of God as having daughters is in large part due to the existing, religious milieu in which the text was revealed, as goddesses—in particular Lat, 'Uzza and Manat, considered to be God's daughters (Q. 53:19–23)[115]—were a part of pre-Islamic Arabian theology.[116]

Fathers: Earthly Surrogates of God?

Not only does the Qur'an avoid portraying God as a heavenly patriarch but also, in its treatment of parenthood, refuses to privilege fathers over mothers. According to the Qur'an, Barlas points out, the main reason behind the Arabs' rejection of Muhammad's prophecy was their practice of blindly following in the footsteps of their fathers:[117]

---

[112] Asma Barlas, 'Texts, Sex, and States: A Critique of North African Discourses on Islam', in *The Arab-African and Islamic Worlds: Interdisciplinary Studies*, eds. Kevin Lacey and Ralph Coury (New York: Peter Lang, 2000), 108–9.

[113] Barlas, *Islam, Muslims, and the US*, 120.

[114] Barlas, *'Believing Women' in Islam*, 98.

[115] It is important to note that the statement within this passage, 'Are you to have males and He females? That, then, will be an unfair division', is meant to be ironic, given the great shame that the pre-Islamic Arabs associated with the birth of daughters, leading them to bury their daughters alive—a practice that the Qur'an roundly condemns (Q. 16:58–9). See Asad, *The Message of the Qur'an*, 926–7.

[116] Ali and Leaman, 43.   [117] Barlas, *'Believing Women' in Islam*, 120.

When they are told, 'Follow what God has sent down,' they say, 'We will rather follow what we have found our fathers (*aba'ana*) following.' What, even if their fathers (*aba'uhum*) neither applied any reason nor were guided? (Q. 2:170)

While the obvious critique can be made here that Barlas' gendered reading of this verse treats the term *aba'ana* (our fathers) literally, rather than using its wider, conceptual meaning (our *fore*fathers or our ancestors), her argument that this passage challenges patriarchal conventions remains persuasive. For unquestioning obedience—on the part of both men and women—to established norms, to existing configurations of power, is a core aspect of patriarchal practice. Indeed, the Arabs equated what was normative (ethical) with whatever they found their forefathers doing, while the Qur'an introduced, as Izutsu aptly phrases it, 'a new morality entirely based on the absolute Will of God.'[118] Furthermore, Barlas argues, the text's condemnation of the misogynistic tradition of female infanticide, or the pre-Islamic Arabian custom of burying newborn daughters alive (Q. 16:58–9; 81:8–9), undercuts father-right in traditional patriarchies: that is, the base assumption that the father exercises ownership over his children, who function as his personal property, permitting him to do whatever he wants with them.[119] But the text, Barlas observes, not only refuses to ascribe to fathers 'any real or symbolic privileges that it does not accord mothers',[120] but it actually elevates mothers over fathers. For instance, while the Qur'an states the importance of showing kindness and respect to one's parents, it singles out mothers in particular, expressing empathy for the pains of pregnancy and childbirth that the mother alone has to endure:[121]

We have enjoined the human being concerning his parents. His mother carried him through weakness upon weakness, and his weaning takes two years. Give thanks to Me and to your parents. To Me is the return. But if they urge you to ascribe to Me as partner that of which you have no knowledge, then do not obey them. Keep their company honourably in this world and follow the way of him who turns to Me penitently.

---

[118] Izutsu, 45–6.   [119] Barlas, *'Believing Women' in Islam*, 180–1.
[120] Barlas, 'The Qur'an and Hermeneutics', 31.
[121] Barlas, *'Believing Women' in Islam*, 175. The Qur'an's sensitivity to the difficulties of childbearing is best captured in Jesus' birth, in which God, through a divine messenger, comforts Mary (Q. 19:22–6).

Then to Me will be your return, whereat I will inform you concerning what you used to do. (Q. 31:14–15)

As this passage shows, however, at the same time as children owe their parents respect, it is God's authority that constitutes the final word, trumping all other forms of allegiance. What differentiates one's relationship with God from that of one's parents, writes Barlas, is that the former is to be worshipped, and thus owed obedience, while the latter deserve courtesy, compassion, mercy (Q. 17:23–4).[122] The rebellion of Prophet Abraham against his polytheist father, which we will examine below, is perhaps the most compelling example of a Qur'anic story that draws out both teachings.

Prophetic Paradigms: Abraham and Muhammad

Abraham emerges as a central prophetic figure in Barlas' exegesis, exemplifying the Qur'an's emphasis on God's rule over father's rule. Abraham's break with his father is narrated in the following verses:

> And mention in the Book: Abraham. He was a truthful one, a prophet. When he said to his father, 'O my father! Why do you worship that which neither hears nor sees, and is of no avail to you in any way? O my father! A knowledge has come to me that has not come to you. So follow me that I may guide you to a right path. O my father! Do not worship Satan. Indeed, Satan is disobedient to the all-Beneficent. O my father! I am afraid that a punishment from the all-Beneficent will befall you, and you will become Satan's accomplice.' He said, 'Abraham! Are you renouncing my gods? If you do not desist, I shall stone you. So go away from me for a while.' He said, 'Peace be on you! I shall plead with my Sustainer to forgive you. Indeed, he is gracious to me. I dissociate myself from you and whatever you invoke besides God. I will supplicate to my Sustainer. Hopefully, I will not be disappointed in supplicating to my Sustainer.' (Q. 19:41–8)

This seminal passage, comments Barlas, demonstrates that the Qur'an, by subverting the authority of Abraham's father, is at odds with the structuring of traditional patriarchies, which rest on the indisputable sovereignty of fathers.[123] Moreover, she hastens to clarify, these verses do not simply substitute the authority of disbelieving

---

[122] Ibid, 174.   [123] Barlas, 'The Qur'an and Hermeneutics', 27–8.

fathers with believing ones, but rather firmly establish the supremacy
of God's rule, as evidenced further by the fact that while Abraham's
prophetic descendants are praised in the text, neither he nor they are
valorized *as* fathers.[124] In sum, the very person who is routinely
referred to, even celebrated, as the Great Patriarch—a label that the
Qur'an never uses—himself engaged in an acutely *anti*-patriarchal
act: splitting with his own father. Even Esack, an outspoken advocate
of gender justice, falls into the trap of paternalizing this prophet:

> Abraham, mentioned sixty-nine times in the Qur'an, emerges as the
> common father of the people of the book with the Muslim community
> also being the children of this great patriarch.[125]

On the contrary, Barlas writes, the Qur'an employs gender-neutral
language when describing Abraham: specifically, it uses the term
imam (Q. 2:124),[126] referring to one who acts as a leader and spiritual
guide of the people. It is important to note here that while *imam* is
grammatically masculine (the feminine form would be *imama*) the
term is, conceptually speaking, gender-neutral. This is clearly not the case
with the word 'father'—such as when Abraham states in the above
passage: 'O my father' (*ya abati*)—which is both grammatically and
conceptually masculine. While Barlas only discusses Abraham as
imam, the text uses a number of titles to describe this prophetic
figure, all of which are, significantly, gender-neutral. On various
occasions, for example, Abraham is referred to, even by himself, as
a *hanif* (Q. 3:67; 6:79; 16:120), denoting one who has abandoned
everything in order to commit him or herself to God:[127] a devout
monotheist. In addition to *hanif*, Abraham is venerated as *khalilullah*,
or the friend of God (Q. 4:125).[128]

---

[124] Barlas, *'Believing Women' in Islam*, 113.
[125] Esack, *The Qur'an: A User's Guide*, 153.
[126] Barlas, *'Believing Women' in Islam*, 114–15. The term *imam*—literally, one who
stands in front—has taken on very different meanings in Sunni and Shi'a Islam. In the
former, it refers to a prayer leader or, more generally, used as a title of respect when
addressing an Islamic scholar, while in the latter it can refer either to a prayer leader,
to an Islamic scholar or (in the specific case of Twelver Shi'a Islam) to one of the
twelve divinely-appointed Imams, starting with Imam Ali, the cousin and son-in-law
of Prophet Muhammad, and ending with Imam Muhammad al-Mahdi, who remains
in occultation.
[127] Siddiqui, 75.
[128] It is precisely because of this epithet that the Palestinian city of Hebron,
wherein Abraham lived, is referred to in Arabic as *Khalil*.

Just as Abraham is denied symbolic fatherhood, so is Muhammad, who is, in fact, denied not only symbolic but *actual* fatherhood (understood both as having a father and in the patriarchal sense of fathering sons). This scriptural silence—that is, the absence of portrayals of the Prophet in distinctly paternalistic terms—speaks volumes for Barlas, affirming the Qur'an's opposition to father-rule, to the consecration of fathers as earthly surrogates of God.[129] Q. 33:40— 'Muhammad is not the father of any of your men, but he is the Apostle of God and the Seal of the Prophets'—is the most important passage that she draws upon in this respect. While Barlas acknowledges that the specific historical circumstances of this verse suggest that it sought to clarify Muhammad's relationship to Zayd b. Haritha, his adopted son,[130] she argues that, on a deeper reading, this verse undercuts patriarchal representations of the Prophet as a symbolic father of the faithful.[131] Yet exegetes have continued to paternalize the prophet, reading fatherhood into this passage despite its categorical disavowal of Muhammad as any type of father figure. For example, the renowned English translator and commentator of the Qur'an, Muhammad Asad (d. 1992), asserts that this passage confirms the Prophet's status as 'the spiritual father of the whole community', as opposed to a physical one, thereby refuting claims of lineal descent as a sign of righteousness.[132] Asad falls into this trap yet again when translating Q. 33:6. His translation reads: 'The Prophet has a higher claim on the believers than [they have on] their own selves, [seeing that he is as a father to them] [*sic*] and his wives are their mothers.'[133] Asad is a useful barometer for gauging established, scholarly understandings of scripture, as he anchors his explanatory notes in the inherited exegetical tradition. His parenthetical addition—'[seeing that he is as a father to them]'—is thus not putting forth his own original exposition, but rather echoing the opinions of earlier commentators,

[129] Barlas, 'The Qur'an and Hermeneutics', 30.
[130] Zayd was a child-slave purchased by Muhammad, who set him free and adopted him as his own son. Zayd would later marry Zaynab bint Jahsh. Their marriage, however, was a rocky one, eventually leading to divorce. The Prophet married Zaynab shortly afterwards. He became deeply worried, however, about what people might say. Q. 33:40 essentially underscored Muhammad's adoption of Zayd, clarifying that the same marriage restrictions that apply to blood relatives do not hold for adopted/legal ones, as marriage to the former spouse of one's biological child is forbidden. See Asad, *The Message of the Qur'an*, 725.
[131] Barlas, *'Believing Women' in Islam*, 121.
[132] Asad, *The Message of the Qur'an*, 726.   [133] Ibid, 718.

in particular Abu al-Qasim al-Zamakhshari (d. 1144) and Isma'il ibn Kathir (d. 1373).[134] But Muhammad, adds Barlas, is not only denied symbolic fatherhood, but also, as history has shown, actual fatherhood:

> Given that the Prophet is not sacralised as father, is it also a mere coincidence that he loses his father, Abdullah, in his own infancy, and all his sons in theirs; that only his daughters survive, at a time and in a place when people view girls as a curse?[135]

Her discussion on how such aspects of Muhammad's life are at variance with traditional patriarchy is an illustrative example of how she incorporates the *sira* (prophetic biography) into her thinking, using historical accounts to complement her Qur'anic reading. Indeed, the Prophet's personal lifestyle, Barlas observes, was surprisingly gender egalitarian—especially given the machismo of his times—partaking in household chores, such as preparing his own meals, and never physically or verbally abusing his wives.[136]

A Hermeneutical Irony

This reference to prophetic biography is also revealing, however, because it indicates that Barlas' engagement with extra-Qur'anic Islamic texts is markedly selective, anecdotal. Like Esack, Engineer, and Wadud, when she draws upon other texts she does so in an unsystematic and utilitarian fashion, the ultimate criterion for judging the validity, the worth of these texts merely being whether their substantive content can supplement (her own reading of) the Qur'an. As the Islamic scholar Aysha Hidayatullah, referring to 'feminist' exegetes' inconsistent treatment of the *hadith*, observes:

> In some cases, the exegetes are inclined to cite certain Hadith reports positively without scrutinizing their historical authenticity when they support the just treatment of women, and they use them to buttress their interpretations of the Qur'an. In other cases, they argue for the inauthenticity of Hadith reports that demean women, rejecting those reports and maintaining that the Qur'an must be prioritized over them.[137]

---

[134] Ibid.   [135] Barlas, *'Believing Women' in Islam*, 121.
[136] Ibid, 125.
[137] Hidayatullah, 213. While Hidayatullah uses the term feminist, I place feminist in quotation marks here because, as shown in the preceding chapter and later on in

Thus, there is little interest in, or even appreciation for, the integrity of extra-Qur'anic sources as complex, discursive traditions in their own right, and with rich legacies of interpretive engagement. Barlas' usage of the historic example of Umm Salama, in particular Umm Salama's questioning of the Qur'an as a hermeneutical model with which to seek new answers from the text, is another compelling case in point. For the Occasions of Revelation (*asbab al-nuzul*) literature, which catalogue the contexts in which Qur'anic verses were revealed, is part and parcel of the wider *hadith* corpus, and therefore is of doubtful authenticity. If we cannot be certain that Umm Salama questioned the text—this account may be fabricated—why is her enquiry so crucial to Barlas' commentary, elevated to the level of a hermeneutical paradigm? Given Barlas' criticism of the *hadith* as a genre, her emphasis on Umm Salama betrays a lack of internal consistency in her exegesis. In other words, at the same time as Barlas calls for a holistic reading of scripture, employing sophisticated reading strategies and accenting the text's underlying principles, she herself, ironically, partakes in an atomistic hermeneutic of picking-and-choosing when it comes to other Islamic texts and traditions. The same critique can be levelled against Esack's, Engineer's, and Wadud's commentaries.

QUR'AN AND GENDER II: MODERN PATRIARCHY

From Biological Sex to Politicized Gender

The Qur'an not only undermines traditional configurations of patriarchy, but also 'modern' understandings of the term. By modern patriarchy, Barlas refers to those discourses and practices that justify gender inequality on the grounds that men and women have different biologies.[138] The central question that Barlas poses, then, is as follows: does the text politicize biological sex, prescribing specific social roles for men and women? Though the Qur'an, she concludes, 'recognizes sexual *differences*, it does not propagate a view of sexual

---

this chapter, Wadud and Barlas both explicitly reject identifying as feminists. See also my discussion of terminology—under the subsection 'Language and its Discontents'—at the beginning of Chapter 4.

[138] Barlas, *'Believing Women' in Islam*, 1.

differentiation; that is to say, the Qur'an recognizes sexual specificity but does not assign it any gender symbolism.'[139] To put it in simpler terms, the text does not depict males and females in terms of social characteristics—masculinity and femininity—outlining a normative, gendered division of labour.[140] Paralleling Wadud's emphasis on *taqwa* (piety) as the sole measure of human merit,[141] Barlas writes that the only type of differentiation that the Qur'an makes is 'ethico-moral', and thus irrespective of one's anatomy.[142] In her hermeneut-ical emphasis on distinguishing between biological sex and politicized gender, Barlas has clearly been influenced by feminist theory (despite her rejection of *identifying* as feminist, as we will see later in the chapter). This critical distinction between sex ('the biological fact') and gender ('the social fact') was an intellectual breakthrough in the 1970s, undermining the usage of anatomical arguments to rationalize women's subjugation.[143] Womanhood and femininity, feminists argued, were not innate qualities stemming from women's physical makeup but constructed categories, produced through socialization, through lived experience. To quote the famous words of the French feminist Simone de Beauvoir: 'One is not born, but rather becomes, a woman.'[144] This is not to imply, however, that one is an autonomous agent, free to simply choose whichever gender one desires. As the American feminist Judith Butler has noted, while gender is socially construed—a verb rather than a noun, a doing rather than a being—it is a performative act that is closely regulated by a complex web of power relations that not only discipline the subject who takes on gender roles, but actually create and recreate this subject through the very act of doing, hence problematizing notions of a self-aware, self-existing agent.[145]

[139] Barlas, 'Women's Readings of the Qur'an', 266.
[140] For a pioneering study of how masculinities are constructed in Islam, see Amanullah De Sondy, *The Crisis of Islamic Masculinities* (London: Bloomsbury, 2014), in particular Chapter 3: 'The Failed Search for a Single Qur'anic Masculinity'.
[141] Wadud, *Qur'an and Woman*, 36–7.
[142] Barlas, 'Texts, Sex, and States', 102.
[143] R.W. Connell, *Gender* (Cambridge: Polity Press, 2008), 33–4.
[144] Simone de Beauvoir, *The Second Sex* (New York: Vintage Books, 1989), 267. It is worthwhile noting here that the first edition of this landmark book was published in 1949, and thus predates feminist theoretical distinctions between sex and gender, biology and sociality.
[145] Judith Butler, 'Subjects of Sex/Gender/Desire', in *Feminisms*, eds. Sandra Kemp and Judith Squires (Oxford: Oxford University Press, 1997), 285.

On Mothering, Polygamy, and Veiling

Since we have already discussed the Qur'an's elevation of mothers over fathers, the topic of motherhood is an appropriate point of departure to explore Barlas' argument. Is this not evidence of the text's reduction of women to mothers? Firstly, counters Barlas, whereas patriarchies glorify mothers, privileging women who have given birth over those who have not, they never elevate mothers over fathers, who remain the centrepiece of this oppressive system.[146] Secondly, while modern patriarchies portray mothering as the sole function of women, the Qur'an does not present women as only being mothers.[147] Indeed, a number of women who never bore children became highly influential figures in the first Muslim community. Barlas gives the example of Ayesha bint Abu Bakr (d. 678)—a wife of Muhammad—who, despite never becoming a mother, is one of the most revered personalities in Islam and a role model for Muslim women.[148] As *hadith* scholars have shown, Ayesha played a seminal role in the formation of the *hadith* literature, relating roughly 2,200 reports.[149] As we saw in the preceding chapter, Wadud, when highlighting the Qur'an's emphasis on bearing rather than rearing, also drew upon Islamic history. Specifically, she pointed to Amina, the Prophet's mother, who did not partake in her child's rearing, giving him to a wet-nurse, Halima—an action that, significantly, did not lead to any stigma, to any 'charge of un-motherliness' in the biographical accounts.[150] Furthermore, Barlas continues, the Qur'an does not politicize the act of giving birth. That is, it does not portray childbirth as a form of divine retribution against women.[151] This stands in contrast to the Old Testament, which presents the ordeal of childbirth as a perpetual punishment for women, brought about by Eve's enticement (Gen. 3:11–16):

> He [God] said, 'Who told you that you were naked? Have you eaten of the tree of which I commanded you not to eat?' The man said, 'The

[146] Barlas, *'Believing Women' in Islam*, 179.   [147] Ibid.   [148] Ibid.
[149] Jonathan Brown, *Hadith: Muhammad's Legacy in the Medieval and Modern World* (Oxford: Oneworld, 2009), 19. Brown provides the following quantitative breakdown of the five leading *hadith* transmitters: Abu Hurayrah (5,300), Ibn 'Umar (2,600), Anas bin Malik (2,300), Ayesha (2,200), and Ibn 'Abbas (1,700).
[150] Wadud, *Inside the Gender Jihad*, 127–8.
[151] Barlas, *'Believing Women' in Islam*, 175.

woman whom you gave to be with me, she gave me fruit of the tree, and I ate.' Then the Lord God said to the woman. 'What is this that you have done?' The woman said, 'The serpent deceived me, and I ate.' . . . To the woman He said, 'I will surely multiply your pain in childbearing; in pain you shall bring forth children. Your desire shall be for your husband, and he shall rule over you.'[152]

By foregrounding the absence of this narrative—portraying childbirth as punishment, thereby politicizing female biology—in the Qur'an, Barlas makes a novel contribution to the earlier work of Wadud and Hassan. As we have seen, these scholars underscored the absence in the Qur'an of the biblical understanding that (a) Eve was created from Adam's rib, showing that they were both created from a 'single soul' (Q. 4:1) and, therefore, that women and men are ontologically the same; and that (b) Eve persuaded Adam to eat from the Tree, as the Qur'anic narrative presents this act of disobedience as a collective one, in which both partners were equally culpable.[153]

According to Barlas, the Qur'an does not license polygamy. Like Wadud,[154] she makes this case by using historical criticism and careful, textual analysis. Quoting Q. 4:2–3—the polygamy verse (4:3), as well as the one that immediately precedes it—she comments that not only did the text's approval of having up to four wives actually restrict the number of wives that a man could take in that time (theoretically, men could have an unlimited number of spouses) but also that the Qur'an's objective, as the precise wording of the passage reveals, was to ensure justice for female orphans.[155] The verses read:

---

[152] The New Testament provides a slightly different take on this story, for while it affirms the Genesis narrative of Eve's enticement, it represents childbearing as an ordeal that will *save* women in the Hereafter (1 Tim. 2:11–15). It is important to note that Christian feminists have challenged such biblical texts that extol silence and submission on the part of women. See, among others: Elisabeth Schüssler Fiorenza, *Discipleship of Equals: A Critical Feminist Ekklesia-logy of Liberation* (New York: Crossroad Publishing Company, 1993); Elisabeth Schüssler Fiorenza, *In Memory of Her: A Feminist Theological Reconstruction of Christian Origins* (New York: Crossroad Publishing Company, 1994), first published in 1983; and Rosemary Radford Ruether, *Sexism and God-Talk: Towards a Feminist Theology* (Boston: Beacon Press, 1993), also first published in 1983.

[153] Wadud, *Qur'an and Woman*, 19–20 and 24–5; Hassan, 'An Islamic Perspective', 98 and 103–4.

[154] Wadud, *Qur'an and Woman*, 83.

[155] Barlas, *'Believing Women' in Islam*, 191.

Give the orphans their property, and do not replace things of your own that are bad with things that are good among theirs, and do not eat up their property by mingling it with your own property, for that is, indeed, a grave crime. (4:2) If you fear that you will not deal justly with the orphans, then marry women that you like, two, three, or four. But if you fear that you will not be able to deal justly with them, then only one, or what your right hands possess. That makes it likelier that you will not be unjust. (4:3)

This focus on female orphans brings us back to the question of historical context. This verse was revealed in a situation wherein male guardians were exploiting orphans under their care and, thus, the Qur'an proposed marriage as a way of rectifying the problem, 'the assumption being that marriage gives the husband a stake in the honest management of his wife's property.'[156] The Qur'an's espousal of polygamy, then, is tied to a specific moment of crisis in the burgeoning Muslim community and not applicable for all times. Paralleling Wadud,[157] Barlas also makes a holistic reading, noting that social justice is a theme that permeates the text's discourse on polygamy. For in addition to ensuring that justice is meted out to orphans, it states that a man is not allowed to marry more than one wife if he feels that he 'will not be able to deal justly with them', adding later on that even if he wanted to treat them equally, he would be unable to do so (Q. 4:129).[158] The absence of justice in polygamous relationships therefore rules out the possibility of having multiple spouses. It is important to note, however, that Barlas does not simply rehash Wadud's interpretive insights. By reflecting upon these verses in light of modern patriarchy, Barlas is able to push a liberating exegesis of the polygamy verse further. Many Muslims who support polygamy claim that it is in the inherent nature of men to desire multiple partners, as one woman cannot possibly satisfy the incessant male libido. Yet nowhere in the above verses, Barlas observes, are the 'sexual nature or needs' of men or women mentioned, showing that polygamy does not serve a sexual function.[159] That is, there is no connection made between polygamy and desire. Indeed, the Qur'an, she argues, does not distinguish between male and female sexualities.[160] By not framing its discussion on polygamy in terms of male desire, the Qur'an refuses

---

[156] Ibid.   [157] Wadud, *Qur'an and Woman*, 83.
[158] Barlas, *'Believing Women' in Islam*, 191. Q. 4:129 is incorrectly cited as Q. 4:125.
[159] Ibid.   [160] Barlas, 'Women's Readings of the Qur'an', 264.

to politicize male biology, to make a wider, social statement about men's bodies. This returns us to the construction of gender as a category, for not only do women become women but so, too, do men become men, acquiring manhood and masculinity through everyday performative acts,[161] from getting into fights with other men and driving powerful cars to withholding one's emotions in the face of pain and having sex with multiple partners.

Just as the Qur'an does not sanction polygamy, Barlas argues, there is no scriptural basis for the female headscarf, referred to today as the *hijab*. But just because there is no scriptural basis for the veil—an exegetical argument that we will unpack shortly—this does not mean that Barlas views the veil as necessarily being oppressive. For what the veil can mean is contingent upon one's environment: in certain contexts, particularly secular ones, the veil can become an empowering symbol of protest, of asserting 'independence, visibility, and difference', while in other contexts it can be 'a socially-enforced mode of subordination to men'.[162] There are two Qur'anic passages that are commonly cited to justify the veil. They are provided below:

O Prophet! Tell your wives and your daughters and the women of the faithful to draw closely over themselves their wraps (*jalabibihinna*). That makes it likely that they will be recognized and not be troubled, and God is all-Forgiving, all-Merciful. If the hypocrites, those in whose hearts is a sickness, and the rumourmongers in the city, do not desist, We will surely rouse you against them. Then they will not be your neighbours in it except for a while. (Q. 33:59–60)

Tell the believing men to lower their gaze and to guard their private parts. That is more decent for them. God is well aware of what they do. And tell the believing women to lower their gaze and to guard their private parts, and not to display their charms, except for what is outward, and let them draw their veils (*khumurihinna*) over their breasts, and not display their charms except to their husbands, or their fathers, or their husband's fathers, or their sons, or their husband's sons, or their brothers, or their brothers' sons, or their sisters' sons, or

---

[161] Connell, 4.

[162] Asma Barlas, 'Embodying Islam and Muslims: Religious and Secular Inscriptions', in *The Body Unbound: Philosophical Perspectives on Politics, Embodiment, and Religion*, eds. Marius Timmann Mjaaland, Ola Sigurdson, and Sigridur Thorgeirsdottir (Newcastle, UK: Cambridge Scholars Publishing, 2010). This book chapter was accessed on 16 September 2014 from Barlas' personal website: www.asmabarlas.com/papers.html

their women, or their slave women, or male attendants lacking sexual desire, or children that are still unaware of women's nakedness. Let them not thump their feet to make known their hidden ornaments. Turn to God in repentance, O believers, so that you may be felicitous. (Q. 24:30–1)

These passages, Barlas comments, reflect two very different types of injunctions, the former historically contingent and the latter universally applicable. The precise wording of Q. 33:59–60 clearly indicates that it was addressing a particular situation and, therefore, needs to be read in light of this context. Specifically, non-Muslim men—'the hypocrites, those in whose hearts is a sickness, and the rumour-mongers in the city'—were harassing Muslim women on the streets. This was in large part due to the culture of a slave-owning society, as slaves (who were traditionally uncovered) were seen as open to sexual approach.[163] The Qur'anic commandment to cover was thus meant 'to make Muslim women visible to non-Muslim (*jahili*) men as being sexually unavailable.'[164] While Q. 33:59–60 reflects a call to veil relating to a specific set of circumstances,[165] Q. 24:30–1, the language of which is markedly broad in nature, represents a principle applicable to all times and places. Like Wadud,[166] Barlas argues that the veil is an essentially ethical concept, or what she calls 'a sexually moral and modest praxis', and not something that can be reduced to mere physical attire,[167] which is contextually bound. Not only is this a form of veiling that applies, as the wording of Q. 24:30–1 shows, to both men and women—indeed, men are addressed first—but it also presumes, Barlas adds, that men and women are, in fact, free to mix with one another, for how else can the injunction to lower one's gaze make sense if the sexes are segregated?[168] While Barlas offers a scripturally grounded rereading of veiling, she erroneously claims that the Arabic word *hijab* (literally, a screen or curtain) does not occur in the Qur'an.[169] To be sure, *hijab* is never used to refer to a headscarf.

---

[163] Barlas, 'Women's Readings of the Qur'an', 268.   [164] Ibid.

[165] The understanding of the veil as being a universal head-covering was, as the historian Leila Ahmed has shown, introduced into Muslim societies through Sassanian and Middle Eastern Christian communities, wherein veiling and segregation were prevalent practices amongst upper-class women. See Ahmed, 5.

[166] Wadud, *Inside the Gender Jihad*, 219.

[167] Barlas, *'Believing Women' in Islam*, 56.

[168] Barlas, 'Women's Readings of the Qur'an', 268.

[169] Barlas, *'Believing Women' in Islam*, 53.

However, it does appear in three distinct senses: firstly, as a partition between Muhammad's wives and the faithful, who were ordered to address his wives from behind a curtain (Q. 33:53); secondly, as a barrier that emerges between the believers and the pagans when the Qur'an is recited (Q. 17:45); and, finally, as a screen separating humankind and God, who would never speak to a human directly, but rather through divine inspiration, a curtain (*hijab*) or a messenger (Q. 42:51).[170]

Closely tied to veiling is the issue of female sexuality. The sad irony behind the Qur'anic mandate to veil, laments Barlas, is that although its intent was to confront *male* sexual immorality—namely, non-Muslim men harassing Muslim women—it has since devolved into a patriarchal obsession with women's sexual conduct.[171] Indeed, a central assumption underlying Muslim conservatives' support for female veiling, ranging from the headscarf that exposes the face and hands to the *burqa*, covering the entire body, is that women's bodies are 'sexually corrupting to those who see them; it is thus necessary to shield Muslim men from viewing women's bodies by concealing them.'[172] This idea of women's bodies as being too alluring, too sexually robust (and, conversely, of men as being morally weak and thus vulnerable to temptation when exposed to women's bodies) is intrinsically connected to a wider view of sex as being unclean, impure, indecent. This problematic approach to sexuality, she argues, has more in common with Judaism and Christianity than the Qur'an—which makes no such claim—finding its way into Islamic thought through such extra-scriptural sources as the *hadith* and *tafsir*.[173] A recurring theme, therefore, in women's gender egalitarian readings of the Qur'an (recalling Wadud's and Hassan's commentaries of the Creation Story and the Events of the Garden) is the contrasting of the Qur'an with the Bible, in particular the Old Testament, critically discerning the dissimilarities between the two. In so

---

[170] Ali and Leaman, 50–2. With regard to Q. 42:51, Moses and the burning bush are a classic example of God speaking to humankind from behind a curtain, while Jesus' miraculous speech as a newborn and Gabriel's correspondence with Muhammad are examples of inspiration and messengership, respectively.

[171] Barlas, 'Women's Readings of the Qur'an', 268.

[172] Barlas, *'Believing Women' in Islam*, 54.

[173] Ibid, 151–2. Although Barlas explicitly mentions both Judaism and Christianity, the former—as Christopher Rowland has pointed out to me—is actually closer to Islam in this respect.

doing, they have unearthed the lasting effects that biblical exegesis has had on Qur'anic exegesis as a field. On the contrary, Barlas notes, the Qur'an has a very different take on sexuality, approaching sex as 'fulfilling and wholesome in itself, that is, outside of its procreative role.'[174] According to the text, she observes, the purpose of sexual intimacy is the attainment of tranquillity (*sukun*), without making any reference to reproduction (Q. 30:21).[175] The verse reads:

> Among His signs is that He created for you mates (*azwajan*) from your own selves that you may take comfort in them (*litaskunu ilayha*), and He ordained love and mercy between you. There are indeed signs in that for a people who reflect.

This passage not only illustrates vividly the compatibility of sexuality and religion, argues Barlas, but acknowledges that men and women have the same sexual natures,[176] as reflected in the Qur'an's usage of the gender-neutral term: 'mates' (*azwaj*, sing: *zawj*). That is, the text does not differentiate between male and female sexualities. As will be shown shortly, however, this claim has become a point of contention amongst Muslim progressives.

Revisiting a Difficult Verse

Q. 4:34, as witnessed in the preceding chapter on Wadud, is arguably the most challenging passage for Qur'anic commentators reading for gender justice. This subsection will explore core aspects of this verse, analysing how exactly Barlas grapples with them hermeneutically, beginning with the opening section, which reads: 'Men are the guardians (*qawwamun*) of women, because of the advantage God has granted some of them over others and by virtue of their spending out of their wealth.' Interpreters of the Qur'an, critiques Barlas, have read sexual differentiation into this statement, insisting that men are guardians because they have greater physical strength, rationality, even virtue than women.[177] Yet this passage does not make any claims about the innate superiority of men. Echoing Wadud,[178] Barlas foregrounds the historical context of this verse, pointing out the explicit connection drawn between male authority and financial

---

[174] Ibid, 153.   [175] Ibid.   [176] Ibid, 153–4.
[177] Barlas, 'The Qur'an and Hermeneutics', 17–18.
[178] Wadud, *Qur'an and Woman*, 70–1.

resources: that is, the husband's role as family breadwinner.[179] But since the society that we live in today is drastically different, she concludes, with women becoming financial earners next to men, the husband's guardianship is effectively nullified. In addition to historical criticism, Barlas uses textual holism as an interpretive strategy, arguing that a patriarchal reading of men as guardians is at variance with other gender-egalitarian verses in the Qur'an, such as Q. 9:71, describing men and women as each other's protectors (*awliya'*):[180]

> The believing men and the believing women are protectors (*awliya'*) of one another: they enjoin what is right and prohibit what is wrong. They maintain the prayer, give the poor rate, and obey God and His Messenger. It is they to whom God will soon bestow His mercy. Indeed, God is all-Mighty, all-Wise.

Alongside Q. 4:34, there is another verse that conservative Muslims routinely reference when making sweeping claims of male superiority: specifically, Q. 2:228, which refers to men as having a 'degree' (*daraja*) over women. Paralleling Wadud yet again,[181] Barlas reads this passage in its *entirety*, demonstrating that the word *daraja* is not used to signify 'male ontological superiority' but a husband's rights in divorce.[182] The verse reads:

> The divorced women shall undergo, without remarrying, a waiting period of three monthly courses: for it is not lawful for them to conceal what God may have created in their wombs, if they believe in God and the Last Day. And during this period their husbands are fully entitled to take them back, if they desire reconciliation. The wives have rights similar to the obligations upon them, in accordance with honorable norms, and men have a degree *(daraja)* over them. And God is All-Mighty, All-Wise.

However, whereas Wadud interprets the husband's right as being able to pronounce a divorce without outside arbitration, as opposed to the wife who requires the mediation of a judge,[183] Barlas writes that the husband's right is being able to rescind the divorce.[184] Here, she draws upon the explanatory notes of Asad, the English translator of

[179] Barlas, *'Believing Women' in Islam*, 186.
[180] Barlas, 'The Qur'an and Hermeneutics', 18.
[181] Wadud, *Qur'an and Woman*, 68.
[182] Barlas, 'The Qur'an and Hermeneutics', 16–17.
[183] Wadud, *Qur'an and Woman*, 68.
[184] Barlas, 'The Qur'an and Hermeneutics', 17.

the Qur'an introduced earlier on. Asad argues that because the husband is the maintainer of the family, he exercises the right to revoke a divorce first.[185] So just as male guardianship is negated in a new context wherein women are no longer confined to the home so, too, is male privilege in divorce proceedings. Q. 4:34 and 2:228, then, cannot be divorced from their original revelatory setting. And herein lies a key argument in Barlas' commentary: namely, that *difference* does not necessarily entail *inequality*, for the Qur'an's sometimes different treatment of men and women, as exemplified by these two verses, is not rooted in wider biological claims of men as being the superior sex and women the inferior one, but rather reflect the existing division of labour in a patriarchal society.[186]

The wife's obedience to her husband is another contentious aspect of Q. 4:34, or, to be more precise, of mainstream understandings of it. The passage, including the first part on male guardianship, reads:

> Men are the guardians of women, because of the advantage God has granted some of them over others and by virtue of their spending out of their wealth. So righteous women are obedient (*qanitatun*), safeguarding what is unseen (*hafizatun lil-ghaybi*) of what God has enjoined them to guard.

Citing Wadud, Barlas argues that although the vast majority of interpretations of *qanitat* (literally, obedient women) assert that the husband is the object of obedience, it is God, and God alone, who is worthy of obedience.[187] In order to substantiate this argument, Wadud undertook a holistic approach, exploring how the same term is used in other parts of the Qur'an. In so doing, she showed that other occurrences of *qanitat* and its linguistic derivatives are used solely to denote (male and female) obedience to God (Q. 3:17; 33:35; 66:12).[188] *Hafizatun lil-ghayb* (literally, safeguarding what is unseen) is another hotly disputed term in this verse. Gender egalitarian female readers have argued that this phrase refers to women 'who fulfil their religious obligations and protect their faith, as God has guarded it.'[189]

---

[185] Asad, *The Message of the Qur'an*, 61.
[186] Barlas, *'Believing Women' in Islam*, 198–9.
[187] Barlas, 'Women's Readings of the Qur'an', 263.
[188] Wadud, *Qur'an and Woman*, 74. Although Wadud does not include Q. 16:120 here, it is interesting to note that this verse, which we cited earlier when discussing Abraham's rebellion against his father, describes Abraham as a *qanit* (an obedient one).
[189] Ali, *Sexual Ethics and Islam*, 119.

Yet most commentators have understood this phrase as being women who, in the absence of their husbands, protect their chastity and their husband's property—an interpretation that was influenced by a widely circulated and inauthentic *hadith* report:[190]

> The Messenger of God said: 'The best of women is the one who pleases you if you look at her, obeys you if you order her, and if you are away from her, she guards herself and your property.' Then the Prophet recited verse 34 of *Surat al-Nisa'* ['Chapter of the Women', Chapter 4].[191]

Though Barlas does not make an original contribution to this discussion, reiterating the ideas of Wadud, she could have advanced a gender-just reading of *qanitat* and *hafizatun lil-ghayb*. For while Wadud relied on a *textual* argument, analysing how such terms are employed in other parts of scripture, Barlas could have made a *theological* one, reinterpreting them in light of her earlier thesis that the Qur'an is at loggerheads with traditional patriarchy, refusing to portray men as earthly surrogates of a Heavenly Father. Because divine self-disclosure categorically rejects any representation of God as a father figure, and because men can never partake in God's sovereignty and undivided unity, a theologically sound interpretation of *qanitat* and *hafizatun lil-ghayb* must necessarily direct women's obedience and loyalty to God, alone.

The most controversial aspect of Q. 4:34 is the final segment of the verse, a literal rendering of which (as we have seen previously) gives a man license to beat his wife. The verse, in its entirety, reads:

> Men are the guardians of women, because of the advantage God has granted some of them over others and by virtue of their spending out of their wealth. So righteous women are obedient, safeguarding what is unseen of what God has enjoined them to guard. As for those wives whose misconduct you fear, (first) advise them, and (if ineffective) keep away from them in the bed, and (as a last resort) beat them (*idribuhunna*). Then if they obey you, do not seek any course (of action) against them. Indeed, God is all-Exalted, all-Great.

---

[190] Ibid.

[191] The earliest appearance of this report can be found in the *musnad* (*hadith* collection) of Abu Dawud al-Tayalisi (d. 819), which is significant, as the report does not appear in the *sahihayn*, or the two 'authentic' *hadith* collections of Bukhari and Muslim. This *hadith* has resurfaced in classical and medieval Qur'anic exegesis, most notably in the Great Commentary (*al-Tafsir al-Kabir*) of Abu Ja'far al-Tabari (d. 923). I am grateful to Mustafa Abu Sway of al-Quds University for providing the text and citations of this report.

Barlas grapples with this last portion using two signature hermeneutical moves. Firstly, she reads this passage extratextually, underscoring the patriarchal setting of revelation, in which violence against women was widespread. As she puts it:

> At a time and in a society in which a man would inherit his father's wives, bury his new-born daughter alive in the sand, and beat a woman at will, verse 4:34, even if read as permission to strike a wife in specific circumstances, could not have seemed like a license or unethical.[192]

Secondly, she reads this verse intratextually, arguing that an interpretation that mandates wife-beating violates wider Qur'anic principles pertaining to marriage, such as its call for 'love and mercy' (*mawaddatan wa rahma*) between spouses (Q. 30:21), even instructing partners who are in the midst of divorce to act graciously with one another (Q. 2:237).[193] As discussed in the preceding chapter, Wadud initially came to terms with Q. 4:34, taking into account the original context of revelation and concluding that this verse constituted a severe restriction on male violence against women.[194] This reading was unable to satisfy Wadud, however, leading her to later 'say "no" outright to the literal implementation of this passage.'[195] Yet literalism, interjects Barlas, is a hermeneutical impossibility, for 'so long as a word can have more than one meaning there is no such thing as a literal reading.'[196] In other words, whereas Wadud eventually rejects this last part of the verse, Barlas questions why 'beat them' is privileged as the literal translation of *idribuhunna*? She departs from Wadud, then, by analysing the term *idribuhunna* holistically, exploring how it is employed elsewhere in the text. Citing Q. 38:44, she shows that this term is also used in a distinctly symbolic fashion.[197] Referring to Prophet Job, the verse reads:

---

[192] Asma Barlas, *Re-Understanding Islam: A Double Critique*, Spinoza Lectures presented by the University of Amsterdam (Amsterdam: Van Gorcum, 2008), 16.

[193] Barlas, 'Women's Readings of the Qur'an', 264.

[194] Wadud, *Qur'an and Woman*, 76.

[195] Wadud, *Inside the Gender Jihad*, 200. Upon making this statement, Wadud put forth a textually holistic argument that parallels that of Barlas, arguing that any physical strike against women would run counter to such core Qur'anic values as 'justice' and 'human dignity' (203).

[196] Barlas, *Re-Understanding Islam*, 23.

[197] Barlas, '*Believing Women*' in Islam, 188. The legal scholar Azizah al-Hibri also cites Q. 38:44 when dealing with domestic violence. See Azizah Y. al-Hibri, 'Muslim

We told him: 'Take a small bunch of grass in your hand and then with it strike (*idribbihi*) your wife, but do not break your oath.' Indeed, We found him to be patient. What an excellent servant and one who would always turn unto Us!

According to classical commentators, Job vowed to beat his wife with a hundred lashes, as she had cursed God on account of his painful tribulations.[198] When he was healed, God instructed him to take 'a small bunch of grass' and to symbolically strike his wife with it once (*idribbihi*), thereby fulfilling his promise without physically harming her.[199] But 'the best' reading of *idribuhunna* insofar as Q. 4:34 is concerned, concludes Barlas, is not symbolic hitting but 'confinement' (that is, restricting the wife to her home) as the Qur'an prescribes this action when discussing how husbands should deal with adulterous wives (Q. 4:15).[200] This specific rendering of *idribuhunna* is questionable, however, since Q. 4:15 uses a different word altogether: *amsikuhunna* (confine them).

Critical Interpretation or Apologetic Argument?

Barlas' exegesis of Q. 4:34 betrays the limits of her radical hermeneutic, for despite her otherwise critical rereading, she idealizes the text. By idealize I mean that she seeks to completely reconcile contemporary understandings of gender justice with a text that emerged in late antiquity, and thus within a society that had a markedly different conception of gender relations. As shown in Chapter 2, a central grievance that Esack has with the Qur'an is its androcentrism,[201] addressing men, who become the subject of divine discourse, thereby reducing women to objects that are acted on. Going back to our discussion on Q. 4:34, irrespective of whether *idribuhunna* is interpreted as '[physically] beat them', '[symbolically] beat them', that is, spell out a lesson for them, or 'confine them', men remain the text's audience and women passive objects in the third person—an absent 'them'—who are to be checked, rebuked, disciplined. Wadud also

---

Women's Rights in the Global Village: Challenges and Opportunities', *Journal of Law and Religion* 15:1/2 (2000–1): 64–5.

[198] Asad, *The Message of the Qur'an*, 789.
[199] Barlas, *'Believing Women' in Islam*, 188.   [200] Ibid, 188–9.
[201] Esack, 'Islam and Gender Justice', 195.

takes issue with this problematic aspect of the Qur'an and highlights its androcentric discourse on sexuality, as illustrated in Q. 2:223—'Your women are a tillage (*harth*) for you, so come to your tillage whenever you like'—portraying male sexuality as assertive and dominant, female sexuality as acquiescent and submissive.[202] This verse clearly conflicts with Barlas' claim that the text does not differentiate between male and female sexualities.[203] And yet she dismisses any critiques of androcentrism. Since the text was revealed in a context wherein men held power, she rebuts, it had to speak in terms of this reality, clarifying that to 'deal with a historical contingency is not to advocate it as a timeless norm.'[204] But her own research reveals that the Qur'an provocatively pushed the boundaries of its own context, speaking *of* women and men in egalitarian terms and even speaking *to* women directly, as exemplified by Umm Salama's verse (Q. 33:35). In other words, when it comes to matters of faith, good deeds, and divine recompense, the Qur'an explicitly addresses both sexes. But if the Qur'an is willing to use such gender-inclusive language with regard to belief, why does it speak solely to men when discussing sexuality? For instance, the text's discourse on marriage—a partnership that is public, unlike sexual intercourse, which is private and confined to the home—is acutely androcentric, portraying men as 'marrying' and women as being 'married' (Q. 2:221).[205] Even the so-called polygamy verse is inescapably male-focussed. Although women's gender egalitarian readings have cogently demonstrated that the sanctioning of polygamy presumes a historical crisis wherein female orphans were being exploited, and thus is not an open license for having multiple wives, men remain the audience of these verses and it is up to them to elect, to initiate marriage: 'If you fear that you will not deal justly with the orphans, then marry women that you like: two, three, or four' (4:3).[206] Hence, when it comes to sexuality, of which marriage is part and parcel, the Qur'an *does* make social

---

[202] Wadud, *Inside the Gender Jihad*, 193. Q. 2:187 is another example of the text's androcentric approach to sexuality, speaking to husbands and permitting them to enter their wives during the nights of fasting.

[203] Barlas, 'Women's Readings of the Qur'an', 264.

[204] Barlas, *Re-Understanding Islam*, 25.

[205] Ali and Leaman, 42.

[206] I am grateful to Christopher Rowland for alerting me to the androcentric nature of this passage.

statements about male and female bodies, politicizing their different biologies.

The roots of Barlas' apologia can be found in her essentialization of the Qur'an, that is, approaching it as a text that is innately liberating and thus can only be liberating. As the Islamic scholar Kecia Ali has observed, Barlas' anti-patriarchal interpretation refuses to acknowledge the legitimacy of the need to wrestle with divergent Qur'anic readings, in particular patriarchal ones, which are too readily reduced to 'misreadings'.[207] Indeed, while Barlas states at the beginning of her Commentary that her intention is 'not to deny that the Qur'an can be read in patriarchal modes',[208] she ends up making precisely this argument a few pages later, insisting that an 'exegesis that reads oppression, inequality and patriarchy into the Qur'an should be seen as a misreading, a failure in reading, since it attributes to god *zulm* [oppression] against women.'[209] In her essentialist approach to scripture, Barlas shares common ground with Engineer. As was seen in Chapter 3, Engineer presents the Qur'an as an ancient 'charter of rights for women', championing complete gender equality.[210] He even goes so far as to claim that there is not a single verse that can be used to support the oppressive status quo.[211] In other words, when the status quo does draw upon the Qur'an for Islamic legitimacy, it is merely manipulating the text's *real* meaning, which is an invariably liberating one. Though both Barlas and Engineer resort to apologetics, it is important to appreciate the very different ways in which these two exegetes essentialize the text, as Barlas does so in a far more sophisticated manner. Not all essentialist arguments are the same; some are articulated more rigorously than others. Whereas Engineer reads scripture in a selective and inconsistent fashion, Barlas commences her exegesis with a theological reflection—making God's justice, unity and unrepresentability her hermeneutical points of departure—and then forwards textual interpretations in light of this liberating theology. For 'basing our readings of the Qur'an on a theologically sound view of God opens up infinite, and infinitely liberating, ways of encountering scripture.'[212] The problem with

[207] Ali, *Sexual Ethics and Islam*, 132.
[208] Barlas, *'Believing Women' in Islam*, 4.   [209] Ibid, 14.
[210] Engineer, *Islam and Liberation Theology*, 33.
[211] Engineer, *On Developing Theology of Peace in Islam*, v.
[212] Barlas, 'Holding Fast by the Best in the Precepts', 20.

this approach, however, is that it serves to undermine the letter, the substance, the specificity of the text, allowing the reader to explain away anything that contradicts her/his view of a just deity.

ISLAM: A DOUBLE CRITIQUE

Between a Rock and a Hard Place

This final section will unpack the scope of Barlas' discourse on justice. A theme that continuously resurfaces in her writings is her commitment to speaking truth to power in both Muslim and non-Muslim Western contexts.[213] This is an intellectual that occupies two uneasy subject positions: the one as a believing woman in a patriarchal Muslim community, the other as a Muslim in a racist, Western-dominated world. She succinctly sums up this dual grievance as follows:

> As a Muslim woman I thus find myself precariously balanced on the inhospitable terrain between the (ostensibly religious) sexism of conservative Muslims and the (secular) racism of the liberal Western society in which I live. My quarrels, therefore, are necessarily with both.[214]

Barlas' oppositional role in both contexts is effectively encapsulated in a volume titled, *Re-Understanding Islam: A Double Critique* (2008)— a collection of two lectures that she delivered in 2008 as part of the Spinoza lecture series at the University of Amsterdam. The first lecture is essentially a summary of her gender-egalitarian reading of the Qur'an, a project clearly targeted at the wider Muslim community, while the second unpacks the problematic ways in which non-Muslim Westerners have represented Islam and Muslims, thereby addressing a different audience altogether.[215] While I have used the

---

[213] While she acknowledges that the West is an ideologically loaded term, plagued with essentialist assumptions and premised on a reductive representation of a primitive East, she uses it because it reflects 'an actual existing hegemony that characterizes itself as Western.' See Asma Barlas, 'Globalizing Equality: Muslim Women, Theology, and Feminisms', in *On Shifting Ground: Middle Eastern Women in the Global Era*, ed. Fera Simone (New York: Feminist Press, 2005), 108.

[214] Barlas, *Islam, Muslims, and the US*, 14.

[215] Barlas, *Re-Understanding Islam*, 31. The first lecture, delivered in May 2008, was titled 'Believing Women in Islam: Between Secular and Religious Politics and

subjects of these twin lectures as a heuristic tool to illustrate her commitment to 'double critique', it is important not to portray Barlas' exegetical work on the Qur'an as being targeted solely at Muslims. As she notes at the beginning of her Commentary, she undertook this study in order to challenge both conservative Muslims and secular feminists, who cannot see the Qur'an as being anything but a patriarchal, indeed blatantly misogynistic, text.[216] Confronting European and North American discourses on Islam is crucial given the long history of the West's demonization of Islam and Muslims. Barlas notes, for example, that Prophet Muhammad's vilification as a terrorist in Islamophobic circles is not simply a contemporary phenomenon, but has deep roots stretching back to medieval Christendom, in which he was attacked as an imposter, a fanatic, and even the Antichrist.[217] As a result, when writing on Islam, especially in European languages, the Muslim intellectual has to think against the grain of an entire vocabulary—an epistemology—that posits her/his religion as being irredeemably conservative, irrational, backward. Conversely, argues Barlas, such representations serve to vindicate the West, which comes to stand for everything that Islam is not, and never will be:[218] liberal, reasoned, civilized. And it is precisely in order to escape such racist dichotomies that she unmasks injustice in both Muslim and non-Muslim contexts, showing that oppressive systems like patriarchy are not exclusive to Muslim societies. As she puts it with regard to violence against women:

> As someone who was born in the so-called Muslim world and who now lives in the so-called West, I am as horrified by practices like 'honour' killings in some Muslim societies as I am by the fact that a woman is sexually assaulted every 2 minutes in the US.[219]

Theology', and the second, delivered in June 2008, was titled 'Would Spinoza Understand Me? Europe, Islam, and the Mirror of Difference'.

[216] Barlas, *'Believing Women' in Islam*, xii.

[217] Barlas, *Re-Understanding Islam*, 39. For two pioneering historical studies of Western representations of Islam, see Norman Daniel, *Islam and the West: The Making of an Image* (Oxford: Oneworld, 2009), first published in 1960; and R.W. Southern, *Western Views of Islam in the Middle Ages* (Cambridge, MA: Harvard University Press, 1962).

[218] Barlas, *Re-Understanding Islam*, 32.

[219] Ibid, 18. She adds that what initially drew her to the issue of violence against women was not violence perpetrated in the name of Islam, but rather the European practice of witch-burning, which lasted between the fifteenth and eighteenth centuries and claimed the lives of almost one million women.

This section will demonstrate that it is this commitment to double critique that forms the critical point of departure for Barlas' comprehensive approach to social justice, drawing connections between different forms of suffering and resistance.

9/11 and Empire

The attacks of 11 September 2001 are arguably the single most important event, at least in the past decade, that has framed discussions on Islam. Paralleling Esack, who sharply criticized liberal Muslims for failing to challenge the presumption that America's suffering ought to be 'the axis around which the earth rotates',[220] Barlas locates 9/11 firmly within the framework of global politics, thus rejecting any notion that it marked a 'unique event' in history.[221] Ascribing any uniqueness to 9/11, she writes, is inextricably bound to the racist idea that Americans themselves are unique, that their pain is somehow more important than that of the rest of the world.[222] Drawing on the timely article of the Chilean writer Ariel Dorfman—'America's No Longer Unique'—Barlas points out that the USA perpetrated its own 9/11 in Chile.[223] Here, she is referring to 11 September 1973, when the USA backed a military coup that overthrew the socialist and democratically elected president Salvador Allende and brought into power the dictatorship of Augusto Pinochet. While, as has been shown throughout this chapter, Barlas takes issue with literalist readings of scripture, she emphasizes the universality of extremism—not only being present in non-Islamic religions but also in secular discourse and practice—and points to the underlying socioeconomic roots of such interpretations:[224]

> extremism needs to be understood in the broader context of a racist, unjust and oppressive global political economy that is the outgrowth of both centuries of Western imperialism and of many existing US policies.[225]

---

[220] Esack, 'In Search of Progressive Islam Beyond 9/11', 82–3.
[221] Barlas, *Islam, Muslims, and the US*, 17.   [222] Ibid, 21.
[223] Asma Barlas, 'September 11, 2001: Remember Forgetting', *Political Theology* 12:5 (2011): 729–30. For Dorfman's article, see: Ariel Dorfman, 'America's No Longer Unique', *Counterpunch*, 3 October 2001, available at: http://www.counterpunch.org/2001/10/03/america-s-no-longer-unique/ accessed 17 September 2014.
[224] Barlas, *Islam, Muslims, and the US*, 67–8.   [225] Ibid.

For Barlas, then, 9/11 is first and foremost a political event. Though Muslims can be terrorists, depictions of terrorism as uniquely Islamic, as being the simple outcome of Muslim religious fundamentalism renders invisible the oppressive contexts in which terrorism transpires.[226] Furthermore, the USA has found a justification to shape Islamic discourse ever since. The USA, Barlas laments, has appropriated Islam as a tool of imperial policy, creating a stifling dichotomy—the 'moderate' versus 'militant' Muslim—which has nothing to do with religious interpretation but rather is defined purely on the basis of one's political allegiance.[227] The moderate Muslim is pro-American; the militant Muslim anti-American. Calling for gender reform is a central part of this colonial project, portraying Muslims and Islam as being innately patriarchal and promoting inclusive and liberal (read acquiescent and apolitical) interpretations. So whereas Americans had very little interest in Muslim reformist movements prior to 9/11, Islamic reform suddenly became a fashionable topic. In fact, Barlas recalls that she was having great difficulty locating a publisher for her manuscript on the Qur'an. Following 9/11 and the subsequent surge of interest in Muslim women, however, she was successfully able to secure one.[228] In her critical awareness of the ideological politics of Islam, and of Islam and gender in particular, Barlas departs significantly from Wadud. As described in the preceding chapter, when discussing 9/11 Wadud not only subscribed to such a moderate/militant Muslim binary, or what she referred to as 'the face of love and life' versus 'the face of evil and destruction',[229] but she also singled out Muslim *men* as being responsible for planning the attacks,[230] thus connecting this event with patriarchy in Muslim communities.

As Barlas' discourse on 9/11 suggests, she is highly critical of US imperialism. Moreover, her criticism—as seen earlier with regard to Chile's 9/11—moves beyond the Middle East and Muslim-majority countries, noting how the USA has undertaken military interventions throughout the world.[231] What is so provocative, so audacious about

---

[226] Asma Barlas, 'Jihad = Holy War = Terrorism: The Politics of Conflation and Denial', *The American Journal of Islamic Social Sciences* 20:1 (Winter 2003): 46–62. This article was accessed on 17 September 2014 from Barlas' personal website: http://www.asmabarlas.com/papers.html

[227] Barlas, *Islam, Muslims, and the US*, 29.   [228] Ibid, 33.

[229] Wadud, *Inside the Gender Jihad*, 5.   [230] Ibid, 228.

[231] Barlas, *Islam, Muslims, and the US*, 60.

US empire-building is the veneer of liberalism that sugar-coats it. As Barlas words it:

> Wanting control of the world is nothing new. What is perhaps new is that the West and the United States want to be loved as they go about the business of making the world subservient to themselves by any means necessary, for how else can one explain the plaintive question, Why do they hate us?[232]

Indeed, echoing Said,[233] Barlas argues that portrayals of Islam and the West as being diametrically opposed are a direct epistemic outgrowth of Western global dominance,[234] sustained today by American fire-power. This dichotomy is deeply problematic, she observes, not only because Islam and the West are simply incongruent as categories, the former being a religion and the latter a 'geographic space/identity', but it is also based on the racist presumption of 'radical difference.'[235] That is, the essentialist idea that there is something fundamentally different between the Westerner and the Muslim, as if the two are hermetically sealed, occupying different worlds. The very term—'the Muslim world'—is inherently flawed, objects Barlas, since 'Muslims live in the same world as everyone else.'[236] Furthermore, this phrasing presumes that religion is the most important determinant of Muslim life, ignoring key differences amongst the world's one billion plus Muslims rooted in race, culture and political orientation, among others.[237] It is important to note here that Barlas' discourse on world politics cannot be divorced from her anti-patriarchal exegesis. For it is impossible to conceptualize and mainstream gender-egalitarian readings of the Qur'an without a wider democratization of Muslim societies,[238] which are plagued with highly authoritarian regimes that routinely clamp down on human rights and basic freedoms. Consequently, numerous Muslim reformists—as different as Rachid Ghannoushi in Tunisia, Mohsen Kadivar in Iran, and Nasr Hamid Abu Zaid in Egypt, to name but a few—have either lost their jobs,

---

[232] Ibid, 58.
[233] See Edward Said, *Orientalism* (New York: Pantheon Books, 1978) and Edward Said, *Covering Islam: How the media and the experts determine how we see the rest of the world* (New York: Pantheon Books, 1981).
[234] Barlas, 'Reviving Islamic Universalism', 243–4.   [235] Ibid.
[236] Barlas, *Islam, Muslims, and the US*, 57.   [237] Ibid.
[238] Barlas, 'Reviving Islamic Universalism', 249–50.

been imprisoned, or have been forced into exile.[239] However, the dismantling of domestic dictatorship will be tremendously difficult, if not impossible, mourns Barlas, given America's backing of despotic rulers throughout the globe.[240] Rereading scripture is thus intrinsically tied to domestic politics that, in turn, are shaped by the international status quo.

On Class and Race

An analysis of politics is meaningless without paying attention to questions of class. As Barlas puts it: 'to study political institutions *qua* institutions—that is, without analyzing the class matrices in which they are embedded—is to neglect a vital dimension of politics.'[241] In fact, her first book, titled *Democracy, Nationalism, and Communalism: The Colonial Legacy in South Asia* (1995), is a Marxist—to be more precise: a Gramscian—study of the development of British, Hindu, and Muslim sociopolitical institutions in colonial India.[242] Gender, too, cannot be divorced from class. Barlas' approach to gender issues in light of socioeconomic realities can be seen in her critical analysis on the impact of globalization in general, and of new information technologies in particular, on the lives of Muslim women. Sidestepping the conventional line of argument that modernity will necessarily exert

[239] Kamrava, 24. Ghannoushi (b. 1941) is a Tunisian Islamist and a co-founder of *Harakat al-Nahda* (The Renaissance Movement), which is currently the largest political party in Tunisia. An outspoken critic of then-president Habib Bourguiba, Ghannoushi was imprisoned from 1981–4, serving a second term from 1987–8. He was eventually forced to leave for Europe as a political exile, and recently returned to his home country following the 2011 Tunisian Revolution, which overthrew President Zine El Abidine Ben Ali's regime. Kadivar (b. 1959) is a reformist Shi'a cleric and a prominent leader in the opposition movement in Iran. Because of his religious critiques of Khomeini's theocratic writings, in 1999 Kadavar was imprisoned for eighteen months. Abu Zayd (d. 2010) was an Egyptian scholar of the Qur'an. Due to his research, which situated the text within the broader history of Arabic literature rather than religion per se, an Egyptian court charged him with apostasy. Furthermore, the court ruled that he must divorce his wife, Ibtihal Yunis, as a Muslim woman according to Islamic law cannot be married to a non-Muslim man. As a result, they were forced to go into political exile in the Netherlands.
[240] Barlas Interview, 2009. I suspect that, following the revolutions that have swept the Arab world since 2011, she has become more optimistic of the possibility of breaking the shackles of American power.
[241] Barlas, *Democracy, Nationalism, and Communalism*, 203.
[242] Ibid, ix. This work grew out of her doctoral dissertation at the University of Denver, Colorado.

a positive influence on Muslim women, she not only points out that such technologies must be accompanied by 'a fundamental epistemic shift in how Muslims interpret and practice Islam',[243] but also questions how applicable such technologies are to the majority of humankind, since the widening gap between the rich and the poor makes it unlikely that most people will even have access to such technologies.[244]

Given Barlas' Marxist background and her emphasis on socio-economic deprivation, it is curious that markedly liberal terms like individualism and individuality surface at various points in her exegesis. Accenting the Qur'an's discourse on the genderless basis of 'moral praxis'—that God does not differentiate between women and men, judging them solely on their deeds—she argues that this is an example of scriptural support for 'individuality' and, borrowing a phrase used by the Qur'anic scholar Barbara Stowasser, 'ethical individualism'.[245] And as individuals, concludes Barlas, Muslims are 'free moral agents'.[246] This connection between individuality and autonomy is best summed up in the following passage, which Barlas approvingly quotes from the French-Algerian Muslim intellectual Mohammad Arkoun (d. 2010). A Qur'anic reading based on individuality, Arkoun claims:

[creates] an infinite space for the promotion of the individual beyond the constraints of fathers and brothers, clans and tribes, riches and tributes; the individual becomes an autonomous and free agent, enjoying a liberty guaranteed by obedience and love lived within the community.[247]

This stress on the individual is understandable, for a key grievance that Barlas has with the politics of authority in contemporary Islam is that whenever individual interpretations do not line up with established, communal ones—that is, those of the *umma* (the global Muslim community)—the former is subordinated to the latter, thereby confusing 'communal norms with Qur'anic norms'.[248] The representation of the individual in the above passage as 'an autonomous and free agent' is problematic, however, for a couple of reasons. Firstly, it subscribes

---

[243] Barlas, 'Globalizing Equality', 91.   [244] Ibid, 93.
[245] Barlas, *'Believing Women' in Islam*, 130.   [246] Ibid, 118–19.
[247] Mohammad Arkoun, as cited in Barlas, *'Believing Women' in Islam*, 119.
[248] Barlas, 'Still Quarrelling over the Qur'an', 33.

to the fiction of the self-fulfilling subject, to the agent who is in complete control of her/his destiny, thereby ignoring the social circumstances that confine, indeed define, agency, of which moral agency is part and parcel. Secondly, the Qur'an conceives of righteousness in acutely communal terms: that is, to one's ethical relations with the wider human family (Q. 2:177; 90:8–17; 107:1–7). In other words, it is the community—not the individual—that is the centrepiece of moral agency. As Barlas herself notes, the text 'defines moral personality in terms not only of '*ibadah* [worship], but also in terms of responsibilities to the *ummah*, and that the two are connected and inseparable.'[249]

In addition to global politics and economic inequality, race figures prominently in Barlas' thinking. While she undoubtedly experienced racism as a Muslim living in the USA, especially in the aftermath of 9/11, her critiques focus on her disorienting experience as a Coloured Muslim *woman* in feminist circles dominated by White women and largely blind to racial politics.[250] This insensitivity is most evident in feminist representations of the veil, which is invariably portrayed as a symbol of women's oppression. Although, as we have seen, Barlas critiques the mainstream Muslim practice of veiling, arguing that it has no scriptural basis, she also criticizes feminists, for whom 'the exposed/naked body is represented as the free/liberated body, leading many to see clothed bodies as unfree/imprisoned bodies.'[251] Her discourse on the headscarf, therefore, is a compelling example of her commitment to engage in double critique, challenging the privilege of both Muslim men and non-Muslim White women. In her deep-seated grievances with feminism, Barlas shares common ground with Black feminists, who have foregrounded the racial and class dimensions of women's suffering.[252] In so doing, Black women, as well as women of colour from the global South, have had a lasting impact on feminism as a field, which has shifted to a more comprehensive approach to oppression, incorporating questions of race and sexuality,

[249] Barlas, *'Believing Women' in Islam*, 148.
[250] Asma Barlas, 'Engaging Islamic Feminism: Provincializing Feminism as a Master Narrative'. In *Islamic Feminism: Current Perspectives*, ed. Anitta Kynsilehto (Tampere, Finland: Tampere Peace Research Institute, 2008), 17.
[251] Barlas, *'Believing Women' in Islam*, 160.
[252] bell hooks, 'Feminism: A Movement to End Sexist Oppression', in *Feminisms*, eds. Sandra Kemp and Judith Squires (Oxford: Oxford University Press, 1997), 23.

class and empire.[253] Yet despite these important transformations in feminism, Barlas refuses to identify as feminist. She explains her position as follows:

> I am troubled by the extent to which feminism as a discourse has foreclosed the possibility of theorizing sexual equality from within alternative paradigms. An obvious sign of this is the fact that one can't avoid being called a feminist any time one speaks of liberation or equality, no matter what sort of language one speaks in. . . . In a sense, then, it is the very inclusivity of feminism—its attempt as a meta and master narrative, to subsume and annihilate all conversations about equality—that I found both imperializing and reductive.[254]

That is, feminism has attained hegemony over anti-patriarchal thought, making it difficult even to think of non-sexist languages and practices outside of its totalizing framework—a dynamic not so different from Marxism's hegemony over anti-capitalist critique. As we saw in the last chapter, Wadud also refused to identify as a feminist, using the qualified label 'pro-faith, pro-feminist'.[255] While Barlas acknowledges her intellectual debts to feminism as a liberating mode of thinking—indeed, her thesis that the Qur'an is at odds with modern patriarchy and its politicization of women's biology has clearly been informed by feminist theory—she chooses to self-identify in distinctly Qur'anic terms, referring to herself as a 'believing woman'.[256]

Twin Fundamentalisms

Feminism is also problematic because of the secularism that underpins it. Barlas has had a bitter, first-hand experience of feminism's antagonism towards religion. In our interview, she recounted the following incident:

---

[253] For examples, see Butler; Chandra Talpade Mohanty, *Feminism without Borders: Decolonizing Theory, Practicing Solidarity* (Durham, NC: Duke University Press, 2003); and Zillah Eisenstein, *Against Empire: Feminisms, Racism, and the West* (London: Zed Books, 2004).

[254] Barlas, 'Engaging Islamic Feminism', 21–2.

[255] Wadud, *Inside the Gender Jihad*, 79.

[256] Barlas, 'Engaging Islamic Feminism', 16. This Qur'anic term refers to Umm Salama's verse (Q. 33:35).

Now lately when I went back to Pakistan on a post-doc in 1999, the women I met who are feminists and who are involved in the Women's Action Forum (WAF) and Shirkat Gah, you know, so many NGOs. Most of them don't want to touch Islam with a 10-foot pole. When I made a presentation on my work, one of the women in the audience said very loudly, she just got up and said: *Yeh to perhi likhi mawlani hai* [Urdu]. "This is an educated female mulla," is what she told me. You're no better than a female educated mulla because, you know, to speak about the Qur'an is already to be an obscurantist in the eyes of the liberated, feminist women in Pakistan.[257]

Her grievances, therefore, are not just with White feminists, but also Muslim feminists. In order to differentiate between Muslim women who utilize a religious framework to fight against patriarchy and Muslim women who rely upon a secular language of universal human rights, gender activists have suggested the terms 'Islamic feminism' to describe the former and 'Muslim feminism' to refer to the latter.[258] However, given that leading intellectuals like Wadud and Barlas do not identify as feminists, this classification system is misleading. As we have seen, Wadud also takes issue with the secularity of feminism, which is precisely why she opts for the phrasing 'pro-faith, pro-feminist'.[259] In fact, Barlas observes insightfully, secular feminist portrayals of Islam—that it is a monolith, that it can only be interpreted in one way—are strikingly similar to those of Muslim conservatives, thereby reifying oppressive understandings of Islam.[260] In so doing, secular feminists have made it more difficult for Muslim women to secure their rights in the name of Islam. Feminism reflects a wider problem within secularism. For 'secular fundamentalists', writes Barlas, 'suffer from an absence of doubt about their own

---

[257] Barlas Interview, 2009. The Women's Action Forum (WAF) is a feminist organization in Pakistan. Founded in 1981 in Karachi, the group has established chapters in cities throughout the country. WAF espouses a comprehensive approach to women's rights. Its activities include awareness raising about pressing women's issues like domestic abuse; political lobbying against sexist legislation; and providing a general forum wherein different women and women's groups can network. Shirkat Gah—an Urdu term meaning 'a place of participation'—is a Pakistani women's organization that was established in 1975. It seeks to empower women by making them full and equal members of society. Among the organization's many activities are lobbying for more gender-egalitarian legislation and policies; the provision of legal assistance and counselling to women in crisis situations; and the production and dissemination of educational literature on sexual oppression.

[258] Ali and Leaman, 37–8.   [259] Wadud, *Inside the Gender Jihad*, 79–80.

[260] Barlas, 'Texts, Sex, and States', 112.

positions, to which they adhere uncritically, while advocating critical engagements with religion.'[261] For example, she notes that despite secularist portrayals of religion as being inherently violent, secularism has been equally, if not more, guilty of bloodshed, pointing to the two world wars, fascism, and the Nazi holocaust.[262] Indeed, secularism as a discourse needs to construct a fundamentalist, religious Other in order to justify its own 'civilizing project'.[263] Secular modernity and religious fundamentalism, therefore, are inextricably linked. In her criticism of secularism, Barlas stands in contrast to Engineer. As we saw in Chapter 3, Engineer idealizes secularism, upholding it as a neutral language to counter communal violence between Hindus and Muslims.[264] He thus overlooks the crucial question of *who* gets to define the secular, which in the Indian context has historically been, and continues to be, the prerogative of Hindus.

This is not to imply, of course, that religions are bastions of pluralism. In fact, most Muslims are convinced that Islam exercises a monopoly over truth, constituting *the* path towards God. Challenging this chauvinistic claim, Barlas argues that the Qur'an acknowledges the universality of revelation, as God sent prophets to every nation.[265] Islam, then, is a continuation of a long historical chain of divine disclosure. Paralleling Engineer, she points to Q. 5:48 in particular, which celebrates religious diversity:[266]

> We have sent down to you the Book with the truth, confirming what was before it of the Book and as a guardian over it. So judge between them by what God has sent down, and do not follow their desires against the truth that has come to you. For each community among you We have appointed a law and a way of life, and had God wished He would have made you one community, but He wished to test you by that which He gave you. So take the lead in all good works. To God shall

---

[261] Barlas, *Re-Understanding Islam*, 25.   [262] Ibid, 18.

[263] Barlas, *Islam, Muslims, and the US*, 112.

[264] Engineer, 'Secularism and its Problems in India'.

[265] Barlas, 'Reviving Islamic Universalism', 246. Although she does not provide any Qur'anic citations to substantiate this specific argument, there are two verses that support this idea that revelation was sent down to multiple peoples: Q. 35:24 claims that divine messengers have been sent to all nations without exception, while Q. 40:78 clarifies that the Qur'an only discusses a select number of prophets, leaving out others. The text, therefore, makes no claim of providing a comprehensive listing of the prophets.

[266] Barlas, *'Believing Women' in Islam*, 145–6. She incorrectly cites this verse as Q. 5:51.

be the return of you all, whereat He will inform you about that which you used to differ.

So not only does the Qur'an acknowledge the legitimacy of other faith traditions, at least monotheistic ones (the people of the above mentioned 'Book'), but it also states that the presence of diverse religions is actually a part of the divine plan, for 'had God wished He would have made you one community.' In addition to embracing the validity of other religions, Barlas appreciates that they, too, are subject to interpretation. If Islam can be read in multiple modes, so can other faith traditions. She observes, for instance, that Christianity has historically been interpreted in drastically different ways, contrasting the tyranny of the Inquisition and the genocide of indigenous South America, justified in the name of Christ, to the radical liberation theologies that emerged in the mid-twentieth century.[267] Her discourse on religious pluralism, moreover, is a compelling example of how she is willing to use extra-Qur'anic texts when these texts work to affirm 'the best' meanings of scripture. Specifically, she refers to the medieval Sufi scholar ibn 'Arabi and his meditations on the unity of God[268]—a theological concept that, as discussed earlier, Barlas reflects upon extensively. According to ibn 'Arabi, all revealed religions, irrespective of their divergent *forms*, are, in essence, one.[269] To put it another way: while followers of different faiths have embarked upon paths that may or may not overlap, they are all ultimately united by their shared destination: God.[270]

The brunt of Barlas' writings on religious pluralism, however, centres on the importance of fostering genuine inclusivism within the Muslim community. Pointing to Q. 2:256—'There is no compulsion in religion'—Barlas argues that no Muslim has the right to force any type of moral conduct upon a fellow Muslim.[271] By reading Q. 2:256 through the lens of *intra*religious relations, Barlas, like Wadud,[272] departs from common understandings of this verse, which have restricted its meaning to *inter*religious relations: namely,

---

[267] Ibid, xi.   [268] Barlas, 'Reviving Islamic Universalism', 248–9.
[269] Ibid, 249.
[270] Ibid. Barlas is referring here to ibn 'Arabi's notion of *wahdat al-wujud* (the unity of existence).
[271] Barlas, *'Believing Women' in Islam*, 55.
[272] Wadud, *Inside the Gender Jihad*, 81–2.

as prohibiting forced conversion to Islam.[273] Indeed, writes Barlas, in order for a Muslim's submission to God to be meaningful, to carry any 'moral weight' it has to be voluntary.[274] It is precisely for this reason that she (re)defines Islam, which literally means submission, as 'willed submission to God.'[275] Earlier on we saw Barlas, when exploring the Qur'an's opposition to patriarchy, expound on Abraham's relationship with his father. Here, in making a case for the voluntary basis of faith, she returns to Abraham, but this time examines his role *as* father, in particular his response to God's command to sacrifice his child. The story is narrated below:

> When he [Abraham's son] was old enough to go about with him, he said, 'O my son! I see in a dream that I am sacrificing you. Consider, then, what is your view? (*fa-undhur madha tara*).' He said, 'Father! Do whatever you have been commanded. If God wishes, you will find me to be amongst the patient ones.' So when they had both submitted to God's will, and he had laid him down on his forehead, We called out to him, 'O Abraham! You have fulfilled the vision! Thus do We reward the virtuous! That was a manifest test.' Then we ransomed him [Abrahams' son] with a great sacrifice, and left for him [Abraham] a good name in posterity. Peace be on Abraham! Thus do we reward the virtuous. Indeed, he was one of our faithful servants.[276] (Q. 37:102–111)

Barlas comments that this passage not only demonstrates that the Qur'an undermines the rule of fathers—Abraham cannot simply do as he pleases with his son, first seeking his opinion and consent ('Consider, then, what is your view?')—but it also illustrates vividly the voluntary nature of faith.[277] For in order for the sacrifice to be meaningful, his son had to be willing to go along with it. Abraham's request for his son's perspective thus cannot be read as a perfunctory, insignificant exercise. Rather, it was a genuine act of consultation and

---

[273] Asad, *The Message of the Qur'an*, 69–70.
[274] Barlas, *Islam, Muslims, and the US*, 136.
[275] Barlas, *'Believing Women' in Islam*, 235.
[276] It is interesting to note that the passage does not specify the name of the child. However, the next verse goes on to state 'And We gave him the good news of the birth of Isaac, a prophet, one of the righteous' (Q. 37:112), thereby suggesting that Ishmael was the older son and the one referred to in Abraham's sacrifice. This is in line with mainstream Muslim understandings of the story. There is a point of disagreement, therefore, between the Qur'anic and biblical accounts, as the latter explicitly posits Isaac as Abraham's only son at the time and the one who was to be sacrificed (Gen. 22:1–3).
[277] Barlas, 'The Qur'an and Hermeneutics', 29.

mutual interpretation.[278] Barlas' discourse on pluralism within the Muslim community, moreover, is yet another example of her willingness to use extra-scriptural sources. While she cites ibn 'Arabi when discussing interreligious pluralism, she draws upon the insights of the medieval theologian al-Ghazali when calling for intrareligious pluralism.[279] Al-Ghazali lived in a time when Muslim theologians were constantly attacking one another, hurling accusations of heresy while positing their own theological positions as authentic. But no school of thought, interjected al-Ghazali, can claim a monopoly over truth, for all theologies are interpretations that are historically conditioned and, thus, cannot be conflated with divine revelation.[280] This was a profound insight, particularly for someone writing in the eleventh and twelfth centuries, and, as has been seen throughout this book, one that is echoed today by Qur'anic readers of justice.

CONCLUSIONS

Like Esack's, Engineer's, and Wadud's readings, the Qur'an stands at the very heart of Barlas' liberationist exegesis. Because Muslim scripture reflects the actual speech of God, it ought to function as the definitive criterion (*al-furqan*) in shaping our understandings and practices of Islam. Therefore, all Muslims, irrespective of their level of learning, have the solemn responsibility and, in fact, the fundamental right to interpret this central Islamic text, allowing it to speak to their own lives. Barlas is highly critical of other Islamic texts such as the *hadith* and exegetical tradition, the historic elevation of which has blurred the distinction between human interpretation and divine disclosure. Unlike Wadud, who has called for a renewed engagement

---

[278] Asma Barlas, 'Abraham's Sacrifice in the Qur'an: Beyond the Body', in *Conference Proceedings: Religion and the Body* (Turku, Finland: Donner Institute for Research in the History of Religion, Abo Akademie University, 2011), 4–11.

[279] Barlas, 'Reviving Islamic Universalism', 247–8. When discussing al-Ghazali, Barlas consults the work of the Islamic scholar Sherman A. Jackson, *On the Boundaries of Theological Tolerance in Islam: Abu Hamid al-Ghazali's Faysal al-Tafriqa Bayna al-Islam wa al-Zandaqa* ['The Decisive Criterion for Distinguishing between Islam and Masked Infidelity'], trans., annotated and introduced by Sherman A. Jackson (Oxford: Oxford University Press, 2002).

[280] Barlas, 'Reviving Islamic Universalism', 246–7.

with the *shari'a*, Barlas categorically dismisses the legal tradition, arguing that it is too patriarchal to sustain serious reform. There are a number of hermeneutical strategies that emerge in her commentary. Interpreting for the present is a key strategy, and one that she shares with all the commentators considered in this study. The task of the interpreter, according to Barlas, is to understand and implement the teachings of scripture in light of her/his own experiences and lived realities. Here, Barlas draws inspiration from Umm Salama, who boldly questioned scripture, relating the Qur'an to her own subject position as a woman. Muslims must follow in the footsteps of Umm Salama, approaching the Qur'an in terms of their own problems, for the text cannot speak to new contexts unless new questions are asked of it. But not all answers are equally legitimate; some are more relevant than others. A truly contextual exegesis, then, is one that gleans 'the best' meanings from the Qur'an. And because God, as the author of that text, is a just and compassionate deity, the best meanings must necessarily uphold justice. In order to interpret the Qur'an in the present time, to arrive at the best meanings, it is essential to distinguish between the text's timeless principles and its historical particulars. Paralleling Wadud, Barlas argues that this can be achieved by undertaking a holistic approach—that is, reading the Qur'an as an integrated whole—and a historically sensitive one, situating the text within its original setting of revelation. That both Wadud and Barlas rely heavily upon textual holism and historical criticism (strategies that play relatively minor roles in Esack's and Engineer's *praxis*-centred exegeses) suggests that these twin hermeneutical strategies form a crucial and distinctive component of women's gender egalitarian readings of the Qur'an.

Indeed, throughout this chapter I have shown the striking similarities between Wadud's and Barlas' exegeses. At the same time, however, I have argued that while the works of these two interpreters tend to be conflated, as if they are simply doing the same thing, they are actually engaged in substantively different projects. For whereas Wadud explores the topic of woman in the Qur'an, examining such themes as the Creation Story and depictions of the Hereafter, Barlas interrogates the relationship between the text and patriarchy. And it is her systematic and original reflection on this relationship that constitutes her lasting contribution to women's gender egalitarian readings of the Qur'an. Specifically, she argues that the text is at variance with both 'traditional' and 'modern' manifestations of patriarchy. In traditional/religious contexts, patriarchy entails representations of God as Father and, by extension, of real fathers as earthly surrogates of this heavenly patriarch. By reflecting upon the nature of divine self-disclosure—that is, how God describes God's self in scripture—Barlas is able to make a theological case for the Qur'an's opposition to patriarchy. Like Esack, Engineer, and Wadud, she emphasizes the absolute justice of God. As a just and compassionate deity, God cannot, by definition, show an affinity for men as the socially privileged sex. *Tawhid* is the most important feature of such self-disclosure. Because God is One, divine sovereignty is indivisible. When men station themselves as spokespersons, as intermediaries of God they impinge upon this sovereignty and, in so doing, violate *tawhid*. God is not only described in the Qur'an as unpairable, but also unrepresentable. Therefore, portrayals of God in gendered terms, such as being a fatherly or motherly figure (both of which are absent in the text), undermine Islamic monotheism. That Wadud, too, reflects upon the sociopolitical implications of *tawhid* is significant, disclosing the centrality of this paradigm in Muslim women's gender egalitarian exegesis. Just as God is not portrayed as Father in the Qur'an, fathers themselves are not elevated over mothers. In fact, although the text speaks in terms of 'parental' rather than 'paternal' rights, it singles out mothers, showing sensitivity to the pains of pregnancy and childbirth. Furthermore, prophets are never venerated as fathers. Abraham emerges as a key prophetic paradigm in Barlas' exegesis. The rebellion of the so-called Patriarch against his own father—an action that clearly runs counter to patriarchal logic and its consecration of father-rule—exemplifies the sovereignty of God over that of fathers. Nor, for that matter, is Abraham himself celebrated *as* father. Rather, he is referred to in gender-neutral terms, such as *imam* (leader), *hanif* (monotheist), and *khalilullah* (the friend of God). While Abraham was refused symbolic fatherhood, Muhammad was denied both symbolic and actual fatherhood. For not only is Muhammad never presented as a figurative father of the Muslim community—despite the claims of commentators to the contrary—but he also, as the biographical sources record, lost all his sons in their infancy. Although this last observation is demonstrative of Barlas' interest in using extra-Qur'anic Islamic sources, it also shows that her engagement with such texts, like all the exegetes studied in this book, is inconsistent, selectively picking and choosing whichever aspects of these traditions can corroborate her own readings of scripture. There is little appreciation, then, for these texts as sophisticated, discursive traditions in their own right, as intellectual disciplines with complex histories of hermeneutical engagement and contention. Given her criticism of atomistic interpretations of Muslim scripture, it is paradoxical that she applies the same approach towards extra-Qur'anic Islamic texts.

The Qur'an is also at odds with modern/secular forms of patriarchy. That is, while the text recognizes sexual difference, it does not subscribe to a politics of sexual differentiation, politicizing (and thus engendering) women's biology. Barlas fleshes out this argument by examining a number of women's issues, including polygamy, sexuality, and the headscarf. Her analysis of polygamy is illustrative of how she parallels Wadud's exegesis while building on it in novel ways. Like Wadud, she reads the relevant verses in their totality, noting their emphasis on justice and equal treatment towards the wives, which, as the Qur'an later goes on to state, is an impossibility. Echoing Wadud again, she unpacks the verses' immediate historical context, showing that male guardians were exploiting female orphans under their care. These verses, then, addressed a specific crisis in the first Muslim community; they are historically particular, not universally applicable. But the Qur'an's discourse on polygamy, Barlas observes, also makes no mention of sexual desire, stating that it is a part of men's nature to have multiple partners, thereby making wider gendered statements about the male body. Conversely, it never claims that it is in women's nature to share a single husband. Barlas draws extensively upon textual holism and historical criticism when wrestling with Q. 4:34, or the so-called Beating Verse. Highlighting its contextual backdrop, she argues that since this verse was revealed in a society in which violence against women was widespread, it should be read as a restriction on, and not a license for, domestic abuse. Barlas also employs a textually holistic approach, pointing out that the controversial term *idribuhunna* and its various linguistic derivatives are used in diverse ways in other parts of scripture, and thus cannot be defined solely as 'beat them'. Her exegesis of Q. 4:34, however, betrays her tendency to idealize the Qur'an's discourse on gender relations, for however *idribuhunna* is redefined, men remain the subjects of the text, acting upon women who, in turn, become passive objects. Barlas refuses to acknowledge the manifest androcentrism of the text, at least in matters pertaining to sexuality. It is here that a key difference emerges between Barlas on the one hand and Esack and Wadud on the other, as the latter are critical of the Qur'an's presumption of male audiences. In its apologia for Muslim scripture, Barlas' exegesis is similar to Engineer's. The underlying problem with both their interpretations is that they end up essentializing the text. For them, the Qur'an (and, by extension, Islam) can only be liberating; readings to the contrary are simply misreadings.

In a remarkably similar fashion to all the commentators considered in this book, Barlas has a comprehensive approach to social justice, drawing connections between different forms of suffering. And the point of departure for this wider commitment to liberation, I have argued, is her engagement in 'double critique': that is, opposing not only oppressive discourses and practices in Muslim communities, but also in non-Muslim Western societies, especially the USA. Paralleling Esack, she argues that post-9/11 America has appropriated Islam as a tool of empire, creating a stifling binary between the moderate Muslim, who is American-friendly and supportive of Islamic reform, and the militant Muslim, who is anti-American and religiously conservative. Barlas, as a Muslim woman devoted to securing justice for all people, finds herself caught between a rock and a hard place. The following passage deftly sums up her deep-seated frustrations:

> For criticizing Muslim interpretive violence, I am courted as a moderate Muslim but, for criticizing the US's political violence, I am denounced as a militant anti-American. Where then is the space for Muslim-Americans like me to live in accordance with our religious and political principles and beliefs?[281]

Her commitment to double critique is an attempt to carve out such an alternative, third space, wherein she can speak truth to power in multiple contexts of oppression. Barlas' discourse on feminism is a compelling example of double critique. Just as she wrote her gender-just commentary to challenge conservative Muslim readers, she also had secular feminists in mind, for whom Islam is irredeemably patriarchal, even misogynistic. Like Wadud, she criticizes feminism for its secular biases. Indeed, and in contrast to Engineer, Barlas takes issue with secularism as a whole, pointing out its hypocritical tendency to engage religion critically while lacking any doubt in its own assumptions. Her critique of the feminist movement, which has been headed by White women and therefore catered to their own lived

---

[281] Barlas, *Islam, Muslims, and the US*, 34.

experiences, also reflects the centrality of race in her thinking, constantly foregrounding her own subject position as a Coloured Muslim woman. Though her earlier research focussed on class, it is important to note that questions of economic inequality continue to play a role in her analysis. For, as her writings on US imperialism, 9/11, and feminism show, power relations are inextricably intertwined; one category of oppression, whether it is that of racism, patriarchy, or poverty, cannot be engaged without the others. Finally, she embraces religious pluralism, arguing that Islam is not the only path towards God, but rather one of numerous callings. But the most essential aspect of pluralism is intrareligious pluralism, or the acceptance of interpretive diversity within the Muslim community. Like all the exegetes examined in this study, Barlas is keenly aware that any potential of implementing, of mainstreaming her liberating readings, lies in cultivating a culture of mutual respect and understanding amongst Muslims.

6

Conclusions

On Thematic Readings

INTRODUCTION

In this final chapter, I would like to reflect on the significance of this study. While the continued social relevance of the Qur'an, especially in terms of speaking to problems of injustice, is clearly demonstrated by the writings of Esack, Engineer, Wadud, and Barlas, here I would like to explore how their interpretations can offer new insights into the Qur'anic genre called 'thematic commentary' (*tafsir mawdu'i*). Specifically, I argue that liberationist and women's gender egalitarian readings provide three critical insights into this genre: (a) the desire to partake in a direct engagement with scripture and, thus, one that is unmediated by the historic exegetical tradition; (b) the conscious foregrounding of the subject position of the reader in the task of interpretation, suggesting a critical linkage between thematic reflection and contextual theology; and (c) the seminal role that print culture has played in shaping the craft of commentary, massifying both the producers and consumers of religious knowledge. To clarify, my principal interest in this chapter is not to posit arguments about the origins, the emergence of thematic commentary,[1] nor are the arguments that I do forward categoric, applicable to all thematic reflection. Rather, my principal aim is to use liberationist and

---

[1] Thematic commentary predates the exegetes studied in this book, and thus the question of origins is beyond the scope of this study. For example, Mahmud Shaltut (d. 1963)—the former rector of the Islamic university of Al-Azhar in Cairo—was interested in and composed thematic commentary. See Kate Zebiri, *Mahmud Shaltut and Islamic Modernism* (Oxford: Clarendon Press, 1993).

women's gender egalitarian interpretation as a point of departure to discern some wider tendencies within thematic commentary of the Qur'an.

Direct Engagement with Scripture

Thematic commentary has become a prominent genre in contemporary Qur'anic exegesis. Conventional commentaries are referred to as *tafsir musalsal* (literally, 'linked' commentary), as they commence with the first verse of the first chapter, continuing in a sequential manner to the last verse of the final chapter, and therefore are usually large, multivolume works.[2] However, not all sequential commentaries cover the entire text, but rather specific chapters or parts. The Egyptian Qur'anic exegete Muhammad Abduh (d. 1905) is a case in point, producing sequential commentaries on select sections of the text, such as the first chapter (*Surat al-Fatiha*, or the Chapter of the Opening) and the last part (*Juz' 'Amma*), which is comprised of thirty-seven chapters.[3] In contrast to this linear format, thematic commentary focuses, as its name suggests, on a particular subject. As we have seen, all the commentators considered in this book read scripture thematically, exploring topics like socioeconomic liberation, gender justice and religious pluralism. To be sure, thematic commentaries do not necessarily have to centre on a single subject and can address a host of different topics. For instance, Rahman—whose hermeneutic we have encountered at various points in this study— authored a highly influential thematic commentary on Muslim scripture, titled *Major Themes of the Qur'an* (1980). The chapters in this

---

[2] Jane D. McAuliffe, 'The Tasks and Traditions of Interpretation', in *The Cambridge Companion to the Qur'an*, ed. Jane D. McAuliffe (Cambridge: Cambridge University Press, 2006), 183.

[3] Rotraud Wielandt, 'Exegesis of the Qur'an: Early Modern and Contemporary.' In *Encyclopaedia of the Qur'an*, ed. Jane D. McAuliffe (Georgetown University, Washington, DC). Consulted online on 8 May 2012. *Juz'* (pl: *ajza'*) literally means a 'part', and is one of the ways in which Muslims have sectioned the Qur'an. Altogether there are thirty parts, allowing Muslims to recite the entire Qur'an in a month, such as in Ramadan. The last part—popularly known as *Juz' 'Amma*—consists of the shortest chapters and amongst the first that Muslims memorize. It takes its name from the first verse of the chapter that it begins with. Referring to the promise of resurrection and the Hereafter, the verse reads: 'About what do they question each other *('amma yatasa'aluna)*?' (Q. 78:1).

commentary were devoted to different, and yet clearly interrelated, topics, such as 'God', 'Man in Society', 'Eschatology', and 'Prophethood and Revelation'.[4] While the majority of thematic commentaries are nonlinear, it is worthwhile noting the work of an exegete who has reflected on the Qur'an thematically but in a distinctly linear fashion: namely, the Egyptian Islamic scholar Muhammad al-Ghazali (d. 1996). Beginning with the first chapter and ending with the last, al-Ghazali approached each chapter as a unified, cohesive unit, unpacking its dominant themes and linking them together as he moved, sequentially, through the text.[5] Furthermore, although thematic commentary has become an increasingly popular mode of exegetical reflection, it is important not to portray conventional, verse-by-verse commentary as being in decline. On the contrary, it remains a robust and influential mode of reading scripture. For example, Qutb and Mawdudi—two pioneering figures in Islamist thought encountered earlier—wrote sequential Qur'anic commentaries that have attained mass circulation amongst Muslims.[6] Indeed, Mawdudi's commentary is currently 'one of the most widely read sources of its kind in Urdu',[7] while Qutb's may well be 'the most widely translated and distributed Islamic book of all time'.[8]

A key insight that the exegeses of Esack, Engineer, Wadud and Barlas reveal in terms of thematic commentary is the desire to engage the actual text of the Qur'an rather than its historic interpretation. As has been seen throughout this book, they all underline the privileged status of the Qur'an as the Word of God. This critical differentiation between scripture and its interpretation is most pronounced in the gender egalitarian readings of Wadud and Barlas, the former pointing out the fallibility of the exegetical tradition as a thoroughly human

---

[4] Rahman, *Major Themes of the Qur'an*, ix.

[5] Muhammad al-Ghazali, *A Thematic Commentary of the Qur'an*, trans. Ashur A. Shamis (Virginia: International Institute of Islamic Thought, 2000), x.

[6] Muhammad Qasim Zaman, *The Ulama in Contemporary Islam: Custodians of Change* (Princeton: Princeton University Press, 2002), 39. See Sayyid Qutb, *In the Shade of the Qur'an*, 18 vols., trans. and ed. Adil Salahi and Ashur Shamis (Markfield, Leicestershire: The Islamic Foundation, 2015) and Sayyid Abul A'la Mawdudi, *Towards Understanding the Qur'an: Abridged Version of Tafhim al-Qur'an*, ed. and trans. Zafar Ishaq Ansari (Markfield, Leicestershire: The Islamic Foundation, 2008).

[7] Sayyed Vali Reza Nasr, 'Mawdudi and the Jama'at-i Islami: The Origins, Theory and Practice of Islamic Revivalism,' in *Pioneers of Islamic Revival*, ed. Ali Rahnema (London: Zed Books, 2008), 104.

[8] Johannes J.G. Jansen, as quoted in Zaman, 39.

construct, and thus limited to the contextual baggage of the exegete,[9] while the latter goes even further by arguing that the conflation of scripture and interpretation effectively erases 'the distinction between God and humans'.[10] This desire to engage the text directly, however, is not restricted to the exegetes examined in this book. Rather, it characterizes the craft of thematic commentary. Consider Rahman's exegesis. Throughout the commentary, he makes extensive references to the Qur'anic text, as exemplified by the following excerpt that explores the issue of free will:

> There is no doubt that the Qur'an does make frequent statements to the effect that God leads aright whom He will and leads astray whom He will, or that God has 'sealed up' some people's hearts to the truth, etc. (2:8, 142, 213, 272; 14:4; 16:93; 24:35; 28:56; 30:29; 35:8), although more often it says that 'God does not lead aright the unjust ones,' 'God does not guide aright the transgressors,' 'God guides aright those who listen, are sincere, fear God.' (2:26, 258, 264; 3:86; 5:16, 51, 67, 108; 6:88, 144; 9:19, 21, 37, 80, 109; 12:52; 13:27; 16:37, 107; 28:50; 39:3; 40:28; 42:13; 46:10; 61:5: 'when they went crooked, God bent their hearts crooked' (61:7; 62:5; 63:6). [sic] This means that man does something to deserve guidance or misguidance.[11]

In fact, in the entire work there are only three references to classical and medieval commentators: two referring to al-Tabari,[12] one to ibn Taymiyya.[13] This emphasis on the actual letter of scripture can also be found, though to a lesser extent than in thematic interpretation, in sequential Islamist commentaries. The exegesis of Qutb is an illustrative example, as he shows little interest in the inherited interpretive tradition, seeking instead to understand the Qur'an through the Qur'an itself, as well as the *hadith*.[14] Such direct engagement with scripture stands in sharp contrast to classical commentary, which was based on interpreting the text through earlier exegetical writings.

---

[9] Wadud, 'Alternative Qur'anic Interpretation and the Status of Muslim Women', 11.

[10] Barlas, '*Believing Women' in Islam*, 79.

[11] Rahman, *Major Themes of the Qur'an*, 15.

[12] Ibid, 74; 76–7.   [13] Ibid, 31–2.

[14] McAuliffe, 'The Tasks and Traditions of Interpretation', 200. On Qutb and the Qur'an, see Ronald Nettler, 'A Modern Islamic Confession of Faith and Conception of Religion: Sayyid Qutb's Introduction to the *Tafsir, fi Zilal al-Qur'an*', *British Journal of Middle Eastern Studies* 21 (1994): 102–14. For a comprehensive intellectual biography of Qutb, see John Calvert, *Sayyid Qutb and the Origins of Radical Islamism* (New York: Columbia University Press, 2010).

Indeed, a commentary was so dependent on its predecessors that the Qur'anic scholar Walid Saleh has described classical exegesis as a 'genealogical tradition', for each commentary was in a 'dialectical relationship' with the interpretive tradition as a whole and, therefore, cannot be studied in isolation of this tradition.[15] To put it another way: classical exegesis was not so much a commentary of the Qur'an as a commentary of (past) commentaries. This hermeneutic, moreover, was not restricted to scripture, but extended to other traditions like the *shari'a*, which 'developed largely by means of interpretive elaborations on basic [legal] texts.'[16]

Textual holism, or a commitment to an integrated reading of the Qur'an, is intrinsically connected to thematic commentary's direct engagement with the text. As discussed in the preceding two chapters, Wadud and Barlas have deep-seated grievances with the traditional format of verse-by-verse commentaries and call for a more holistic approach to scripture, claiming that the text itself supports such a unified reading.[17] The lack of textual holism in the interpretive tradition was actually a key motivational force behind Rahman's commentary, which argues that a thematic approach can yield greater insight into the Qur'an's worldview, or its 'cohesive outlook on the universe'.[18] Another leading exponent of thematic exegesis, the Egyptian intellectual Hassan Hanafi (b. 1935), echoes Rahman's thesis, writing that thematic commentary can uncover the underlying message—the conceptual heart—of the Qur'an, while linear and sequential commentaries hastily jump from one theme to the next without accumulating meanings, without connecting them together in a systematic way.[19] They are, to use Rahman's wording,

---

[15] Saleh, 14–15.

[16] Brinkley Messick, *The Calligraphic State: Textual Domination and History in a Muslim Society* (Berkeley: University of California Press, 1993), 30. Insofar as my book is a study of Muslim writings on the Qur'an—that is, a commentary of commentaries—it adheres (admittedly inadvertently) to a classical hermeneutic.

[17] Wadud, *Qur'an and Woman*, xii; Barlas, 'The Qur'an and Hermeneutics', 24. While Barlas devotes more attention to the Qur'an's 'auto-hermeneutics'—a reading strategy that will be discussed in detail shortly—than the other exegetes in this book, Wadud also makes an autohermeneutical claim by describing her holistic reading as 'hermeneutics of *tawhid*', thereby invoking the Qur'an's central theme: namely, the undivided unity of God.

[18] Rahman, *Major Themes of the Qur'an*, xi.

[19] Massimo Campanini, *The Qur'an: Modern Muslim Interpretations*, trans. Caroline Higgit (London: Routledge, 2011), 75. For the original citation, see Hassan

'atomistic'.[20] The arguments forwarded by Wadud, Barlas, Rahman, and Hanafi betray a curious paradox of exegesis: specifically, that in order for an interpretation to be holistic, providing insight into the text's wider worldview, it has to be partial, qualified, thematic. Conversely, conventional verse-by-verse commentaries are atomistic precisely because they are encyclopaedic and exhaustive. Indeed, thematic interpretation and textual holism are inextricably linked; there is an underlying, dialectical interplay between the two. To be sure, I am not claiming that the origins of textual holism, as a reading strategy, are to be found in thematic exegesis, but rather that the nature of thematic reflection necessitates a holistic reading strategy, and vice versa. Textual holism is an inescapable aspect of thematic exegesis because of the nature of the thematic task, as the exegete needs to sift through the entire text with a particular subject in mind, relating the various component parts together in a coherent manner. This is especially acute in the context of Muslim scripture (as opposed to, for instance, the Bible, which is comparatively more linear) since the Qur'an is markedly achronological, with various historical figures, communities, and episodes spread out in different parts of the text. The Exodus—which, as we saw in Chapter 2, is the principal paradigm of Esack's liberation theology— is a case in point. The Qur'an does not relate the entire life of a prophet in one piece, the sole exception being Joseph, whose story appears in a single extended narrative in Q. 12:3–101.[21] While Moses is mentioned roughly 140 times,[22] making him the most cited prophet in the Qur'an, these references are scattered in forty-four different places in the text.[23] So when Esack wanted to examine Moses' life, he had no choice but to engage in a holistic reading, working through the full text and carefully piecing together the various accounts.

Hanafi, 'Method of Thematic Interpretation of the Qur'an', in *Islam in the Modern World*, ed. Hassan Hanafi (Cairo: Anglo-Egyptian Bookshop, 1995), 407–28.

[20] Rahman, *Islam and Modernity*, 2.
[21] Sells, 15. The Qur'an, of course, has its reasons for this eclectic treatment of prophetic narratives. Rather than presenting a comprehensive account of a given prophet's life, the text presumes prior knowledge of these figures and events—through the Old and New Testament narratives—drawing upon select aspects of their lives in order to flesh out wider lessons.
[22] Esack, *The Qur'an: A User's Guide*, 154. [23] Sells, 15.

The Role of Experience in Thematic Interpretation

Liberationist and women's gender egalitarian readings of the Qur'an also reflect the increasingly important role of experience in interpretation, as the reader consciously foregrounds her/his subject position. In the commentaries of Esack, Engineer, Wadud, and Barlas, there is nothing random about their choice of themes; rather, that choice is directly contingent on the struggles facing these exegetes in their everyday lives. Sexism is an obvious example. Wadud's and Barlas' hermeneutical focus on woman and patriarchy, respectively, is clearly related to their own experiences of oppression and marginalization *as* Muslim women, and it is from this subject position that they expound the text. Their identity is a central component of their readings. While Engineer is not as explicit about his subject position and its role in shaping his liberationist exegesis, he was initially drawn to questions of social justice because of his own formative experiences growing up in an oppressive context. Ruling with impunity, the religious head of the Dawudi Bohras exploited the community, for example, by imposing heavy taxes on its members in order to consolidate his family's financial standing.[24] As already described, this eventually led to a widespread rebellion against his authority, in which Engineer played an integral part.[25] Esack, however, is the most explicit commentator when it comes to highlighting his own subject position, to showing the critical connections between his lived realities and choice of themes in interpretation. Consider the very format of his Commentary. The first two chapters are not even devoted to the Qur'an—the text comes later—but to the history of South Africa and the South African Muslim community, and to providing an overview of Esack's own life, especially as an early victim of apartheid and an active participant in the struggle against it.[26] These chapters demonstrate vividly that his interest in topics like social liberation, religious pluralism and gender justice is not mere interest, but intimately tied to his own lived experiences. He recalls, for instance, that as a child growing up in the ghettos of the Cape Flats, he was

---

[24] Engineer, *On Developing Theology of Peace in Islam*, 171–2.
[25] Engineer Interview, 2010.
[26] See 'Introduction: In Humble Submission to the Almighty God' and 'Chapter One: The Context: Muslims in the Cape', in Esack, *Qur'an, Liberation, and Pluralism*, 1–48.

constantly touched by the humanity of his Christian neighbours, instilling in him 'a deep awareness of the intrinsic worth of the religious other.'[27] This awareness was reaffirmed during the struggle against apartheid, in which interreligious solidarity was a prominent feature.[28] Furthermore, the roots of Esack's commitment to gender justice, and to a comprehensive justice in general, lie in the suffering of his mother. As he recounts painfully, his father abandoned his mother when Esack was only three weeks old, leaving her to support six children.[29] As a result, she was forced to work from dawn till dusk as an underpaid factory worker, eventually succumbing to her circumstances.[30]

This hermeneutical move of using experience as a point of departure for scriptural reflection is largely due to recent developments in the understanding of the interpretive task. In classical Islamic thought, the quest for knowledge was viewed as an objective undertaking. As discussed in Chapter 2, this understanding was exemplified by the age-old scholarly distinction between *al-tafsir bi'l-ma'thur* (commentary based on transmitted texts, referring to the inherited, exegetical tradition and *hadith* literature) and *al-tafsir bi'l-ra'y* (commentary based on opinion), the former treated as an authentic and legitimate mode of interpretation and the latter frowned upon as fanciful conjecture, unless firmly rooted in the exegetical tradition.[31] Traditional Christianity, too, approached interpretation as 'a kind of objective science of faith', delineating two principal sources of theological reflection (*loci theologici*)—biblical scripture and the intellectual tradition—and both of which were understood as fixed and unchanging.[32] The twentieth and early twenty-first centuries, however, witnessed significant advances in the understanding of the hermeneutical task, particularly in the field of biblical studies, calling into question the assumed neutrality of the exegete. The German philosopher Hans-Georg Gadamer (d. 2002), for example, pointed out that the reader cannot occupy some sort of pristine, stable, and objective vantage point, as if questions of instability lie solely in the text and in its past interpretations, for all readers exist within the flux of history and, therefore, read the Bible through the limitations of their own

[27] Ibid, 3.   [28] Ibid, 8.   [29] Ibid, 1–2.   [30] Ibid, 2.
[31] McAuliffe, 'The Tasks and Traditions of Interpretation', 189–90.
[32] Stephen B. Bevans, *Models of Contextual Theology* (Maryknoll, New York: Orbis Books, 2008), 3–4.

contextual horizons.[33] This critical insight—that all interpretation is inescapably subjective, contextual—has now become mainstream in the field of hermeneutics.[34] As the Christian theologian Stephen Bevans eloquently puts it:

> There is no such thing as 'theology'; there is only *contextual* theology; *feminist* theology; *black* theology, *liberation* theology, *Filipino* theology, *Asian-American* theology, *African* theology, and so forth. Doing theology contextually is not an option.[35]

To be sure, there is a crucial difference between the epistemological acknowledgement that 'theology is contextual'—that is, that all interpreters are informed by their contextual baggage, such as their socioeconomic, racial, and gendered background—and 'contextual theology', which *explicitly* centres that contextual baggage in the act of interpretation.[36] By foregrounding their own contextual realities, liberationist and female gender egalitarian interpreters of the Qur'an are located squarely within this second category.

It is precisely its emphasis on a specific topic (or set of related topics) that makes thematic commentary a far more effective, exegetical vehicle through which interpreters can centre their own contexts than traditional verse-by-verse commentary. For while in a sequential mode of interpretation the exegete must respond to one verse after another, and is thus restricted to the content of successive passages, in

---

[33] David Jasper, *A Short Introduction to Hermeneutics* (Louisville, Kentucky: Westminster John Knox Press, 2004), 108.

[34] This development in exegesis is a long and complex story, one that lies outside the scope of this chapter. I would like to highlight here, however, that twentieth-century understandings of the task of interpretation that unsettled the stability, the supposed neutrality of the interpreter were not so much a response to classical scholarship as to deeply objectivist practices of biblical reading that became mainstream in the eighteenth and nineteenth centuries. Greatly influenced by the Enlightenment and its emphasis on reason and scientific enquiry, interpreters approached the Bible increasingly as a historical object of study—a text no different from any other—drawing on tools like historical criticism and literary analysis to uncover its *real* meaning, to discover the *real* Jesus. For pioneering examples of this approach, see David Friedrich Strauss (d. 1874), *The Life of Jesus, Critically Examined*, 3 vols., trans. George Elliot (Cambridge: Cambridge University Press, 2010) and Ernest Renan (d. 1892), *The Life of Jesus* (London: Watts, 1935). On the emergence of hermeneutics as a discipline, see Anthony C. Thiselton, *Hermeneutics: An Introduction* (Grand Rapids, Michigan: W.B. Eerdmans Pub. Co., 2009) and Jasper.

[35] Bevans, 3.

[36] Angie Pears, *Doing Contextual Theology* (London: Routledge, 2010), 1.

a thematic format the exegete can be more pro-active, starting 'from the application of his [*sic*] own questions to the text'.[37] This is not to imply that the exegete did not have a say in classical, sequential exegesis, as there was always an interpretive choice in terms of what aspect of a particular Qur'anic passage to reflect upon, like its grammatical composition, legal ramifications, and theological underpinnings, and the exegete's own interests would often determine the approach taken.[38] Nor is this to suggest that all thematic commentary is an explicit exercise in contextual theology. (I use the word explicit here because all exegesis is, of course, inescapably contextual.) In fact, a significant number of thematic commentaries continue to subscribe to acutely objectivist notions, such as 'scientific exegesis' (*tafsir 'ilmi*)— an apologetic body of thematic commentary that seeks to prove the compatibility of the Qur'an and natural science.[39] Rather, my argument is that thematic commentary has become an increasingly popular form of scriptural reflection because it complements a contextual theological approach, acting as a powerful medium through which the exegete can reflect on her/his own context, give this context thematic expression and then use these themes as an analytical framework to engage the text.

But because contextual theology remains on the margins of Qur'anic exegesis, liberationist and female gender egalitarian exegetes, as has been seen throughout this book, have had to evoke Islamic paradigms in order to legitimize their overtly contextualist readings. As discussed in the previous chapter, Barlas describes her exegesis as an 'auto-hermeneutic',[40] or a form of interpretation that uncovers the ways in which scripture calls for its own interpretation. In her commentary, Barlas drew great inspiration from the Prophet's wife Umm Salama, whose critique of the androcentric nature of the Qur'an (which was still in the process of being revealed) resulted in the revelation of Q. 33:35, explicitly mentioning women in a parallel fashion alongside men. That God responded favourably to, rather than ignored or castigated, Umm Salama's criticism represented, for Barlas, a moment in 'divine pedagogy', for just as Umm Salama

---

[37] Wielandt.

[38] McAuliffe, 'The Tasks and Traditions of Interpretation', 183.

[39] Stefan Wild, 'Political Interpretation of the Qur'an', in *The Cambridge Companion to the Qur'an*, ed. Jane D. McAuliffe (Cambridge: Cambridge University Press, 2006), 281.

[40] Barlas, *'Believing Women' in Islam*, 205.

reflected upon her own subject position as a woman when engaging the text so, too, should all Muslims (women and men) raise new questions when reading the Qur'an, drawing upon their own intellect, concerns, and needs.[41] Though Barlas reflects on the Qur'an's auto-hermeneutics more extensively than the other commentators in this book, in certain ways they all make autohermeneutical claims. When accenting the role of *praxis* in exegesis, and thus the importance of the reader's realities, Esack also appeals to the roots, arguing that this mode of reading was how the first Muslims engaged the Qur'an. The text was not revealed at a single moment, he points out, but rather came down gradually over an extended period of twenty-three years—what Esack refers to as 'progressive revelation'—addressing specific situations, problems, and difficulties that emerged in the burgeoning Muslim community.[42] The Qur'an, then, not only spoke to their context, but its language was continuously reshaped by it. Chapter 4 discussed how Wadud saw her own acutely layered experience of oppression—that is, being a woman, Black and poor, as well as a single mother—in Hagar, who becomes a key paradigm in Wadud's writings. Specifically, she discerned in Hagar, a Black slave abandoned in the desert and forced to find water for her child, the plight and suffering of the 'homeless, single parent.'[43] While Engineer is silent on the contextual dimensions of the Qur'an's autohermeneutics, he still references the text to legitimize his own interpretive methodology. For example, Engineer locates his *praxis*-based approach within scripture, pointing to Q. 4:95, which elevates the *mujahid* (or one who partakes in struggle) over those who sit at home.[44]

Lasting Effects: The Rise of Print Culture

There are two aspects of the Qur'anic commentaries of Esack, Engineer, Wadud, and Barlas that struck me over the course of my research: namely, their brevity and accessibility. Historically, commentaries were encyclopaedic in scope, massive exegetical works that would usually run up to twenty dense volumes.[45] Indeed, there are

---

[41] Barlas, 'Holding Fast by the Best in the Precepts', 21.
[42] Esack, *Qur'an, Liberation, and Pluralism*, 54.
[43] Wadud, *Inside the Gender Jihad*, 143.
[44] Engineer, *Islam and Liberation Theology*, 6.
[45] McAuliffe, 'The Tasks and Traditions of Interpretation', 183.

references in Islamic biographical dictionaries—a prominent literary genre in Muslim history—of commentaries comprised of fifty to even one hundred volumes.[46] It is precisely because classical commentaries were so vast that scholars were forced to produce what Saleh has termed '*madrasa* commentaries', or abridged versions of well-known commentaries that could practically be taught to students in Islamic seminaries.[47] The length of traditional commentaries stands in sharp contrast to those of contemporary liberationist and gender egalitarian female exegetes, which are single-volume works and, thus, significantly shorter: Esack's *Qur'an, Liberation and Pluralism* is 288 pages; Barlas' '*Believing Women' in Islam* is 254 pages; and Wadud's *Qur'an and Woman* is 118 pages. While Engineer does not have a single work that focuses solely on the Qur'an—his exegesis is spread out in a number of books—they, too, are relatively compact: *Islam and Liberation Theology* is 238 pages; *On Developing Theology of Peace in Islam* is 200 pages; and *The Rights of Women in Islam* is 183 pages. In addition to their brevity, I was struck by how easily I could access their writings, all of which were available for purchase through book markets. In terms of acquisition, my labours as a researcher were minimal. In the past, however, learning was, physically speaking, an immensely demanding vocation. A medieval scholar was essentially an itinerant traveller, constantly setting off for distant lands to gain knowledge. Consider the journeys of the medieval scholar ibn 'Arabi:

> So the great Spanish mystic Ibn Arabi (b. 1165) travelled from Murcia to Seville, to Tunis, to Fez, to Cordoba, to Almeria, to Tunis again, to Cairo (twice), to Jerusalem (twice), to Mecca (twice), to Baghdad (twice), to Mosul, Malatya, Sivas, Aksaray, Konya, and Damascus where he died in 1240.[48]

It is important to note here that scholars did not travel merely to acquire various texts and obscure manuscripts, but rather to read these intellectual works with other scholars. Unlike the modern world, in which the written word is the dominant mode of knowledge transmission, learning was historically defined by oral culture. For writing 'was not the mechanical representation of an author's meaning, and in this sense there was no simple "presence" of an author in

---

[46] Saleh, 20.   [47] Ibid, 21.
[48] Francis Robinson, 'Technology and Religious Change: Islam and the Impact of Print', *Modern Asian Studies* 27 (1993): 237.

a text.'[49] In order to be read, then, a text had to be read out loud in the presence of its author or a scholar who had an *ijaza* (license) to teach that specific text, which he would have acquired either by studying the text with its author or another scholar who had done so.[50] In this section, I will argue that these twin aspects of the commentaries examined in this book—brevity and accessibility—reflect the lasting impact that print culture has exercised on Qur'anic exegesis in general and on thematic Qur'anic exegesis in particular.

Over the past two centuries, the printing press has become a formidable force in Muslim societies. Printing emerged in the Islamic world in the nineteenth century, taking off in South Asia in the 1820s and 1830s and in the Ottoman Empire, Iran, and Egypt in the second half of the century.[51] The very first question that the researcher faces, then, is what explains the roughly 350-year gap between the rise of the press in the Islamic world and Christian Europe, wherein printing emerged in the late fifteenth century, playing a key role in the Protestant Reformation (1517–1648)? According to the historian Francis Robinson, the answer lies in the privileged place of orality in traditional Islamic learning, for the printed word challenged the oral word, undermining 'what was understood to make knowledge trustworthy, what gave it value, what gave it authority.'[52] In fact, it

---

[49] Timothy Mitchell, *Colonising Egypt* (Berkeley: University of California Press, 1988), 150.

[50] Robinson, 237–8. On modes of learning in the medieval Muslim world, see Jonathan Berkey, *The Transmission of Knowledge in Medieval Cairo: A Social History of Islamic Education* (Princeton: Princeton University Press, 1992) and Konrad Hirschler, *The Written Word in the Medieval Arabic Lands: A Social and Cultural History of Reading Practices* (Edinburgh: Edinburgh University Press, 2012). For a classic study of the continued importance of orality in traditional Islamic education in the twentieth century—focussing on learning practices in the Moroccan city of Marrakesh in the 1920s and 1930s—see Dale F. Eickelman, 'The Art of Memory: Islamic Education and its Social Reproduction', *Comparative Studies in Society and History* 20 (1978): 485–516.

[51] Robinson, 232–3.

[52] Ibid, 234. Historians have also pointed out that print took longer to spread in the Muslim world due to the technical difficulties of reproducing a cursive, ligatured script with early forms of movable type. As a result, lithography emerged faster in Muslim societies, such as in Southeast Asia. See Michael Laffan, *The Makings of Indonesian Islam: Orientalism and the Narration of a Sufi Past* (Princeton: Princeton University Press, 2011). For two important anthropological studies on the impact of print culture, focussing on Jordan and Yemen, see Andrew Shryock, *Nationalism and the Genealogical Imagination: Oral History and Textual Authority in Tribal Jordan* (Berkeley: University of California Press, 1997) and Messick, *The Calligraphic State*.

was because of the potential threat that the printing press posed to religious authority that the *'ulama* became the first Muslims to exploit the press, publishing their own tracts in order to reach new audiences and consolidate their authority.[53] The rise of print has been accompanied since the mid-twentieth century by the steady spread of state-sponsored mass education, which has increased the literacy rate considerably.[54] In the Arab Middle East, for instance, mass education emerged in the 1950s in Egypt and Morocco and in the early 1970s in Gulf countries like Oman and Yemen.[55] As a result, by the late 1980s 'a critical mass of people with post-secondary education, capable of sustaining an expanded internal market for newspapers, periodicals, and books, began to emerge.'[56] Although the literacy rate in modern Muslim societies is significantly higher than at any point in history, one should be careful not to over-estimate this phenomenon and, thus, the influence of print. India, Bangladesh, and North Yemen are illustrative examples of the limited reach of the press, in which literacy rates in the early 1990s were 36 per cent, 20 per cent, and 14 per cent, respectively.[57]

The rise of print culture and popular literacy has led to a remarkable expansion in the ranks of Islamic knowledge production.[58] As the anthropologist Dale Eickelman and political scientist James Piscatori have observed, a distinguishing feature of contemporary Islam is that 'discourse and debate about Muslim tradition involves people on a mass scale.'[59] Despite the initial attempts of the *'ulama* to harness the press, this technology, as numerous scholars of contemporary Islam have indicated, has served to subvert religious hierarchy.[60] Today, the *'ulama* are no longer the sole, even principal,

---

[53] Robinson, 240. [54] Taji-Farouki, 14.
[55] Eickelman and Piscatori, 40.
[56] Ibid, 39. [57] Robinson, 250.
[58] While my focus in this section is on print media and its seminal impact on Qur'anic exegesis, it is important to note that new media technologies—such as cassettes, satellite, video, and the internet—have also exerted a lasting influence on contemporary Islam. See, among others: Charles Hirschkind, *The Ethical Soundscape: Cassette Sermons and Islamic Counterpublics* (New York: Columbia University Press, 2006); Dale F. Eickelman and John W. Anderson eds., *New Media in the Muslim World: The Emerging Public Sphere* (Bloomington, Indiana: Indiana University Press, 2003); and Gary R. Bunt, *iMuslims: Rewiring the House of Islam* (Chapel Hill: University of North Carolina Press, 2009).
[59] Eickelman and Piscatori, 39.
[60] Robinson, 245; Eickelman and Piscatori, 43; Taji-Farouki, 13; Peter Mandaville, *Global Political Islam* (London: Routledge, 2007), 309.

interlocutors of Islamic thought. Rather, a new class of Muslim intellectuals educated in seemingly secular fields such as medicine and engineering, history and literature, journalism and the social sciences have entered the exegetical circle, vigorously debating the meaning of Islam.[61] It is within this specific context that we need to situate the exegetes in this book, all of whom have been trained in the so-called secular university, with the notable exception of Esack who also attended a *madrasa*. This new class of interpreters, moreover, employ modes of reading that differ considerably from those of traditional Islamic scholarship, exhibiting little interest in the inherited, interpretive tradition, either out of ignorance or because this tradition, so they argue, is simply out of touch with the problems and needs of the contemporary world.[62] As we have seen, all the exegetes considered in this study, especially Wadud and Barlas, share this critique. Indeed, the very bypassing of the tradition constitutes a radical challenge to the *'ulama*'s authority, for the commentary was a core, discursive site wherein authority was historically reproduced. The following passage by the Islamic historian Muhammad Qasim Zaman deftly demonstrates the interplay between traditional exegesis—in this case, a commentary of *hadith* based on the lectures of the South Asian scholar Rashid Ahmad Gangohi (d. 1905)—and the construction of the *'ulama*'s authority as a class:

> But it is not only Rashid Ahmad's presence, or his personal authority, that is perpetuated through this commentary. Muhammad Yahya, who wrote down the lectures; his son Muhammad Zakariyya, who added an introduction and glosses to his commentary; and Abu'l-Hasan 'Ali Nadwi (d. 1999), the former rector of the Nadwat al-'Ulama of Lucknow and the most influential Indian religious scholar of his generation . . . who added a short biography of Muhammad Zakariyya to it, are all part, in varying measures, of a select group that this commentary helps to consolidate, celebrate, and link both with the earliest generations of Islam, and with other scholars of all times engaged in the venture of transmitting similar materials. Each scholar, dead or living, shares some of the lustre of the others and adds some of his own authority to this company.[63]

[61] Wild, 278.   [62] Ibid.
[63] Zaman, 52. Gangohi's work is an exegesis of *Sahih al-Bukhari*, a central *hadith* collection in Sunni Islam.

It should be hardly surprising, then, when mainstream traditional scholars criticize new readings of the Qur'an that engage the text directly, as traditionalists are well aware that they have much to lose in terms of religious authority. That being said, it is important to underline that although print has allowed new communities to interpret scripture who would otherwise have been excluded from Islamic knowledge production, in particular women,[64] the *'ulama* have also benefited greatly from print technology, which has enabled them to gain access to Islamic texts that would have been rare commodities in the manuscript age, as well as provided them with a cheap and efficient means with which to spread their own interpretations.[65]

Print culture not only democratized the producers of Islamic knowledge, but also drastically enlarged its audiences: that is, the consumers of Islamic knowledge. This development can be discerned most acutely in the growing number of commentaries that were written for the expressly public media of journals and newspapers. For instance, the Qur'anic exegesis of Abduh and Rashid Rida (d. 1935)—two pioneering Islamic reformists—first appeared in the Egyptian journal *al-Manar* (The Light Stand) between 1927 and 1935,[66] and is precisely why it is referred to as *Tafsir al-Manar*, or the Commentary of *al-Manar*. Muslim South Asia provides another compelling example of the movement of Qur'anic exegesis from private scholarly circles to the domain of mass media. Earlier this chapter noted the widely distributed commentary of the Islamist thinker Mawdudi, titled *Understanding the Qur'an* (*Tafhim al-Qur'an*). Like Abduh's and Rida's exegesis, *Understanding the Qur'an* first appeared in a journal that was edited by Mawdudi and in which, over the course of thirty years (1942–72), he published a running exegesis of the entire text.[67] Upon completion, the various journal articles were collected and compiled into book format. That one of the most influential interpreters of the Qur'an was a journalist—Mawdudi worked as an

[64] There are, of course, historical exceptions to this patriarchal tendency, especially with regard to the mystical tradition. See al-Sulami.

[65] Zaman, 54.

[66] Wild, 280. In addition to his exegetical contributions to *al-Manar*, Abduh—a traditional scholar trained at the Cairo-based Islamic University of al-Azhar—was chief editor of the official newspaper of the Egyptian state, *al-Waqi'a al-Misriyya*. See Yvonne Haddad, 'Muhammad Abduh: Pioneer of Islamic Reform', in *Pioneers of Islamic Revival*, ed. Ali Rahnema (London: Zed Books, 2008), 32.

[67] Nasr, 103–4.

editor for numerous newspapers throughout his career, such as *The Muslim*, the official media mouthpiece of the Society of Indian 'Ulama (*Jami'at-i 'Ulama-i Hind*)[68]—is significant, reflecting the massification of Islamic discourse in general and of Qur'anic exegesis in particular. The looming presence of the West was a key factor that spurred Abduh and Mawdudi to try to reach out to and influence a larger audience. Indeed, the Qur'anic scholar Stefan Wild has argued that modern Muslim exegesis cannot be understood without appreciating the global context in which it has emerged: namely, the superior military and economic might of the modern West.[69] Abduh's chief objective was to prove to Muslims that Islam was compatible with modernity, portraying Islam as, to borrow the words of the historian Yvonne Haddad, 'the champion of progress and development'.[70] Similarly, Mawdudi wrote in an environment wherein young Muslims, impressed by the achievements of the West, were adopting Western lifestyles and therefore, in order to counter this devious trend, targeted his commentary not at the *'ulama* but at the average, lay Muslim reader.[71] In addition to journals and newspapers, books have become an increasingly popular medium for Islamic discourse, especially in the Middle East and South Asia, which have undergone an Islamic revival since the 1970s. Not to be confused with lengthy, dense, and costly scholarly works, these 'Islamic books' are often short, attractively designed, and cheap, thereby being accessible and appealing to a mass readership that lacks advanced literary skills.[72] It is difficult to over-emphasize the popularity of such religious literature. Focussing on topics like Qur'anic exegesis, the *shari'a*, and women's issues, these books have acquired an enormous readership, especially amongst university students.[73]

And it is this broader context that can provide critical insight into the current state of Qur'anic commentary and, specifically, the

---

[68] Ibid, 100. It is interesting to note that although Mawdudi always identified as a journalist and layperson, he actually completed the *Dars-i Nizami*, the standard *madrasa* curriculum in South Asia. This aspect of Mawdudi's life, moreover, only became known after his death. See ibid, 101.

[69] Wild, 276–7.   [70] Haddad, 46.

[71] Saeed, *Interpreting the Qur'an*, 17.

[72] Eickelman and Piscatori, 40. As the authors note, the French Arabist Yves Gonzalez-Quijano was the first to coin this term.

[73] Dale F. Eickelman and Jon W. Anderson, 'Print, Islam, and the Prospects for Civic Pluralism: New Religious Writings and their Audiences', *Journal of Islamic Studies* 8 (1997): 55.

increasing popularity of thematic commentary. The massification of Islamic discourse, with millions of Muslims now able, via a publication market, to access Islamic texts, has fundamentally diversified the craft of commentary, significantly shortening exegesis and shifting from a full-scale, encyclopaedic treatment to a partial, thematic one. These transformations were inevitable, for the commentary had to adapt to its new audiences, which were not only exponentially larger but also unschooled in complex, scholarly methods of exegesis.[74] Whereas a traditional scholar might have had the time and training to read a convoluted, twenty-volume work, this was simply not an option for the overwhelming majority of lay readers. Clarity and conciseness now became key features, for in order for a text to be read, to gain widespread distribution, it had to respond effectively to the demands of its readers, being able to capture and to sustain their interests—a feat that would be difficult to achieve with a lengthy, dense text. (Indeed, a key reason why a number of modern sequential commentaries are popular, particularly those of Mawdudi and Qutb, is because of their lucid and engaging prose, deliberately aimed at these new lay audiences. Print culture, therefore, has also exerted an influence on full-scale, sequential exegesis itself, diversifying its writing styles.) Clarity and conciseness are actually defining traits of the Islamic books that have become popular in recent decades, written in clear prose—sometimes even in the local vernacular language—and strikingly compact, mostly taking the form of manuals, pamphlets, and primers.[75] Thus, while the encyclopaedic commentary is not in decline, its form is somewhat anachronistic—it was designed for a completely different audience. A child of its time, it addressed (or at

---

[74] This dynamic has been reinforced with the emergence of new media technologies such as the internet, which has made it possible for anyone, irrespective of educational level, to access effortlessly the Qur'an and other Islamic texts—often in the form of brief articles and discussion threads/forums—and to partake in religious debate from the comfort and privacy of one's home. Television has, of course, played a key role in accelerating the massification of Islamic discourse, most notably with the rise of popular televangelists like the Egyptian Amr Khaled (b. 1967). Khaled has become something of a phenomenon in the Arab street, despite the fact that he has no traditional Islamic training, having studied accounting at Cairo University. The argument could be made that it is precisely Khaled's lay background (in addition to his exploitation of satellite television) that has enabled him to secure such massive followings, imbuing him with a certain earthly appeal—a worldly relevance—to the average, uneducated Muslim listener.

[75] Eickelman and Piscatori, 42–3.

least was originally designed to address) a small, closely knit circle of scholars. Its sheer breadth and the disparate, disconnected nature of its verse-by-verse hermeneutic are at variance with contemporary needs for lucidity, succinctness, and the ability to speak to a mass readership. In contrast, thematic exegesis, by focussing on a specific subject or set of related subjects rather than offering a comprehensive exposition, is not only considerably shorter but can centre on issues that are of pressing concern and relevance, or merely of general interest, to its readers. This form of commentary, then, is closely tied to the modern phenomena of print culture and mass literacy, of new producers and consumers of Islamic knowledge.

In this section, I have used the thematic approaches of the interpreters examined in this book as a point of departure to make a larger argument about thematic commentary and its relationship to print culture. In doing so, however, I do not mean to imply that their writings are situated within the type of popular Islamic literature that we have discussed above. Rather, all the exegetes considered in this book, with the exception of Engineer, are academics and publish with university or academic trade presses like Oxford University Press (Wadud), University of Texas Press (Barlas), and Oneworld Publications (Esack). As such, their commentaries belong to a genre within contemporary Islamic literature that speaks to a more elite readership that is familiar with their complex hermeneutical methods and theoretical frameworks.[76] That being said, their commentaries are still shaped by external factors. Indeed, there are remarkable parallels between the forces exerted on their writings and on popular Islamic literature. Clarity and marketability, for instance, have become crucial criteria for academic publication houses. Discussing the transition from doctoral dissertation to book, Gregory Colón Semenza—a scholar of medieval English literature—writes:

> editors will be focussed on numerous practical considerations. How much need is there for such a book? Is this book likely to sell? How much work will the press need to ready the book for publication? Whereas jargon may sound intelligent to you, it will likely suggest to an editor your inability to communicate clearly. . . . In constructing a

---

[76] Taji-Farouki, 15.

prospectus, you must communicate the marketability of the project without surrendering its intellectual integrity.[77]

In certain ways, the transformation of a thesis into a book—shifting from an audience of a handful of examiners to hundreds, even thousands, of readers—is a microcosm of our preceding discussion on the movement of Islamic discourse from restricted scholarly circles to a mass readership. As noted in the above passage, in order to be accessible to specialists in other fields, as well as lay readers, an academic book needs to be able to 'communicate clearly' and without 'jargon'. Secondly, while contextual information may need to be added in order to make the book comprehensible to those in other disciplines, the process is, essentially, one of 'pruning', such as removing the literature review section, long discussions of methodology, and extensive footnoting.[78] Conciseness is especially acute in trade publishing, as it is more difficult to maintain the reader's interest over a lengthy work.[79] So just like mainstream print culture, the demands of academic print culture are at variance with the voluminous and convoluted nature of traditional exegesis. Thematic commentary, on the other hand, with its eschewal of encyclopaedic comprehensiveness and focus on select topics, is simply more compatible as an exegetical format. Moreover, traditional commentary's approach of reading one verse after another without amassing meanings in a systematic way, and of mustering prior interpretations without necessarily offering new ones, conflicts with academia's accent on advancing knowledge, on forwarding original arguments.[80]

---

[77] Gregory Colón Semenza, *Graduate Study for the 21st Century: How to Build an Academic Career in the Humanities* (New York: Palgrave Macmillan, 2005), 219.

[78] Beth Luey, *Handbook for Academic Authors* (Cambridge: Cambridge University Press, 2010), 40–1.

[79] Ibid, 161–2.

[80] This actually reflects a paradox in the relationship between the scale and nature of knowledge in traditional learning on the one hand and contemporary academia on the other. For despite the majestic size of traditional Qur'anic commentaries, and of medieval Islamic scholarly works in general, their aims were markedly modest, humble: to seek (*talaba*) and to preserve (*hafaza*) knowledge rather than the grander objective of originating knowledge, of forwarding bold and entirely new understandings. Conversely, the culture of contemporary academia celebrates, indeed is defined by, originality and radical creativity while, at the same time, emphasizing succinctness and lucidity. I am grateful to James McDougall for this insight.

CONCLUSIONS

Liberationist and women's gender egalitarian readings of the Qur'an
are clearly significant in terms of demonstrating the contemporary
social relevance of Islam's sacred text. But these readings are also
significant, I have argued, because they provide critical insights into
thematic exegesis of the Qur'an. Firstly, they reflect the desire to
partake in a direct engagement with scripture, unmediated by the
commentaries of classical scholars. This mode of reading marks a
historical rupture with past exegetical practices, which, as a genealogical tradition, were basically interpretations *of* interpretations. Part
and parcel of such a direct engagement with the Qur'an has been the
tendency to read the text holistically. This holistic hermeneutic is
closely tied to the character, the structure of thematic exegesis, as the
reader must sift through the entire text with a specific subject in mind,
piecing together the various fragment parts.

Secondly, the interpretations of these exegetes reveal the centrality
of one's subject position in thematic reading. There is nothing random about the choice of topic, as this choice is directly informed
by the environment, struggles, and problems facing the reader. So
Wadud and Barlas, as women living in patriarchal societies, focus on
gender equality; Esack, as an activist engaged in an anti-apartheid
movement characterized by interfaith solidarity, explores the twin
themes of liberation and pluralism; Engineer, as a Muslim living in an
environment plagued with communal conflict between Hindus and
Muslims, examines social justice, peaceful reconciliation, and interfaith relations. Thematic commentary is an effective exegetical vehicle
for such 'contextual theology'—that is, the conscious foregrounding
of one's context in the hermeneutical process—as the interpreter can
focus on those topics that speak directly to her/his interests and
needs. There is a critical synergy, then, between thematic reflection
and contextual theology.

Finally, the interpretations of these exegetes reflect an underlying
relationship between thematic commentary and print culture. Print
culture has played a fundamental role in shaping Qur'anic exegesis.
The emergence of the printing press in Muslim societies, coupled
with the spread of mass education and thus dramatically higher rates
of literacy, exploded the ranks of Islamic knowledge production.
Non-traditionally trained exegetes like engineers, physicians, and
humanities scholars now began to partake in the interpretive task.

Print culture did not only massify the producers of Islamic knowledge but also its consumers, as Qur'anic commentaries increasingly appeared in public media like journals, newspapers, and popular books. It is within this wider milieu that we need to appreciate the appeal of thematic commentary. Though sequential commentaries are hardly in decline, the thematic model is simply more compatible with a print market that accents clarity, conciseness, and the ability to sustain the interests of, and speak to the issues facing, a large and largely lay audience.

Select Glossary

'Adl	A Qur'anic term for justice, alongside *qist*.
Ahl al-Kitab	Literally, the People of the Book. This is a Qur'anic term that refers to monotheistic communities that received revelation prior to Islam, such as Jews and Christians, thereby differentiating them from polytheists.
'Amil	A Dawudi Bohra term denoting a traditionally trained Islamic scholar who executes the wishes of the *da'i*. Cf. the entry on *'da'i'*.
'Aml al-salihat	Righteous works.
'Aqida	Islamic creed or doctrine.
'Aql	Intellect or intelligence.
Asbab al-nuzul	The Occasions of Revelation literature, which records the various contexts wherein Qur'anic verses were revealed.
Aya (pl.: *ayat*)	Literally sign, referring to a Qur'anic verse.
Da'i	A Dawudi Bohra term referring to the representative of the hidden *imam*, who is in seclusion. Mohammed Burhanuddin (r. 1965–2014) was the 52nd *da'i*.
Dalits	Literally the Crushed People, denoting the so-called Untouchables of the Hindu caste system.
Dawudi Bohras	A sub-sect of Shi'a Ismai'ili Islam based largely in India and with a membership of approximately one million followers. According to the Dawudi Bohras, their twenty-first *imam*—Tayyib abi al-Qasim (b. circa 1130)—disappeared and went into seclusion. Since this time, a hereditary line of *da'is* has represented the hidden *imam*. Cf. the entries on *'da'i'* and 'Shi'a Islam'.
Fiqh	Islamic jurisprudence.
Fitra	Human nature, referring to the innate inclination of all human beings towards goodness.
Fuqaha' (s.: *faqih*)	Islamic jurists.
Hadith (pl.: *ahadith*)	A reported saying or action of Prophet Muhammad.
Halaqa (pl.: *halaqat*)	Religious study circle.

Hermeneutics	In this book, the term is used in two distinct senses: the first as the *way* in which a text is interpreted and the second as the *study* of the strategies and problems of interpretation.
Hijab	Literally, a screen or curtain. This term is commonly used by Muslims to refer to the female headscarf.
Ihya' al-sunna	The revival of the *sunna*.
Ijtihad	Technically a legal device in the *shari'a*, *ijtihad* is now often used to refer to independent, critical reasoning in Islamic reformist thought.
Imam	This term has multiple meanings. Literally it means one who stands in front, denoting a prayer leader. Imam can also be used as an honorific title for a religious scholar. The most significant usage of the term, however, is in the context of Shi'a Islam. Cf. the entry on 'Shi'a Islam'.
Iman	Belief or faith in God.
Iman bi-l ghayb	Belief in the unseen.
Islah wa tajdid	Reform and renewal.
Islam	Literally submission, that is, to the one God.
Islamism	In this book, the term is defined as a type of religious activism that seeks to establish an Islamic state, whether through militant or peaceful, democratic means.
Isra'iliyat	A genre in the Islamic intellectual tradition that refers to prophetic stories and narratives derived from biblical (literally, Israelite) literature.
Jahiliyya	Commonly translated in English as the Age of Ignorance, this term refers to pre-Islamic Arabian society.
Jihad	Literally, struggle. This term includes both physical combat and inner, spiritual exertion.
Karbala	A shrine city in Iraq. The term is often used to denote a historic battle (680) that took place in the same city, which, at the time, was an open plain. Here, Husayn ibn Ali—the grandson of Prophet Muhammad and third *imam* of Shi'a Muslims—rebelled against the caliph Yazid. Husayn and his small band of followers were brutally massacred.
Khilafa	This term has two distinct meanings. Caliphate, or the Sunni institution of political leadership following the Prophet's death, is the most common understanding of

the term. In a Qur'anic context, *khilafa* means trusteeship, that is, the idea that God, at the beginning of time, appointed humankind as trustee (*khalifa*) of the Earth. Humankind, then, will be accountable for its role as trustee on the Final Day.

Kufr Generally translated as disbelief but also entailing the notion of ingratitude, of rejecting a gift.

Madrasa A traditional Islamic seminary.

Matn The substantive content of a *hadith*.

Maulana Literally, our master. This is a term of respect that is often used in South Asia to address a traditional Islamic scholar.

Mujahid One who partakes in *jihad*.

Mu'min (pl: *mu'minun*) One who believes.

Muslim Literally, a submitter. That is, one who submits him/herself to God.

Nafs Soul.

Praxis The idea that theology ought to emerge in the midst of the collective struggle against oppression, and is characterized by a dialectical hermeneutic of action–reflection–action.

Qist A Qur'anic term for justice, alongside *'adl*.

Qital Fighting in warfare.

Sadaqa Charity.

Salafiyya An Islamic reformist movement that emerged over the past two centuries and which emphasizes a return to the original practice of the *salaf*, or the first generations of Muslims.

Salah Islamic ritual prayer, performed five times a day by Sunni Muslims, three times a day by Shi'a Muslims.

Salam Peace.

Sanad (pl.: *isnad*) A *hadith* report's chain of narration. The *isnad* are classified into various levels of reliability, such as *sahih* (authentic), *hasan* (good), and *da'if* (weak).

Shari'a Literally the Way, denoting the inherited, legal tradition of Islam.

Shi'a Islam A minority branch of Islam that believes that the leadership of the Muslim community after the Prophet's death should have fallen to Ali ibn abi Talib (d. 661), the cousin and son-in-law of the Prophet, since authority, according to Shi'a Muslims, is vested within the Prophet's family. Ali is referred to as the first *imam* (spiritual guide). Different Shi'a groups follow different hereditary lines of *imams*.

Shirk   The association of partners with God and, thus, the antithesis of *tawhid*.

Sira   The inherited corpus of biographical literature on Prophet Muhammad.

Sisters in Islam (SIS)   An influential Muslim women's organization in Malaysia that advocates for women's rights through an Islamic framework.

Sufism   The mystical tradition of Islam. 'Sufism' is the anglicized version of the Arabic term *tasawwuf*.

Sunna   This is a widely used shorthand for *sunnat al-nabi*, the custom or precedent of Prophet Muhammad.

Sunnat al-awwalin   Literally, the precedent of the ancients, referring to earlier peoples who had shunned the prophets and, as a result, were destroyed by God.

Sunnat Allah   The custom or precedent of God.

Sunni Islam   The majority branch of Islam that follows the *sunna* of the Prophet and his companions, as opposed to Shi'a Islam, which follows the Prophet and his family. In terms of leadership institutions, Sunni Islam was distinguished by the caliphate (*khilafa*), an office that governed the Muslim community after the Prophet's death. Unlike the imamate (cf. entry on 'Shi'a Islam'), the caliphate did not explicitly combine religious and political authority, although of course it, by virtue of being the political and symbolic head of Muslims, still had wider religious implications.

Tadrij   Progressive revelation. A term that Esack uses, *tadrij* refers to the fact that the Qur'an was not revealed at one moment but rather gradually over a period of twenty-three years (*c.* 610–32), addressing various problems and issues as they emerged within the burgeoning Muslim community.

Tafsir   Literally interpretation, referring to the historic exegesis of the Qur'an.

Tafsir 'Ilmi	Scientific commentary of the Qur'an, seeking to reconcile natural science with scripture.
Tafsir mawdu'i	Thematic commentary of the Qur'an.
Tafsir musalsal	Sequential, verse-by-verse commentary of the Qur'an.
Taqwa	Piety or God-consciousness.
Tawhid	The central tenet of Islam, referring to the unity of God.
'Ulama (s: *'alim*)	Literally those who know, denoting the historic, traditionally trained interpreters of Islam.
'Ulama al-nusus	Text scholars, or traditional Muslim scholars and, thus, those who have expertise in various Islamic texts like the Qur'an, the *hadith* and the *shari'a*.
'Ulama al-waqi'	Context scholars, or specialists trained in so-called secular fields like the humanities, social sciences and natural sciences.
'Ulum al-hadith	The traditional sciences of the *hadith*.
'Ulum al-Qur'an	The traditional sciences of the Qur'an.
Umma	Literally, community or nation. This term is often used by Muslims to refer to the global Muslim community.
Usul al-fiqh	The roots or principles of Islamic jurisprudence.
Yawm al-din	Literally the Day of Religion, referring to the Day of Judgement.
Zaka	The annual almsgiving.
Zina	Illicit sexual relations, such as premarital sex and adultery.
Zulm	Oppression.

Bibliography

Works by Amina Wadud

———. 'On Belonging as a Muslim Woman'. In *My Soul is a Witness: African American Women's Spirituality*, ed. Gloria Wade-Gayles. Boston: Beacon Press, 1995.

———. 'Sisters in Islam: Effective Against All Odds'. In *Silent Voices*, eds. Doug A. Newsom and Bob J. Carrell. Lanham, Maryland: University Press of America, 1995.

———. 'Towards a Qur'anic Hermeneutics of Social Justice: Race, Class and Gender' *Journal of Law and Religion* 12 (1995–6), 37–50.

———. 'Teaching Afrocentric Islam in the White Christian South'. In *Black Women in the Academy: Promises and Perils*, ed. Lois Benjamin. Gainesville: University Press of Florida, 1997.

———. "An Islamic Perspective on Civil Rights Issues." In *Religion, Race, and Justice in a Changing America*, eds. Gary Orfield and Holly Lebowitz. New York: Century Foundation Press, 1999.

———. *Qur'an and Woman: Rereading the Sacred Text from a Woman's Perspective*. Oxford: Oxford University Press, 1999.

———. 'Alternative Qur'anic Interpretation and the Status of Muslim Women'. In *Windows of Faith: Muslim Women Scholar-Activists in North America*, ed. Gisela Webb. Syracuse, New York: Syracuse University Press, 2000.

———. 'Roundtable Discussion: Feminist Theology and Religious Diversity' *Journal of Feminist Studies in Religion* 16:2 (2000), 90–100.

———. 'Beyond Interpretation'. In *The Place of Tolerance in Islam*, eds. Khaled Abou El Fadl with Joshua Cohen and Ian Lague. Boston: Beacon Press, 2002.

———. 'American Muslim Identity: Race and Ethnicity in Progressive Islam'. In *Progressive Muslims: On Justice, Gender, and Pluralism*, ed. Omid Safi. Oxford: Oneworld, 2003.

———. 'What's Interpretation Got To Do With It: The Relationship between Theory and Practice in Islamic Gender Reform'. In *Islamic Family Law and Justice for Muslim Women*, ed. Hjh Nik Noriani Nik Badlishah. Kuala Lampur: Sisters in Islam, 2003.

———. 'Qur'an, Gender and Interpretive Possibilities' *Hawwa* 2:3 (2004), 316–36.

———. 'Citizenship and Faith'. In *Women and Citizenship*, ed. Marilyn Friedman. Oxford: Oxford University Press, 2005.

———. 'Aisha's Legacy: The Struggle for Women's Rights within Islam'. In *The New Voices of Islam: Rethinking Politics and Modernity: A Reader*, ed. Mehran Kamrava. Berkeley: University of California Press, 2006.

——. *Inside the Gender Jihad: Women's Reform in Islam*. Oxford: Oneworld, 2006.

—— ed. *Introduction to Islam: A Reader*. Dubuque, Iowa: Kendall/Hunt Publishers, 2007.

——. 'Foreword: Engaging *Tawhid* in Islams and Feminisms' *International Feminist Journal of Politics* 10:4 (2008), 435–8.

——. 'Islam beyond Patriarchy through Gender Inclusive Analysis'. In *Wanted: Equality and Justice in the Muslim Family*, ed. Zainah Anwar. Petaling Jaya, Malaysia: Musawah, 2009.

——. 'American by Force, Muslim by Choice' *Political Theology* 12:5 (2011), 699–705.

——. 'The Authority of Experience'. Keynote address at the conference, 'Muslim Women and the Challenge of Authority', Boston University, Boston, 31 March 2012.

——. 'The Ethics of *Tawhid* over the Ethics of *Qiwamah*'. In *Men in Charge? Rethinking Authority in Muslim Legal Tradition*, eds. Ziba Mir-Hosseini, Mulki Al-Sharmani, and Jana Rumminger. London: Oneworld, 2015.

Works by Asghar Ali Engineer

——. 'Women and Administration'. In *Proceedings: National Seminar on the Status of Woman in Islam*. New Delhi: Bait-al-Hikmat, 1983.

—— ed. *Islam and Revolution*. Delhi: Ajanta Publications, 1984.

——. *Islam and Liberation Theology: Essays on Liberative Elements in Islam*. New Delhi: Sterling Publishers, 1990.

——. *The Rights of Women in Islam*. New York: St. Martin's Press, 1992.

——. 'Islam, Women, and Gender Justice'. In *What Men Owe Women: Men's Voices from World Religions*, eds. John C. Raines and Daniel C. Maguire. Albany, New York: State University of New York Press, 2001.

——. *Rational Approach to Islam*. New Delhi: Gyan Publishing House, 2001.

—— ed. *The Gujarat Carnage*. New Delhi: Orient Longman, 2003.

——. 'Dalit-Muslim Dialogue'. *Secular Perspective*, 16 August 2004. Accessed 12 August 2016. http://www.csss-isla.com/wp-content/uploads/2015/06/August-16-31-04.pdf

——. 'Islam and Pluralism'. In *The Myth of Religious Superiority: A Multifaith Exploration*, ed. Paul F. Knitter. Maryknoll, New York: Orbis, 2005.

——. *On Developing Theology of Peace in Islam*. New Delhi: Sterling Publishers, 2005.

——. 'Israeli Aggression and the World'. *Secular Perspective*, 1 August 2006. Accessed 12 August 2016. http://www.csss-isla.com/wp-content/uploads/2015/06/August-1-15-06.pdf

——. 'Kashmiri Youth and Prospects of Peace'. *Secular Perspective*, 1 September 2006. Accessed 12 August 2016. http://www.csss-isla.com/wp-content/uploads/2015/06/Septe-1-15-06.pdf

——. 'Women's Plight in Muslim Society'. *Secular Perspective*, 1 November 2006. Accessed 12 August 2016. http://www.csss-isla.com/wp-content/uploads/2015/06/November-1-15-06.pdf

——. 'Secularism and its Problems in India'. *Secular Perspective*, 1 December 2007. Accessed 12 August 2016. http://www.csss-isla.com/wp-content/uploads/2015/06/December-1-15-07.pdf

——. 'How Secular is India Today?' *Secular Perspective*, 16 October 2008. Accessed 12 August 2016. http://www.csss-isla.com/wp-content/uploads/2015/06/October-16-31-08.pdf

——. *Islam: Misgivings and History*. New Delhi: Vitasta Publishing, 2008.

——. *A Living Faith: My Quest for Peace, Harmony and Social Change: An Autobiography of Asghar Ali Engineer*. New Delhi: Orient Blackswan, 2011.

——. *The Prophet of Non-Violence: Spirit of Peace, Compassion and Universality in Islam*. New Delhi: Vitasta Publishing, 2011.

Works by Asma Barlas

——. *Democracy, Nationalism and Communalism: The Colonial Legacy in South Asia*. Boulder, Colorado: Westview Press, 1995.

——. 'Texts, Sex, and States: A Critique of North African Discourses on Islam'. In *The Arab-African and Islamic Worlds: Interdisciplinary Studies*, eds. Kevin Lacey and Ralph Coury. New York: Peter Lang, 2000.

——. 'Muslim Women and Sexual Oppression: Reading Liberation from the Qur'an' *Macalester International* 10 (Spring 2001), 117–46.

——. 'The Qur'an and Hermeneutics: Reading the Qur'an's Opposition to Patriarchy' *Journal of Qur'anic Studies* 3 (2001), 15–38.

——. *'Believing Women' in Islam: Unreading Patriarchal Interpretations of the Qur'an*. Austin: University of Texas Press, 2002.

——. 'Jihad = Holy War = Terrorism: The Politics of Conflation and Denial' *The American Journal of Islamic Social Sciences* 20:1 (Winter 2003), 46–62.

——. 'Amina Wadud's Hermeneutics of the Qur'an: Women Rereading Sacred Texts'. In *Modern Muslim Intellectuals and the Qur'an*, ed. Suha Taji-Faruqi. Oxford: Oxford University Press, 2004.

——. *Islam, Muslims, and the US: Essays on Religion and Politics*. New Delhi: Global Media Publications, 2004.

——. 'Globalizing Equality: Muslim Women, Theology, and Feminisms'. In *On Shifting Ground: Middle Eastern Women in the Global Era*, ed. Fera Simone. New York: Feminist Press, 2005.

——. 'Reviving Islamic Universalism: East/s, West/s, and Coexistence'. In *Contemporary Islam: Dynamic, not Static*, eds. Abdul Aziz Said,

258 *Bibliography*

Mohammad Abu-Nimr, and Meena Sharify-Funk. London: Routledge, 2006.

——. 'Women's Readings of the Qur'an'. In *The Cambridge Companion to the Qur'an*, ed. Jane McAuliffe. Cambridge: Cambridge University Press, 2006.

——. 'Still Quarrelling over the Qur'an: Five Interventions' *International Institute for the Study of Islam in the Modern World (ISIM) Review* 20 (Autumn 2007), 32–3.

——. 'Engaging Islamic Feminism: Provincializing Feminism as a Master Narrative'. In *Islamic Feminism: Current Perspectives*, ed. Anitta Kynsilehto. Tampere, Finland: Tampere Peace Research Institute, 2008.

——. '"Holding Fast by the Best in the Precepts": the Qur'an and Method'. In *New Directions in Islamic Thought: Exploring Reform and Tradition*, eds. Kari Vogt et al. London: I.B. Tauris, 2008.

——. *Re-Understanding Islam: A Double Critique*, Spinoza Lectures presented by the University of Amsterdam. Amsterdam: Van Gorcum, 2008.

——. 'Embodying Islam and Muslims: Religious and Secular Inscriptions'. In *The Body Unbound: Philosophical Perspectives on Politics, Embodiment, and Religion*, eds. Marius Timmann Mjaaland, Ola Sigurdson, and Sigridur Thorgeirsdottir. Newcastle, UK: Cambridge Scholars Publishing, 2010.

——. 'Abraham's Sacrifice in the Qur'an: Beyond the Body'. In *Conference Proceedings: Religion and the Body*. Turku, Finland: Donner Institute for Research in the History of Religion, Abo Akademi University, 2011.

——. 'September 11, 2001: Remember Forgetting' *Political Theology* 12:5 (2011), 727–36.

——. 'Does the Qur'an support gender equality? Or, do I have the autonomy to answer this question?' In *Negotiating Autonomy and Authority in Muslim Contexts*, eds. Monique Bernards and Marjo Buitelaar. Leuven, Belgium: Peeters, 2013.

Works by Farid Esack

——. 'Three Islamic Strands in the South African Struggle for Justice' *Third World Quarterly* 10 (1988), 473–98.

——. *But Musa Went To Fir-aun! A Compilation of Questions and Answers about the Role of Muslims in the South African Struggle*. Maitland, South Africa: Call of Islam, 1989.

——. 'Contemporary Religious Thought in South Africa and the Emergence of Qur'anic Hermeneutical Notions' *Islam and Christian-Muslim Relations* 2:2 (1991): 206–26.

——. 'Qur'anic Hermeneutics: Problems and Prospects' *The Muslim World* 83:2 (1993): 118–41.

——. "Between Mandela and Man Dalla, Kafirs and Kaffirs: Post-Modernist Islamic Reflections in a Post Apartheid South Africa" *Reviews in Religion and Theology* 2:3 (1995): 24–7.

——. *Qur'an, Liberation, and Pluralism: An Islamic Perspective of Interreligious Solidarity Against Oppression.* Oxford: Oneworld, 1997.

——. *On Being a Muslim: Finding a Religious Path in the World Today.* Oxford: Oneworld, 1999.

——. 'Islam and Gender Justice: Beyond Simplistic Apologia'. In *What Men Owe Women: Men's Voices from World Religions,* eds. John C. Raines and Daniel C. Maguire. Albany, New York: State University of New York Press, 2001.

——. 'In Search of Progressive Islam Beyond 9/11'. In *Progressive Muslims: On Justice, Gender, and Pluralism,* ed. Omid Safi. Oxford: Oneworld, 2003.

——. 'Religio-Cultural Diversity: For What and With Whom? Muslim Reflections from a Post-Apartheid South Africa in the Throes of Globalization'. In *Cultural Diversity in Islam,* eds. Abdul Aziz Said and Meena Sharify-Funk. Lanham, Maryland: University Press of America, 2003.

——. *HIV, AIDS and Islam: Reflections based on Compassion, Responsibility and Justice.* Cape Town: Positive Muslims, 2004.

——. *The Qur'an: A User's Guide.* Oxford: Oneworld, 2005.

——. 'The Contemporary Democracy and the Human Rights Project for Muslim Societies: Challenges for the Progressive Muslim Intellectual'. In *Contemporary Islam: Dynamic, not Static,* eds. Abdul Aziz Said, Mohammad Abu-Nimr, and Meena Sharify-Funk. London: Routledge, 2006.

——. 'Care in a Season of AIDS: An Islamic Perspective'. In *Restoring Hope: Decent Care in the Midst of HIV/AIDS,* eds. Ted Karpf, Jeffrey V. Lazarus, and Todd Ferguson. New York: Palgrave Macmillan, 2008.

——. 'Muslims Engaging the Other and the Humanum'. In *Proselytization and Communal Self-Determination in Africa,* ed. Abdullahi A. An-Na'im. Eugene, OR: Wipf and Stock, 2009.

——. 'Open Letter'. *Jewish Peace News,* 2009. Accessed 3 September 2012. jewishpeacenews.blogspot.com/2009/04/farid-esacks-open-letter-is-inscribed. html

—— and Sarah Chiddy eds. *Islam and AIDS: Between Scorn, Pity and Justice.* Oxford: Oneworld, 2009.

—— and Nadeem Mahomed, 'Sexual Diversity, Islamic Jurisprudence and Sociality' *Journal of Gender and Religion in Africa* 17:2 (2011): 41–57.

——. 'The Territory of the Qur'an: 'Citizens', 'Foreigners', and 'Invaders'. In *Observing the Observer: The State of Islamic Studies in American Universities,* eds. Mumtaz Ahmad, Zahid Bukhari, and Sulayman Nyang. Herndon, VA: International Institute of Islamic Thought, 2012.

——. "The Portrayal of Jews and the Possibilities for Their Salvation in the Qur'an." In *Between Heaven and Hell: Islam, Salvation, and the Fate of Others,* ed. Mohammad Hassan Khalil. Oxford: Oxford University Press, 2013.

——. "Islam, Children, and Modernity: A Qur'anic Perspective." In *Children, Adults, and Shared Responsibilities: Jewish, Christian, and Muslim Perspectives,* ed. Marcia J. Bunge. Cambridge: Cambridge University Press, 2014.

——and Nadeem Mahomed, "The Normal and Abnormal: On the Politics of Being Muslim and Relating to Same-Sex Sexuality" *Journal of the American Academy of Religion*. Advance Access published 24 July 2016, doi: 10.1093/jaarel/lfw057

Interviews

Barlas, Asma. Interview by Shadaab Rahemtulla and Sara Ababneh. Ithaca, United States: 20 August 2009.

Engineer, Asghar Ali. Interview by Shadaab Rahemtulla. Oxford, United Kingdom: 12 June 2010.

Esack, Farid. Interview by Shadaab Rahemtulla and Sara Ababneh. Oxford, United Kingdom: 16 November 2009.

Wadud, Amina. Interview by Shadaab Rahemtulla. Bergen, Norway: 26–27 November 2009.

Secondary Sources

'A Common Word between Us and You (Summary and Abridgement)'. Accessed 3 September 2012. www.acommonword.com/index.php?lang=en&page=option1

Abi Talib, Ali ibn. *Peak of Eloquence: Nahjul Balagha, with Commentary by Ayatollah Murtada Mutahhari*, edited by Yasin T. al-Jibouri. Elmhurst, New York: Tahrike Tarsile Qur'an, 2009.

Abou El Fadl, Khaled. *Speaking in God's Name: Islamic Law, Authority and Women*. Oxford: Oneworld, 2001.

——. Foreword to *Inside the Gender Jihad: Women's Reform in Islam*, by Amina Wadud. Oxford: Oneworld, 2006.

Abugideiri, Hibba. 'Hagar: A Historical Model for "Gender Jihad."' In *Daughters of Abraham: Feminist Thought in Judaism, Christianity, and Islam*, eds. Yvonne Y. Haddad and John L. Esposito. Gainesville: University Press of Florida, 2001.

Afsaruddin, Asma. *The First Muslims: History and Memory*. Oxford: Oneworld, 2008.

Agnes, Flavia. 'The Supreme Court, the Media, and the Uniform Civil Code Debate in India'. In *The Crisis of Secularism in India*, eds. Anuradha D. Needham and Rajeswari S. Rajan. Durham, US: Duke University Press, 2007.

Ahmed, Akbar. *Jinnah, Pakistan and Islamic Identity: The Search for Saladin*. London: Routledge, 1997.

Ahmed, Leila. *Women and Gender in Islam*. New Haven: Yale University Press, 1992.

Akhtar, Shabbir. *A Faith for All Seasons*. Chicago: Ivan R. Dee, 1990.

——. *The Final Imperative: An Islamic Theology of Liberation*. London: Bellew, 1991.

——. *The Qur'an and the Secular Mind: A Philosophy of Islam*. Abingdon, UK: Routledge, 2007.

——. *Islam as Political Religion: The Future of an Imperial Faith*. Abingdon, UK: Routledge, 2011.

Al-Baghdadi, al-Khatib. *Tarikh Baghdad* [A History of Baghdad]. Beirut: Dar al-Kutub al-'Ilmiyya, n.d.

Al-Ghazali, Muhammad. *A Thematic Commentary of the Qur'an*, translated by Ashur A. Shamis. Herndon, Virginia: International Institute of Islamic Thought, 2000.

Al-Hibri, Azizah Y. 'An Introduction to Muslim Women's Rights'. In *Windows of Faith: Muslim Women Scholar-Activists in North America*, ed. Gisela Webb. Syracuse, New York: Syracuse University Press, 2000.

——. 'Muslim Women's Rights in the Global Village: Challenges and Opportunities'. *Journal of Law and Religion* 15:1/2 (2000–2001), 37–66.

Al-Nawawi, Yahya ibn Sharaf. *The Complete Forty Hadith of Imam al-Nawawi*, translated by Abdassamad Clarke. London: Ta-Ha Publishers, 2009.

Al-Sulami, Abu 'Abd al-Rahman. *Early Pious Women: Dikhr an-niswa al-muta'abbidat as-sufiyyat*. Edited and translated from the Riyadh manuscript with introduction and notes by Rkia E. Cornell. Louisville, Kentucky: Fons Vitae, 1999.

Ali, Abdullah Yusuf. *The Holy Qur'an: Text, Translation and Commentary*, 2nd US ed. New York: Tahrike Tarsile Qur'an, 1988.

Ali, Ahmed. *Al-Qur'an: A Contemporary Translation*. Princeton: Princeton University Press, 1993.

Ali, Kecia. *Sexual Ethics and Islam: Feminist Reflections on Qur'an, Hadith, and Jurisprudence*. Oxford: Oneworld, 2006.

—— and Oliver Leaman. *Islam: The Key Concepts*. London: Routledge, 2008.

Amanat, Abbas and Frank Griffel eds. *Shari'a: Islamic Law in the Contemporary Context*. Stanford: Stanford University Press, 2009.

An-Na'im, Abdullahi. *Islam and the Secular State: Negotiating the Future of the Shari'a*. Cambridge, MA: Harvard University Press, 2010.

Asad, Muhammad. *The Message of the Qur'an*. Bristol: The Book Foundation, 2003.

Asad, Talal. *Genealogies of Religion: Discipline and Reasons of Power in Christianity and Islam*. Baltimore: Johns Hopkins University Press, 1993.

——. *Formations of the Secular: Christianity, Islam, Modernity*. Stanford: Stanford University Press, 2003.

Austin, Allan D. *African Muslims in Antebellum America: Transatlantic Stories and Spiritual Struggles*. London: Routledge, 1997.

Awde, Nicholas ed. *Women in Islam: An Anthology from the Qur'an and Hadiths*. New York: Hippocrene Books, 2005.

Barazangi, Nimat Hafez. *Woman's Identity and the Qur'an: A New Reading*. Gainesville: University Press of Florida, 2004.

Beinart, William. *Twentieth-Century South Africa*. Oxford: Oxford University Press, 2001.

Berkey, Jonathan. *The Transmission of Knowledge in Medieval Cairo: A Social History of Islamic Education*. Princeton: Princeton University Press, 1992.

Bevans, Stephen B. *Models of Contextual Theology*. Maryknoll, New York: Orbis Books, 2008.

Bhalotra, Sonia and Barnarda Zamora. 'Social Divisions in Education in India'. In *Handbook of Muslims in India: Empirical and Policy Perspectives*, eds. Rakesh Basant and Abusaleh Shariff. Oxford: Oxford University Press, 2010.

Boff, Leonardo and Clodovis Boff. *Introducing Liberation Theology*. Maryknoll, New York: Orbis Books, 1999.

Boyer, Ernest. *Scholarship Reconsidered: Priorities of the Professoriate*. San Francisco: Carnegie Foundation for the Advancement of Learning, 1990.

Bradstock, Andrew and Christopher Rowland eds. *Radical Christian Writings: A Reader*. Oxford: Blackwell Publishers, 2002.

Brown, Daniel W. *Rethinking Tradition in Modern Islamic Thought*. Cambridge: Cambridge University Press, 1999.

Brown, Jonathan. *Hadith: Muhammad's Legacy in the Medieval and Modern World*. Oxford: Oneworld, 2009.

Bulliet, Richard W. *The Case for Islamo-Christian Civilization*. New York: Columbia University Press, 2004.

Bunt, Gary R. *iMuslims: Rewiring the House of Islam*. Chapel Hill: University of North Carolina Press, 2009.

Butler, Judith. 'Subjects of Sex/Gender/Desire'. In *Feminisms*, eds. Sandra Kemp and Judith Squires. Oxford: Oxford University Press, 1997.

Calvert, John. *Sayyid Qutb and the Origins of Radical Islamism*. New York: Columbia University Press, 2010.

Campanini, Massimo. *The Qur'an: Modern Muslim Interpretations*, translated by Caroline Higgitt. London: Routledge, 2011.

Chakrabarty, Dipesh. *Provincializing Europe: Postcolonial Thought and Historical Difference*. Princeton: Princeton University Press, 2000.

Chaudry, Ayesha S. *Domestic Violence and the Islamic Tradition: Ethics, Law and the Muslim Discourse on Gender*. Oxford: Oxford University Press, 2013.

Clarence-Smith, William G. *Islam and the Abolition of Slavery*. Oxford: Oxford University Press, 2006.

Colaiaco, James A. *Martin Luther King Jr: Apostle of Militant Nonviolence*. New York: St. Martin's Press, 1988.

Commins, David D. *The Wahhabi Mission and Saudi Arabia*. London: I.B. Tauris, 2009.

Connell, R.W. *Gender*. Cambridge: Polity Press, 2008.

Cragg, Kenneth. *A Christian-Muslim Inter-Text Now: From Anathemata to Theme.* London: Melisende, 2008.

Curtis IV, Edward E. *Muslims in America: A Short History.* Oxford: Oxford University Press, 2009.

Dabashi, Hamid. *Islamic Liberation Theology: Resisting the Empire.* London: Routledge, 2008.

Daly, Mary. *Beyond God the Father: Toward a Philosophy of Women's Liberation.* Boston: Beacon Press, 1993.

Daniel, Norman. *Islam and the West: The Making of an Image.* Oxford: Oneworld, 2009.

Dawood, N.J. *The Koran,* 7th rev. ed. London: Penguin Books, 2000.

De Beauvoir, Simone. *The Second Sex.* New York: Vintage Books, 1989.

De Sondy, Amanullah. *The Crisis of Islamic Masculinities.* London: Bloomsbury, 2014.

DeLong-Bas, Natana J. *Wahhabi Islam: From Revival to Reform to Global Jihad.* Oxford: Oxford University Press, 2004.

Desai, Sonalde and Veenu Kulkarni. 'Unequal Playing Field: Socio-Religious Inequalities in Educational Attainment'. In *Handbook of Muslims in India: Empirical and Policy Perspectives,* eds. Rakesh Basant and Abusaleh Shariff. Oxford: Oxford University Press, 2010.

Diouf, Sylviane. *Servants of Allah: African Muslims Enslaved in the Americas.* New York: New York University Press, 1998.

Dorfman, Ariel. 'America's No Longer Unique' *Counterpunch* 3 October 2001. Accessed 17 September 2014. http://www.counterpunch.org/2001/10/03/america-s-no-longer-unique/

Duderija, Adis. *Constructing a Religiously Ideal 'Believer' and 'Woman' in Islam: Neo-traditional Salafi and Progressive Muslims' Methods of Interpretation.* New York: Palgrave Macmillan, 2011.

Eickelman, Dale F. 'The Art of Memory: Islamic Education and its Social Reproduction' *Comparative Studies in Society and History* 20 (1978): 485–516.

—— and James Piscatori. *Muslim Politics.* Princeton: Princeton University Press, 1996.

—— and Jon W. Anderson. 'Print, Islam, and the Prospects for Civic Pluralism: New Religious Writings and their Audiences' *Journal of Islamic Studies* 8 (1997), 43–62.

—— and Jon W. Anderson eds. *New Media in the Muslim World: The Emerging Public Sphere.* Bloomington, Indiana: Indiana University Press, 2003.

Eisenstein, Zillah. *Against Empire: Feminisms, Racism, and the West.* London: Zed Books, 2004.

Ernst, Carl W. *Following Muhammad: Rethinking Islam in the Contemporary World.* Chapel Hill: University of North Carolina Press, 2003.

Esposito, John L. *The Islamic Threat: Myth or Reality?* Oxford: Oxford University Press, 1999.

Euben, Roxanne L. and Muhammad Q. Zaman eds. *Princeton Readings in Islamist Thought: Texts and Contexts from al-Banna to Bin Laden.* Princeton: Princeton University Press, 2009.

Fisher, Alan G.B. and Humphrey J. Fisher. *Slavery in the History of Black Muslim Africa.* London: Hurst and Company, 2001.

Freire, Paulo. *Pedagogy of the Oppressed.* Translated by Myra Bergman Ramos. London: Penguin Books, 1996.

Frye, Marilyn. 'Some Reflections on Separatism and Power'. In *Feminist Social Thought: A Reader*, ed. Diana T. Meyers. London: Routledge, 1997.

Gandhi, M.K. *Non-Violent Resistance (Satyagraha).* Mineola, New York: Dover Publications, 2001.

Goddard, Hugh. *A History of Christian-Muslim Relations.* Edinburgh: Edinburgh University Press, 2000.

Grey, Mary. 'Feminist Theology: A Critical Theology of Liberation'. In *The Cambridge Companion to Liberation Theology*, ed. Christopher Rowland. Cambridge: Cambridge University Press, 2007.

Gross, Rita. 'Feminist Theology: Religiously Diverse Neighbourhood or Christian Ghetto?' *Journal of Feminist Studies in Religion* 16:2 (2000), 73–8.

——ed. 'Roundtable Discussion: Feminist Theology and Religious Diversity' *Journal of Feminist Studies in Religion* 16:2 (2000), 73–131.

Guha, Ranajit. 'On Some Aspects of the Historiography of Colonial India'. In *Selected Subaltern Studies*, eds. Ranajit Guha and Gayatri Chakravorty Spivak. Oxford: Oxford University Press, 1988.

Gutiérrez, Gustavo. *A Theology of Liberation: History, Politics, and Salvation.* Maryknoll, New York: Orbis Books, 1973.

Haddad, Yvonne. 'Muhammad Abduh: Pioneer of Islamic Reform'. In *Pioneers of Islamic Revival*, ed. Ali Rahnema. London: Zed Books, 2008.

Hammer, Juliane. 'Identity, Authority, and Activism: American Muslim Women Approach the Qur'an' *The Muslim World* 98 (2008), 443–64.

Hanafi, Hassan. 'Method of Thematic Interpretation of the Qur'an'. In *Islam in the Modern World*, ed. Hassan Hanafi. Cairo: Anglo-Egyptian Bookshop, 1995.

Hassan, Riffat. 'An Islamic Perspective'. In *Women, Religion and Sexuality: Studies on the Impact of Religious Teachings on Women*, ed. Jeanne Becher. Philadelphia: Trinity Press International, 1990.

Hasso, Frances S. 'Discursive and Political Deployments by / of the 2002 Palestinian Suicide Bombers / Martyrs' *Feminist Review* 81 (2005), 23–51.

Hidayatullah, Aysha A. *Feminist Edges of the Qur'an.* Oxford: Oxford University Press, 2014.

Hirschkind, Charles. *The Ethical Soundscape: Cassette Sermons and Islamic Counterpublics.* New York: Columbia University Press, 2006.

Hirschler, Konrad. *The Written Word in the Medieval Arabic Lands: A Social and Cultural History of Reading Practices.* Edinburgh: Edinburgh University Press, 2012.

Holy Bible: English Standard Version, Anglicized Edition. London: Collins, 2007.

hooks, bell. 'Feminism: A Movement to End Sexist Oppression'. In *Feminisms*, eds. Sandra Kemp and Judith Squires. Oxford: Oxford University Press, 1997.

'Human Development Report 1998'. *United Nations Development Program.* Accessed 23 September 2012. http://hdr.undp.org/en/reports/global/hdr1998/

Huntington, Samuel P. *The Clash of Civilizations and the Remaking of the World Order.* London: Touchstone Books, 1998.

Hyder, Syed Akbar. *Reliving Karbala: Martyrdom in South Asian Memory.* Oxford: Oxford University Press, 2006.

Izutsu, Toshihiko. *Ethico-Religious Concepts in the Qur'an.* Montreal: McGill-Queen's University Press, 2002.

Jackson, Sherman A. *On the Boundaries of Theological Tolerance in Islam: Abu Hamid al-Ghazali's Faysal al-Tafriqa Bayna al-Islam wa al-Zandaqa* [The Decisive Criterion for Distinguishing between Islam and Masked Infidelity]. Translated, annotated and introduced by Sherman A. Jackson. Oxford: Oxford University Press, 2002.

Jalal, Ayesha. *The Sole Spokesman: Jinnah, the Muslim League and the Demand for Pakistan.* Cambridge: Cambridge University Press, 1994.

Jasper, David. *A Short Introduction to Hermeneutics.* Louisville, Kentucky: Westminster John Knox Press, 2004.

Jenkins, Betty C. and Susan Phillis. *Black Separatism: A Bibliography.* Westport, Connecticut: Greenwood Press, 1976.

Johns, Anthony H. 'Let my people go! Sayyid Qutb and the Vocation of Moses' *Islam and Christian-Muslim Relations* 1:2 (1990), 143–70.

Kamrava, Mehran ed. *The New Voices of Islam: Rethinking Politics and Modernity: A Reader.* Berkeley: University of California Press, 2006.

Keddie, Nikki R. *Modern Iran: Roots and Results of Revolution.* New Haven: Yale University Press, 2003.

Kelly, Jill E. '"It is because of our Islam that we are there": The Call of Islam in the United Democratic Front Era' *African Historical Review* 41:1 (2009): 118–39.

Khan, Yasmin. *The Great Partition: The Making of India and Pakistan.* New Haven: Yale University Press, 2008.

Kugle, Scott Siraj al-Haqq. *Homosexuality in Islam: Critical Reflection on Gay, Lesbian, and Transgender Muslims.* Oxford: Oneworld, 2010.

Laffan, Michael. *The Makings of Indonesian Islam: Orientalism and the Narration of a Sufi Past.* Princeton: Princeton University Press, 2011.

Lamptey, Jerusha T. *Never Wholly Other: A Muslima Theology of Religious Pluralism.* Oxford: Oxford University Press, 2014.

Lawrence, Bruce. *The Qur'an: A Biography*. London: Atlantic Books, 2006.
—— ed. and James Howarth trans. *Messages to the World: The Statements of Osama bin Laden*. London: Verso, 2005.
Lockman, Zachary. *Contending Visions of the Middle East: The History and Politics of Orientalism*. Cambridge: Cambridge University Press, 2004.
Luey, Beth. *Handbook for Academic Authors*. Cambridge: Cambridge University Press, 2010.
Magubane, Bernard. 'Introduction: The Political Context'. In *The Road to Democracy in South Africa* Vol. 1, ed. South African Democracy Education Trust. Cape Town: Zebra Press, 2004.
Mamdani, Mahmood. *Good Muslim, Bad Muslim: America, the Cold War, and the Roots of Terror*. New York: Pantheon Books, 2004.
Mandaville, Peter. *Global Political Islam*. London: Routledge, 2007.
Marsden, Magnus. *Living Islam: Muslim Religious Experience in Pakistan's North-West Frontier*. Cambridge: Cambridge University Press, 2005.
Massad, Joseph. 'Re-Orienting Desire: The Gay International and the Arab World' *Public Culture* 14:2 (2002): 361–85.
Mattson, Ingrid. *The Story of the Qur'an: Its History and Place in Muslim Life*. Oxford: Blackwell Publishing, 2008.
Mawdudi, Abul A'la. *Towards Understanding the Qur'an: Abridged Version of Tafhim al-Qur'an*. Edited and translated by Zafar Ishaq Ansari. Markfield, Leicestershire: The Islamic Foundation, 2008.
McAuliffe, Jane D. 'Reading the Qur'an with Fidelity and Freedom' *Journal of the American Academy of Religion* 73 (2005), 615–35.
—— ed. *The Cambridge Companion to the Qur'an*. Cambridge: Cambridge University Press, 2006.
——. 'The Tasks and Traditions of Interpretation'. In *The Cambridge Companion to the Qur'an*, ed. Jane D. McAuliffe. Cambridge: Cambridge University Press, 2006.
McCloud, Aminah Beverly. *African American Islam*. New York: Routledge, 1995.
Mernissi, Fatima. *The Veil and the Male Elite: A Feminist Interpretation of Women's Rights in Islam*. New York: Basic Books, 1991.
Messick, Brinkley. *The Calligraphic State: Textual Domination and History in a Muslim Society*. Berkeley: University of California Press, 1993.
Mir-Hosseini, Ziba. *Islam and Gender: The Religious Debate in Contemporary Iran*. London: I.B. Tauris, 2000.
Mitchell, Timothy. *Colonising Egypt*. Berkeley: University of California Press, 1988.
Mohanty, Chandra Talpade. *Feminism without Borders: Decolonizing Theory, Practicing Solidarity*. Durham, NC: Duke University Press, 2003.
Nasr, Sayyed Vali Reza. 'Mawdudi and the Jama'at-i Islami: The Origins, Theory and Practice of Islamic Revivalism'. In *Pioneers of Islamic Revival*, ed. Ali Rahnema. London: Zed Books, 2008.

Needham, Anuradha D. and Rajeswari S. Rajan eds. *The Crisis of Secularism in India*. Durham, US: Duke University Press, 2007.

Nettler, Ronald. 'A Modern Islamic Confession of Faith and Conception of Religion: Sayyid Qutb's Introduction to the *Tafsir, fī Zilal al-Qur'an*' *British Journal of Middle Eastern Studies* 21 (1994): 102–14.

Omar, Rashied. Faculty website. Accessed 13 August 2016. http://kroc.nd. edu/facultystaff/Faculty/rashied-omar

Pal, Amitabh. *'Islam' means Peace: Understanding the Muslim Principle of Nonviolence Today*. Santa Barbara, California: Praegar, 2011.

Palombo, Matthew. 'The Emergence of Islamic Liberation Theology in South Africa' *Journal of Religion in Africa* 44 (2014): 28–61.

Pandey, Gyanendra. *The Construction of Communalism in Colonial North India*. Delhi: Oxford University Press, 1990.

Pears, Angie. *Doing Contextual Theology*. London: Routledge, 2010.

Qara'i, Ali Quli. *The Qur'an, with a Phrase-by-Phrase Translation*. London: Islamic College for Advanced Studies Press, 2004.

Qutb, Sayyid. *In the Shade of the Qur'an*. 18 vols. Translated and edited by Adil Salahi and Ashur Shamis. Markfield, Leicestershire: The Islamic Foundation, 2015.

Rab, Abdur. *Exploring Islam in a New Light: An Understanding from the Qur'anic Perspective*. New York: iUniverse, 2008.

Rahemtulla, Shadaab. 'Im Schatten des Christentums? Die Herausforderung islamischer Befreiungstheologie' [In the Shadow of Christianity? The Challenge of an Islamic Liberation Theology]. In *Gott und Befreiung. Befreiungstheologische Konzepte in Islam und Christentum* [God and Liberation: Concepts of Liberation Theology in Islam and Christianity], eds. Klaus von Stosch and Muna Tatari. Paderborn, Germany: Schöningh, 2012.

——. 'Toward a Genuine Congregation: The Form of the Muslim Friday Prayer, Revisited'. In *Only One is Holy: Liturgy in Postcolonial Perspectives*, ed. Cláudio Carvalhaes. New York: Palgrave Macmillan, 2015.

Rahman, Fazlur. *Islam and Modernity: The Transformation of an Intellectual Tradition*. Chicago: University of Chicago Press, 1982.

——. *Major Themes of the Qur'an*. Minneapolis: Bibliotheca Islamica, 1994.

Ramadan, Tariq. *To Be a European Muslim: A Study of Islamic Sources in the European Context*. Markfield, Leicestershire: The Islamic Foundation, 1999.

——. *Western Muslims and the Future of Islam*. Oxford: Oxford University Press, 2004.

——. *Radical Reform: Islamic Ethics and Liberation*. Oxford: Oxford University Press, 2009.

Renan, Ernest. *The Life of Jesus*. London: Watts, 1935.

Riches, John. *The Bible: A Very Short Introduction*. Oxford: Oxford University Press, 2000.

Ricoeur, Paul. *Hermeneutics and the Human Sciences: Essays on Language, Action and Interpretation,* edited and translated by John B. Thompson. Cambridge: Cambridge University Press, 1998.

Roberts, Adam and Timothy Garton Ash. *Civil Resistance and Power Politics: The Experience of Non-Violent Action from Gandhi to the Present.* Oxford: Oxford University Press, 2009.

Robinson, Francis. 'Technology and Religious Change: Islam and the Impact of Print' *Modern Asian Studies* 27 (1993), 229–51.

Rouse, Carolyn Moxley. *Engaged Surrender: African American Women and Islam.* Berkeley: University of California Press, 2004.

Rowland, Christopher ed. *The Cambridge Companion to Liberation Theology.* Cambridge: Cambridge University Press, 2007.

—— and Jonathan Roberts. *The Bible for Sinners: Interpretation in the Present Time.* London: Society for Promoting Christian Knowledge, 2008.

Ruether, Rosemary Radford. *Sexism and God-Talk: Towards a Feminist Theology.* Boston: Beacon Press, 1993.

Saeed, Abdullah. 'Fazlur Rahman: A Framework for Interpreting the Ethico-Legal Content of the Qur'an'. In *Modern Muslim Intellectuals and the Qur'an,* ed. Suha Taji-Farouki. Oxford: Oxford University Press, 2004.

——. *Interpreting the Qur'an: Towards a Contemporary Approach.* London: Routledge, 2006.

——. *The Qur'an: An Introduction.* London: Routledge, 2008.

Safi, Omid ed. *Progressive Muslims: On Justice, Gender, and Pluralism.* Oxford: Oneworld, 2003.

——. *Memories of Muhammad: Why the Prophet Matters.* New York: HarperOne, 2009.

Said, Edward. *Orientalism.* New York: Pantheon Books, 1978.

——. *Covering Islam: How the media and the experts determine how we see the rest of the world.* New York: Pantheon Books, 1981.

——. *Peace and its Discontents: Essays on Palestine in the Middle East Peace Process.* New York: Vintage Books, 1995.

Saleh, Walid A. *The Formation of the Classical Tafsir Tradition: The Qur'an Commentary of al-Tha'labi (d. 427/1035).* Leiden: Brill, 2004.

Sayyed, Khalid. *The Qur'an's Challenge to Islam: The Clash Between the Muslim Holy Scripture and Islamic Literature.* Dooagh, Ireland: Checkpoint Press, 2009.

Schüssler Fiorenza, Elisabeth. *Discipleship of Equals: A Critical Feminist Ekklesia-logy of Liberation.* New York: Crossroad Publishing Company, 1993.

——. *In Memory of Her: A Feminist Theological Reconstruction of Christian Origins.* New York: Crossroad Publishing Company, 1994.

Scott, David and Charles Hirschkind eds. *Powers of the Secular Modern: Talal Asad and his Interlocutors.* Stanford: Stanford University Press, 2006.

Segundo, Juan Luis. *Liberation of Theology*. Maryknoll, NY: Orbis Books, 1976.

Sells, Michael. *Approaching the Qur'an: The Early Revelations*. Ashland, Oregon: White Cloud Press, 1999.

Semenza, Gregory Cólon. *Graduate Study for the 21st Century: How to Build an Academic Career in the Humanities*. New York: Palgrave Macmillan, 2005.

Shaikh, Sa'diyya. 'Exegetical Violence: *Nushuz* in Qur'anic Gender Ideology' *Journal for Islamic Studies* 17 (1997), 49–73.

——. 'Knowledge, Women and Gender in the Hadith: A Feminist Approach' *Islam and Christian-Muslim Relations* 15 (2004), 99–108.

——. 'A *Tafsir* of Praxis: Gender, Marital Violence, and Resistance in a South African Community'. In *Violence Against Women in Contemporary World Religions: Roots and Cures*, eds. Daniel Maguire and Sa'diyya Shaikh. Cleveland, OH: Pilgrim Press, 2007.

——. 'In Search of *al-Insan*: Sufism, Islamic Law, and Gender' *Journal of the American Academy of Religion* 77:4 (2009), 781–822.

——. *Sufi Narratives of Intimacy: Ibn 'Arabi, Gender, and Sexuality*. Chapel Hill: The University of North Carolina Press, 2012.

Shani, Ornit. *Communalism, Caste and Hindu Nationalism: The Violence in Gujarat*. Cambridge: Cambridge University Press, 2007.

Shari'ati, Ali. 'On the Sociology of Islam: The World-View of Tawhid'. In *Introduction to Islam: A Reader*, ed. Amina Wadud. Dubuque, Iowa: Kendall/Hunt Publishing, 2007.

Sharp, Gene. *The Politics of Nonviolent Action*. 3 vols. Boston: Peter Sargent Publishers, 1973.

Shryock, Andrew. *Nationalism and the Genealogical Imagination: Oral History and Textual Authority in Tribal Jordan*. Berkeley: University of California Press, 1997.

Shugar, Dana R. *Separatism and Women's Community*. Lincoln, Nebraska: University of Nebraska Press, 1995.

Siddiqui, Abdur Rashid. *Qur'anic Keywords: A Reference Guide*. Markfield, Leicestershire: The Islamic Foundation, 2008.

Sisters in Islam. *Are Muslim Men Allowed to Beat their Wives?* Kuala Lumpur: Sisters in Islam, 1991.

——. *Are Women and Men Equal before God?* Kuala Lumpur: Sisters in Islam, 1991.

Sonbol, Amira E. 'Rethinking Women and Islam'. In *Daughters of Abraham: Feminist Thought in Judaism, Christianity, and Islam*, eds. Yvonne Y. Haddad and John L. Esposito. Gainesville: University Press of Florida, 2001.

Southern, R.W. *Western Views of Islam in the Middle Ages*. Cambridge, MA: Harvard University Press, 1962.

Stowasser, Barbara Freyer. *Women in the Qur'an, Traditions, and Interpretation.* Oxford: Oxford University Press, 1994.

Strauss, David Friedrich. *The Life of Jesus, Critically Examined.* 3 vols. Translated by George Elliot. Cambridge: Cambridge University Press, 2010.

Taji-Farouki, Suha ed. *Modern Muslim Intellectuals and the Qur'an.* Oxford: Oxford University Press, 2004.

Talbot, Ian. *Pakistan: A Modern History.* New York: St. Martin's Press, 1998.

The Monotheist Group. *The Natural Republic: Reclaiming Islam from Within.* Breinigsville, PA: Brainbow Press, 2009.

Thiselton, Anthony C. *Hermeneutics: An Introduction.* Grand Rapids, Michigan: W.B. Eerdamns Pub. Co., 2009.

Thompson, Leonard. *A History of South Africa.* New Haven: Yale University Press, 2000.

Von Denffer, Ahmad. *'Ulum al-Qur'an: An Introduction to the Sciences of the Qur'an.* Leicestershire, UK: The Islamic Foundation, 2007.

Webb, Gisela ed. *Windows of Faith: Muslim Women Scholar-Activists in North America.* Syracuse, New York: Syracuse University Press, 2000.

Wielandt, Rotraud. 'Exegesis of the Qur'an: Early Modern and Contemporary.' In *Encyclopaedia of the Qur'an*, ed. Jane D. McAuliffe, Georgetown University, Washington DC. Consulted online on 8 May 2012.

Wielenga, Bastiaan. 'Liberation Theology in Asia'. In *The Cambridge Companion to Liberation Theology*, ed. Christopher Rowland. Cambridge: Cambridge University Press, 2007.

Wild, Stefan. 'Political Interpretation of the Qur'an'. In *The Cambridge Companion to the Qur'an*, ed. Jane D. McAuliffe. Cambridge: Cambridge University Press, 2006.

Wolfe, Michael ed. *Taking Back Islam: American Muslims Reclaim their Faith.* Emmaus, Pennsylvania: Rodale Press, 2004.

X, Malcolm and Alex Haley. *The Autobiography of Malcolm X.* London: Penguin, 2001.

Young, Robert. *Postcolonialism: An Historical Introduction.* Oxford: Blackwell Publishing, 2001.

YouTube. 'Female Imams – Morocco'. Accessed 22 September 2011. http://www.youtube.com/watch?v=Qgk5JFGUkRw

Yuksel, Edip. *Manifesto for Islamic Reform.* Breinigsville, PA: Brainbow Press, 2009.

Zaman, Muhammad Qasim. *The Ulama in Contemporary Islam: Custodians of Change.* Princeton: Princeton University Press, 2002.

Zebiri, Kate. *Mahmud Shaltut and Islamic Modernism.* Oxford: Clarendon Press, 1993.

Index of Qur'anic Citations

Index

Note: Footnotes in page entries are indicated by 'n'.

poor, the 19, 47, 48, 52, 67, 69, 75, 81,
 82, 92, 97, 108, 128, 136, 141,
 148, 149, 154, 159, 200,
 213, 226
Positive Muslims 36
postcolonial perspective 39
poverty 2, 8, 12, 48–50, 52, 57, 67, 69, 75,
 100, 147, 149, 160, 225
power 3, 11, 26, 33, 34, 44, 47, 52, 74, 77,
 81, 91, 93, 98, 126, 143, 162–4,
 184, 186, 192, 205, 207, 209,
 224, 225
powerless 20, 48, 52, 67, 91
pragmatism 105, 111, 113, 168, 169
praxis 49, 50, 69, 93, 96, 109, 157, 181,
 197, 213, 221, 236
 -based reflection 3, 20
 between application and 110–13
 and faith 42
 and gender relations 37, 38
 and Gutiérrez 20
 as *jihad* (struggle) 29, 49
 theology emerging through
  struggle 251
prayer 24, 57, 65, 68, 101, 126, 133–5,
 147, 153, 200, 251
pre-Islamic Arabia 87, 127, 185,
 186, 250
precedent 5, 57, 71, 78 n. 107, 124
 n. 121, 252
 sunnat al-awwalin (of earlier
  communities) 57, 252
 sunnat Allah (of God) 57, 252
 sunnat an-nabi (of the Prophet) 57
pregnancy 169, 186, 222
premarital sex 169, 253
Prince Alwaleed bin Talal Center for
 Muslim-Christian
 Understanding 42, 43
print culture 4
 rise of 236–45
private property 72, 104
privilege 5, 29, 64, 68, 69, 72, 77, 91, 106,
 127, 142, 146, 149, 159, 160,
 164, 170, 175, 178, 182, 186,
 201, 214, 222, 228, 238
pro-faith, pro-feminist 97, 141, 215
profit, prioritising over human
 welfare 36
progressive revelation (Esack) 15, 21, 50,
 176, 236, 252
progressive values 97, 160

prophetic Islam 32, 33, 35
prophetic paradigms 187–90
 Abraham 187–9
 Muhammad 189–90
prophetic reports 13, 14, 58, 63, 92, 104,
 153, 157
Prophet, the, *see* Muhammad, Prophet
'Prophetic' solidarity 10, 31–5
prophetic biography 190
prophetic prayer 57
prophets 26, 41, 48, 52, 71, 72, 79, 132,
 167, 176, 217, 217 n. 265,
 222, 252
protest 43, 47, 74, 91, 95, 142, 196
Protestant Reformation 238
Protestantism 27
punishment 52, 58, 59, 71, 121, 147, 167,
 169, 187, 193, 194
purification 34
puritanism 30

qanitat (obedient women) 201, 202
Qaramita 72
qawwamun (guardians) 127, 199
qist (justice) 66 n. 61, 249, 251
qital (fighting in warfare) 88, 251
queer identity politics 39–40
queer Muslims 38, 40
queer rights 78
Qur'an
 'articulation of divine will' 102
 'atomistic' readings of 172
 difference between Qur'anic text and
  exegesis 101–2
 extratextuality 173
 gender egalitarian interpretation 2 n.
  3, 8, 29, 37, 38, 61, 97–8, 162,
  176, 221, 222, 226, 227, 228
 grammatical composition 106
 modern patriarchy 191–2
 oral text 87–8
 saying no to literal wording of 129–31
 sunna as 'living embodiment' of 103
 traditional patriarchy 178–80
 as transcendent and historical
  text 102
 see also apologetics; apologia;
  historical criticism; holistic
  and intratextual reading of
  Qur'an; praxis
Qutb, Sayyid 17, 25 n. 65, 30, 228,
 229, 243

Made in the USA
Middletown, DE
26 May 2020